Dachau and t

1933- --

Vol. II   Studies and Reports

# Dachau and the Nazi Terror
# 1933–1945

## Vol. II   Studies and Reports

Edited by
Wolfgang Benz and Barbara Distel

Dachau 2002

Published for the
Comité International de Dachau, Brussels

ISSN 0934-361 X
ISBN 3-9808587-1-5

© Verlag Dachauer Hefte
Alte Römerstrasse 75
85221 Dachau
Printed by: Fuldaer Verlagsanstalt

# Contents

# Preface

The Dachauer Hefte, established in 1985 and published with the moral authority of the Comité International de Dachau, carries the subtitle "History" of Nazi Concentration Camps: Studies, Reports, Documents. Devoted to all aspects of National Socialist persecution, the journal is not limited to events directly connected to the concentration camp at Dachau.

Articles by contemporary witnesses who experienced the horror of Dachau, Auschwitz and Buchenwald, of Treblinka and Theresienstadt and other camps are followed in this second volume of the English edition by articles, unabridged and selected from 16 issues of the Dachauer Hefte between 1985–2000, from 12 scholars of various disciplines engaged in establishing and analysing the history of National Socialist persecution and oppression. It is the intent of the Dachauer Hefte — and this English edition shall also give expression to this — to overcome the boundary between academic scholarship and the recollections of survivors. The goal is to hold a dialogue between survivors and historians in the service of enlightenment.

The texts presented in this edition shall contribute to this endeavour.

*Wolfgang Benz, Barbara Distel*

Barbara Distel

# 29 April 1945

## The Liberation of the
## Concentration Camp at Dachau

The liberation of the concentration camp at Dachau by units of the US Army
was a tremendously moving event for everyone involved. It marked the end
of the camp's twelve year history, a history of oppression and suffering, of
misery and death, but also of resistance and survival, of tenacity and mutual
support.

Attempting to approach the matter forty years later is not easy. At first
glance it seems as though time had simply passed it by, as though the problems
of 1985 had hardly anything in common with issues topical in 1945. Has
the drama of those days retained its significance only for those few survivors
celebrating the 40th anniversary of their liberation?

Dachau is the place where the 'SS State' began, which was to lead to
the mass extermination in Auschwitz. But here too it fell, when on 29 April
1945, as the last but one of the concentration camps, it was liberated.

Today, as we inquire into the causes and conditions which made 'Dachau' and finally 'Auschwitz' possible, we must also tackle the problems of the
disastrous end that was at the same time a deliverance which was the result
of the twelve preceding years.

In attempting to reconstruct the course of events, the most important
source of information is found in the reports of surviving prisoners written
largely in the initial years after the liberation. Many of them are now out
of print; others were never even published.[1] Through the liberators of the
camp films and pictures were made available, illustrating that in the end
the camp in Dachau looked just like all the other sites of the Holocaust.
The SS bureaucracy broke down in the spring of 1945. Although the camp
files were kept up to the last day, in many instances incriminating evidence
was destroyed at the last minute, so that documents which would have
answered many as yet unresolved questions are no longer available.

---

1  On the territory of the former concentration camp at Dachau a memorial was
   erected in 1965. Affiliated with it are a library and an archive where all documents
   at all related to the history of Dachau concentration camp are collected.

In the last phase of the Second World War, when it became clear that the military defeat of the German army could no longer be avoided, the prisoners' situation and living conditions at Dachau concentration camp also changed drastically.

By 1944, as an increasing number of concentration camp inmates were put to work in the factories of Germany's war industry, the number of work commandos and subsidiary camps had grown to over 120. In the winter of 1944/45 another 44 were added. At that time many of the 'old Dachauers', i.e. the German political prisoners, who had been imprisoned for a number of years, were kept in one of those subsidiary camps. Moreover, in November 1944, several hundreds of them were recruited for so called 'probation units' and sent to the front, so that only very few prisoners lived to see the final months and the liberation of Dachau. In the end Polish and Soviet inmates accounted for the largest national groups.

The beginning of the last act of the Dachau drama, with its final toll of far beyond 15,000 lives, is marked by the outbreak of the typhus epidemic in December 1944, from which 3,000 prisoners had died by January 1945.

There was not enough room for the numerous patients, and conditions of hygiene were disastrous. There was no nutritious food, no dressings, and medication neither to prevent nor to treat the disease. Prisoner nurses and doctors fell victim to the epidemic, as did the inmates of other work commandos. The Dutch writer, Nico Rost, wrote in his secret diary, "… I have asked almost all doctors about the mortality rate in the case of typhus fever: under the age of 35 it hovers around 40 %, over the age of 45 and especially under the prevailing conditions it is 80 %. Moreover, in most cases other diseases, such as thrombosis, ear infections and paralysis complicate the situation even more …"[2]

In the course of the winter of 1944/45 the situation continued to deteriorate through transports of prisoners arriving from other camps, which had been evacuated on account of approaching Allied troops. In January the first to be moved off westward in an attempt to avoid the approaching Red Army were the Auschwitz inmates. In March the inmates of the subsidiary camps situated around the Natzweiler camp in Alsace were evacuated and moved off eastward in an attempt to keep them from the Western Allies. Between January and March and until the end of April, when Dachau was the only concentration camp, except Mauthausen, that had not yet been liberated, thousands of prisoners arrived there. The conditions under which they arrived were always the same: totally exhausted human beings, who had marched for days and sometimes for weeks or who had been jammed in railroad cars, exposed to cold, hunger and disease, dragged themselves into

2    Nico Rost, Goethe in Dachau, Berlin 1948. New Edition Hamburg 1981, p. 201.

the camp. But in Dachau there was neither adequate accommodation nor sufficient food, on the contrary, these arrivals only added to the devastating circumstances that already existed, and the number of deaths continued to grow. "The death lists are becoming longer and longer. At least four times a day I have to go and see the clerk of Block 30, the sick block, which is nearly finished, to pick up a list of the most recent deaths ...", Nico Rost wrote in his diary on 4 March 1945.[3]

By that time the prisoners knew as did their SS guards that the fall of the SS empire was imminent, and that the days of Dachau concentration camp were also numbered. The Czechoslovakian clergyman Bedrich Hoffmann, who also secretly kept a diary, characterized the atmosphere in February 1945 as follows: "... The SS men who used to come up to the blocks to check on us made an effort to point out to the inmates that they always meant well with them and that in actuality they were their best friends ..."[4]

As far as the prisoners were concerned, these final weeks were a race against time, a race which thousands of them ended up losing. And apart from the question as to whether they would succeed in holding out until the liberators arrived with food and medical treatment they increasingly feared that there were plans to liquidate all prisoners. Rumors and conjectures circulated in the camp, and the fear that the SS would not even shy away from mass murder in order to eliminate the witnesses of their crimes grew stronger.

That an evacuation of the more than thirty thousand inmates would itself be a death sentence was something they had been made clear to them by the transports of evacuees from other camps all winter long. Of course they also asked themselves where the Dachau camp should be evacuated to anyway, after units of the Western Allies had already crossed the Rhine and finally the Danube as well. The representatives of the national prisoners' groups began to meet in secret in order to discuss how a possibly planned mass murder of the inmates could be prevented. At the time they could do nothing but wait, compile information and keep an eye on the SS.

Suddenly, at the end of March 1945, several hundred German clergymen were released. The reason why 170 others had to stay behind was not clear. On 4 April the Danish and Norwegian prisoners were handed over to the Swedish Red Cross. But in contrast to these hopeful events, was the fact that the executions continued and, above all, that the epidemic continued to spread, and that each additional day lowered the prospects of survival for the ill and weak.

3    Ibid, p. 194.
4    Bedrich Hoffmann, A Kdo vás Zabije ..., Prerov 1946, unpublished translation by Ernest Bornefeld (Dachau Archive No.A.o. 031).

For in Dachau, as in other concentration camps, there was a class system which spread the prospects of survival unevenly among the prisoners, in particular during the final phase. There was a small group of prisoners in privileged positions who did not suffer from hunger and therefore were not as prone to disease as others. On the one hand, the majority of the prisoners who worked in the various commandos were underfed, but in many cases they had held out until then by helping each other, for example, by sharing packages from the Red Cross. On the other hand, there was a steadily growing number of the so called 'unassigned', who received smaller rations of food; these included the sick and those who, though they were not assigned to work, had to spend the day outdoors because they were not allowed to stay in the barracks.

As of mid April, the cannon fire of the approaching front could be heard at Dachau camp. The SS had discontinued handing out the Red Cross's packages to the prisoners. At the camp's headquarters, documents were burned. SS squads on guard searched the inmates' huts. From Flossenburg and other camps the so called special inmates were brought in to Dachau. They were prominent German opponents to the NS regime, above all from circles such as the resistance group '20 July 1944' and its supporters, who were taken into so called 'Sippenhaft' custody (liability of all members of a family for the crimes of one member), high ranking individuals of both the military and the Church from various countries and foreign politicians like Leon Blum and Kurt Schuschnigg and their wives. These prisoners — a group of special prisoners also existed at the Dachau camp — were kept separate and accommodated under much better conditions than the ordinary prisoners. Now they were just as uncertain about their fate and were fearful of falling victim to a fanatic 'Durchhalteideologie' (ideology of persistance) so shortly before the end. As late as 9 April some of the leading resistance fighters of the '20 July 1944' group were executed in Flossenbuerg.

On 23 April 1945 for the first time the work commandos no longer left the camp at Dachau. Towards noon the more than two thousand Jewish prisoners were ordered to stand in formation on the parade ground and to get ready for march off. "This means evacuation and they are going to start with the Jews ...", Nico Rost wrote.[5] On that day the Jewish inmates did not leave the camp. They had to wait at the parade ground until the following day, when they were loaded into railroad cars, which by 26 April had still not left the site.

On 24 and 25 April, no evacuation marches left Dachau camp, but more than 2,000 survivors of a 'death march' from Hersbruck, a Flossenbuerg subsidiary camp, arrived. Now the prisoners impatiently waited for the

5    Nico Rost, op. cit., p. 227.

almost daily air-raid warning, which would make a march off impossible and with which they hoped to be able to delay the evacuation of the camp until the arrival of the liberators.

On 26 April, in spite of ever clearer indications that they were about to break up, by applying force the SS once again succeeded in maintaining their control over the camp at Dachau. Although the representatives of the national groups were determined to sabotage the evacuation of the camp in any way possible, and although those responsible for the various work commandos were taking advantage of the increasingly chaotic situation to delay the carrying out of orders by the SS and gain time, they had to follow the order issued on the morning of 26, according to which the 'Reichs-deutschen' and Soviet prisoners, as well as the Jewish prisoners, also had to stand in formation on the parade ground and get ready for march off.

By prolonging the distribution of the food rations, the departure could be delayed by hours; some of the prisoners even managed to hide, mainly in those huts the SS avoided for fear of contracting a disease. However, as becomes evident from statistics on the camp, 6,887 prisoners in groups of 1,500 had left the camp, with "Oetztal" as their destination. The prisoners themselves did not know where they were going. It can no longer be ascertained how many of the prisoners died on this march. The survivors were not rescued by American soldiers until 2 May. "Joy and hope have vanished in the camp", a Belgian prisoner wrote after their departure.[6] A total of 137 of the prominent special prisoners were transported in buses and trucks. Their first stop was a camp of war prisoners near Innsbruck and, with the help of members of the German Wehrmacht, they were finally able to convince the SS men accompanying them that it would be best to hand over the well-known prisoners to the Allies unharmed.

At last, on 4 May, they were able to be taken over unharmed by units of the US Army at a hotel near Niederndorf in South Tyrol.[7] The last commander at Dachau also left the camp on 26 April. He drove to the castle at 'Itter', a Dachau subsidiary camp in the Tyrol, where he shot himself in the head on 27 April. Although additional evacuations were ordered on 27 and 28 April, the prisoners, ready for march off, did not leave the camp. Again there was an air-raid warning and most of the members of the SS began to leave Dachau quickly after having removed prisoners' valuables and undistributed Red Cross packages from the special storage room.

6    Arthur Haulot/Ali Kuci, Dachau, Brussels 1945. New Edition, Brussels 1985; unpublished translation by Gustav Görsch (Dachau Archive No. 10083), p. 18.
7    Cf. Memories of this transport: Reise durch den letzten Akt, Isa Vermehren, Hamburg 1946. New edition Hamburg 1979, pp. 140; Von Preußen nach Europa, Lebenserinnerungen, Stuttgart 1968, pp. 174; The Venlo Incident, London 1950, pp. 221.

At the same time, several thousand prisoners arrived who were being evacuated from Dachau's subsidiary camps, and from Flossenbuerg and Buchenwald. Many of them died immediately upon arrival at the camp, others were so weakened that they simply collapsed on the parade ground. Once again, the situation regarding provisions deteriorated rapidly.

The representatives of the national prisoners' groups, who continued to meet in secret and discuss developments, at that point realized that the main goal was no longer to prevent the evacuation of the camp, but to survive on the remaining food until the arrival of the liberators, and to avoid panic. From then on, a group of prisoners guarded and patrolled the prisoners' huts. Yet the prisoners' fear of falling victim to a massacre by the SS persisted until the end. Almost all the reports written about the final days and the liberation of the concentration camp at Dachau mention that the prisoners gained knowledge of an order issued by Heinrich Himmler on 14 April 1945 to evacuate the camp immediately and to prevent any prisoner from falling into the hands of the enemy alive. It was not until after the end of the war that it became known that, apart from this order, at least two different plans for the extermination of the prisoners before the arrival of the Allies had existed.

On 27 April a representative of the International Red Cross was sent from the town of Uffing in Upper Bavaria to Dachau, on a mission personally to distribute food packages directly among the prisoners and to see to it that the camp be handed over to the Americans. However, the assistant to the camp's commander, who was still present, did not grant him permission to enter the protective custody camp.

On 28 April the noise of tanks coming from the city of Dachau could be heard at the camp. At the same time, by means of hidden radio sets, the prisoners were informed through repeated announcements on the radio that day about the 'liberation of Bavaria' (Freiheitsaktion Bayern),[8] calling for a peaceful handover of Munich to the US Army. It was not until after their liberation that the prisoners found out that those calls had actually caused the 'Dachau rebellion': here, too, a group of opponents to the regime had prepared for peaceful transition. Among them were prisoners from the concentration camps who had escaped work commandos located outside the camp and who had hidden in the city of Dachau. After a group of twenty to thirty men had occupied the city hall for a few hours they were surrounded by SS units. Most of the rebels were able to escape; six of them, among them three prisoners from concentration camps, were executed on City Hall Square.[9]

8    Aufstand in Dachau, Adolf Maislinger, unpublished (Dachau Archive No. 7676).
9    Die Sechs vom Rathausplatz, Hans Holzhaider, Dachau 1982. Nico Rost, loc. sit., p. 242.

In the morning of 29 April, the prisoners found that the entire SS had apparently left. On one of the buildings in the vicinity of the neighboring SS camp a white flag could be seen. "The SS have put up a white flag! At the entrance of the camp. The excitement among us is indescribable. Anybody who can is running to 'the parade ground' from where the flag can be seen ...", Nico Rost wrote in his diary that morning.[10] However, the machine guns up on the watch towers were still manned and the feeling of being threatened had not yet disappeared.

The representatives of the national prisoners' groups, who in the meantime had formed the International Dachau Committee, no longer had to hide. "We are in permanent session. The first proclamation has been drafted. It calls on the comrades to remain calm. It appeals to them to stay in their blocks and wait for further instructions ...", the French prisoners' representative, Edmont Michelet, reported.[11] In the course of the morning, the noise of approaching and departing tanks could be heard. At the same time, the prisoner Karl Riemer of Augsburg was attempting to make his way to the American commander of the small town of Pfaffenhofen approximately thirty kilometers away in order to direct his attention to the prisoners' desperate situation at Dachau concentration camp. On 26 April, along with a group of seventeen prisoners, he had escaped from the camp with the help of a squad in charge of emptying trash cans. Their mission was to go and get the Americans to come to the camp as quickly as possible. The group was separated on the way and when Karl Riemer finally reached Pfaffenhofen he was alone. In a report from 11 May 1945 he describes his encounter with the American commander at Pfaffenhofen: "He had me describe the situation from the moment the abduction in the mountains took place. I urged him to rescue the remaining prisoners in the camp and described the circumstances to him. Every moment was important and not a moment was to be lost ... After questioning me on a few matters concerning the reason why I had been sent to the camp, etc., he dismissed me, promising immediate help ..."[12]

Colonel Felix Sparks of the Third Battalion of the 157th Infantry Association of the 45th Infantry Division reported that he and his soldiers had been on their way to Munich when they were ordered via radio to first liberate the concentration camp at Dachau. Upon arrival, the first thing they found in the vicinity of the SS camp was a parked train of forty cars,[13] but not

10  Nico Rost, loc. sit., p. 242.
11  Die Freiheitsstraße, Edmont Michelet, Stuttgart, no year (1960), p. 249.
12  Amerikaner helfen, Karl Riemer, unpublished report from 11 May 1945 (Dachau Archive No. 7560).
13  Felix L. Sparks Dachau and its Liberation, unpublished (Dachau Archive No. 20202). The figures on the number of train cars given in the various reports and publications vary considerably.

until they had approached did they realize that it was full of dead prisoners. Most likely it was the last evacuation transport from Buchenwald. The German prisoner Walter Leitner reported that among the approximately two thousand bodies, seventeen survivors were found,[14] but that the best medical treatment could not keep them alive. This atrocious discovery, even before reaching the prisoners' camp, most deeply shocked the American soldiers. Colonel L. Sparks reported that many of them broke out in tears or vomited, although they belonged to a battle tried unit. Whether Colonel Sparks and his men were the first to climb over the walls of and arrive at the camp to liberate it, or General Linden, who came driving through the entrance gate with a vanguard of the 42nd Rainbow Division, among whom was also an American war correspondent, will be impossible now to prove with ultimate certainty.[15]

Nico Rost depicted the arrival of the liberators as follows: "It started at three o'clock! The tormenting silence was suddenly broken by the noise of machine gunfire and the rattle of handguns, vigorously answered by firing from the SS watchtowers. The shooting was coming closer and closer and became increasingly fierce. I went to the death chamber and climbed onto the flat roof with the help of a ladder. Dr van D. already stood up there and even Steensma, despite having only one leg, came climbing up. The Americans were approaching! We could clearly see them in the distance in the bushes! They were approaching extremely slowly and carefully, their machine guns in firing position, every now and then aiming at the SS watchtowers, from which they were fiercely fired at, despite the white flags and rags ... It was 5.28 sharp according to the headquarters clock when the big gate opened ..."[16] All reports written by prisoners describe that at the same time soldiers were firing from the towers, in the process of which a Polish prisoner was hit fatally. According to all reports SS soldiers were also taken down from the towers by American soldiers and shot immediately. It was found that they were not the former guards of the camp, but that they had either been transferred to this unit only shortly before or brought in from the SS disciplinary camp located near the protective custody camp. Colonel Sparks wrote that a total of approximately two hundred SS soldiers had been detained, and some of them shot on the spot.[17] As soon as the prisoners

---

14    Die letzten Tage im Konzentrationslager Dachau, Walter Leitner, unpublished (Dachau Archive No. 7675).

15    Arthur Haulot/Ali Kuci, loc. sit.; Hermann Langbein: ... Nicht wie die Schafe zur Schlachtbank, Frankfurt 1980. In numerous reports written by prisoners, General Linden's arrival coincides with that of the American reporter.

16    Nico Rost, loc. sit., p. 243.

17    Felix L. Sparks, loc. sit. There are varying and contradictory accounts on the execution of SS guards by members of the US Army. It is unlikely to be determined

had grasped the fact that the liberators were present in the camp, anybody who could manage to stand on his own two feet rushed to the parade ground in order to see the soldiers with his own eyes, salute them, thank them or simply to cheer them from a distance. "Oh, this overwhelming and unforgettable moment," the Belgian Arthur Haulot wrote,[18] and the German prisoner Edgar Kupfer-Koberwitz, whose diary notes are among the most impressive documents about the camp at Dachau, depicts the moment of liberation as follows: 'The Americans are here! The Americans are in the camp! Hurrah, hurrah, they are at the parade ground!' Everybody is in motion. The sick are leaving their beds, those who are almost well, and the block personnel are running out into the block road, jumping out of the windows, climbing over wooden fences, rushing to the parade ground. From the distance, all the way to here, you can hear the shouting and cheering. They are shouts of joy. Everyone is continuing to run around. Everybody has expressions of excitement on their transfigured faces. 'They are here, we are free, free!' We all can hardly believe it, but we hear the cheering outside. Comrades are coming back, out of breath, telling us: 'The Americans are at the parade ground. They are shooting the SS. The camp has been taken over, we are free.' Even the severely ill are getting out of their beds, stumbling towards the windows. Comrades are coming towards me: Frenchmen, Russians, Jews, Italians. We are kissing each other like brothers and congratulating each other. Many have tears in their eyes. We tightly grab each others' hands: 'Free, free!'".[19]

They had survived, they had been rescued.

Only slowly did the immense problems of taking care of 32,000 malnourished prisoners, of providing medical treatment for thousands, and checking the typhus epidemic come to the fore again. For in Dachau too, as the prisoner Jorge Semprun, liberated at Buchenwald, had put it, "the end of the camp by no means meant the end of the dying".[20] Thus, in May 1945 alone, over 2,000 prisoners died at Dachau.

Yet many of them who had survived the camp soon felt the urge to make sure that what happened at this place would not fall into oblivion. After all, it was thanks to their efforts that the former concentration camp with its diverse history (after the last prisoners had left the camp, war crime trials were held there by US military authorities for three years, and in 1948 the grounds served as a refugee camp) was turned into a memorial on the 20th anniversary of its liberation.

exactly how many people died during the battles for the liberation of the concentration camp at Dachau.

18  Arthur Haulot/Ali Kuci, loc. sit., p. 29.
19  Edgar Kupfer Koberwitz, Die Mächtigen und die Hilflosen, Vol. 2, Stuttgart 1957, p. 254.
20  Jorge Semprun, Die große Reise, Hamburg 1964, p. 75.

Hermann Weiss

# Dachau and International Public Opinion

## Reactions to the Liberation of the Camp

> *"I've always thought*
> *they exaggerated*
> *to make us hate the Krauts."*

Shortly after the National Socialist seizure of power, the foreign press had already made the National Socialist concentration camps a subject of their reports. The foreign press based their description of the conditions in German concentration camps to some considerable extent on the testimony of released prisoners who had escaped from Germany and published reports about their experiences.

In order to counteract negative foreign propaganda concerning concentration camps, the SS soon proceeded to have German journalists write faked positive reports about the camps.[1]

Common to all reports about German concentration camps in both the German press and the foreign press was the fact that their accuracy was not verifiable for foreigners and that Allied propaganda about atrocities during World War I actually proved positive for the Germans in the formation of public opinion in western countries. Reports such as the one published by the London Times on 16 December 1939, about the alleged plan of the Germans to establish a type of Jewish state in occupied Poland in a "concentration zone" around Lublin, to which all German, Austrian, Czech and most

---

[1] Especially typical is a five-page "Special Report" of the *Illustrierter Beobachter* of 3 December 1936 about the camp at Dachau. An assortment of photographs of stubblybearded, shorn heads held in unfavorable poses with corresponding captions under the pictures, as well as downright idyllic photographs of camp life were to suggest to the observer that in reality disreputable "sub-humans", meaning Communists, loafers and professional criminals, were to be rehabilitated through work in this place, which was a model of order and cleanliness. In the two-page illustrated report "about a concentration camp" in the *Münchner Illustrierte Presse* of 3 August 1939, which consists entirely of pictures of the work of prisoners in the concentration camp Dachau, particular attention is drawn to this in order to counteract the "most hair-raising things" in the descriptions in the foreign press.

Polish Jews were to be deported — altogether around 2,27 million people — in order to be gradually exterminated there, were so far beyond the power of human imagination, at least in the western democracies, that the Times made the attenuating remark that although such a massacre of European Jews might well firm with the Nazis' imaginary world, even they would not be able fully to carry it out.[2]

The British government also took into consideration that certain things were just as inconceivable to its citizens and, in a directive from the Ministry of Information of 25 July 1941, warned political journalists not to risk their credibility with too drastic reporting.

In this evaluation of the effect that the reports of atrocities would have the fact that ideological opponents had with the outbreak of the Second World War become declared enemies, who were no longer to be treated according to standards of fairness but rather according to criteria of psychological warfare, clearly also played a part. But even though one could assume that in the Allied countries people were in principle aware of the system followed in the National Socialist concentration camps, the treatment in the Allied and nonpartisan press of the first eye-witness accounts from the death camp at Auschwitz shows how little credence was given to details of National Socialist persecution and extermination measures which exceeded the power of human imagination. It was, for example, not until the summer of 1944, eleven months before the end of the war, that a report launched to an international public through all possible channels, received a widespread response in the press.[3]

For this reason the first reports from Allied correspondents to appear in western newspapers since April 1945 were a shock to the international public. After the capture of the death camp at Auschwitz the world was given its first foretaste of the cold-bloodedly executed, criminally inhumane world the system of the National Socialist "death mills" concealed. On 28 January 1945, one day after the capture, the Soviet Pravda drew attention to what had happened. On 1 February, as a supplement to a report from the front, Pravda printed a report of thirty lines about the size of the camp, the number of inmates and the nutritional condition of the liberated prisoners. This was followed the next day by a two-column report in which the numbers of victims were made public. On 14 February, in a report

---

2   See: Martin Gilbert, Auschwitz and the Allies, New York 1981, p. 14.
3   The so-called Wetzler-Vrba-Report, which contains the accounts of three prisoners who escaped from Auschwitz, appeared in extracts in June and July 1944, in the Swiss press in 383 articles and reprints. See: John S. Conway, Frühe Augenzeugenberichte aus Auschwitz, in: Vierteljahrshefte für Zeitgeschichte 27 (1979), p. 278, footnote 35; see also Gilbert, op. cit., p. 10 and 272–281.

about the work of the Polish commission for disclosure of the NS crimes in Auschwitz, Pravda published details of the extermination machinery, the gas chambers and crematoria, and also of the reuse of the hair, the gold fillings and the clothes of the dead prisoners.

Finally, on 7 May, when detailed reports on the German concentration camps captured by western Allied troops were already appearing in the press of the western Allied countries, Pravda followed once more with a two-page article about Auschwitz, which was rather sparsely illustrated with two photographs. Here for the first time the number of 4 million prisoners killed there was quoted.[4]

In Great Britain the first reports about concentration camps appeared on 12 April 1945. They were written by correspondents of the westem Allies who were eye-witnesses after the liberation of the concentration camp at Buchenwald, which was close to Weimar. Three days later, the German army surrendered the concentration camp Bergen-Belsen, which was situated between Celle and Soltau south of the Lüneburger Heide. Bergen-Belsen was for months so overcrowded with transports from other camps, among them Auschwitz and Buchenwald, that the conditions which the Allied troops encountered there surpassed everything they had seen until then or were still to see. In March 1945 more than 18,000 prisoners died there; in the first two weeks of April before the liberation more than 9,300 died, among them many women.[5]

In the reporting, however, Buchenwald remained in first place not only because it had been liberated earlier, but also because it was dangerous to enter Bergen-Beisen due to the typhus epidemic which was raging through the camp. After several smaller news items and photographs concerning Buchenwald, Bergen-Belsen and subsidiary camps such as Nordhausen and Ohrdruf,[6] there appeared in the London Times of 28 April 1945, a two-column report on the visit of a delegation of British members of Parliament and American congressmen to Buchenwald. In this article the story already

4   Although the lack of adequate sources makes it impossible to state exact figures, the computation from camp files and transport lists existing for certain periods and from the use of all other relevant sources and statistical material show the number of killed to be between one and two million. See Ino Arndt/Wolfgang Scheffler, Organisierter Massenmord an Juden in nationalsozialistischen Vernichtungslagern, in: Vierteljahrshefte für Zeitgeschichte 24 (1976), p. 134.

5   See: Eberhard Kolb, Bergen-Belsen, in: Studien zur Geschichte der Konzentrationslager, Stuttgart 1979, p. 151.

6   Concerning Buchenwald see the "Times" of 18 and 19 April (photographs) and 23 April 1945. A report about the filming for newsreels in Buchenwald appeared in the "Times" of 1 May 1945. Concerning Bergen-Belsen see the "Times" of April 19, 1945.

surfaced about lamp shades made of human skin which had a egedly been found there.[7] The delegation of congressmen and members of Parliament had come to Germany at the explicit request of the Allied supreme commander, General Eisenhower. According to a report in the New York Herald Tribune of 21 April, he was of the opinion that information about the living conditions in these German camps should be circulated as widely as possible in the USA. The same issue of the newspaper also carried a report on conditions in Bergen-Belsen, which was illustrated with photographs. A few days later, on 29 April, the Herald Tribune published a first summary of Buchenwald. It stated that the function of Buchenwald was primarily of a political nature, that is to eliminate Europe's political elite. To that end opponents of National Socialism were killed by a combination of underfeeding and heavy labor, by abuse, beatings and torture, unbelievably overcrowded sleeping quarters and by diseases like typhus and tuberculosis. Reports on the visits of various delegations of congressional representatives and leading members of the press also take up substantial space in the American press. On 7 May 1945 the magazine Life published a pictorial report including some particularly shocking photographs from Bergen-Belsen and Buchenwald. This report certainly did not fail to have an effect on the American public.

Information about the SS prison camps in Germany was by no means as extensive on the Continent of Europe as it was in the Anglo-Saxon countries. Relatively detailed reports about Buchenwald were followed, mostly, by only short notices about the liberation of the other camps. One example is from the *Neue Zürcher Zeitung* which printed a full report of the Swiss News Agency on 26 April 1945. On the next day this was supplemented with a two-column article by its own correspondent. It followed on 1 May with a short dispatch from United Press about the liberation of the concentration camp at Dachau:

"A first view of the extensive installation of the concentration camp Dachau, which was liberated yesterday, and the SS community lying beside it, provides essentially the same picture as in Buchenwald. Around 32,000

---

7   Conclusive evidence of this has still not been put forward. The allegations in connection with treated human skin, which played a particularly important part in the trial of Ilse Koch, the wife of the notorious camp commander of Buchenwald, Karl Koch, are in our context not so much to be seen as a problem of the sensationalist press, but more as an example of how much the image of the Germans suffered in the eyes of the international public after the reality of the concentration camps beeame known. A fair, scholarly discussion of the problem of human skin preparations from concentration camps can be found in: Arthur L. Smith jr., Die Hexe von Buchenwald. Der Fall Ilse Koch, Cologne 1983, especially pp. 102–105 and 123–137.

prisoners were freed, many of them in a pitiful condition and practically starved to death. The prisoners had been treated according to the same barbarian methods as in the other concentration camps already eaptured. The usual gas chambers, crematoria, torture chambers, whipping posts, and gallows were to be found. In addition there was found in Dachau a train of 50 cars, all of which were packed with corpses ... The survivors, insofar as they are able to travel, will now be transferred with American ambulances to improvised hospitals near the Czechoslovakian border. An honorable burial is to be given to the dead.

In the English press, too, the reportage on Buchenwald was far more detailed than on Dachau, although neither camp was liberated by British troops. On 23 April, already before the liberation of Dachau, the *Manchester Guardian* published a letter that reads almost like an introduction to what was later to be demanded of the public in understanding and self-examination, it was written by a German emigrant who knew the camp at Dachau from personal experience.

Before I was so lucky as to come to this country as a refugee in the summer of 1939, the Gestapo had sent me from one concentration camp to another for several years. I will recall one incident which was significant not only when it occurred, in 1938, but up to a few months ago in this very country, Great Britain.

In May 1938, a batch of prisoners arrived at Dachau (near Munich). Amongst them was the editor of a well-known Viennese Socialist paper (I cannot give the names, as I have simply forgotten them). We asked him:

'You have been visited by our comrades who have been released previously, you have even printed and published their reports. Why did you not act accordingly?'

His reply was:

'I have to admit that we received numerous reports about the conditions in these concentration camps. Some of them we even published. But, to tell you the truth, we did not believe them!'

That is the point. Not only in Vienna but all over the world nobody believed us. The cruel realities were unimaginable. Now the world is bound to believe. Why not earlier? How many lives could have been saved!

o. Winter, Huddersfield"

The capture of Dachau and the liberation of the prisoners on 29 April was followed on 1 May by the first press information which was based entirely on news agency reports. While the London *Times*, using a Reuter dispatch, added nothing new to the information in the *Neue Zürcher Zeitung*, the report in the *Manchester Guardian* on the same day, published under the headline "32,000 Freed at Dachau — SS Guards Attacked", contained some additional information:

The capture of the notorious concentration camp near Dachau, where approximately 32,000 persons were liberated, was announced in yesterday's S.H.A.E.F. communique. Three hundred SS guards at the camp were quickly overcome, it said.

A whole battalion of Allied troops was needed to restrain the prisoners from excesses. Fifty railway trucks crammed with bodies and the discovery of gas chambers, torture rooms, whipping posts, and crematoria strongly support reports which had leaked out of the camp.

An Associated Press correspondent with the Seventh Army says that many of the prisoners seized the guards' weapons and revenged themselves on the SS men. Many of the well-known prisoners, it was said, had been recently removed to a new hide-out in the Tyrol.

Prisoners with access to the records said that 9,000 died of hunger and disease, or were shot in the past three months, and 4,000 more perished last winter.

As well as this notice, in the same issue the *Manchester Guardian* dedicated an editorial to the camp at Dachau:

"Dachau has the infamous distinction of being the first Nazi concentration camp. Hitler came to power on 30 January 1933. Within six weeks the president of the Munich police announced that Dachau was being prepared for political prisoners — Communists and 'Marxists' — for whom it was impossible to find room in the State prisons. Dachau was to hold 5,000. From that time onwards Dachau was a name at which to tremble. Into it went a steady stream of political prisoners of all sorts, from Communists to Nazis who had fallen foul of all their authorities, and Jews. It was one of the show places of the Nazi system, in which, under proper guidance, visitors were permitted to see the 'educational work' by which the politically backward were converted into good German citizens. But the visitors never saw the whole nor did they see what happened in those dark detention cells and overcrowded dormitories or on the work parties. The details of what Dachau was like before 1939 are well known. We published several accounts at the time and they were confirmed by the evidence in the Government's White Paper of October 1939. What has happened in the five and a half long years since we are now hearing from the American liberators."

The most thorough coverage of Dachau appeared understandably in the American press. After all, American soldiers had liberated the camp; additionally, as in Great Britain, Dachau was in the US a synonym for the coercion and persecution of National Socialist Germany. The American public and the American soldiers at the fronts which were still being desperately held, above all by SS troops, were very greatly agitated by the reports so far published about the atrocities in the concentration camps which had already been liberated.

The first press reports about the liberation appeared in the issues of 1 May, two days after the liberation — Dachau was taken on a Sunday. The individual articles agreed with one another on many details; but they deviated from each other in strikingly many points which could easily have been verified. Concurrence appeared to be greater with information which apparently came from prisoners' accounts and which could be based on the prisoners' internal camp information system, for example, statements about the numbers of evacuation transports in the last days or of deaths in the final months before the liberation.

There are more contradictory statements in the events directly observed by American war correspondents, for example, in the number of railroad cars on the sidings of the camp filled with people who had starved,[8] in the descriptions of combat actions in the camp itself, in the number of SS guards killed or taken prisoner, the reactions of the prisoners and the GIs toward the SS men. The drama of events which have just taken place and the portrayal dominated by the narrow field of personal observation necessarily produces a different relation to objectivity than the epic report focusing on events lying farther in the past and based on a series of similar or identical testimonies.

Before all the US press reports, which are available to everyone, the information service of the 42nd US Infantry Division, the Rainbow Division, deserves to be reprinted here. It was intended only for the officers and a small group of specialists in the Division. The report was produced as a one-page hectographed leaflet. On the back it carries the headline "42nd Infantry Division — World News — Tuesday, 1 May 1945":

"Dachau is no longer a name of terror for hunted men. 32,000 of them have been freed by the 42d Rainbow Division. The crimes done behind the walls of this worst of Nazi concentration camps now live only to haunt the memories of the Rainbow men who tore open its gates and first saw its misery, and to accuse its SS keepers of one of the worst crimes in all history.

When Infantrymen of the 42d Division fought their way into Dachau against fanatical SS troops who met deserved violent deaths along the moats, behind the high fences and in the railyards littered with the bodies of fifty carloads of their starved victims, these hardened soldiers expected to see horrible sights. But no human imagination ... could have been prepared for what they did see there ...

---

8   Nico Rost. Goethe in Dachau. Literatur und Wirklichkeit, München, n. d. The transport train of Jewish prisoners, which was to have left Dachau on 24 April, could at first not leave the camp for days because of a lack of locomotives and because of low-flying aircraft. At the liberation on 29 April the train with cattle cars, which the US troops found, was however an evacuation transport from Buchenwald.

Seasoned as they were by long acquaintanceship with stark reality, these trained observers gazed at freightcars full of piled cadavers ... and they could not believe what they saw with their own eyes.

Riflemen accustomed to witnessing death had no stomach for rooms stacked almost ceiling-high with tangied human bodies adjoining the cremation furnaces, looking like some maniac's woodpile ...

Ten days before the arrival of the Rainbow Division fifty carloads of prisoners arrived at Dachau from the Buchenwald concentration camp in a starving condition after 27 days without food. When Buchenwald was threatened by advancing American troops the Nazis hurriedly crowded about 4,000 of their prisoners into open flatcars unfit even for cattle. 27 days later — days of exposure to freezing weather without anything to eat, a trainload of human suffering arrived at Dachau ...

In these stinking cars were seen the bodies of these prisoners too weak even to get out. A few tried, and they made a bloody heap in the door of one of the cars. They had been machine gunned by the SS ...

Some of the cars had been emptied and the bodies carted to the crematory. In one room adjoining the furnace-room on the left they were neatly stacked. 'The stripped corpses were very straight. But in the room on the right side they were piled in complete disorder, still clothed.

These on the right were just as they were dumped out of the freight cars where they had died of starvation.

It was incredible that such things could happen today, but there was the visible proof.

It was unbelievable that human beings were capable of perpetrating such unspeakable atrocities, but there were the men who did it. The SS.

At least 25 and perhaps 50 were beaten to death by inmates who struck with all the fury of men who suddenly release years of pent-up hate.

Someone said there were 14 in the canal. One in a railroad car had no face left.

Now the SS Guards were dead. But their deaths could not avenge the thousands dead and dying there in Dachau.

Those tortured dead can only be avenged when our world is aroused so much by what the 42d uncovered at Dachau and by what others have found at the other Dachaus scattered throughout Germany, that never again will any party, any government, any people be allowed to mar the face of the earth with such inhumanity."

In the *Rainbow Reveille*, obviously the Division newspaper of the 42nd US Division, there appeared ten days later, on 11 May, an article about the concentration camp whose title "This Was Dachau" already suggested a more distant view. The author attempted to link the still fresh experiences of the days of the liberation with the historical development in National

Socialist Germany, with the expansion of the concentration camp Dachau and with the simultaneous disintegration of moral norms to produce an historical overview of the phenomenon of the concentration camp:

"In the year 1933, near the pleasant, conventional suburb of Munich called Dachau, a prison was established. It began in the form of wooden barracks in a barbed wire enclosure, and was called a 'concentration camp'.

It was the beginning of the New Order in Europe. As the power of the new Chancellor, Adolf Hitler, grew, the camp at Dachau grew with it. Grim, grey-black walls rose around it, closing it in from the rest of the world. Horrible sounds, babbling, animal-like screams of pain, sometimes came to the ears of the citizens of the suburb from the direction of the sinister camp... As the years passed, more and more thousands were herded into the vast torture-chamber. Few ever left it alive. Similar open sores erupted elsewhere on the face of Germany, at Buchenwald and Landsberg and a dozen other places, but Dachau was the oldest, and the biggest.

On 30 April 1945, American soldiers ended Dachau's 12-year reign of terror, and men of the 42d Division saw for themselves, when they overran the camp, what was probably the greatest concentration of human misery in the history of the world ...

All the prisoners were political prisoners, but not all were foreign. Many were Germans. Many were Germans who had been there from the first, for twelve years. They had survived only because they could work. Those who became too weak to work, who broke an ankle or an arm, perhaps, got no food. Either they starved to death, or went to the crematory.

Why was Dachau established? What had these men done to cause the Germans to send them to such a place? There is not one but various answers to this question. Some were there because they had dared to stand up for their convictions, as opposed to the vile theories of Hitler's New Order. Others were there because they were Jews ...

Others in Dachau had been sent there simply because they had been denounced by some enemy with political connections, perhaps merely a disgruntled neighbor or some business competitor ...

Unnatural as were the horrible crimes committed at Dachau, they were the natural outcome of the Germans' belief in themselves as a master race, a natural outcome of their contempt for the political and religious beliefs of all who differed with them. What was violated at Dachau was not only the bodies of countless victims of the master-race bullies. The spirit of democracy, of decency and tolerance was also consumed in the flames of its hideous crematories ..."

Although an extensive textual criticism is not intended, it does seem important here to draw attention to some points which are either typical of the articles compiled here or which need supplementary explanation.

What, in comparison to memoirs, is rather disagreeably noticeable is the attempt, understandable in the medium of the newspaper, of the journalists to put together some hastily gathered information, without precise background knowledge, to make an interesting article. Language difficulties alone meant that it was often not possible for the reporters to assess the reliability of their informants. And this explains reports about mass gassing in the one gas chamber of the camp. Since the prisoners, apart from certain squads, could not go into the crematorium structures — at least as long as they lived — it is understandable that they took the numerous executions carried out in the crematorium to be in part gassings and after the liberation gave testimony to this effect. In fact, the gas chamber in the crematorium at the camp Dachau was never put to use. In Dachau no gassing took place.[9]

Of course, one could not expect an exhaustive study of the concentration camp Dachau from the reporters "of the first hour". The details reported often have a very random character, in some articles one clearly sees, for example with the repetition of facts which had already been described, that the authors were under time pressure. This explains the frequent contradictions in details. In the *Rainbow World News* of 1 May, it is, for example, reported that the train with the Buchenwald prisoners arrived in Dachau already ten days before the liberation of the camp. But in a later report of the *Rainbow Reveille* of 11 May, they say only four days. In addition to this, of course, is the widespread lack of knowledge about Germany in general and about the concentration camps in particular, which leads to the consequence that the camp Landsberg, one of the many subsidiary camps of Dachau, is called an independent camp like Dachau itself or Buchenwald.

In this matter, the daily newspapers differ in no way from the military bulletins and newspapers — aside from literary style, where the professional papers clearly have the advantage. The first newspaper reporters and news correspondents came to the camp directly with the fighting troops; because it was Sunday, however, their reports did not appear until two days later. On 1 May, the *New York Times* simply brought a shortened report from the Associated Press:

"Dachau, Germany's most dreaded extermination camp, has been captured and its surviving 32,000 tortured inmates have been freed by

9    Concerning crematoria and gas chambers, see the contribution of Barbara Distel in: Nationalsozialistische Massentötung durch Giftgas. Eine Dokumentation, hrsg. v. Eugen Kogon/Hermann Langbein/Adalbert Rückerl u. a. Frankfurt/M. 1983, p. 277–280; also a contribution by Günther Kimmel, Das Konzentrationslager Dachau. Eine Studie zu den nationalsozialistischen Gewaltverbrechen, in: Bayern in der NS-Zeit, Bd. 2, hrsg. v. Martin Broszat/Elke Fröhlich, München/Wien 1979, p. 391 f., 407.

outraged American troops who kilied or captured its brutal garrison in a
furious battle ...

The troops were joined by trusty prisoners working outside the barbed-
wire enclosures. Frenchmen and Russians, grabbing weapons dropped by
slain guards, acted swiftly on their own to exact full revenge from their
tormentors.

The sorting of the liberated prisoners was still under way today but the
Americans learned from camp officials that some of the more important captives had been transferred recently to a new hideout, probably in the Tyrol ...

Prisoners with access to records said that 9,000 captives had died of
hunger and disease or been shot in the past three months and 14,000 more
had perished during the winter. Typhus was prevalent in the camp and the
city's water supply was reported to have been contaminated by drainage
from 6,000 graves near the prison.

A short time after the battle there was a train of thirty-nine coal cars
on a siding. The cars were loaded with hundreds of bodies and from them
was removed at least one pitiful human wreck that still clung to life. These
victims were mostly Poles and most of them had starved to death as the
train stood there idle for several days. Lying alongside a busy road nearby
were the murdered bodies of those who had tried to escape.

Bavarian peasants — who traveled this road daily — ignored both the
bodies and the horrors inside the camp to turn the American seizure of
their city into an orgy of looting. Even German children rode by the bodies
without a glance, carrying stolen clothing ...

The camp held 32,000 emaciated, unshaven men and 350 women
jammed in the wooden barracks. Prisoners said that 7,000 others had been
marched away on foot during the past few days. The survivors went wild
with joy as the Americans broke open their pens ...

Bodies were found in many places. Here also were the gas chambers
— camouflaged as 'showers' into which prisoners were herded under the
pretext of bathing — and the cremation ovens. Huge stacks of clothing
bore mute testimony to the fate of their owners ...

The Americans stormed through the camp with tornadic fury. Not a
stone's throw from a trainload of corpses lay the bleeding bodies of sixteen
guards shot down as they fled.

In the mess hall of the guards' barracks, food was still cooking in the
kitchen. One officer was slumped over a plate of beans, a bullet through
his head. Nearby was a telephone with the receiver down and the busy
signal still buzzing. Outside the power house were the bodies of two
Germans slain by a Czech and a Pole working in the engine room.

The main part of the camp is surrounded by a fifteen foot wide moat
through which a torrent of water circulates. Atop a ten foot fence is charged

barbed wire. When Lieut. Col. Will Cowling of Leavenworth, Kan., slipped the lock in the main gate, there was still no sign of life inside this area. He looked around for a few seconds and then a tremendous human cry roared forth. A flood of humanity poured across the flat yard which would hold a half dozen baseball diamonds — and Colonel Cowling was all but mobbed. He was hoisted to the shoulders of the seething, swaying crowd of Russians, Poles, Frenchmen, Czechs, and Austrians, cheering the Americans in their native tongues ...

The joyous crowd pressed the weight of thousands of frail bodies a-gainst the wire, and it gave way at one point. Like a break in a dam, the prisoners rushed out, although still penned in by the moat. Three tried to climb over the fence, but were burned to death on the top wire, for the current still was on. Two guards fired into the mass from a tower, betraying their presence. American infantrymen instantly riddled the Germans."

The *Chicago Daily Tribune* printed a more complete impression of the Associated Press report in its edition of the same day, here the reactions of the German population are also reported:

"Correspondents and infantry men found 39 open type railroad cars on a siding that ran thru the walls of the camp.

At first glance the cars seemed loaded with dirty clothing. Then one saw feet, heads and bony fingers. More than half the cars were full of bodies, hundreds of bodies ...

The best information available was that this trainload of prisoners, mostly Poles, had stood on the tracks several days and most of the prisoners had been starved. Others had been shot thru the head. Clothing had been torn from some and their wasted bodies bore livid bruises. Some had tried to escape; their bodies lay along the tracks five or six steps way. One, shot thru the head, was astride a bicycle.

This spectacle was outside the walls of the camp, along a widely traveled road inside the city of Dachau where Bavarians passed daily.

The civilians were looting an SS warehouse nearby, passing the death train with no more than curious glances at the American soldiers."

One woman, the correspondent of the *New York Herald Tribune*, Marguerite Higgins, produced the most impressive report about conditions in the camp.[10]

Of all the articles of the daily press which have been reviewed here, hers is not only the most vivid, but also the most reliable. More precisely

---

10   Her entrance into the enclosed camp area while the fighting was still going on is also mentioned in printed memoirs; see Edgar Kupfer-Koberwitz, Die Mächtigen und die Hilflosen. Als Häftling in Dachau, Bd. 2: Wie es endete, Stuttgart 1960. p. 257; Johann Steinbock, Das Ende von Dachau, Salzburg 1948, p. 28; Yéfime, Die letzten Tage in Dachau, in: Wort und Tat, September 1947, p. 103.

than any of her colleagues she described the special features of the crematorium, its hidden, inaccessible location, the executions through shooting in the neck, the torture of hanging by the hands; indicatively, she did not report about gassing. The details in her article serve an informative purpose and are not to the same extent as with many of her colleagues filled with striking embellishments; her accounts have been confirmed by memoirs and results of research:

"Troops of the United States 7th Army liberated 33,000 prisoners this afternoon at this first and largest of the Nazi concentration camps ...

This correspondent and Peter Furst, of the army newspaper 'Stars and Stripes', were the first two Americans to enter the inclosure at Dachau, where persons possessing some of the best brains in Europe were held during what might have been the most fruitful years of their lives.

While a United States 45th Infantry Division patrol was still fighting a way down through SS barracks to the north, our jeep and two others from the 42d Infantry drove into the camp inclosure through the southern entrance. As men of the patrol with us busied themseives accepting an SS man's surrender, we impressed a soldier into service and drove with him to the prisoners' barracks. There he opened the gate after pushing the body of a prisoner shot last night while attempting to get out to meet the Americans.

There was not a soul in the yard when the gate was opened. As we learned later, the prisoners themselves had taken over control of their inclosure the night before, refusing to obey any further orders from the German guards ... The prisoners maintained strict discipline among themselves, remaining close to their barracks so as not to give the SS men an excuse for mass murder.

But the minute the two of us entered a jangled barrage of 'Are you Americans?' in about sixteen languages came from the barracks 200 yards from the gate. An affirmative nod caused pandemonium.

Tattered, emaciated men, weeping, yelling and shouting 'Long live America!' swept toward the gate in a mob. Those who could not walk limped or crawled. In the confusion, they were so hysterically happy that they took the SS man for an American. During a wild five minutes he was patted on the back, paraded on shoulders and embraced enthusiastically by prisoners. The arrival of the American soldier soon straightened out the situation.

I happened to be the first through the gate, and the first person to rush up to me turned out to be a Polish Catholic priest, a deputy of August Cardinal Hlond, Primate of Poland ...

In the excitement ... some of the prisoners died trying to pass through electrically charged barbed wire. Some got out after the wires were decharged and joined in the battle when some ill-advised SS men holding out in a tower fired upon them. The prisoners charged the tower and threw all six SS men out the window. After an hour and a half of cheering, the crowd was calmed down enough to make possible a tour of the camp. The only American prisoner, a flyer, with the rank of major, took some of the soldiers through.

According to prisoners, the most famous individuals who had been at the camp had been removed by SS men to Innsbruck ...

The barracks at Dachau, like those at Buchenwald, had the stench of death and sickness. But at Dachau there were six barracks like the infamous No. 61 at Buchenwald, where the starving and dying lay virtually on top of each other in quarters where 1,200 men occupied a space intended for 200. The dead — 300 died of sickness yesterday — lay on concrete walks outside the quarters and others were being carried out as the reporters went through ...

The crematorium and torture chambers lay outside the prisoner inclosures. Situated in a wood close by, a new building had been built by prisoners under Nazi guards. Inside, in the two rooms used as torture chambers, an estimated 1,200 bodies were piled.

In the crematorium itself were hooks on which the SS men hung their victims when they wished to flog them or to use any of the other torture instruments. Symbolic of the SS was a mural the SS men themselves had painted on the wall. It showed a headless man in uniform with the SS insigne on the collar. The man was astride a huge inflated pig, into which he was digging his spurs.

The prisoners also showed reporters the grounds where men knelt and were shot in the back of the neck ...

Just beyond the crematorium was a ditch containing some 2,000 more bodies, which had been hastily tossed there in the last few days by the SS men, who were so busy preparing their escape they did not have time to burn the bodies.

Below the camp were cattle cars in which prisoners from Buchenwald had been transported to Dachau. Hundreds of dead were still in the cars due to the fact that prisoners in the camp had rejected SS orders to remove them."

Even after the liberation American newspapers still published articles about living conditions in the former concentration camp Dachau, which were only slowly getting back to normal. Of chief interest was everyday life in the camp with all its torments. But in the reports the revenge of the prisoners on their torturers also found a sympathetic response. A good example for this is the report which the *New York Times* published on 2 May, under the headline, "Dachau Inmates Get Revenge on Nazi Torturers. SS Men Are Found Slain. Beaten to a Pulp. Their Middle Fingers Cut Off":

"A terrible vengeance met SS (Elite Guard) tormentors guarding the Dachau concentration camp when they fell into the hands of some of the infuriated inmates.

Bodies in SS uniforms were found in a half-dozen places, beaten to a pulp, the middle fingers cut from their hands before or after death.

Many inmates displayed their own mutilated hands from which fingers had been severed, and swore their Nazi guards did this to them to add to their torment.

The incongruous sight in this stinking den of sadistic Nazi torture and extermination of helpless prisoners is a variety of signs admonishing inmates and others how to behave and be sanitary. In the filthy crematory where the bodies of the slain were destroyed, for instance, was a big sign reading: 'Cleanliness is a special obligation here. Therefore don't forget to wash your hands.'

At the entrance gate ... prisoners faced a huge sign on the administration building roof informing them: 'there is only one way to freedom. Its milestones are obedience, industry, cleanliness and love for one's people.'

The inmates were marked with letters indicating their nationality and with colored triangles indicating the nature of the offenses with which they were charged, For instance, 'T' meant they were Poles. A green triangle meant they were accused of a criminal offense, pink meant homosexual, red stood for political, black for so-called social or anti-social prisoners.

Their food consisted of a slice of bread and a bowl of watery soup daily ... The barracks were overcrowded, with two prisoners to a narrow bunk. The death rate normally was 112 to 135 a day.[11]

Buildings for the SS guards and administrative staffs occupied at least four times as much space as the narrow inner compound for prisoners ...

Electrically charged barbed wire and a water-filled ditch surrounded the inmates' compound. Guard turrets and concrete bunkers were placed along the ditches, from which SS guards safely could fire upon the prisoners in event of a wholesale escape attempt. Hangings, they said, were done publicly. But when prisoners were beaten to death, this was done secretly."

The prominent figures from all over Europe, some of whom had lived for years in the concentration camp Dachau and who were evacuated in the last hours before the liberation, filled the newspaper columns for some days still. With the title, "Odor of Death Still Pervades Dachau Camp", the *Chicago Daily Tribune* published an A. P. report on 3 May:

"The stench of corpses, filth, and pollution, the perils of typhus and the horrible spectacle of the 'living dead' still pervaded the Nazis' Dachau prison camp today. But American troops and military government officials

---

11  The number of over 100 dying daily certainly is correct for the months after January 1945. The prison camp recorder Domagala registered a total of 27,839 dead for the years 1940–1945 alone, not including those executed, who were not listed in the camp books. The International Trace Service Arolsen registered a total of 31,951 dead. See: Kirrunel, op. cit. p. 385, footnote 167.

have moved in and started to cleanse it of the filth. There is food for the hungry, and those who smoke receive cigarettes.

The Americans learned that many more of the notables ... were spirited from the camp to a stronghold in the Tyrol, Austria, just before the advancing Americans liberated Dachau. Among these was Nicholas Kallay, former Hungarian premiers who had been believed dead.

A niece of Russian Foreign Minister Molotov, listed as Aleksel Hokorin; a son of Italian Marshal Pietro Badoglio; a German General von Falkenhausen, and at least one member of the Krupp industrial family were among those also reported removed from Dachau."

A further A. P. report from the headquarters of the 6th US Army, which the *New York Times* published on 7 May, was concerned in as much detail as was possible at the time with the contradictory behavior of the SS in the clearance of the camp, which had not been completed, and cited once again the evacuation order[12] of Himmler, which is also often mentioned in memoirs, but is no longer available today:

"Gestapo Chief Heinrich Himmler ordered the evacuation of the notorious Dachau concentration camp on 14 April and the extermination of all its inmates to prevent any witnesses to German inhumanity falling into Allied hands, the Sixth Army Group said in an official statement tonight.

The commander at Dachau suggested to Himmler that the camp be turned over to the Allies, the announcement said it was learned through documents seized by the United States Seventh Army. Himmler replied with an order prohibiting such a move and concluded, over his own signature:

'No prisoner shall be allowed to fall into the hands of the enemy alive. Prisoners have behaved barbarously to the civilian population at Buchenwald' (The Buchenwald camp was liberated by the Americans the week before the Himmler order was written).

No explanation was given immediately why the camp was not evacuated as ordered by Himmler and why stacks of dead prisoners and long rows of the barely living victims were left to betray the German brutality."

The effect of the many corpses, marked by hunger and brutality, which still lay in and around the camp, on the soldiers of both Divisions who had captured the camp was graphically described in a report in the US Army newspaper *Stars and Stripes* on 3 May 1945:

"Fifty boxcars still stand on a spur track beside the Dachau prison camp. Twenty are filled with human bodies killed during the past week. Some are wrapped in filthy rags, others completely nude.

12  Published as an appendix in Rost, op. cit. p. 310. See the contribution of Stanislaw Zámečník in Dachauer Hefte, No. 1.

Many doughboys who took Dachau with the 42d and 45th Divs. surveyed the mournful sight today and talked about it in hushed, shocked tones. Pvt. John Mackisin, of Youngstown, Ohio, in the 232 FA Bn., said:

'I've always thought they exaggerated to make us hate the Krauts. Now I know these things are true. More Gls should see this with their own eyes. It would harden us up a lot.'

Doughboys cast angry glances in the direction of German civilians passing by the freight ears ... They avoided looking in the direction of the trainload of corpses and pretended they did not know they were there.

All along the track lay corpses which had fallen out of the cars. Not one good German had the decency to stop and cover a body with a sheet. They seemed to think it none of their affair.

The Dachau crematorium is a long low brick structure with a tall smokestack from which smoke poured day and night. The gas chamber is 20 feet square and has 18 nozzles across the ceiling which look like shower outlets ...

The guards told the murder-house victims to undress and prepare to shower. They entered the room nude and when the room was full, the door was shut tight and the gas turned on while attendants watched the death throes through a telescopic device in the wall.

Adjoining to the death house is a dog kennel where 122 huge dogs were kept to torment prisoners. The dogs were Great Danes, shepherds, Wolfhounds and boxers. SS men frequently stripped prisoners and hung them up for the dogs to jump at while they tapped the prisoners' testicles with sticks. When the dogs leaped up and tore off a man's organs, SS men howled and patted the dogs and gave them meat. Many dogs now lie dead beside the kennels where doughboys shot them.

Cremating was done by habitual criminals who were fed well while on detail and promised liberty and parole after several months of good service. But the Nazis played a wry joke on their helpers. When parole time came they were pushed into the gas chambers themselves.

The biggest headache of the Dachau camp commander, who ran all camps in Bavaria and Austria[13] was the shortage of fuel for ovens. When

---

13   The subsidiary camps or detachments belonging under the authority of the con-
     centration camp Dachau were scattered across wide areas of Bavaria, mainly,
     south of the Danube and in the western half of Austria. Since subsidiary camps
     such as Landsberg or Kaufering are repeatedly treated as independent concentra-
     tion camps in Allied press reports, the attribution of a kind of supervisory function
     over the Bavarian and Austrian concentration camps is probably based on this
     fact. A list of all the Dachau subsidiary camps can be found in Kimmel, op. cit.,
     p. 381–383. The former camp commander of Dachau, SS battalion leader (SS-
     Sturmbannführer) Martin Gottfried Weiss, had become "unemployed" as the
     commander of the concentration camp Lublin due to the advance of the Red

coal was lacking, people were taken from the gas chamber and thrown in a great pit within the camp where 8,000 now lie."

It is even more obvious in the article in the army newspaper than in the one already cited from the *New York Herald Tribune* of 2 May that at least some Americans had in the meantime learned to distinguish between the "good" and the "bad" Germans in the camp itself, between those imprisoned for political reasons and the criminals of the camp. For good reasons this was at first true only of the inmates of the prison camp and even towards them there was some resentment, the "bad" Germans rubbed off on the "good". This can also be seen indirectly in a report from the *New York Herald Tribune* of 12 May, which appeared with the headline, "34 Nations Represented Among the Dachau Inmates. Official Check Sets Total at 31,601 Prisoners":

"A reminder of the wholesale enslavement of people of many nations which was practiced by the Germans came today in an announcement at Supreme Headquarters that among the 31,601 prisoners at Dachau, an official check has shown, were persons of thirty-four nationalities.

Those imprisoned at this infamous German camp were Poles, Russians, French, Slovenes, Italians, Czechs, Belgians, Hungarians, Dutch, Austrians, Greeks, Spaniards, Luxemborgers, Iranians, Croats, Norwegians, Serbs, Rumanians, Slovaks, Lithuanians, Albanians, Letts, Estonians, Bulgarians, Portuguese, Sudetans, annexed Germans, Armenians, Swiss, Arabs, Danes, Irakians, Maltese and Finns.

There were also 2,539 Jews whose distinct nationalities were not given.

Germans (Reichsdeutsche) do not appear at all in this listing. Nonetheless, the Germans and the Austrians, with together over 6,000 prisoners, made up the fourth largest group among the nations in the camp even in 1945. The largest group was the Poles (almost 15,000), then the Russians (over 13,500) and then the Hungarians (around 12,000). The Germans formed a larger group than the French, the Italians or the Lithuanians."[14]

How difficult, even impossible, it had become for Americans to form an objective judgement about Germany and the Germans, precisely because of the increasing number of publications[15] about what had happened in

Army. He was ordered to return to Dachau shortly before the end of the war to support the actual camp commander, SS head battalion leader (SS-Obersturm-bannführer) Eduard Weiter. Whether he occupied such a position or if Weiter made the practice of such a position possible, cannot be substantiated documentarily. See: Kimmel, op. cit., p. 373 f.

14  See: Statistik der Nationalitäten im Konzentrationslager Dachau und seiner Außen-lager vom 16.-26. April 1945 aus der Lagerschreibstube; original is at the IST Arolsen, a copy is in the museum of the memorial site at Dachau, No. 845.

15  Magazine articles illustrated with photographs from the camps deserve mention here, for example, "Army Talks", 4th year of publication, no. 9 from 10 July 1945, issued by ETOUSA, the high command of the American Army in Europe. It

the concentration camps, is shown by an article about the findings of American publishers and newspaper editors who had returned from viewing Buchenwald, Dachau and other camps. The article was published in the *New York Times* on 9 May:

"American editors and publishers who were flown to Europe at the suggestion of Gen. Dwight D. Eisenhower to investigate German atrocities returned here yesterday morning, convinced that peace terms for Germany must be harsh.

Spokesmen for fifteen of the original delegation of eighteen newspaper and magazine executives asserted that published reports of the horrors and tortures perpetrated in German concentration camps at Dachau and Buchenwald were 'all too true.' ...

Joseph Pulitzer, editor and publisher of *The St. Louis Post-Dispatch*, voiced the sentiment of his colleagues, when ... he said:

'We were asked to go there to verify the conditions reported in the press. We found they were not exaggerated. As a matter of fact, they were understated. I am for a just but very severe peace as far as the Germans are concerned.'

'I'd say it couldn't be too severe,' Norman Chandler, publisher of the *Los Angeles Times*, added.

Gideon Symour, executive editor of *The Minneapolis Star Journal*, said: 'We've got to police Germany for the next twenty years, if the American people will stand for it.' ...

Stanley High, associate editor of *Reader's Digest*, said: 'We found no feeling of remorse among the Germans. If you talk to a German now, you wouldn't think there are any Nazis left — or at least only one, and that would be Hitler or the fellow next door.'

Mr. Pulitzer said he did not see how the average German could help not 'knowing of conditions when they saw thousands of these peoples being shipped out to work every day.' All Americans should see the atrocity pictures and newsreels, he added, declaring: 'The greater the shock to the American people, the better will be the realization of the horrors.'

The group expressed impatience with the theory that such pictures should not be shown in 'family theatres.' William L. Chenery, publisher of Collier's

placed a photograph of the main entrance of the camp Dachau at the front of a "Report about German Death Mills". See also articles in "Life" from 14 May 1945, in "Collier's" from 15 and 23 June 1945 and the most detailed and vivid one in "Time" from 7 May 1945. – Cf. also the documentary film about the concentration camps with which the US Army confronted the German population. See Brewster S. Chamberlin, Todesmühlen. Ein früher Versuch zur Massen-"Umerziehung" im besetzten Deutschland 1945–1946, in: Vierteljahrshefte für Zeitgeschichte 29 (1981), p. 420–436.

Magazine, said that 'if some people have to endure these atrocities, certainly other peopie can look at them.'"

As a reaction to the horror of the camp, the occupation powers had begun to draw upon the German guards and in some cases even the male inhabitants of the surrounding communities for cleaning out the concentration camps. The German language New York newspaper *Der Aufbau* reported on a compulsory visit which had been ordered by the Military Government for the German civilian population, including 30 dignitaries of the city of Dachau under the heading "The Jewish Flag Flies above Dachau":

"The correspondent of the JTA reports from Dachau: 'The blue-white Zionist flag flies above the watch tower of this feared concentration camp. When I came here to make observations about the fife of the Jewish inmates of the camp, it turned out that the American troops were still having to fight serious adversities in order to clean away the terrible conditions which the Germans have created in Dachau. Many things are still crying out for improvement, but nonetheless, 1,000 of the 2,539 Jews are already under hospital care. Dr. Benjamin Zacharin, a very well-known surgeon from Kaunas, who works in the camp hospital, explained to me that, with the appropriate care, most of them would survive.

All the camp inmates, Jews and non-Jews, are terribly impatient to leave the camp. However, that will not be possible yet for some time since 500 cases of typhus have appeared here ... The Jews themselves are not represented in the international camp committee. They have constructed their own Zionist 'center' under the direction of Chaim Kagan, who earlier headed the statistical office of the city Kaunas.

Lt. William Montague, a former film producer from Hollywood, ... has just completed, after ten days' work, filming the Dachau murder factory.

The population of Dachau maintains that it had no idea what was going on behind the electric barbed wire, only a few steps away. The lieutenant was able to bring a group of more than 30 leading citizens of the city of Dachau into the camp and to photograph the reactions reflected in their faces. Some fainted, as is shown in the film; others held handkerchiefs in front of their noses, and those, who were still able to speak as they left the camp, whispered outside again and again, 'unbelievable'."

A document of a special kind is represented by the comprehensive article by the London correspondent of the Polish newspaper Rzeczpospolita of 29 May 1945, which he had telegraphed to his editors on 17 May. The report is reprinted here in a shortened form, especially with personal references to relatives of the prisoners in Poland omitted:

"I am sending today the first report about my visit to Dachau in the capacity as the accredited correspondent of 'Rzeczpospolita' ...

Somewhat less than one kilometer before the gate of the concentration camp, the road divides into two directions. The one to the left goes to the city of Dachau with 15,000 inhabitants. The other one to the right goes to the concentration camp Dachau with twice the number of inmates. The sign with the inscription 'to the concentration camp' points out the way — and above this sign there is a colorful bas-relief which depicts the well-known picture of the German painter Spitzweg, 'The Three Merry Musicians'. The first plays a violin, the next a bass and the third a trumpet — all three frisk merrily about, showing the way to hell — to the concentration camp Dachau. Can one imagine a greater cynicism? ... We drive along a wonderful, magnificent avenue as if we were approaching a palace. On both sides stands a row of modern luxury-houses. These are the dwellings of the SS criminals. Finally, we arrive at the camp gate. We cannot drive farther because of the typhus and the outbreak of lice which prevail in the camp grounds. Therefore, at the entrance we have to undergo a special procedure: inoculation against typhus and spraying with insecticide. While standing in line, I speak in Polish to a camp translator from the group of camp inmates. I had, of course, recognized him as being Polish by the white-red badge in his buttonhole and the letter 'T' on the obligatory red background on his jacket. I have in my life often seen people who are happy and touched, but it is difficult for me to describe the rapture of this Pole when I addressed him in his mother tongue. It turns out that he is a priest ... He tells me that the American troops captured the camp on Sunday, 29 April, at 6:00 pm, three hours before the intended massacre of the prisoners, which had been set for 9:00 pm. In one of the guard houses abandoned by the Germans there was found an order of Himmler from 14 April. In answer to the question of the head squad leader (Obergruppenführer) Pohl, under whom all the concentration camps stood, about the future fate of the camp Dachau, Himmler ordered: 'There is no question of surrender. The camp is to be evacuated immediately. No prisoner shall be allowed to fall into the hands of the enemy alive. Prisoners have behaved barbariously to the civilian population in Buchenwald, signed Himmler.' ...

In this moment the car of the current American commander arrives. It is Colonel Joyce, who gives instructions, in concise military words, about conduct on the camp grounds and about relations with the former prisoners. The colonel has not yet come to an end, when, suddenly, his driver rushes up to me and excitedly shakes my hand. It turns out that he was also a prisoner — the Pole Zenon Tim ...

Finally, we got to the camp. The way leads through a wide avenue to an area surrounded with barbed wire which had formerly been electrified. In the middle a walled double gate with a high watch tower. Behind the gate a wide area, behind that, to the left, a long street with barracks on both sides. The grounds and the street are filled with people. A beautiful, warm day, and thousands of former prisoners are walking, conversing in various languages, sunning themselves and enjoying freedom, still for the time being in an area surrounded with barbed wire because of the epidemics and contagious diseases in the camp. For the time being the former prisoners are not allowed to leave the camp unauthorized ... Their faces are emaciated, their eyes sunken and with many of them, their eyes are glowing with fever. In prisoners' clothing with long white and blue stripes or in ragged suits, the former prisoners give the appearance of being creatures from another world. ... Those inside the barracks, who on the tenth day of their freedom are still not able to enjoy the sun, lie motionless on the plankbeds, barely able to lift their heads. Only now and then do their eyes reveal a certain interest in the new world surrounding them. They are closer to death than to life. Still today, the tenth day of freedom, 125 persons die each day in the camp, as reported to me by the American senior medical officer of the camp.. On the tenth day of freedom 32,250 of the former prisoners of Dachau are still alive ...

At the end of my visit in the camp I was still the witness of a terrible proceeding, that is, the removal of the dead from the crematorium. In the last weeks of their murderous activities, the Hitler criminals ran out of coal which was necessary for burning the corpses. The corpses had simply been thrown on a pile in the crematorium, where they have lain for three weeks. When the Americans opened the crematorium, a terrible sight was offered to them: five-thousand decomposing bodies, attacked by worms from which arose a horrible odor. At present the bodies are buried in mass graves — 400 daily. From the city Dachau Germans have been mobilized to clear the bodies out of the crematorium. I was still a witness to the heartless impassivity with which the Germans cleared out those bodies and how with complete detachment, they threw them like wooden blocks on the open wagons — each time, thirty bodies on a wagon drawn by two horses. When twelve wagons were loaded in this way, the train of wagons, driven by the Germans, began to move toward the gate, along the main road through the streets of the city of Dachau to the cemetery — to the mass grave. On the wagons lay, visible for all, charred corpses and skeletons, covered over only with thin skin, with the stink of decomposing bodies. Witness to the shame and proof of the crimes of the Germans."

The mass of readers' letters on the themes of tyranny, war and dictatorship are devoted to the conquered Germans and above all to the concentration camps. An exemplary collection of such remarks was published by the *New York Herald Tribune* on 24 April 1945 under the eloquent headline "Hell on Earth", with the sub-title "Shocked and Enraged Reactions of Readers, to the Mass Atrocity of the Nazis". "What citizen of the civilized world can hear the names 'Germany' and Japan' without a feeling of rejection? Why don't we extinguish these names forever from the family of nations?'" asked one indignant reader. And the American delegation of publishers declared in a common resolution on their return from Germany, that the German people could not be released from their part in the responsibility for these crimes. And furthermore, a just punishment was demanded for the leading figures of the Third Reich and the German general staff, for the party functionaries, all members of the Gestapo and the SS. The demand was also made that for sheer reasons of justice and for the future of world peace these people be indicted as war criminals on the basis of their official positions (*Chicago Daily Tribune*, 6 May 1945).

The idea of the collective guilt of the German people was once more enormously popularized in the foreign press at the end of the war through the discovery of the concentration camp horror. Almost all peoples of continental Europe had, through a long-term process of habituation, accommodation and the development of counter-reactions, to a degree internalized the "normal" hardships of war and the pecularities of the National Socialist race and minority politics, so that to them the discovery of the SS prison-camp system only represented a gradual intensification of what they already believed the Germans capable of. But the exposure of the net of concentration and death camps shocked the American public in a totally different proportion. Many Americans of German descent felt themselves to be in a situation of collective consternation. America had a high percentage of European emigrants, many of them Jews, who by now formed part of public opinion with their own personal interest in the future fate of the Germans. Moreover at the end of the Second World War America had a position of undisputed moral supremacy in the world. The USA thus not only took a leading part in preparing and conducting of the International Military Tribunal in Nuremberg, but in their twelve subsequent Nuremberg war crimes trials against the leadership elite of the Third Reich they also surpassed all similar trials of other Allied states against former Axis powers, both in the rank of the accused as well as in the political importance of the trials. There is a clear line of development from the reporting about the persecution and extermination measures in the camps of the SS to the Nuremberg trials, the so-called Dachau trials and finally even to the series of trials against Nazi criminals in German courts. In this line of development lies the importance of the reporting about Dachau, Buchenwald and other camps rather than in the historical sources of individual accounts, which often raise as many questions for historians as they answer.

Wolfgang Benz

# Between Liberation and the Return Home

## The Dachau International Prisoners' Committee and the Administration of the Camp in May and June 1945

When Liberation came, the concentration camp changed from a place of imprisonment, exploitation and annihilation under the control of the SS to the "autonomous Republic of Dachau under American protection".[1] This peculiar social entity existed for about six weeks and ended with the departure of the last exprisoners some time in June 1945.[2]

But as far as externals were concerned, for most of the prisoners the situation after 29 April, the day of the Liberation, did not differ much from before. Even if the threat from the SS had ceased, the danger to life continued, from typhus and typhus fever, from the shocking sanitary conditions and from the corpses that lay about everywhere and the removal of which was still in progress a week after the Liberation. Nor did the Liberation mean liberty, at least not the liberty to leave the camp area.

Under the date of 29 April 1945, a declaration was promulgated, from which the "Comrades" — this was now the official designation and form of address — discovered that "as the supreme representatives of the prisoners of all nations and for the preservation of order, an International Prisoners' Committee has been formed" which decreed, among other things, the following with immediate effect: "The supreme executive organs of the camp are the Camp Elder and the Camp Secretary. All their instructions, which are given with the approval of the International Prisoners' Committee,

1 Edmond Michelet, Die Freiheitsstraße. Dachau 1943–1945, Stuttgart, n. d. (1960), p. 252.
2 The exact point in time cannot be established on account of the bad state of the records; the Italians were still in Dachau at the end of June; it is possible that there were still stateless persons and some people too ill to be moved in the camp area or at the evacuation points much later. As an indication, c.f. the Communique 1/45 of 3. 7. 45, in which Jan Domagala as "Camp Secretary" announced rules of behaviour in the name of the "Camp Office of Dachau" (Collection of the Instructions of the International Prisoners' Committee, Archive of the Dachau Memorial Site).

are to be carried out at once. The entire police force is under the command of the Camp Elder and is to ensure peace and security with all the means at its disposal. Any infringement will be punished immediately in the strictest manner."[3]

And a few days later the Camp Elder made it known that the commander of the American Liberation army had issued this decree: "Anyone found outside the camp without a pass will be shot" and the Camp Elder added that the "Commandant demanded the strictest discipline, quiet and order within the camp as well."[4]

The situation of this social entity consisting of people of many nations was without precedent. In many ways it no doubt resembled a medieval town in which the plague had raged, but where in contrast to the latter over-population also prevailed. The imprisonment suffered together had, as was soon revealed, by no means resulted in an awareness of equality and fraternity among all the inmates, and not all regarded patience and solidarity as the most important virtues demanded by the situation.

The task faced by the International Prisoners' Committee as legislative and executive organ of self-government at the same time was gigantic. 32,000 former prisoners from nearly all the countries in Europe had not only to be fed and clothed, they had to be issued with a provisional proof of identity, and for many of them a home country had first to be found: for the Spaniards, for example, who had fought against Franco, for the Yugoslavs who had become Italian citizens through no action of their own or who, as opponents of Tito, had no wish to return to their homeland. There were Greeks and Albanians in Dachau who were listed as Italians; there were Lithuanians, Estonians, Latvians and Ukrainians who were claimed by the Soviet Union against their will; there were nearly 10,000 Poles and over 2,000 Jews in the camp, the nationality of some of whom was the subject of controversy. To say nothing of those unfortunate young men from Belgium, Norway and Holland who had let the Nazis seduce them into service with the Waffen-SS, then deserted and had finally arrived in Dachau as prisoners. In those cases where their compatriots did not make short work of them on the spot, terrible things awaited them when they arrived home.[5]

Spontaneous vengeance also threatened all those prisoners who had acted as agents of the SS; numerous capos, the overseers, met their fate in the same hour that brought liberation to their victims.

The first meeting of the prisoners' committee after the Liberation, which took place in the presence of the commander of the American troops, Lt. Col.

3   Idem.
4   Idem, Announcement of the ce, undated.
5   Michelet, Die Freiheitsstrafe, p. 258 f.

Fellenz, on the evening of 29 April 1945, or perhaps not until the morning of 30 April,[6] was taken up with the problem of preventing the chaos that was threatening for the reasons mentioned. In this meeting, the American commander handed over all authority in the camp to the President of the committee, Patrick O'Leary. The Americans wanted to restrict themselves to providing protection in relation to the outside world; they promised to take over the supply of provisions in a few days' time. The camp Elder, Oskar Müller, a German Communist, an inmate of many years' standing who combined an essential honesty with stubbornness, and the Camp Secretary, Jan Domagala, a Polish priest, were designated as the executive agents of the camp. The camp police was put under the command of Gustav Eberle "until further notice".

The first and most important decrees issued by the Committee were:
1. "Nobody is permitted to leave the camp".
2. "Any weapons in the camp must be handed in to the office immediately".
3. "Arbitrary actions, acts of personal vengeance etc. will be punished at once with the most vigorous measures."

The commandos necessary for supplying the camp (the term "commandos" was retained from the terminology of the time before the Liberation, and officials involved in the internal self-administration also continued to be called "capos") were able to leave the grounds with passes. The Prisoners' Committee established three sub-committees which were to be responsible for food (Jan Marcinkowski), discipline (Oskar Juranic) and disinfection and sanitation (Frantisek Blaha). This was the first organizational framework the International Prisoners' Committee provided for the Camp.

The Committee itself had been formed before the Liberation, indeed it had existed as an underground organization for some time before the arrival of the Americans, and had taken over the internal control of the camp immediately before they appeared. Its activities in the last week of April had consisted of sabotaging the evacuation transports out of Dachau, of offering help to those arriving from other camps until the very end (for instance, the 400 women from Landsberg, who arrived on 23 April, and the 120 women from Auschwitz, who arrived in Dachau on 26 April). Their

6    The "Report on the first meeting of the International Prisoners' Committee in the liberated camp at Dachau" is undated. As stated there, the report was to be "made public in the most important languages in the course of the morning" which makes the early morning of 30 April seem the probable date. All the subsequent reports which have the character of minutes of meetings, are dated. They are in the archive of the Memorial Site of the Concentration Camp, and subsequent quotations refer to these.

assistance consisted of organizing food and blankets. The representatives of the national groups had been preparing in particular to resist the expected final annihilation action of the SS against the whole camp. The Committee maintained a well-functioning underground communications network, through which instructions for the ultimate emergency could be spread and through the branches of which news from the SS camp hierarchy could also be gathered.

In the night of 28 to 29 April, when it became clear to the men that the greater part of the guard had vanished, the first "official" meeting of the International Prisoners' Committee took place.[7] The first goal was to organize survival until the arrival of the Allied troops. Enormous difficulties would continue after the Liberation or only become apparent then, namely the health of the 32,000 prisoners, two thirds of whom were ill and debilitated, the supply of food, the absence of medicines and medical equipment. Apart from that, the atmosphere in the multi-national community of the camp was characterized by explosive emotions. "What is important now," wrote Haulot and Kuci, the chroniclers of these events, "is to snatch these 32,000 people from the jaws of death so that they may return home alive and recover from their physical and spiritual sufferings in their home countries. That is the task that lies before us, and that we want to try to fullfil. Under the chairmanship of Major O'Leary, we constituted ourselves as the International Prisoners' Committee, and from that moment on regarded ourselves as the only legitimate authority in the camp ..."[8]

There were fourteen members who, as representatives of the individual nations (or of the national committees), constituted the IPC, the generally accepted abbreviation of the International Prisoners' Committee. Its

7    Cf. the account in Arthur Haulot and Ali Kuci, Dachau (July 1945, unpublished translation in the archive of the Memorial Site, Dachau) p. 25: "At 11.30 p. m. fifteen men gathered as quietly as possible in Block 24: the Canadian, Patrick O'Leary; the Englishman, Tom Groome; the American, René Giraud; the Frenchman, Michelet; the Yugoslavs, Jurenic and Popovic; the Poles, Maczewski, Domagala and Kokoszka; the Czech, Blaha; the Dutchman, Boelard; the German, Müller; the Austrian, Kothbauer; the Belgian, Haulot; the Albanian, Kuci. The Russian General Michailov was unable to appear on account of illness." Michelet, Freiheitsstraße, p. 258 f. on the other hand, dates the first full meeting of the International Prisoners' Committee as being on the morning of 29 April "in the library of the first room of Block 2, on the left avenue, that is, the one nearest to the 'jour house' [the camp gate]". Cf. also Arthur Haulot., "Lagertagebuch" (Camp Diary), in: Dachauer Hefte, 1, Introduction and entry of 29. 4. 1945. Haulot there dates the beginning of the Committee at 6th April, 1945. Cf. also Nico Rost, Goethe in Dachau, Munich, 1946, p. 296 f.

8    Haulot/Kuci, Dachau, p. 26.

composition soon changed[9] and the body became smaller and smaller in the course of the repatriation of national groups. Until 7 May, Patrick O'Leary, who represented Great Britain, was President. Arthur Haulot (Belgium) and Edmond Michelet (France), both Resistance fighters who made political careers for themselves after their return home, were the Vice-Presidents. The writer Giovanni Melodia represented Italy, Oskar Juranic represented Yugoslavia, the Soviet Union was represented by Nikolai Michailov, a general who for some curious reason had escaped the fate of so many high-ranking Russian officers as German prisoners of war. Georg Pallavicini spoke for Hungary, Alfons Kothbauer for Austria, Dr Ali Kuci sat on the committee for Albania (and for the small groups of peoples from the Balkans, later for Greece as well) — he achieved remarkable things as the person in charge of the press and cultural matters, having been Minister for Information in his homeland. Josef Kokoszka represented the Poles and the delegate of the Czechs was Frantisek Blaha, a doctor who plays an extremely praiseworthy role in many of the memories of the suffering in Dachau. Norway, Holland, Luxemburg and Spain also had representatives on the IPC at various times, As a result of objections from General Michailov, members of individual nationalities of the USSR such as the Lithuanians were not separately represented. Nor did the more than 2,000 Jews have their own representative at first, since their national status was not easy to clarify. And the 1,100 German prisoners were not represented as a nation in the first instance either.

While the Austrians celebrated a national rebirth with red-white-red flags and insignia and demonstrated a new selfconfidence before everybody in the camp,[10] the Germans had become outcasts. Their two-fold identity — as compatriots of the SS and as companions in suffering for, in most cases, many years of imprisonment in the concentration camp — now sent them to the bottom end of the camp community. They had no flag when the whole camp broke out in a sea of bright national colours (the liberated prisoners had found large quantities of material for them in the stores and workshops of the SS), and the German language, yesterday the only official idiom, retreated entirely into the background. Despite this, of course, German remained an important means of communication in the

9   The composition of the IPC was made public in the proclamation of 29 April. Fourteen representatives were named; the following information is verified by the minutes of the meetings. Some uncertainties (including in the spelling of some of the names) could not be removed. Thus, for instance, the American and the Englishman mentioned by Haulot/Kuci do not appear; it is also unclear from what date the Greek representative belonged to the I PC, and from when until when the "small groups of Balkan peoples" had their own delegates.

10   Johann Steinbock, Das Ende von Dachau, Salzburg 1948, p. 34 f.

Babylonian confusion of Dachau, within the new government of the camp as well as in interaction with the outside world.[11]

"The first have become the last," wrote former prisoner No. 16921 Karl Adolf Gross in his diary on 30 April. This was, he wrote, somewhat unfamiliar to the Germans who even as prisoners still belonged to the "master race and noble class". And Gross continued: "Just between ourselves, we have to be glad that they did not bash our skulls in; did not the various kinds of pashas, moguls, pharaohs, capos and those on fatigues do all they could to encourage the mistaken notion that there is no difference among the Germans whether they be SS-Führer or prisoners, that they are all the same block-heads and all belong into the bull family? For our pashas had right up to the end been chosen almost exclusively from among the Germans, and did they do anything to destroy this notion? Certainly, the SS is not in the least exonerated by this. On the contrary, it is evidence of the cunning they employed in that they had direct maltreatment replaced more and more by the cruelty of the prisoners to one another, thus building human weakness and malice into their system".[12] For this reason the fact that a German exercised the functions of "Camp Elder" is a more a miracle than an accident. This fact can perhaps be better explained by the personal qualities of the anti-fascist Oskar Müller, who had only been appointed to the office shortly before by the SS, and had then, in close cooperation with the still illegal national committees, made preparations to prevent the catastrophe feared by all — the massacre they expected of the retreating SS in the final hours before the arrival of Allied troops.[13] Oskar Müller, an energetic and political man (later, from October 1945 to December 1946, he was Minister for Labour in the first post-war government in Hesse), succeeded the notorious Armenian Johann Meanssarian, who had been removed from the position as Camp Senior by the SS in the middle of April 1945 and had been executed by firing squad on the orders of the US commander immediately after the Liberation, together

11  At the 7th meeting of the WC on 8 May, the French representative Michelet had declared that French had to be the prevailing language for the negotiations of the Committee. As in the founding conference of the UNO in San Francisco, English, Russian and French were to be the official languages; for practical reasons, German could be retained as a fourth one. The Belgian Haulot, who presided, noted that all previous meetings had been held in French, English and German, he himself always translated from German to French and vice versa.

12  Karl Adolf Gross, Fünf Minuten vor zwölf. Des ersten Jahrtausends letzte Tage unter Herrenmenschen und Herdenmenschen. Dachauer Tagebücher des Häftlings Nr. 16921, Munich n. d. (1947), p. 216.

13  Cf. "Einer von 'Nacht und Nebel'. Was Arthur Haulot zu Dachau sagt", in: Süddeutsche Zeitung, 18. 12. 1945. See also Hermann Langbein, ... nicht wie die Schafe zur Schlachtbank. Widerstand in den nationalsozialistischen Konzentrationslagern 1938–1945, Frankfurt 1980, p. 382.

with the German Wernicke, capo of the camp police.[14] Even in view of the vengeance that was wreaked everywhere in the concentration camps against the former prisoners who had been given functions by the grace of the SS, it was remarkable that a German Camp Senior was able to retain his authority. Finally, on 6 May, a German committee was also formally constituted.[15]

There were several reasons why the gate of the camp remained closed for most prisoners after the Liberation and why for many, it took weeks before they were free. While fighting continued in Southern Germany, there were no means of transport available for the former prisoners and at the very least they would have been in danger on their homeward journey. But the population of the area surrounding the camp had to be protected from marauding liberated prisoners wanting to make up for the deprivation they had suffered. (It was not possible to prevent this entirely despite all precautions, but the depredations of plundering camp inmates in the Dachau hinterland did not come anywhere near the grave fears.)

Apart from the difficulties with transport, the state of health of most of the prisoners was a decisive obstacle to their returning home; even the constitution of the apparently healthy proved not to the drastic improvement in nourishment after a few days. Typhus and typhus fever had been epidemic for months in any case. This fact, together with the catastrophic hygienic conditions, prompted the Americans to place the entire camp under quarantine. A further reason for maintaining the prison-like conditions lay in the fact that former guards and officials from the ranks of the SS as well as of the prisoners, had disappeared in the camp, hoping to escape justice by wearing prisoners' clothes.

All this, and not least the repatriation question, characterized the situation and the problems between Liberation and the return home. There was an absolute contrast between the high spirits of the Liberation and the bureaucratic procedures which the Americans had thought up with the

14 Report of the first meeting of the IPC; Meanssarian, born in Saloniki, stateless spy and Gestapo agent, had not become camp Elder until the beginning of 1945. The policecapo Wemicke was a former member of the SA in the Horst Wessel-Sturm, who had got into the concentration camp as a result of criminal offences. These two had created an atmosphere in the camp in April, "which was supposed to lead to an explosion. 'Our way lies with the SS', they emphasized again and again and tried to gain control of the camp with a group of 500 dark elements. Had this been successful, the consequence would have been a devastating bloodbath." (Oskar Müller, So wurden 33,000 befreit, in: Mitteilungsblätter der Lagergemeinschaft Dachau, December 1970.) Meanssarian and Wernicke were the two officials of the camp hierachy who were removed by the illegal prisoners' organization, cf. Haulot, Lagertagebuch, Einführung und Eintragung vom 29. 4.1945 Introduction and Diary entry of 29. 4. 1945.

15 K. A. Gross, Fünf Minuten vor zwölf, p. 242 f.

best of intentions and which they implemented in cooperation with the national prisoners' committees.

Reports and chronicles of the concentration camp at Dachau usually end at the latest with the description of the festivities on 1 May 1945, when on the parade ground of the camp in the middle of a forest of flags and banners, the Liberation and imminent end of the war were festively celebrated with speeches in fifteen languages.[16] But the celebrations — many national groups also celebrated the Liberation in their own separate functions — were followed for most inhabitants of the camp by periods of waiting that were hard to bear. In the late afternoon of 1 May, the third meeting of the International Prisoners' Committee took place. On this occasion, the American Captain Martin Agather elaborated (in German) the approaching struggle with redtape in the following words: "The main thing is that you get home as soon as possible. So that we can do this as quickly as possible, we would like you all to give us a little help. We have here a questionnaire. Everyone who is in the Camp has to fill in a questionnaire. So we want you as a group, each from his own nation, to make sure that we get help with these questionnaires. You can choose as many assistants as are necessary. It depends on the size of the group. So that this will happen as quickly as possible, the Major, who is our assistant officer, will check that all questions are correctly answered. I shall show you this evening how this questionnaire is to be filled out. For this reason, I am now distributing the questionnaire to all those present. These questionnaires are printed in English and German and the answers are to be written in block capitals. Pay attention, there are a few questions here that require some explanation. In the question about profession, we mean profession in civilian life. In the question about the place of arrest, we mean the place where the arrest took place. Under details concerning imprisonment, we mean any cruelty that you personally have suffered. An American court will be set up in the camp. All those who have committed atrocities will appear before this court and receive their punishment. On the second page, line six, there is the question: Have you ever been convicted of a punishable offence? This question must be answered precisely. There are some people in the camp who are here because of crimes, we have to know this. The next question refers to anything that relates to the previous question: date, court, trial, date of release from prison — everything has to be answered precisely on the questionnaire. We need four questionnaires for each person. We have to have the questionnaires filled in as quickly as possible, so only one copy of the questionnaire is filled in. As soon as we have the individual questionnaires we will ask you

---

16  Idem, p. 217; Michelet, Die Freiheitsstraße, p. 253 f.; Steinbock, Das Ende von Dachau, p. 36 f.

to have the other three copied on a typewriter and signed by the person filling it in."[17]

A lively discussion developed, in which the representatives of the national groups demonstrated the difficulties faced in filling out of the questionnaires: linguistic problems, since English was one of the rarer languages in the camp, doubtful or no longer valid citizenships, questions of nomenclature. Typical of the requests for further information was that of the Italian Melodia, who wanted to know whether in the case of Italian military prisoners who had been transferred from an Italian military prison to a German concentration camp, the date of the Italian or German arrest was decisive; General Michailov wanted to know which citizenship Russian emigrants had to state, if they had emigrated in 1917 and now wished to return to their old homeland.

Despite all this, the American Captain was confident that the clearance of the camp could be accomplished in 30 days. He already had five thousand forms at his disposal, he was expecting a further 100,000 in the next few days. The clerks and interpreters got to work.

The greatest difficulty in the next few days lay in explaining to the inhabitants of the Camp the limits of their liberty and in keeping these limits effective with appeals and threats. On 2 May the Americans drew the reins in more tightly. An order had come from Eisenhower's headquarters that no-one was permitted to leave the Camp who had not been disinfected. Besides this and despite all precautions inhabitants of the camp who were plundering and loafing about in the town of Dachau were a cause for concern. Anyone found outside the camp without permission would be shot; orders to this effect had been issued to the US troops in Dachau, Captain Agather declared in the meeting of the IPC on the evening of 2 May. Inside the camp as well, conditions were giving cause for concern. Agather implored the men of the International Prisoners' Committee: "There is to be no strife in the camp, rather you ought to live together as good comrades. We do not want to be guards. You are free and you shall live in freedom, only you cannot go out for the time being until the requirements have been met."[18]

In order to restore order and discipline which had started to falter in the camp, the organization of the authority structures responsible for Dachau

17  Report on the 3rd meeting of the I PC, 1. 5. 1945.
18  4th meeting of the IPC, 2. 5. 1945. Some insight into the life of the camp is given by the circular of the Camp Elder to all blocks of 9. 5. 1945: "During a check by American medical personnel, it was observed that cleanliness and hygiene in the individual blocks leaves extraordinarily much to be desired. I therefore order: The cleaning of the blocks will take place in the usual fashion. That is, after waking and breakfast, the rooms and dormitories must be cleared of all comrades insofar as they are not bedridden or ill. The cleaning/fatigue duty will then clean

were tightened on 2 May on the orders of the American commandant. The
commander of the US troops installed himself as the "Camp Commandant",
the president of the IPC became the "Lagerführer" or Camp Leader, and in
this capacity Patrick O'Leary was the executive agent and directly responsible
to the US commandant. On the level below this — "Lagerältester" Camp
Senior and "Lagerkapos" Camp capos — everything remained as it had
been. The "police capo", the chief of the camp's internal police troop, was
given the power to arrest any miscreants immediately. The authority in
legal matters was vested in the person of the Jugoslav Committee member
Juranic as it had been previously; this received complaints, carried out "trials"
and reported on these to the IPC. How seriously the Americans took their
function in preserving security and order can be gauged from all sorts of
complaints and grievances with which the International Prisoners' Committee was obliged to concern itself. For example, the American military
police confiscated a truck laden with spare parts for radios which an official
unit had obtained outside the Camp on the instructions of the IPC. Radio
receivers were vital for the morale in the camp. In another instance, they
would not even allow a unit to leave the camp to acquire clothing, even
though it was properly equipped with the regulation passes. And the
President of the International Prisoners' Committee, Patrick O'Leary, who,
as a British officer, was called urgently to London by telegram, was initially
refused permission to make the journey by the Americans who pointed out
that no-one was allowed to leave the Camp on account of the quarantine
regulations.

Nonetheless, O'Leary was able to leave the camp on the evening of 7
May;[19] this brought about another change in the hierarchy. O'Leary's

dormitory, living room, washroom and latrines most thoroughly. Buckets with
calcium chloride are to be placed in all latrines. The latrine duty is to strew calcium
chloride over the toilet bowl and basin. I remind you once again that, in the
interests of the proper distribution of food, the sick must be brought to room 4,
and if there are too many, to room 3 of each Block. Only in this way is it possible
to hand out normal food for the healthy and semi-solids for the sick. In irresponsible
fashion, in isolated dormitories the ceilings have been destroyed with the intention
of hiding and concealing organized things in the roof. I am making the Block
officials responsible for obtaining new ceiling boards in cooperation with the
Camp Capo in order to repair the damage."

19  5th meeting, 5. 5. 1945 and 6th meeting, 7. 5. 1945. Patrick O'Leary was in
    reality a Belgian, whose name in civil life was Albert Guérisse. He arrived in
    September 1944 from the Natzweiler Concentration Camp and was regarded as
    a Canadian. It was for this reason too that he had become President of the IPC,
    since the rivalries among the French, Poles and Russians for this office were avoided
    by the election of the representative of the smallest national group. O'Leary was
    the only "Canadian" in Dachau. Cf. Langbein, ... nicht wie die Schafe, p. 172.

successor as camp leader was the American lieutenant Charles Rosenbloom; this gave the advantage of very close contact with the American authorities. As a member of the liberating army, however, Rosenbloom could not be a member of the IPC. O'Learys position as President of the International Prisoners' Committee was now taken over by the Russian Michailov. This was actually merely pro forma. In fact, the affairs of the camp government were run by the Belgian Haulot, as they had really been from the start. The composition of the camp government changed a number of times before the disbanding of the Camp. But until 6 June, when the worst was over, Haulot and Rosenbloom provided continuity and efficiency during the concluding work. Haulot, who took over the office of President officially from 26 May after Michailov's departure, does not appear to have had a successor. After this the almost entirely empty Camp was administered solely by the Americans, who tried and sentenced the former masters of Dachau and other concentration camps before military courts there from November 1945 onwards.[20]

The International Committee had shrunk more and more from the end of May. The Czech doctor Frantisek Blaha, who had rendered such outstanding services to the medical care in the camp, left for home on 23 May. (He ran a hospital in Prague until 1968, when he fell into disfavour.) His successor as head of the medical service in the camp was a Dr Dortheimer, who represented the Jews on the IPC. Pallavicini, the Hungarian, went to Paris on 26 May to confer about the repatriation of his countrymen. The majority of the French had left the camp on 22 May; on 26 May the Greeks representative also changed; their delegate on the IPC had been arrested on suspicion of having collaborated with the SS. Ali Kuci, who represented the Rumanians and Bulgarians as well as his own Albanian compatriots, now also took over the representation of the Greeks in the IPC. Kuci remained in the camp until the end and, in his capacity as head of the press and in charge of cultural activities, he provided information and entertainment. (He then returned to Albania and was not heard of again). On 31 May, the Polish representative also changed, because Josef Kokoszka departed. On 2 June the time came for Oskar Müller, the Camp Senior, to return home too; his successor was the Jugoslav Senko Knez who had hept the minutes of the IPC until then and who knew all the

20   The last extant minutes of a meeting of the IPC is dated 31. 5. 1945 (18th meeting); the last plenary meeting of the IPC took place on 6 June, and at this Rosenbloom was discharged. His successors were Captain Smith and Lt. Smolen. On 6 June, it was decided that, instead of the IPC, a sub-committee including the two Americans would meet every morning. Cf. Communique of the 1 PC, NO. 32 of 6. 6. 1945.

languages spoken in the camp. On 5 June Oskar Juranic, the "Minister of Justice" in the camp government, also left Dachau.[21]

One aspect that was not only extremely remarkable but also fairly problematic for the camp community was the nationalism which flared up immediately after the Liberation. It was only natural that the individual national groups should conduct ceremonies on the parade ground to celebrate their survival and freedom. In view of the situation, however, national egoism, and worse still, the occasions on which it manifested itself, were strange and difficult to comprehend. The fact that the Norwegian Rasmus Broch complained in the International Prisoners' Committee that the Norwegian flag had not been hoisted during the celebrations on 1 May was harmless. The French, on the other hand, evidently often made the lives of their comrades of other nationalities thoroughly difficult. On 7 May Haulot declared in the meeting of the Committee that there was French agitation in the camp that could no longer be tolerated. Thus for instance, he said, French officers had repeatedly demanded that their compatriots be admitted into the overfilled sick bay, for which there was neither cause nor justification. At first there had been disagreements about insufficient consideration of the French language and about the inappropriate placement of the Tricolour; the French were of the opinion that their flag should fly next to the American Star-Spangled Banner and the flags of Great Britain and the USSR, but in the spring of 1945 China was regarded everywhere as the fourth nation of the "Big Four" instead of France. A donation of food by the French Army immediately after the Liberation, before the Americans could provide supplies, and the utilization of this assistance for propaganda purposes, kept the International Prisoners' Committee in suspense for some time.[22]

The French representative Michelet liked to revert to fundamentals in questions of prestige, and even compared the Prisoners' Committee with the inaugural conference of the UNO in San Francisco to prove, for example,

21   Cf. especially the 17th meeting of the IPC on 26. 5. 1945, as well as the communiques of the I PC, in which the head of the press section Kuci farewelled the departing national groups and IPC members with cordial words. – At the 15th meeting of the IPC, Dr Schreiber was welcomed as the representative of the Jewish group. Haulot noted that he was invited to all future meetings of the IPC, but did not act "as a delegate of the Jews as a national group", as the Jews hat not been recognized as such a group, "since, in accordance with the current resolutions of the views of the Committee, the Jews belonged to those national groups whose citizens they are. The Jews have established their own information office, of which Dr Schreiber is the head. He takes part in the meetings without the right to a vote."

22   Michelet, Die Freiheitsstraße, p. 252 f. and 256 f.; 7th Meeting of the IPC, 8. 5. 1945 and 12th Meeting 14. 5. 1945.

that the French representative really deserved the presidency of the IPC. When Michelet, in the course of such an argument, complained vehemently that no representative of the French National Committee had been invited to meet the US ambassador to Paris, who had paid an inspection visit to the Dachau camp on 8 May, it was the last straw. Kuci pointed that they had only found out about the event the night before: "If Michelet slept while we worked and slaved away to have everything ready, then he has only himself to blame for the consequences." And Haulot added: "while we made these preparations in the greatest imaginable haste, we really did not have the time to think about all the possible consequences". And he went on, incidentally, there were more urgent matters to be attended to and people ought not to fritter the time away with this sort of thing.

Michelet justified himself by pointing out that his compatriots had been upset, he as a "disciplined member of the Committee" had tried to pacify them and had been able to prevent a protest demonstration. Apart from this the French were among the poorest inhabitants of the camps; this fact and the particular sufferings of the French were acknowledged by the members of the Committee. Frantisek Blaha did remark, however, that, as long as he had been on the Committee, no one had heard a single word from him that referred to his nation in particular: "We must all consider only the well-being of the camp as a whole".[23] Other members of the Committee expressed similar sentiments.

An appeal to practise solidarity and to desist from political demonstrations, to await the procedures involved in disbanding the Camp patiently in order to avoid chaos and anarchy, was issued in the name of the International Prisoners' Committee by the press chief Ali Kuci to the press sections of the national committees. Under the heading: "Two Duties and one Principle: Friendship, Brotherhood and No Politics ..." the article reads as follows:[24]

"Twelve years have passed since this Dachau Camp was founded. Twelve years have passed since Hitler the beast grasped power in Germany. Only twelve years. Years of suffering and monstrous pain. A very small span in the enormous space of countless centuries, but a very sad and depressing chapter of human history ... A Hitler obsessed with power wanted to subjugate the world, and the soil of Germany became the grave of Europe. This our Dachau was a grave too. The grave of hundreds of thousands. And we survived it. And today, we are alive ...

---

23  7th Meeting of the IPC, 8. 5. 1945.
24  IPC, Information and Culture, Central Press Bureau, 8. 5. 1945: To all the Press Bureaus Dachau. Two duties and one Principle: Friendship, Brotherhood and No Politics ... Archive of the Dachau Memorial

We have woken from a long sleep and a terrible dream. The darkness of that long uncertainty and of the macabre scenes of the dream are fresh in our memories: we cannot comprehend the reality. Our conscious mind is incapable of grasping the happiness of liberty.

The most important thing is that we have been returned to life, that we are alive today. And the reason we are alive today is thanks to the friendship and brotherhood that existed in the Camp. We shared all the sorrows and sufferings of the difficult times, but we never hated one another, never spied on one another. In the Nazi-hell, there were no Germans, no Russians, no Poles, no Jugoslavs: here there lived a community of friends and brothers, a family threatened by death on all sides, a society with the same principles and ideals. All had one and the same aim: the death of Hitler's thugs and their supporters. It was for this that we waged war in the high mountains and the wide plains of our homelands. This was the motto of the emaciated in Dachau.

And now we are free. The glorious armies of the Allies have fatally wounded the beast, it lies dying already ...

Tomorrow, we shall return to our home and hearth. We shall find our loved ones and above all our homelands free and independent. It is there that we shall begin our social activities. Not here. Here we are in Dachau, the scene of the cruelty and the mass murders. And in this place, our thoughts would always dwell full of horror with the events of the past. Nothing more. Nothing else. We must give our liberators time to help us and for the wounds of the past to heal. We must make it possible for our representatives to carry out their tasks. No chaos, no anarchy! Those who yesterday betrayed our cause will have to answer before the camp court and will be charged. But the lives of thirty three thousand people so run down as to be mere skeletons must not be placed at risk. Anyone who tries to disturb the peace will be punished by all. Nothing will be forgiven him ...

Here there are only two duties and one principle: friendship, brother-hood and no politics ..."

Naturally, those who had been imprisoned in the Camp for years on account of their political views, as opponents of the Hitler regime or as resistance fighters, could not desist from politics at all or only with difficulty. To demand political abstinence in the situation of the liberated camp was hardly realistic.

The French representatives certainly did exaggerate a little when they anticipated on a lower level, as it were, the sort of obstruction carried out by the French military governor in the Allied Control Council in Berlin from the summer of 1945 onwards. They had made themselves unpopular with the Americans in Dachau because of the constant concern about the prestige of their nation while at the same time showing a great lack of concern about the general situation in the camp. The meeting of 14 May was characteristic. The International Prisoners' Committee was invited to it at the quarters of the American Commandant, Colonel Joyce, who was receiving a visit from General Adams. Lieutenant Rosenbloom introduced the members of the IPC to the General. Michelet, the French representative, was absent. As the items to be discussed included matters of concern to the French, Joyce explicitly stated his regrets at Michelet's absence. When he discovered that the Frenchman had been properly invited, but had declared that he would probably not appear, the American colonel blew a gasket. He complained that Michelet had already failed to comply with a request the previous evening and added that if this were repeated he would have the guards fetch him. Moreover, the situation in the French area was terrible, they disregarded the quarantine regulations, they walked around the hospital with typhus patients and generally behaved as though the kitchen was for them alone.[25]

Because the main occupation for most of the inhabitants of the camp was waiting, discipline was soon in a bad way. To the sorrow of the International Prisoners' Committee, the force exercised by the SS was not automatically replaced with a feeling of solidarity that might have served as a mechanism for regulating the life in the camp. Thus for instance, the Camp Senior Müller reported that during a check on two work commandos, one had been found in the roof, where the men were lying in the sun, while the other had dispersed completely, in order to "organize". (On the following day, the head of the work services, Malczewski, announced — "as an illustration of work morale" — that the entire kitchen unit, consisting of 60 men, had run away.) If it was not possible to bring about order by means of the national committees, Oskar Müller declared, "then we shall have to do what we would like to avoid: to ask the Americans to have guards accompany the individual commandos".[26] This would have meant that the US Army would have had to take over the functions of the SS.

The Americans, however, had enough to do with guarding the camp to maintain quarantine and with processing the questionnaires, As far as the Prisoners' Committee was concerned, they contented themselves with appeals about establishing discipline somehow or other. The continuing looting and refusals to work would have to stop. It happened regularly, IPC-member Malczewski reported, "that, for example, a unit is delegated to clean a hut. In fact, however, no-one is at work, since everybody is busy looting. The Americans say to themselves: we don't really care how long this work, which is supposed to make camp life tolerable, is dragged out by those involved themselves ..."[27]

25   13th Meeting of the IPC, 14. 5. 1945.
26   7th Meeting of the IPC, 8. 5. 1945.
27   8th Meeting of the ICP, 9. 5. 1945.

The food supplied by the US Army caused unforeseen problems as well. The empty tins increased the mountains of rubbish in the camp, the removal of which was so troublesome, and in addition, the army rations encouraged many to cook in the streets of the camp in front of the huts; this was problematical not only for reasons of hygiene, but also because some used boards from the beds and other fittings as fuel.[28] The authority of those responsible for discipline in the camp was naturally limited; the "Camp Police", consisting of former prisoners, could not, for example, control the numerous visitors who wandered around the sick-bay area and made the quarantine pointless, as Dr Blaha complained. He would have preferred to have his patients guarded by GIs: "It is difficult for a prisoner (member of the Camp Police) to send all visitors away. For that, there has to be authority, since a uniform is a uniform and a rifle is a rifle ..."[29]

The "Lagerälteste", Camp Senior Müller, on the other hand, tried to provide authority for his camp police by means of an appeal to common sense and a feeling of community in a circular to the Block Seniors: "The Camp Police is not the old 'Lager Polizei'. The Camp Police is only a voluntary service of your comrades to maintain order and security in the camp. For this reason, people ought not to make difficulties for the Camp Police or to abuse them, but to obey their orders, and, wherever possible, to give them full support. Any justified and true accusations are to be reported in writing to the Camp Senior. The Camp Police will, however, take firm action against undisciplined and malicious elements damaging to the Camp community."[30]

A good leisure activities programme would save half the Camp Police, a member of Kuci's Cultural Section had sighed in the IPC Meeting of 5 May, and Michelet had demanded a resolution of the Committee to solve the question of entertainment and activities during the leisure hours. If the people were to sing and entertain themselves, he said, there would be fewer difficulties with them. This was clear to all the members of the Committee,

---

28　6th Meeting of the ICP, 7. 5. 1945.

29　Idem. On the orders of the newly appointed LF Rosenbloom, the Camp Elder had issued an announcement on 7.5.1945 demanding order and discipline: "The sensible comrades in the camp must stand together and support the general order. In the barracks, rooms, toilets, wash rooms and on the block streets the most painstaking cleanliness must prevail in the interests of the health of all comrades. Any breaking out of a new illness or epidemic will necessarily result in the extension of quarantine." And as a measure to strengthen discipline in the Camp, a "special list" was announced, in wich the LF was to enter the names those who had been insubordinate: "Those comrades reported for lack of order and discipline will be released last from the Camp." Notice dated 7. 5. 1945, Archive of the Concentration Camp Memorial Site, Dachau.

30　Circular of the ce. dated 9. 5. 1945

but the possibilities for doing anything were extremely limited. Above all, there was no space for cultural activities in the overcrowded camp. The problem with making the deer-park established by the SS next to the camp available, for example, was partly that it had to be guarded, since many inhabitants of the camp were only waiting for the opportunity to "escape", quite a few succeeded too, even though the Americans issued strong warnings against leaving the camp for home without papers and without a copy of their questionnaire.

The death statistics in the camp for the months of May and June show how terrible the conditions in the camp were after the Liberation, and in what areas the activities of the camp's self administration and those of the Americans were most urgently required. Jan Domagala, the Polish priest who kept a tally in his capacity as Camp Secretary until 16 June, records 2226 dead for May and in June there were still 192.[31] The removal of the bodies of the dead, which had been lying in the camp's street since April, had still not been completed a week after the Liberation. According to the information supplied by the Camp Senior in the meeting of the IPC on 5 May, 100 to 300 dead were buried every day. Particular concern was caused by those dead who were lying in drainage ditches or were floating in the narrow River Wuerm. This small river between the concentration camp and the Camp of the SS, supplied water to the inhabitants of the camp.[32] The Americans carried out a vaccination campaign against typhus and typhus fever and expended considerable efforts on disinfecting the camp inhabitants and furniture. But in order to improve the sanitary conditions, it was necessary in the first instance to reduce the overcrowding, to separate the sick from the healthy — in so far as it was possible to speak of any "healthy" among the former prisoners — and to create space generally. By including the adjoining SS grounds, where there were, above all, better facilities for admitting the sick, the situation gradually improved. As far as

31  Jan Domagala, Die durch Dachau gingen (translation of the report which appeared in Warsaw in 1957 in the Archive of the Concentration Camp Memorial Site, Dachau). By way of comparison: the death rate in Bergen-Belsen, which was liberated by British troops on 15. 4. 1945, was even higher. Between 15 April and 20 June 1945, approximately 14,000 people died there. Cf. Eberhard Kolb, Bergen-Belsen, Hannover 1962, p. 314 f.

32  The supply of drinking water was a frequent topic at the meetings of the IPC. It is characteristic for the isolation of the inhabitants of the Camp that they thought the river next to the camp in which the bodies floated, was the Isar. Cf. 6th Meeting of 7. 5. 1945. Cf. also the circular of the Camp Elder of 9. 5. 1945, which states inter alia: "Drinking the water is highly dangerous. The pumping station has been damaged by sabotage on the part of the SS. The water supply is taken from a stream in which corpses have been found. We warn all comrades against drinking the water."

possible, the relocation took place in closed national groups, which, however, created new problems again.

While the re-quartering into the outer areas of the camp complex did bring some relief, the greatest improvement in the situation occurred when several thousand men were evacuated to the grounds of an SS-huts near the Schleissheim airfield, about 10 km from Dachau. The exodus began in the middle of May; it had been preceded by intense debates and controversies in the International Prisoners' Committee as to which groups should go to Schleissheim. As Lieutenant Rosenbloom announced, they were to stay in the new surroundings for about a fortnight, at the end of which they were to be repatriated. Quarantine was to be complete for everybody on 28 May, as Blaha had already announced in the meeting of the Committee on 10 May. The arguments now broke out as to which groups should be re-located to Schleissheim. According to Domagala's information, the original camp precincts at that time — on 14 May 1945 — held approximately 4,500 Russians, 3,100 Yugoslavs, 9,000 Poles, 2,200 Italians and 1,100 German nationals. Kuci suggested that all the Poles be re-located, that would solve the problem. Haulot objected that there were not enough healthy Poles (the sick could not and would not be moved), the Italians would be included. Michelet opposed this on the grounds that the Poles were "les doyens du camp", all the functions vital to the operation of the Camp were in their hands and they should remain there so that everything did not get into a mess. Haulot then suggested that the 4,500 Russians, together with the 3,100 Yugoslavs, 1,600 Czechs and 1,100 Germans be moved, but General Michailov protested against this. For the most part, the Russians were hardly fit to be moved, since they had only recently arrived exhausted in Dachau from Buchenwald and Flossenbürg. Apart from this, there were, he maintained, not 4,500, but only 3,500 Russians in the camp, of whom only 2,500 were in a position to be moved. Nor could the Germans be considered for re-location either, because, as Oskar Müller pointed out, they were just being moved to the outer areas of the Dachau Camp. The Czechs were ruled out because their repatriation was imminent.

The suggestion that certain quotas of individual nationalities (Italians, Yugoslavs, Poles and Russians) be moved drew protests first from the Jugoslavian representative; his compatriots had always been badly treated, and now they had got the thin end of the wedge again compared with the French and smaller groups who had gone to the outer precincts of the camp. The Polish representative declared that the Poles had spent the longest time in Dachau and had made the greatest sacrifices. Only the Spaniards and the Italians were prepared to move to Schleissheim. After Lieutenant Rosenbloom had once again emphasized the usefulness of having whole national groups move, and the Polish representative had again expounded why the Poles did not wish to move, the US-Lieutenant consulted his superiors and conveyed the recommendation of the Russian Michailov, that the choice should be left to the American authorities. Rosenbloom was able to inform the Committee at once of the decision of the Commandant, Co. Joyce. The first transport was to leave on 15 May and was to consist of 1,000 Russians, and the first releases home were to be from Schleissheim, even before there were any from Dachau. This enticement had its effect (the accommodation, being former SS-barracks, were said to be better there as well); Oskar Juranic announced that, provided the men there would be released more speedily, he agreed to the re-location of the Jugoslavs to the interim camp, though he would first like to get a better picture of the place for himself.

It was decided to form a commission which would have a Pole, a Jugoslav and an Italian as members representing the national groups who were to move. This commission was to inspect the new camp. The Russians did not appoint a member to the commission; General Michailov had refused with a fine justification: "He said he had no wish to see anything, since he had complete faith in the American authorities. We have voiced our reasons, but if it has been determined that we are to move, then we have complete confidence and it is not up to us to choose or to verify, so an inspection is pointless."[33]

Naturally, the conditions in the Dachau camp did not improve suddenly as a result of the loosening up and of the evacuation to Schleissheim. There were even opinions to the contrary. In the old camp there was a terrible atmosphere, declared IPC member Malczewski on 17 May; those who had been moved to the outer areas had a host of advantages, those who had remained behind were living in a desert. The suggestion that the deer-park of the SS be opened to these people as a recreation area still remained unanswered by the Americans; the re-location campaign to Schleissheim had been stopped, as not sufficient accommodation had been prepared there as yet. Conditions were no different and no better than at the time of the Liberation, the Pole Kokoszka put on record; the people were still sleeping on the floor, the situation was catastrophic, there could be mutinies.[34] Five days later, there were complaints about insufficient and bad provisions, it was suspected that the German population outside the camp was living much better; Lieutenant Rosenbloom tried to dispel these fears.[35]

33   12th Meeting of the IPC, 14. 5. 1945.Because of the move to Schleissheim, three meetings of the IPC took place in the course of 14 May; in the afternoon and the evening, the Committee met in Colonel Joyce's quarters in the presence of General Adams who personally calculated the quotas of those to be moved.
34   15th Meeting of the ICP, 17. 5. 1945.
35   16th meeting of the ICP, 22.5.1945.

In order to improve the atmosphere, the chief of the Press Bureau had taken up his pen again. Under the title "Three Questions and two reasons", Ali Kuci urged perseverance in the name of the International Prisoners' Committee, once again imploring the inmates of the Camp to exercise patience and solidarity:

"When are we going home? This is the question everyone is asking the American authorities, the members of the Prisoners' Commitee etc. The people in this Camp are very eager to find out something about the date they will be repatriated. And they are right. For after so many years of suffering and sadness, we all want to go home. To return immediately to our home and hearth and into the circle of our loved ones, to know and see how our countries and our people are faring now that the black clouds have been driven from the sky over Europe, clouds that have darkened the shining past and future of this continent for so many years.

But why are we not going home? There are very few people who can answer this question. Only those who are familiar with the present circumstances and know what is going on here in Dachau. This group of responsible persons knows the true situation. And they are working day and night to help their comrades and to facilitate their way home.

The living conditions in the Camp have greatly improved in the meantime. Our sick are being cared for as well as at all possible in the American evacuation hospitals. The food they are receiving is of a kind that we could not even imagine hitherto. They are content and full. The majority of those whose fate had been sealed in the SS-time now past are saved and are back in the land of the living. The sick, who had been languishing in the misery of quarantine, are now enjoying reasonable health. Their lives have been saved.

How can we go home? Many Camp inmates are suffering from typhus, tuberculosis and other serious epidemic diseases. That is the state of affairs. If the Americans had tried to evacuate us at once, many — about 80 per cent — would have died on the journey. This is one of the reasons why we were unable to return to our home countries immediately. The lives of many thousands were saved by these wise measures of the American authorities.

And the second reason? The epidemics we would have taken home with us would have seriously endangered health in our own countries. We would have caused misery in the beloved places of our homelands. That would have been unfair.

We have lived for many long years in this place as prisoners and deathly shades. We had the courage and the endurance to survive the greatest sufferings known to the history of mankind. We were the victims of the cruellest tyranny in the world.

But now we are free. And we know that we shall be home in a few weeks. Why such haste? All haste, lack of order and insubordination hampers the work of our liberators and postpones our return home. This is why we should stand united together. This is why we should help each other, we among ourselves and all of us the Americans, who are doing so much for us."[36]

When the article appeared, a silver lining was beginning to appear on the camp horizon. Frantisek Blaha, who took part in a committee meeting for the last time on 22 May (this meeting had even been called especially as a farewell to him), announced that the infectious diseases in the camp — except for the sick bay — had ceased and Michelet added that there were no more cases of typhus among the French. Oskar Müller reported that the situation was improving in the camp, which was becoming emptier and emptier. The day before, 2,200 Russians had left the camp, the remaining 1,100 departed on 22 May; of the Czechs, some of a group of 990 had been repatriated, others evacuated already, the rest in the process of departure. The old camp now contained Poles, Jugoslavs, Italians, some smaller national groups, and Jews with unclear nationalities. In all, the population now amounted to only about 10,000 men, who were gradually better distributed. The deer-park was finally made accessible (until 9 p.m.), though the use of the SS swimming pool had to be prohibited again after a short time because the water was contaminated; living conditions altogether had improved,[37] and for many the camp gates had already opened to freedom. The quarantine had been lifted early; and, much to the amazement of those involved, in the bureaucratic procedures too, the Americans had done an about-face, some details of which anticipated the denazification policy as practised later in the American Occupation Zone.

The 12th of May came to be the dramatic climax in the tug-of-war about the release procedures thought up by the office-desk strategists, of the US Army. Captain I. V. Peterson had invited the Prisoners' Committee to his office in order to thank them for their successful work so far in relation to the filling in of the questionnaires; he expressed the hope that the work would be continued at the same rate. It was "the wish of the office concerned with the collection of information on the inmates of the camp who were to be repatriated, as well as the wish of the American Army, that this work be speeded up as much as possible".

This announcement by the American Captain hinted that for many, release into liberty would not follow immediately upon filling in all the forms: "Those about whom there are no doubts or open questions will be considered for release first. But the questionnaires of those where there are doubts will be retained until everything has been completely resolved."

36 IPC, Information and Culture, Central Press Bureau, Communiqué No. 20, Three Questions and two reasons, 21. 5. 1945.
37 16th Meeting of the ICP, 22. 5. 1945.

For many, the time when they could enjoy freedom again would depend on the astuteness or the goodwill of the CIC officials, the American secret service investigating the "dubious" cases. In view of the background of so many of the Camp inmates, this was a depressing prospect. The former prisoners thus preferred by the hundred to withdraw from camp life regardless of the bureaucracy requiring the filling in of the questionnaire in quadruplicate before release. Captain Peterson issued a stern warning about such unauthorized behaviour, pointing out that, since the fighting had stopped, there was now plenty of personnel available as military police, who would keep a very strict watch to ensure that no-one would get out without permission. Apart from this, those who went home illegally would have difficulties once they got there. Captain Peterson requested that the following information be made clear to the camp inmates: "For every inmate properly released from the camp, one of these four forms is sent to his destination, but there will be no form for anyone who runs away. This will cause him many troubles and much unpleasantness and can even be dangerous for him."[38]

That was at nine o'clock in the morning.

At six in the evening of the same day, another meeting of the Committee took place with very good reason. Haulot, acting as chairman, informed the Committee that Captain Peterson had received new instructions, according to which the camp was now to be cleared in the shortest time possible. The US military authorities had decided to cancel the questionnaire campaign. Only the Germans and the Austrians now had to fill in the tedious forms before being released. Members of other national groups would merely be registered on lists and then be repatriated. The Americans would not interfere in the "special cases" (any longer), it was up to the authorities in their home countries what happened to these people. Major Goormaghtigh, as representative of the US Army, declared emphatically that as soon as a responsible officer appeared with the necessary means of transport, he could have his compatriots. If any country was not in a position to do this, the Americans would transport the people to the border of the country concerned.

In the meantime, there were evidently rumours circulating to the effect that the camp would be cleared within a week. In any case, Lieutenant Rosenbloom appeared in a meeting of the IPC and declared that the Camp Commandant knew nothing about this. A deputation thereupon made its way to ask Colonel Joyce himself. They returned and Major Goormaghtigh assured the Committee that it had been a false alarm. It was certainly true

38   10th Meeting of the IPC, 12. 5. 1945. One illegal return home from Dachau has been described in Floris B. Bakels, Nacht und Nebel. Der Bericht eines holländischen Christen aus deutschen Gefängnissen und Konzentrationslagern, Frankfurt 1979, p. 345 ff.

that the Camp was to be cleared swiftly, but not within a week: "Col. Joyce nearly had a stroke when he heard that according to rumours circulating the camp was to be burnt down within a week. He is simply not aware of the false rumours often flying around the camp so vigorously."[39]

The clearance of the camp was now only a transport problem, since the Americans had completely changed their attitude in the quarantine question as well. Only those actually ill came under it; all the others would have to undergo fourteen days' quarantine when they got home — so the Americans affirmed, and they perhaps even believed it. Haulot welcomed the improvement of the general living conditions in the camp and was pleased that they could now look forward to a logical and practical solution to the repatriation question and that there were no further paper problems.

This did not, however, apply to the Germans and Austrians, and their spokesmen did not conceal their indignation at the discrimination they saw in the fact that they were the only ones to fill in the questionnaires. The representative of the Austrians, Anton Kothbauer from Vorarlberg, said furiously: "If I have understood correctly, we as Austrians are being treated as second-rate or being classed with the Germans — we who actively fought for the Austrian and the Allied cause against Hitlerism in the concentration camps and prisons, some of us who had been deported to Germany as early as 1938! Only yesterday, Radio London reported that Austrian citizens in Czechoslovakia are not to be regarded as Germans and do not fall under the provisions applicable to Germans. As the representative of the Austrians, I wish to express my displeasure at the fact that we, who had to build this Camp in double quick time with blood and sweat, are to be the last to leave. Like many other comrades, I personally fought against National Socialist Germany under Dollfuß and Schuschnigg. I shall probably no longer be able to attend meetings of the International Committee and I shall ask the national committee whether it still has confidence. You cannot appeal to us for years through Radio Moscow, London and America to take up resistance and then not recognize those who end up in prisons and concentration camps as equals."[40]

Major Goorinaghtigh tried to pacify him by pointing out that the questionnaire matter was no more than a formal affair. The main thing he was expecting was a list of suspects — he meant the accomplices of the SS in prisoners' clothing — and assured him that the fact of having been a citizen of the German Reich that had been decisive for the discrimination, and that no sweeping condemnation was intended by it and so there was no reason for indignation.

---

39 11th Meeting of the IPC, 12.5.1945.
40 Ibid.

But Oskar Müller saw it differently. And one of the things that may well have played a part in his reply was the painful awareness of the difference in status which the well dressed representatives of the well-fed US Army without even thinking about it demonstrated at every turn towards the wretched figures of the liberated men: "We German anti-fascists were the first to have borne unspeakable suffering in the prisons and concentration camps for eight and ten years, and it is unjust towards us too that special surveys are made for us.[41]

The representatives of some other national groups had different worries. Thus Pallavicini asked what those who still had no contact with their home countries such as the Hungarians and the Yugoslavs might hope for. (On this and other occasions, the Poles too gave expression to the problem of their unclarified future: which Polish government was to be responsible for them, the government-in-exile in London or the Lublin-Committee, and where should they have themselves repatriated depending on which political direction gained the upper hand?)

Major Goormaghtigh consoled the representatives of those national groups who still had no contact with their governments: "The whole world knows about Dachau. It is a focus of public interest the world over. No-one can maintain that your governments know nothing about Dachau. No doubt they are interested in Dachau. Material difficulties are responsible for their not having made contact. It is extremely difficult to get through a military zone; a long time passes before one can get permission. It is a bureaucratic process. The French have established contact so quickly because their troops are in the vicinity. The fact that the Belgians had contact from the beginning is a result of the coincidence that he himself — not as a Belgian but as an officer of an allied army — had been appointed to deal with repatriation questions here in Dachau."[42]

The imminent return home and the question "What will it be like there?" were also the principal topics in the camp newspaper. From the beginning of May, there existed in Dachau a press scene that was short-lived but extremely diverse. The newspapers, which were published by the national committees, mostly consisted of a few hectographed pages of A 4 format. The paper of the Soviet committee was even handwritten on stencils and duplicated, presumably because there was no typewriter with Cyrillic type available. The Spaniards published a "Boletin de Informacion de los Espanoles Internados en Dachau", the Polish "Glos Polski-Biuletyn Komitetu Polskiego w Dachau" began to appear on 3 May; there was a Greek and a Jugoslavian information sheet; the Italians produced 37 issues of "Gli Italiani in Dachau" up to 29 June 1945, while the paper of the Belgians ("L'Union

41 Ibid.
42 Ibid.

Belge") ceased to appear early in May because of the repatriation, as did the French "Liberté" in which there was more discussion of great political issues than in other Camp newspapers. The Dutch informed themselves (for the last time in issue 11 on 14 May) by means of "De Stem der Lage Landen — Orgaan der Nederlanders in Dachau" and the Luxemburgers were served by "Ons Zeidong" in their own language.

The Austrians had one of the most extensive papers, which however only appeared rarely, though it did change its title in the third (and last) issue: the "Weg und Ziel der Österreicher" (Path and Goal of the Austrians) with the sub-title "Mitteilungsblatt der Österreicher in Dachau" (Information paper of the Austrians in Dachau). The main topic here was the rebirth of the nation, and there was surprisingly detailed reporting about the situation at home.

The German newspaper was called "Der Antifaschist. Stimme der Deutschen aus Dachau" (The Anti-fascist. The Voice of the Germans from Dachau) and it appeared twenty times beginning on 6 May. The last, undated issue, which had contained mainly announcements, short information items and news, was devoted to looking back ("German Anti-fascists did their duty" from the pen of Oskar Müller), but also to the future. The paper closed with the words: "We leave Dachau with the firm conviction that our lives will continue to be devoted to fighting against any form of fascist tyranny and for a free, democratic and anti-fascist Germany."[43]

The words of farewell written by Ali Kuci as head of the press bureau of the International Prisoners' Committee at the beginning of June as a kind of final proclamation, were directed to all those who had suffered in Dachau. They reminded of the past but they also contained optimistic expectations of the future couched in amical pathos: "The people are going home. Many, many have gone home in the last few days and even now many are setting off. In the next few days, Dachau will be deserted, a deserted monastery, which will bear witness of the greatest martyrdom in history to coming generations. Until now it has been a grave. In the twelve years of its existence about a million Europeans have been tortured behind the walls and behind the electrified barbed wire of this gigantic grave. The surviving men are returning home. Their homelands are free and their flags fly proudly in their countries. The great work of reconstruction has already begun. And we must all cooperate with this reconstruction. Happy and full of joy, we leave this hell: it has finished. No more threats, no more fear: Great life is — as they say — awaiting us!"[44]

43  All the Camp newspapers, insofar as they are extant, are in the Archive of the Concentration Camp Memorial Site, Dachau.
44  IPC, Information and Culture, Central Press Bureau, Communiqué No. 30, 2. 6. 1945.

Ute Benz

# Breeding Grounds of the Nation

## "The German Mother and Her First Child" or The Continuing Success of a Parental Guidance Book

The question as to how each of us was fed, wrapped in nappies, cuddled, left alone, was praised or scolded is in general regarded as a personal and not a politically relevant question. In any case, if we are interested in details, we soon reach the limits of our capacity to remember. Images and narrated events focus on the particular, the unique rather than the every-day. They represent pieces in the puzzle which is subject to varied nuances in the process of memory and, almost without our noticing it, they attain a greater significance than those every-day, much less spectacular things that elude conscious consideration. Impressions of early childhood form the basis of human development. In the light of present knowledge, it is no longer possible to believe that they could be simply eradicated by some later awareness. Rather, we have to assume that, in some guise or other, they will continue to have an effect by, for instance, leaving their mark on our basic expectations, fears and desires in our interactions with other individuals and the interaction between the generations. Thus, the question as to what happened in our childhood goes beyond the private sphere and becomes a decidedly topical and political one.

Personal memories are not sufficient for researching the essential formation of the personality. Our considerations must extend to include the ideas each generation has of the relationships between man and woman, parents and children, between the baby and its mother as they apply in any historical situation. For this purpose, books on the care of babies and the rearing of small children provide us with source material of the first order.

If we are to gain a detailed understanding of a political catastrophe like National Socialism in terms of its causes and effects so that any possible repetition may be prevented, then we need to focus our attention on the study of the upbringing accorded to young children. We should, for instance, ask what sort of image society had of mothers as people in their activities and their relationships, how and by whom they were advised, reassured, made to worry, and warned when they sought information. Although many parents think that they bring up their children free from external influences, and simply in accordance with their feelings (an opinion impressively refuted by Elisabeth Badinter in her book "Motherly Love, The History of a Feeling"), nonetheless all those who are new to the business of having children seek help, at the very latest, when problems occur from authorities or in books. They cannot live outside of the conventional conceptions of relationships any more than their children can.

This paper examines what those parents or maturing adults, who wanted to find information in the period after 1933, were able to find out about dealing with babies and young children, what they might have been subjected to involuntarily or what they had forced upon them.

From 1933 onwards, there was neither an unlimited choice of books on childrearing available for purchase, nor was it possible for independent authors to publish without difficulties. No book could be published without the approval of the "Reichsschrifttumskammer" (the central department of literary affairs), which meant both that the educational norms of National Socialist society were given a stamp of official approval and that they were given a far wider distribution among families than would ever have been possible on the free market. It was in this way that books became famous.

*The German Mother and her First Child* is one of those books that became a standard text. It appeared in 1934, published by the F. J. Lehmanns Company, Munich and Berlin. Its author, Johanna Haarer, a doctor born in 1900, died in Munich on April 30, 1988. The book reached a publication run that others can only dream of: by 1941, 440,000 copies had been printed. Under the title *The Mother and her First Child*, the work is currently still on the market, in the impression numbering from 1,222,000 to 1,231,000 copies of the total edition.

A second work by the same author — a direct continuation of the "Baby Book" - appeared in 1936 under the title *Our Small Children*. Two years later it had sold 23,000 copies; this title too, was reissued after 1949 and sold well into the 1970's. In 1937, Dr Haarer published *The Care of Infants For Young Girls* in the Bergbücherei publishing house in Esslingen. A further large work completed the model for German child-care and child-rearing; this appeared under the title *Our Schoolchildren*, Carl Gerber Press in 1950.[1] The titles mentioned thus far could be regarded as objective textbooks free of any political content — at least at first sight. This impression was carefully calculated by Dr Haarer in order not to make mothers-to-be feel insecure. Her aim is to spare expectant mothers any excitement, such

[1]  The presentation which follows is based above all on an analysis of the principal work "Die deutsche Mutter und ihr erstes Kind" ["The German Mother and her First Child"] in its various editions between 1934 and 1987.

as, for example, damaging half-knowledge of medicine". She carefully skates around anything of a political nature.

But there was no ambiguity in her political attitudes in her book *Mother, tell me about Adolf Hitler,* which appeared in the Lehmanns Press in Munich in 1939. This work, with the subtitle: "A Book for Reading Aloud, Telling Stories from and for Reading by Yourself for Small Children and Big Ones" was a success — in 1941, a fourth impression appeared, taking the total print-run to 78,000. Under the claimed intention of presenting the children with the truth, even where it might hurt, with considerable pedagogical skill, the author here presents children with pure Nazi ideology instead of historical information. She makes use of the children's need for role models to present them with a view of history in which the Germans appear as a poor but good and pure people who, against their own wishes, have continuously had to defend themselves against malicious, envious neighbours on the outside as well as against low, dirty, scheming, greedy people in their own country. Jews are associated in the minds of the children with all negative adjectives as the evil ones against whom the only courageous and proper man, namely Adolf Hitler, has at last risen up. Self-adulation, self-justification and the falsification of history cannot be comprehended as lies by children — they want to identify with the hero and to have good and evil distinguished as clearly as in a fairytale. For instance, the son of Veilchensteins, a negative figure which provokes anti-Semitism, is described in such a vile way that the wish has to be awakened in children for a hero who will finally get rid – "of the Veilchensteins, the purveyors of junk and the whole of that lovely lot"[2] once and for all.

Four years after the collapse of the Hitler Reich, Dr Haarer had her book on pregnancy, birth and infant care reprinted by the Lätare Press in Nuremberg under the slightly altered title *The Mother and Her First Child,* — the formerly meaningful adjective, "German," now being regarded as tainted and thus not contributing to sales, was dropped. Since then it has been on the market continuously, having been taken over by the Carl Gerber Press, Munich, in 1951; by 1988 it had reached a distribution of 1.2 million copies. The book has thus remained a long-running success even though the vivacity of the language which characterized the first version has been sacrificed totally to the political purification procedure, in which everything that was no longer opportune was excised. It was gradually modernized, carefully supplemented, nicely illustrated and in time has gained a completely new appearance.

Today, the book appears as a modern work: in an unbroken sequence, regardless of all political events, the name Haarer is a guaranteed brandname

2    Mutter, erzähl von Adolf Hitler [Mother, tell me about Adolf Hitler], (1941), p. 38.

for timeless quality in the German education sphere. Certainly sufficient cause for a critical appraisal. The publisher and the author (whose daughter, Dr Anna Hutzel, has co-operated in the more recent editions), proud of its long-standing success, emphasize in particular the continuity and quality of the book, *The Mother and her First Child*. The publisher lists the editions from 1934 to 1988 — without of course mentioning the year of its first appearance. He points to the book's increased expertise arising from the editorial assistance of female doctors and the continuous adaptation to social changes — at present, for instance, to the changing role of fathers. And indeed, the continuity of the book is a phenomenon that has to be taken seriously even beyond the realm of child-rearing. After a detailed analysis of the editions appearing under Nazi rule, which formed the basis of Dr Haarer's fame, it is interesting to inquire whether there is a continuity in some aspects other than the unchanging recipe of *The German Mother and her First Child* in regard to pregnancy, exercises, birth, infant care, education, many recipes for health, cooking, sewing and knitting — there are even patterns in the book. That is, we need to ask whether there are continuities of another kind as well which might be less of a cause for pride and might well be reconsidered and changed in a way that goes beyond simple editorial changes by all those interested in the topic of the child in our time.

What can we establish today about concepts of child-rearing and human relationships in Germany? In 1934, Dr Haarer directed this programmatic preface ("To the German Woman") to her readers: "In the life of a woman there is probably no time that can be compared in its special quality to those months in which she is expecting her first child, and there is no spiritual or physical experience that can be compared in its significance to that child's birth. Nor is there any experience in the life of a woman that so removes her from her own individual life and places her into the great events of the life of her people the way this step does, a step to the front of the mothers of our people who pass on the stream of life, the blood and inheritance of countless ancestors, the properties of the race and its homelands, the treasures of its language, customs and culture to the next generation and have them rise again there. And there is no time in her life more suited to making the woman experience more indelibly her shared destiny, in a profound relationship with all her sisters, than when it is her task to carry out what has been ordained by her Creator and to fulfil her destiny as a mother. It is as though an invisible hand removes all the artificial barriers erected between women by customs and origins, the notion of caste and class or lack of understanding and selfishness. In the months of pregnancy and on the decisive day of the birth, the same great goal unites all women. In this it does not make any difference whether it is a housewife or a professional woman who is to give life to a child and there is no difference between rich and poor, city or peasant woman, working class or middle class. The mighty natural event takes hold of the strong and courageously positive woman just as much as it does the one who is frightened and doubtful. The life to be born does not ask whether the woman is secure in a marriage and a home or if she does have a hard struggle outside of marriage and the traditional order. Now they are all equal before destiny."[3]

The person who wrote this for millions of women and young girls was not the chief ideologue for women's affairs in the Nazi organization, but an educated woman active as a writer, who had herself just become the mother of twins, and had, for this reason, given up a profession in which women were an exception — that of a doctor — in order to devote herself wholly to her family. She was involved in the NSDAP, but not in any major way: she did not hold any office in the party and indeed did not join the Hitler party until 1937. As a "regional expert for race policy," she was temporarily active in the Nazi Women's Organization, also in the "Mother and Child Relief Organization" and with the NSV. She occasionally published articles in the *Völkischer Beobachter*, the Nazi newspaper.

Dr Haarer could not have directed the programmatic preface of her book to mothers out of personal conviction alone or indeed have achieved any effect with it; nor would the fact that she was drawing on her own experiences as a young mother and housewife suffice as an explanation for this sort of appearance and for the success of her books. But the combination of the two aspects of the mother and housewife together with the authority given by her position as a doctor gave the author a legitimation for her views. It was this combination which, without much assistance from her, but resulting simply from the social status of her profession, raised her views to a position above any doubt into a realm beyond discussion, to the absolutely correct. Although she was not a paediatrician, she was able to appeal to a following where powers of persuasion alone would not have been sufficient; it was as though the fact that she was a doctor, housewife and mother bestowed on her a quality that had no need of proof. Respect for medical knowledge became a vehicle for transmitting things very different from objectively based knowledge, namely political ideology.

The grotesque exaggeration of one's personal experience into a feeling of a feminine community fusing all distinctions seems embarrassing today. Ecstatic enthusiasm speaks through her words and allows one to assume that, in fact, the women were fairly lonely and longed for solidarity and community. Such irrational fantasies of greatness and togetherness can only be understood politically and psycho-analytically. Seen analytically, their energy is fed by unconscious powers in the form of strong desires and

---

3    Johanna Haarer, Die deutsche Mutter und ihr erstes Kind, Munich 1934, p. 5.

fears. For, inseparably linked with such desires for togetherness are immense fears, equally irrational and overwhelming any sensible restraint (to which the author otherwise constantly appeals).

We find massive fears in many places in Haarer's books before 1945, though not in the same place as the desires (where they would be more easily recognized), but split off, apparently not in connection with the desires. We find them, for example, in the chapter on abortion. Here they are concentrated in the evidently quite intolerable concern of those responsible for the "health of the people" in the face of a danger conjured up as threatening the very existence of the people, a danger that had to be feared all the more since it was regarded as stemming from the same origins as the way to salvation, namely from conception. What led to the expectation of happiness for mother and nation alike also led to the fear of ruin through (inherited bad) characteristics. Producing bad genetic characteristics, and what is more, producing them in allegedly uncontrollably large numbers, that is, much more potently, is simply pushed onto "the others," whoever they may be. Haarer lists those with congenital illnesses, political opponents, Marxists — because they would support the seeds of destruction by approving of abortion — and the (bad) women from their own ranks who did not ask for the health certificate ("racial purity") in the choice of their men. At that time, everybody knew that this context amounted to agreement with the anti-Jewish racist policies which the National Socialists shamelessly supported in public. Whether for personal reasons, — because Dr Haarer did not want to adopt a position against her medical colleagues, some of whom might have been Jewish, — or for political reasons, because the author did not want to spoil the ideal world of her readers far removed from party politics with any undisguised language, in any case, the word "Jewish" is not used. Dr Haarer remained within the realm of the general and, as we shall see, this was entirely sufficient to create within women an attitude that was useful to the system.

As a defence against the fears of corruption, which many women had in relation to sexuality for reasons that had nothing to do with politics, women allowed themselves to become committed to harshness by the book, to an ultimately cruel harshness towards themselves and others. Only briefly the harshness is covered over again and again by short postscripts according to which everything the stern mother has to do to her child is, of course, done only out of a spirit of love and respect. Mothers in the Nazi period found themselves inescapably at the mercy of murderous consequences. The women, who were meant to serve life exclusively and who wanted to fulfil this goal, were also obliged, on account of precisely this exclusiveness to condone a selective treatment of life according to which only such life as was healthy had a right to exist and to be worthy of their efforts. Even worse, in the notion of "eradication" as it was used by Haarer for the removal of those who were regarded as being unworthy of life, the mothers were obliged to accept and share a component of hatred for any life and any children who deviated from the norms declared by the authorities. Fear, shock and murder were the inevitable other side of the "worthy of life" coin. What profound anxieties must the mothers have felt or suppressed when they became aware that they were unable to choose their children. Desolate loneliness for mothers with such anxieties. Here the appellative character of Haarer's language no doubt fulfilled a reassuring function.

The Haarer books contain a mass of practical advice. In the Nazi period this is given in a tone of comradeship using the familiar "Du"-Form — or is it an authoritarian tone? The feeling was frequently suggested that the mothers were on a battlefield. Things that might easily be regarded as a bagatelle rapidly assumed the proportions of a test of allegiance, loyalty or betrayal. Any stirrings of independence on the part of the child or gentleness on the part of the mother were immediately regarded as stirrings that should potentially be combated. Mothers were sworn to watchfulness, not so that they would not miss something wonderful, but to be on guard to lest the enemy in the child's room make any inroads on the front. Mothers as guards: "The salvation of the race and of the nation has been placed in the hands of the women."[4]

The birth itself is depicted as the first battle the mother has to survive. "But the woman does not emerge from the struggle without wounds, and like any other wounded person, she is in need of complete rest and attentive care. To use the comparison with the wounded here is no mere play on words. A woman who has just given birth is indeed wounded."[5]

The education and training of the child had to begin immediately after the delivery. For this purpose, Haarer emphatically recommends an early separation of the child from the mother: "But where is the child? ... we urge that he be accommodated away from the mother and brought to her only for feeding. The mother is spared not only much anxiety in this way — she listens only too eagerly to every sign of life of the little being and worries unduly but for the child too, a room of his own is of the greatest advantage." The reasons Dr Haarer gives for this are that the baby is protected from infection and heat loss. But the principal reason lies in the intention of beginning with the education of the child from the very first day: "In addition, the separation of mother and child has extraordinary pædagogical advantages for the child."[6] Breast-feeding — as advocated by Dr Haarer — is placed in the service of early training: "In between feeds, regular and

4    Ibid., p. 8.
5    Ibid., p. 91.
6    Ibid., p. 97.

sufficient pauses must be maintained under all circumstances ... Feeding is to take place at the same times every day." The course of the young mother's whole day is directed by these times. "Never forget: it is with your correct behaviour in this quite crucial question that the proper care and education of your child stands or falls. Regular meals, punctually given at the same time every day, are the decisive beginning in the education of your child."[7]

The baby is left largely to his own devices: "Let the whole family make it a basic rule that they should never concern themselves with the infant without some reason ... avoid loud and vigorous expressions of maternal feelings."[8] If the baby should cry, check what might be wrong. If the baby should cry before a meal: "On no account do we provide the meal sooner, otherwise the child will very rapidly learn to force this again and again, and its regular daily routine is endangered again."[9] If the child cries nonetheless, then — occasionally — one may have recourse to a dummy. If the dummy should fail too, and all matters of care have been ruled out as a cause, then: "dear mother, be hard. Do not begin to pick the child up out of his bed, to carry him, rock him, wheel him up and down or hold him on your lap, let alone feed him. The child will learn with incredible speed that he need only cry in order to bring some sympathetic soul running and become the object of such care. After a short time he will demand this sort of treatment as a right and will give you no peace until he is picked up, rocked and wheeled — and you have the little, but pitiless, tyrant in the house."[10] And further: "Where possible, the child is pushed into a quiet place where he remains alone and is not attended to until the next meal. Often it takes only a few trials of strength between mother and infant — they are the first ones — and the problem is solved. ... All infants should be left alone at night from the beginning."[11]

According to the views of Dr Haarer, the German mother is a strange being. She is a "correct" mother. She is postulated as the model of absolute fulfilment of duty and loyalty, as being imbued with the importance of her pædagogical task and equipped with total self-control as well as the capacity for complete selflessness. "Only a woman of firm character and conscious of her duty, with common sense and a sense of order, regularity, punctuality and cleanliness will be able to bring up her child properly."[12] But would she not, we ask full of consternation today, have to appear to her husband and her children as a very caricature of a real, genuine woman? Especially

7    Ibid., p. 106.
8    Ibid., p. 143.
9    Ibid., p. 145.
10   Ibid., p. 148.
11   Ibid., pp. 148 f.
12   The German Mother (1941), p. 270.

the women themselves must have experienced anxiety, at the very latest when, in comparison with the German super mother, they saw themselves as failures, for instance when their own desire for perfection was placed under great stress by the daily dealings with their children and burst like a soap bubble. Through this book, we see German mothers who were obliged to be afraid of their own impulses, who were constantly to give the impression of being controlled: care machines which, once properly adusted, were to function for a lifetime — a horror vision for all those dependent on her.

While reading this book, we also gain the impression that these mothers were not married to real fathers, but had rather been bound above all in an intimate alliance to the Führerstate, Totally subservient to the state, they were to suppress their own needs, sacrifice themselves along with their children; for its sake deny feelings of weakness or gentleness or imperfections or, at best, to use these as a stimulus for increased efforts in yet more conscientious obedience to all instructions in order to do everything right for the idolized State. As a reward for this and legitimated by a higher vocation, German mothers could then create their own dominion over those dependent on them in the "woman's realm," the household. The rules applying there were no less strict. For their part, they now had actively to combat everything that might endanger or even question their "marriage on a higher level": criticism, individuality or pluralism. For the maintenance of their own value system, it was in evitable that any women who chose to follow different paths were denigrated in devastating terms.[13]

The constantly beseeching tone of Haarer's text in the editions before 1945 (in the post-Hitler era editions, this was replaced by short sentences and countless exclamation marks) often conjures up the image of a parade ground where young pregnant women, lined up in rows, are given the orders applicable for mothers, almost as though the women awaiting the birth of their first child are under threat of an enemy invasion. It is difficult to avoid the impression that they were on the alert not against some external enemy, but against their own children or perhaps their imagined wrong development.

It was suggested to young mothers that decisive battles had to be waged in confinement and in the infant's room, at the "mothers' front of our people" so that later catastrophes would be avoided. "Never forget: it is with your correct behaviour in this quite crucial question that the proper care and education of your child stands or falls."[14] Cleanliness, tidiness and maintenance of the sacred regular daily routine had to be fought for in infancy.

13 For instance in the chapter on abortion, ibid., p. 29.
14 The German Mother (1941), p. 120.

In the toddler stage, the main task was — in addition to the eternal battle for cleanliness — to steer the defiant child between Scylla (longterm defiance) and Charybdis (broken or weakened will). Dr Haarer required an exemplary approach from the German mother: "A great deal will already have been gained if the mother is prepared from the outset for defiance, indeed for the occasional real outburst of defiance and anticipates the danger before it is actually there. Defiance in the playful age passes as it came, but only if the child is handled properly at this time and no serious mistakes occur in the child-rearing process. For this reason, every mother must devote attention and thought to the expressions of defiance of her child. If she does not approach it in the right way, the defiance will take hold. If she breaks it with force, she may deform the healthy will-power of the child."

Preventive measures recommended are: allow the child to use his will to let him do things he can already do, let him carry out small household tasks, for instance, and permit him to let off steam and tire himself out. "We treat the child politely and lovingly. No command-tones at this stage! That would only challenge defiance to surface. We thus restrict commands and prohibitions to what is essential and do not lead the child by the nose. We allow the two great educative forces of habit and example to continue to have their effect. Naturally, the child ought never see anything resembling defiance in us adults. In our daily dealings with the child we show him inconspicuously that we often have to bow to something or give in and that the mother, for example, subordinates her opinion to that of the father. But let there be no song and dance about this, no visible conscious intention. Otherwise it can happen that we attain the exact opposite. No experimentation with different child-rearing methods and above all no rapid changes between goodness and strictness."[15]

At this age too, the political education of the small children is prepared: "The countless inquisitive questions of our little ones provide us, quite informally with the first opportunity of telling them something about our people, our fatherland and our Führer ... They are certainly susceptible to an inkling of human greatness as well as an inkling of the divine. Already at this early age the aims of our State Youth can begin to be a guideline for them — fitting with society, avoiding all self-pity; bravery and courage, obedience and discipline can all be suggested to children at this playful age without any artificiality. After all, basically, no good mother, no good father could wish any other educative ideals on their children."[16]

These samples show the spirit of the upbringing proposed, a linguistic barrage which is evidence of an attitude towards the child that leaves no

15   Unsere kleinen Kinder [Our small Children] (1938), p. 215.
16   Ibid, p. 224.

room for any living growth of relationships. Just as the author admits of no nuances or doubts and knows only demands, so she never recommends trying anything that might be pleasant for mother and child. Dr Haarer's language always conveys an aggressive drive, and with this it reveals a deep mistrust of the relationship of the adult to the newly born child.

What this makes clear above all is that the new space, so longingly hoped for, (and which the politicians had constantly proclaimed) unexpectedly became smaller instead of larger for German women. Inside their own four walls very little more remained for their own development than the purely practical side of life. Here the creativity of the mothers was allowed free rein, in inventing charming details, nice little things, practical and ever more clever objects or actions. It appears that this escape into the practical realm was the only possible escape. Here everything that could be thought, planned or invented was permitted. Little remained for mothers at that time, for ultimately their lives necessarily withered away on the last remaining field of the practical, where dry instructions and inflexible regulations merely prescribed details to be imitated.

What was left? Cleanliness, tidiness and devotion to duty as the principal, but pathetic, sources of pleasure. Nurseries without humour, laughter and gentleness, full of regulation, inflexibility and consistency. We can see how life ultimately atrophied more and more for the (genetically) healthy as well. Relationships inimical to life developed also in the nursery between mother and child.

What had started as mere advice on the regularity of dividing the day and the observance of strict feeding times, namely education to hardness, begins mercilessly in the phase after the first year of life. With pride the author tells of her own two-year old son who, even when he had fallen very badly, would get up by himself and say quite indignantly: "But Fritz does not cry". His mother thinks that she is helping to make life easier for her son in this way, she is thinking in a direct logical line of his future life as a soldier.

The book "Our Small Children" is particularly hard to understand today, because many people have memories filled with suffering from this period. Also, identifying with small children brings with it, even more strongly than in the case of infants, the danger that the mother is seen as the culprit. It is hard to regard them, even in their hardness, as suffering women who, in the rearing of their children, are swearing an oath of allegiance to the state. The scope for mothers thus becomes restricted even more to dogged fulfilment of duty in terms of rules of principle; everything becomes a matter of principle, of legitimacy.

The author expressly warns against tenderness, and here for the first time a sub-clause reveals that she is acquainted with the lack of satisfaction experienced by women, when she writes, "the woman not satisfied in her marriage, for example, should be very careful not to vent her unfulfilled longing for tenderness on her child ... A certain economy in these matters, too, is surely more appropriate to German people and German children. ... To tender mothers unable to change their natures we suggest that they twist any excess of emotion and sentiment into fun and humour." And she goes on: "It continues to be a source of amazement how early children have a sense for joking and teasing. Encouraging this is surely better for their later lives than too great an emphasis on feeling. Humour, a sense of the comic and the capacity to joke can help us over the most difficult situations in life. Continual emphasis on feeling, on the other hand, only makes a difficult situation seem even more problematic and oppressive."[17] Many women aged between 35 and 80 today are only too painfully aware that tenderness was denounced as substitute satisfaction for unsatisfied women, as ingratiating oneself to achieve some end: tenderness was rejected as superfluous cuddling. Did not this sort of upbringing necessarily produce a generation of emotionally starved adults? What fear of tenderness and softness comes to light here! Poor children, poor mothers and fathers, if any need for tenderness has to be twisted into comedy.

Any form of softness and yielding was also condemned: "Even a screaming and resisting child has to do what the mother thinks necessary, and if he continues to behave in a naughty way, he has to be 'put on ice', placed in a room where he can be alone and ignored until he changes his behaviour. It is hard to believe how early and how quickly a child can understand this sort of procedure."[18] The child was not to get anything from the adults' table, no crumb was to be given them, by no-one — just like a dog — so that he will not learn to beg. Unbroken continuity into the eighties — the same advice is repeated in all the editions.

The type of person the society of the time wanted brought up corresponds to the military ambitions of the Nazi state. It was to be a heroic type, imbued with absolute obedience towards the Führer (mother) and his (her) plans, bear pain without complaint and be clean and tidy. Defiance and self-will only create a disturbance, resistance is not tolerated, fitting in is trumps. The final goal is the virtues of the soldier, although they are seldom referred to as such. On the topic of obedience, we find these not expressly stated goals developed in a concentrated form as the goals of education: "Anyone who properly observes children can readily see that they long to be led and that a tendency to obedience is clearly recognizable in the nature of the child along with the tendency to resist."[19]

17   Ibid., p. 179.
18   The German Mother (1934), p. 237.
19   Our small Children (1951), p. 97.

"In the playing stage, obedience must be achieved, that is to say, absolute obedience without distraction, without reward or promises and without
any threats of punishment. ... But never shall we put up with the child
questioning our instructions or complaining or pouting or contradicting."[20]
The modern version of 1951 reads: "If, for instance, the child plays with
his food, we take his plate away and he goes hungry. If he quarrels with his
brothers and sisters, or bothers the adults, then he has to remain alone for
a while ..."[21]

It is unimaginable that mothers might find their way through the
labyrinth of instructions like this. For them the trap snapped shut anyway,
since, if they recalled another principle that also continued to have validity,
the notion that "the natural" was to have precedence, then they probably
followed their own wishes sometimes and threw troublesome instructions
overboard. Insofar as mothers did not have to act out great sadistic needs,
they probably did that all the time anyway. If they possessed a different
horizon of experiences from their own fulfilled childhood, it will not have
been difficult for them. If, on the other hand, they had been subjected to a
strict Wilhelminian, middle class upbringing, they would have had neither
experience nor support. But the less secure the mothers were in these times
of social and political change after World War I, the greater their need for
generally applicable advice and that in Johanna Haarer's book was, after
all, designed for a "Reich" that was to last a thousand years. In this process,
quite a lot may have been simply accepted in accordance with the slogan
"no pain (hard work) no gain (happiness)". If mothers behaved differently
in the nursery, they and the children were later threatened in the kinder-
garten and at school with the confrontation with the public constraints
they had hitherto avoided or toned down. Then only hypocrisy and secrecy
could protect the women's own feeling of naturalness from public criticism.

Many things are painful to today's reader, especially in the chapter on
toilet training. Starting from the principle that "pleasure in cleanliness is
part of every real woman's nature," the author emphasizes that toilet
training must on no account be begun too early because of possible later
consequences; nonetheless, she does regard the end of the first year as the
desirable limit, "unfortunately still not always attainable". It is always the
mother, however, who has failed if the child does not look gratifyingly
cared for. The authority of the doctor coerces the mothers, because,
"Negligence by the mother on the point of cleanliness" is said to have bad
consequences: "Such a child does not develop a healthy repugnance for
everything disgusting. ... But the feeling of disgust is a warning sign that

20   Ibid.
21   Ibid., p. 97.

protects our health. We miss it painfully in our small children at first in any case. For instance, whenever they put all sorts of possible and impossible things into their mouths, we ask ourselves in horror whether they aren't disgusted. So let us help them develop a healthy feeling of disgust. Let us present wetting with urine, soiling with excrement and bad smells to them as something loathsome and let us show them that this sort of thing must always be removed immediately, dirty clothing has to be changed. If we do this tirelessly, we shall soon convert the child to our point of view. He will be more and more unhappy and uncomfortable when he is wet or dirty. He will demand cleanliness. Once we have got this far, we have won half the battle."[22]

For mothers who could not see the logic of this type of argumentation, the daily labour with tiresome nappy-washing in a time before disposable nappies may well have been motivation enough for early toilet training. Anyone for whom this may still not have been sufficient grounds to set herself against the natural needs and capacities of the small child — for these mothers, even bigger guns were provided in the Nazi period: the sight of dirty children was a threat for the whole people. "Anyone who tolerates a dirty, smelly, soiled child in the vicinity is acting against the population goals of our government!" Because, as is claimed, the desire to have a child might be diminished in an onlooker (men or household help or young girls), to the detriment of the preparedness of the men to father children, since they would literally and figuratively be fed up with it and might well think, after the second child: "I'd rather not have any more of them".[23] Mothers were also threatened with worry by their children's attempt to broaden their horizons. "Full of horror the mother sees a child constantly dirty again around her." Horror just because the principles of cleanliness and order appear threatened?

In a situation where negligence and mistakes are immediately declared to be offences against the people, one can only live in constant fear, one has to feel either bad or guilty or a failure and is forced to secrecy or confession. There always is the greatest worry about the future and the past, the fear of being found out later. A vicious circle of feelings of shame and entanglement in guilt which chokes life itself. These feelings of horror and shame would have been appropriate, on the other hand, if they had been permitted to apply to the murderous intentions towards those who has been declared unfit for life. The feeling concerning inhumanity was, however, not experienced where it would have been appropriate, but shifted on to harmless things, such as questions of order, which, in turn, could only attain the values they did in this way.

22  Our small Children (1938), p. 48.
23  Ibid.

The reason why Dr Haarer's books had such wide distribution in the Third Reich was certainly not that the author had anything new to say or recommend. On the contrary, she fulfilled the requirements of her society to a great degree in that her books reinforced, in an easily manageable form, what were/are generally firmly established notions of the child and the natural disposition of woman, woman as the being destined to fulfil the three things which were seen as an indivisible unity at that time: conception, childcare and house-keeping. Across all political divisions, all the parties, as well as the churches, were in agreement on this all the time: the limits of female capabilities were regarded — by the church, by NS-supporters and by atheists — as being in splendid agreement with the aims of God, providence or nature and these limits were set large enough to be able to include a little place for unmarried or childless women within the realm of charity work.

The thought of emancipation must have caused avalanches of anxieties in both men and women during those years: a general call for salvation was heard. With their good sense for security needs that could be exploited politically, the National Socialists were able, as it were, to leap on to a moving train, demand the job of driver and determine the destination. With a few tricks, which could not have been invented better by modern advertising strategists, they presented themselves as saviours in a time of need. They instituted a new type of Olympic sport for Germans — having children as a national sport. While saving money for themselves, they made it possible for all those who had to take on the daily marathon of the tedium of cleaning, washing, patching, changing nappies as a long term stress, to step up finally on to a victors' stand: a bronze stand after four children, a silver one after six and a gold one after reaching the eight-children mark. In recognition of their services, they were awarded a heavily symbolic medal, the "mothers' cross," hung around their necks like soldiers after a victorious battle. Thereafter, they could wear it as a sign of no doubt frequently missed gratitude and social recognition. Today, this attempt to use a piece of decoration to provide reassurance to all the fathers, mothers and siblings who might well have had guilt feelings, often no doubt without admitting them, about their own ambivalence at bringing children into the world in bad times would be regarded as frighteningly cunning.

It is inconceivable that all the desires and fears in the relationship between mother and child could simply have been erased after 1945. There was thus no inner experience for handling freedom and co-determination. Even for those who were shattered by the fact that Germany had been completely ruined politically by the authorities — as a result of the mur-derous consequence of the path declared as being right once and for all. Even for those who had the good will to begin again and longed for democracy, it was impossible psychologically to suddenly devalue the treasure, regarded as a certainty, of the internal relationships they had had in the early mother-child relation. That would have meant that the gods would have had to be seen in their human and pathological involvements. This in turn would have entailed the most profound insecurities and collapse for all those who had sacrificed their lives (as individuals) to their gods (i. e. mothers etc.).

Haarer's concept of bringing up children — and this has to be empha-sized, because what matters here is not to make a single author responsible for a particular educational style — was the concept of German society under National Socialism. It fulfilled the political desires of the Germans for a role in world affairs, security and comprehensibility, health and strength. The consistency demanded of mothers by this concept was to guarantee success: the authority of the mothers and the absolute obedience of the children. As a result, both the mother and the child were troubled: the mother was supposed to hide her feelings, suppress doubts, deny any lack of certainty, and the child for his part too had to divert his aggressions, to find other possibilities for coping with the critical and aggressive feelings inevitably aroused by absolute obedience. Transferring the aggressive feelings, desires, and anxieties which arose in the every-day activities in the parental home, at work, etc., to the outside, to other people (political opponents, outsiders, the sick), was politically encouraged and indeed provoked. A generation brought up to or forced into absolute obedience was allowed to vent its feelings of anger, hatred and murder in a government sanctioned way with a logical conclusion in murder and even mass murder. Viewed from this perspective, society under National Socialism, in order to maintain its fragile internal peace (within the family as well as in the population), needed to discriminate against certain groups to get rid of its own aggressions which it was not able to take out on those who had really caused those feelings — mothers, fathers, superiors. Those in positions of power had to be accepted and protected unconditionally, including their senseless commands.

Are continuities to be found in relation to pregnancy, birth, infant care and upbringing in those of Dr Haarer's books which appeared after 1949? Are old models still in effect under the modernized guise of the current Haarer books? After all, grandmothers and mothers-in-law — since they themselves liked using these books — could gladly and without concern hand them on to their daughters, daughters-in-law and grand-daughters. The practical questions appear as separate problems isolated from the historical background, which save the mothers from having to think about the consequences of their actions.

Baby care as something negligible? Lack of interest because, after all, this was a merely practical question? How is it that this problem has remained for so long outside the discussion of what parents have inherited from the past? Perhaps we are united by a common interest as long as we exclude this phase of life from our critical thinking. The reason for this could lie in the fact that we would all like to retain in our minds an illusion, the idea of a idyll, of an island of happy, cozy togetherness of mother and baby, far removed from any political disturbance — and to a large extent also far removed from the fathers. In the Haarer books, in any case, the father hardly rates a mention until late in the 1980s — neither in the title nor in the cover photo was there any room for him for half a century. The cover photo impressively embodied this idea of the mother-child-idyll. The 1977 edition showed a contentedly sleeping baby, the mother's eye blissfully watching over it; the next edition, 1979, presented the observer with a view of mother and child as a tenderly loving pair touching each other with the lips on shoulder and cheek. Until 1987, both pictures and content continued a relationship model along the lines of the allegedly purely practical, that is, mothers can very well manage the rearing of the child by themselves, the father is required only incidentally. As a result of longer working hours, the absence of the men in the war and as prisoners of war, it had been a necessity for a whole generation of women to be independent in the role of the person bringing up the child alone. Today, it could well be different. Nonetheless, the father remained a marginal figure in the nursery: this problem has continued. In view of the many single parents today, we might ask the psycho-analytical question whether it is possibly not simply a personal decision when parents think that one partner is enough for rearing the child. It is at least conceivable that a whole generation is subject to the compulsion of repeating what it experienced or — seen from the dynamics of the family — is attempting to carry out a task taken over from their parents. According to this the parents have to prove to themselves and to their own parents that they are coping, allegedly better and voluntarily, without the father, or perhaps (still) are searching for another, better father for themselves and their own children.

In the most recent "fully revised and expanded" edition of 1987, at first sight everything seems improved; the tone conveys a different, more relaxed approach to mother and child. The fear that a baby might be spoiled is gone at last — and yet enough relics of the old training and relationships models have remained. For example, the publishers and the authors did react to the new generation of fathers who will not allow themselves to be excluded so easily from the rearing of the child. Now the father has been accorded a place on the cover photo. But in the contents, a change in the mother-father-child-relation has not been achieved. On the contrary, in many questions in which the author apparently goes into caring detail, a specifically one-sided model is carried forward. "But, ask many women, what will my husband's attitude be to it (i. e. pregnancy)? Will he still love me as he has; will the changes in my body not make him turn away from me? Fortunately, most men today have a natural and relaxed attitude to these questions. ... The father has been, as it were, rediscovered in our time, a great help for the mother-to-be".[24]

The father continues to be the man according to whom the woman has to arrange herself. He cannot be expected to have to tolerate any hardships, such as for example, nocturnal disturbances, to which the mothers allegedly become accustomed rapidly: "Despite the disturbance, you (the mother) are well rested in the morning".[25] One cannot expect too much of him during the birth. "Perhaps you are opposed to your husband's being present when your baby is born. Even this is very understandable. Because towards the end of the confinement, the events are somewhat turbulent. You will not always make a beautiful impression during this process."[26]

The relationship between the parents is presented in a surprisingly open way in the chapter "Sexual relationships after confinement": "It will be difficult for many young men to live for weeks in abstinence. You should therefore not be completely deaf to the wishes of your husband and should try to satisfy him by some other means. There are many forms of intimacy and tenderness. If need be, have your gynecologist advise you."[27] Here it is clearly recognizable that two kinds of tradition are continued unquestioned, even where, in comparison to previous editions, liberating openness appears to be the order of the day. The needs of the man have preference, the needs of the women are not even mentioned. But at the same time, the father is excluded from any direct relationship, despite the apparent caring. In case of any problem, his wife is to talk not to him, the husband, but to ask the doctor (a man). In addition to the one-sided partner relationship, a doctor-patient relationship is continued which has a long tradition in Germany. The doctor, the authority, takes precedence. The wife/mother is in an alliance with the representative of authority instead of in a relationship with her partner. Thus the woman is at best confronted with the choice of which authority she is going to decide for. But whatever she chooses, she has to do it right for the man, whether the husband or the doctor-authority.

The other thing that is decidedly embarrassing and annoying is the continuity right up to the most recent edition of the problem of the only child. Here, in established tradition, the parents as well as the only children are quite simply discriminated against. "But you can see again and again how capable and efficient the people are who have grown up with siblings,

---

24  The Mother and her First Child (1987), p. 39.
25  Ibid., p. 143.
26  Ibid., p. 91.
27  Ibid., p. 130.

how difficult and often incapable the excessively pampered and spoiled only children appear by comparison."[28] Pressure by means of anxiety is still applied whenever convincing arguments are absent and political goals need to be veiled.

There is a further continuity from 1934 to the end of the seventies in the specific attitude to those who provide advice and those who seek it. Here, Dr Haarer is continuing a tradition that is wide-spread outside the nursery too. It consists in one person claiming to know exactly how something is done while the other, the lay person, has merely to keep exactly to what is laid down. "It is only when all this has been properly thought through that you and your husband will have real pleasure in the child. ... That is why we ask you to read this book very carefully and to take notice of every piece of advice."[29] The division of roles is strictly maintained and the belief in the doctor's knowledge cements the two positions. "In health matters, we want to advise you well, naturally in accordance with the latest research, without presenting you with dangerous medical half-knowledge."[30] As of 1987, the author promises that she will protect the (female) reader learning from her book from two things: from unnecessary specialized knowledge and unnecessary mistakes. It sounds milder in tone, but has the same basic meaning: we doctors will say what is right, you lay person follow obediently and then all will be well. She demands faith and trust in authority instead of providing information, which may evidently not be given to the reader because it is harmful. Harmful for what? For the position of the doctors? For the mother's peace of mind? As though anxieties could be switched off simply by not informing mothers, handing over the baby, its body so to speak, to the doctor responsible. The mother is still an institution whose function is to do everything right, then she can rest in the knowledge that she has done her best, in accordance with the instructions of the doctor. If something should go wrong, then the doctor was in error or she was not consistent in her efforts, but as an autonomous person responsible to herself, the mother has been excluded.

The impression conveyed by those books by Haarer still available today is ambivalent. So much good advice, but given in such a beseeching tone, so many warnings, so much "must," "ought," "absolutely". The true range of emotion conveyed is the fear of mistakes. There is also a lack of faith of the author in her readers — she thinks them incompetent, lax, unable to carry anything through. How else can we regard the advice given in the chapter on motherhood protection legislation to mothers who are breast-feeding:

28   Ibid., p. 270.
29   The Mother and her First Child (1979), Preface.
30   Idem.

"May we give you the advice that you not exploit it (the motherhood protection legislation) excessively? Otherwise it will lead to a negative attitude to mothers in the work-place and that would be very regrettable."[31] For 54 years — from 1934 to 1988, Dr Haarer has been concluding her books "Mother and First Child" with almost literally the same sentiments, even in the completely revised new editions. In them, she points the reader to current basic directions once again in a more concentrated form, and with this she combines a hidden threat, which can only be interpreted as an intention to make the reader adhere to what she has recommended. Any failings in the character of the child are declared to be avoidable mistakes on the mother's part : "We have no conscious memory of the earliest period of our infancy, it does not begin until later. As a result of research by doctors and psychologists, however, it has been shown that we cannot overestimate the importance of precisely this first period of life. The first experiences and impressions continue to affect the unconscious. It is extremely important that at this time everything is 'right' and 'fits'. The first experience of the other', the first contact with the external world, the satisfaction of the earliest needs such as thirst and hunger, the first necessity of doing something one does not like, and not to do something one would like to do — these things can be crucial for later life. It is not for nothing that we say of people who demonstrate deficiencies of character or mistakes in their behaviour that they were badly brought up."[32] The old German concept of bringing up children was based on the fear of mistakes. It was linked to the absolute desire to do everything right and grounded in the hope of attaining a better future in this way, one free from anxiety, for the next generation. This concept encouraged the tendency of people to divide the world into good and evil, right and wrong, obedience and command, expert and layman, sick and healthy. The search for the only right way, or advice, prevented parents from taking on responsibility for themselves and increased their dependence on those giving advice. It led to the development that the medical authority was burdened with the entire responsibility, and that the lay people, the parents, were relieved of their responsibility for themselves, at the price of dependence on the advice of others to the point of having no say at all. The doctors appeared as powerful, the lay people as powerless, liberated from responsibility but also from liveliness. This concept is still in effect today; it is, for instance, clearly noticeable in advisory centres for parents and children. Where, on the surface, it is a question of the children's problems, a deeper understanding reveals that the parents have

31  Ibid., p. 117. These sentences have been deleted from the 1987 edition.
32  Ibid., p. 249; almost identical with the wording of the most recent edition (1987), p. 270.

lost their liveliness out of fear of having guilt thrust upon them. Their fear of having made a mistake and being made responsible for it represents an obstacle for working with the parents that is difficult to remove. How does a young mother feel at the beginning of her life together with a baby — this new situation in life is certainly exciting enough — when is presented with this sort of thinking? Does she throw the book into a corner as useless and look for something friendlier to read? Does she prefer to rely on her own strength? If she is free from anxiety and has the choice, that may be what happens. Does she not have to be terribly afraid of making a mistake with her newborn, of being an imperfect and bad mother, if every failing of character is attributed to the mother's failings? How is she to escape the temptation of living in the (bad) tradition of the Germans according to which a mother has to do nothing but be a good mother?

Detlef Garbe

# The Purple Triangle

## The "Bibelforscher" (Jehovah's Witnesses) in the Concentration Camps

"There is hardly an analysis or memoir of the concentration camps in which the devout thought, the diligence, the helpfulness and the fanatical martyrdom of the 'Ernsten Bibelforscher' are not related".[1] With these words thirty years ago, Friedrich Zipfel pointed out that in numerous reports of former concentration camp prisoners, the group of "Bibelforscher" (Jehovah's Witnesses) is mentioned and assessed from the perspective of the time. Nevertheless, the persecution of the Jehovah's Witnesses long remained largely unknown in both research and the public. Even the written histories of the concentration camps gave little attention to this group of prisoners, to which the SS had assigned its own category ("purple triangle"). There are no independent analyses; with only one exception,[2] there are no studies on the collective fate of the "Bibelforscher" in the particular concentration camps even today.

Besides the overly discussed disinterest of the German historical study in KZ-historiography, the research interest of the time is probably also responsible for the fact that the authors, in terms of emphasis, mostly inquired into the functional role of particular camps in the KZ system and their political-economic function or directed their attention toward the political prisoners. Certainly other groups, such as the Roma and Sinti and the homosexuals, increasingly found public attention in the 1980s, however an interest of that sort was not expressed in the "Bibelforscher". From the historical research standpoint this is highly regrettable, but in the case of the persecution of Jehovah's Witnesses, it is a question — as Friedrich Zipfel, the first historian interested in the topic, stated — "of a very peculiar occurrence."[3] Also in the

1    Friedrich Zipfel, Kirchenkampf in Deutschland 1933–1945. Religionsverfolgung und Selbstbehauptung der Kirchen in der nationalsozialistischen Zeit, Berlin 1965, p. 175.
2    Kirsten John, Häftlinge im Konzentrationslager in Wewelsburg unter besonderer Berücksichtigung der Ernsten Bibelforscher, Masters Thesis (type-written), Münster 1992.
3    Zipfel, Kirchenkampf, p. 176.

eyes of many fellow prisoners, the "Bibelforscher" were "the most astonishing community ... that there was in the concentration camp".[4]

## On the Persecution of the Jehovah's Witnesses in the "Third Reich"

The beginnings of this Christian denomination, which today numbers 4.5 million believers[5] worldwide, date back to the 1870s. The founder was the US-American Charles Taze Russell who, after his break with the Adventists, proclaimed that Christ had returned invisibly to the people. From now on those faithful to the Lord should assemble and, after a forty-year "harvest period" and the subsequent victory — heralded in the biblical revelations (John's Apocalypse 16:16) — over the "Satanic forces" in the battle of "Armageddon," would erect the salvation-promising "Thousand Year Reich" on earth. Proceeding from Pittsburgh (Pennsylvania), Russell's message, which since 1879 was spread in the periodical "Zion's Watch Tower," first found encouragement on the European continent in the 1890s. In 1897 the main voice ("Der Wachtturm") also appeared in a German edition; five years later, the "Internationale Bibelforscher-Vereinigung" (IBV) opened its first branch in Ebersfeld. At the end of World War I, when the IBV numbered 3,868 "proclaimers" in nearly 100 congregations in the German empire, the religious and governmental authorities — prompted by the growing number of conscientious objectors out of the "Bibelforscher" circle — for the first time became increasingly aware of the denomination's activities. From that point on the "Bibelforscher" in Germany, whose number increased significantly in the post-war years, multiplying by nearly six to 22,535 believers by 1926, were subjected to fierce attacks from the religious apologetic that was propagating the battle against this "sect nuisance," and also from the völkisch and later the National Socialist side. The main criticisms against the IBV included: the new salvation prophesies for the beginning of the peaceful Christian empire; the dogmatic revisions under the second president of the IBV, Joseph Franklin Rutherford, through which Christians owed obedience not to governmental, but to divine authorities; the sermon of the decisive battle of the last days, "Armageddon," and of the approaching decline of the "old world" and its powers of "politics, money and church"; the agitation against "Satan's world empire of false religions" and the denunciation in particular of the pope and the Catholic clergy; the doctrine

4   Heinrich Christian Meier, So War Es. Das Leben im KZ Neuengamme, Hamburg 1946, pp. 31 f.
5   See Jahrbuch der Zeugen Jehovas 1993, ed. Wachtturm Bibel- und Traktatgesellschaft, Selters/Taunas 1993, pp. 33 ff. (further cited as "Jahrbuch" with the year of publication). In the Federal Republic of Germany today, 160,000 people profess to the Jehovah's Witnesses.

of the equality of the races; and the avowal of the Zionist movement as a clear sign of the end-time, as well as "foreign links" to the congregations of the USA. The religious "defense struggle" and the constant agitation of the anti-Semitic völkisch circles against the "Bibelforscher" as "preparing the way for Jewish Bolshevism" eventually succeeded, in that action was taken against the IBV as of 1931 in individual German lands (Baden, Bavaria, Württemburg) by means of police decree and printing bans.

In 1931 the denomination assumed the name "Jehovah's Witnesses"; however, the older names "Bibelforscher" and "Ernste Bibelforscher" long remained in use in Germany.

Even though the ca. 25,000 Jehovah's Witnesses amounted to less than a half percent of the total population, they were considered all the same a grave threat to the "Volk and Nation" and, starting in April 1933, they gradually became the first denomination to be forbidden in all German lands (in Prussia on June 24, 1933). The IBV, whose German headquarters in Magdeburg had hoped to be able to come to an arrangement with the authorities and rulers in the "Third Reich," soon found itself fighting a losing battle.

A very large number of the IBV members did not submit to the prohibition of their confession. Despite the high risk, far more than 10,000 Jehovah's Witnesses persistently carried on the "works of divine service," their gatherings, and the missionary activities, which were especially dangerous, particularly the "house-to-house visitations". No other religious community resisted the National Socialist pressure to conform with a comparable unity and inflexibility. The Jehovah's Witnesses saw in the strict observance of the Christian rules and commandments — in the sense that they understood them — the only God-pleasing path offering them entry to the promised "new world". As their religious postulates were fundamentally incompatible with the demands of the National Socialist-controlled state, the principled and uncompromising IBV-members — almost inevitably — came into sharp opposition to National Socialism, which in turn demanded an unconditional following, claimed all people for itself and denied every deviating ideology its right to exist.

The decisive refusal attitude of numerous Jehovah's Witnesses against the multifarious demands of the regime (required salutes, oath-taking, membership in compulsory NS- organizations) led to a marked intensification of the conflict. After the first arrests in 1933, the "Bibelforscher" community developed structures adapted to the conditions of illegality. They maintained the connections amongst themselves and abroad, organized the extensive smuggling of writings with the help of couriers, and produced underground their periodical "Der Wachtturm" and other printed products with which they supplied the IBV groups and cells nationwide and attempted to win new believers. The Gestapo and the previously rather hesitant judicial system now took more severe action against the Jehovah's Witnesses. Thousands of Jehovah's Witnesses were condemned in the so-called "Bibelforscher process" by the special courts functioning specifically as "political criminal divisions". Above all as of 1935, the especially uncompromising believers — men as well as women — were committed by the hundreds to concentration camps.

The large part of the church community did not let itself be intimidated by the increasing repression. They reacted much more with an intensification of their activities. In this way the Jehovah's Witnesses turned to the population with several nationwide organized pamphlet campaigns in 1936/1937 in order to protest the restriction of their religious freedom and their persecution in the "Third Reich". The regime declared the Jehovah's Witnesses to be "absolutely dangerous enemies of the state" and reacted with a dramatic intensification of the repression. A surprisingly large number of people concerned themselves with the Jehovah's Witnesses' courage to profess; the highest authorities in the judicial system, the police and the SS worked for a while on the "Bibelforscher" question. The state police departments increased their "sect reports" and a "Sonderkommando" of the Gestapo was formed in the Berlin Headquarters.

Although mass arrests of Jehovah's Witnesses took place in August and September 1936 and the head management of the organization was cut off through the arrest of numerous officials, a reorganization of the underground work succeeded. Only with a renewed wave of arrests in the spring and summer of 1937 did the activities of the IBV in the German Empire break down, so that in the years 1938–1939 an organized resistance practically not exist. Not until the war years did the few remaining groups — mostly small circles with a disproportionate number of women — succeed in forming connections with each other and creating firmer organizational structures in specific regions.

During the war the activities of the Jehovah's Witnesses were threatened with the very harshest punishments on the basis of new legal provisions. For they were the only group in the "Third Reich" to propagate conscientious objection as a whole, regardless of the fact that the military courts after the beginning of the war sentenced large numbers of Jehovah's Witnesses to death because of "subversion of the military strength".

As to the extent of the persecution, the following information is available on the basis of newer research:[6] of the 25,000–30,000 persons who professed the Jehovah's Witnesses' faith at the onset of the "Third Reich," approximately 10,000 were detained for some variable length of time. The number of victims

6    See Detlef Garbe, Zwischen Widerstand und Martyrium: Die Zeugen Jehovas im "Dritten Reich". Munich ²1994, pp. 479 ff. The article presented here is based primarily on the results of my dissertation; as one can be referred to that for special evidence and further questions on the persecution of the Jehovah's Witnesses, the footnotes in this text are, as a rule, limited to citations.

killed amongst the German Jehovah's Witnesses is around 1,200; of those approximately 250 — predominantly through military court convictions for refusal to serve — were executed. Thus the Jehovah's Witnesses were of all the religious-ideological groups, after the members of the Jewish faith, the most harshly persecuted by the National Socialist regime.

## The "Purple Triangle" in the Concentration Camps

Starting in 1935, the year in which several hundred Jehovah's Witnesses were committed to the concentration camps Esterwegen, Moringen and above all Sachsenburg (near Chemnitz),[7] the "Bibelforscher" made up its own separate group within the camp society — apart from the Communists, Social Democrats, and other opponents of the regime, as well as the first still relatively few "non-political" KZ-prisoners. In the pre-war years, when the number of occupants in the concentration camps was still relatively small — in the winter of 1936–1937, the total occupancy in the KZs sank to the all-time low of approximately 7,500[8] — the Jehovah's Witnesses comprised numerically a not insignificant group. As a rule their proportion in the total occupancy of the concentration camps at the time totaled between five and ten percent. In part their numbers also were much higher; in particular camps they even made up at times the largest group of prisoners. Of the altogether 433 prisoners in protective custody at Fuhlsbüttel in October 1937, at least 122 (28.2%) were Jehovah's Witnesses,[9] and in Schloß Lichtenberg, the main

7   According to reports, there were about 400 Jehovah's Witnesses under SS control in Sachsenburg and about 120 in Esterwegen in the summer of 1935 (Erwachet!, 11/22/1992, p. 18; Frank Zürcher, Kreuzzug gegen das Christentum, Zürich 1938, pp. 150 f.) In the years 1935–36, it was quite common for most Jehovah's Witnesses to be released from KZ-imprisonment after several months' stay in the camp.

8   Through the increase in committals of both "non-political" KZ-prisoners (the "Asocial"-actions in April and June 1938, the "Jew-action" in November 1938) and opponents to the regime from "annexed" territories (Austria, Sudetenland), the total number of occupants in all the concentration camps up to the beginning of the war climbed to 25,000. See Martin Broszat, "Nationalsozialistische Konzentrationslager 1933–1945", in: Anatomie des SS-Staates. Gutachten des Instituts für Zeitgeschichte. Vol. 2, Munich 31982, pp. 11–133, here pp. 80 f.

9   199 of those in "protective custody" were committed by the criminal police (see Henning Timpke, "Das KL Fuhlsbüttel" in: Studien zur Geschichte der Konzentrationslager, Stuttgart 1970, p. 11–28, here p. 25), so that the Jehovah's Witnesses made up over half the detainees among the 234 Gestapo-prisoners (52.1%). The high proportion of Jehovah's Witnesses in Fuhlsbüttel continued until the spring of 1938. See Detlef Garbe, "Gott mehr gehorchen als den Menschen". Neuzeitliche Christenverfolgung im nationalsozialistischen Hamburg, in: Verachtet — Verfolgt — Vernichtet. Ed. Projektgruppe für die vergessenen Opfer des NS-Regimes, Hamburg 21988, p. 172–219, here p. 195 and p. 216, note 168.

women's camp from December 1937–May 1939 and thus the precursor of Ravensbrück, even over forty percent of the prisoners were members of the Jehovah's Witnesses. There the numbers of the "Bibelforscher" were markedly higher than those of the Communists and Social Democrats.[10]

After the beginning of the war, the share of Jehovah's Witnesses in the total camp occupancy decreased sharply. In the last years of the war, as the total number of prisoners multiplied through the introduction of hundreds of thousands of foreign resistance fighters and forced laborers (December 1942: 88,000, August 1943: 224,000, August 1944: 524,000, January 1945: 718,000[11]), the "Bibelforscher" made up only a very small minority: IBV members made up 5.2% of all prisoners in the KZ Mauthausen in December 1939, in KZ Buchenwald at the same time their number was 3.3%. At the end of 1944 the statistics note 0.12% "Bibelforscher" prisoners in Mauthausen and approximately 0.3% in Buchenwald.[12]

For the KZ base camps during the war the following numerical data are available, which represent not the total number, but rather the respective highest levels of "Bibelforscher" prisoners: Auschwitz (ca. 150), Buchenwald (477), Dachau (ca. 150), Flossenburg (205), Mauthausen (ca. 150), Neuengamme (ca. 100), Ravensbrück (ca. 600), Sachsenhausen (500–600) and Wewelsburg (306). Smaller contingents were present in the KZ base camps Majdanek, Natzweiler, Stutthof and Vught (Herzogenbusch). Altogether, over 3,000 Jehovah's Witnesses were imprisoned in the concentration camps. Of those, about 800 were of non-German nationality: large groups came from the Netherlands (200–250), Austria (200) and

10  Based on the allotment of prisoners' numbers it can be assumed that, in the one and a half years of its existence, altogether 1415 women were admitted to the women's-KZ Lichtenburg. The number of prisoners varied greatly. When the camp was dissolved in May 1939 there were almost 1,000; the statistics name 386 "Bibelforscher" (40.3%), 240 prisoners denoted as "asocials" (25.1%) and 119 as "criminals" (12.4%), 114 "political prisoners in protective custody" (11.9%) and 98 persecuted for so-called "race defilement" (10.2%) . Information from Klaus Drobisch, "Frauenkonzentrationslager im Schloß Lichtenburg," typed lecture, Berlin 1993.

11  Information from Bundesarchiv (Koblenz), NS 3/439; Falk Pingel, Häftlinge unter SS-Herrschaft. Widerstand, Selbstbehauptung und Vernichtung im Konzentrationslager, Hamburg 1978, p. 129 f.

12  The absolute values for Mauthausen run on 12/1/1939: 143 "Bibelforscher" in a total occupancy of 2,772, on 12/31/1944: 85 "Bibelforscher" in a total occupancy of 72426; for Buchenwald on 12/1/1939: 405 "Bibelforscher" in a total occupancy of 12,341, in September 1944 approximately 260 "Bibelforscher" in a total occupancy of 82,239 prisoners. Numerical data from the Bundesarchiv (Koblenz), NS 4 Bu/vorl. 143, Schutzhaftlagerrapport Buchenwald; Evelyn Le Chíne, Mauthausen. The History of a Death Camp, London 1971, pp. 178–190; Pingel, Häftlinge (note 11), p. 282, note 47.

Poland (100), smaller groups from Belgium, France, the Soviet Union, Czechoslovakia and Hungary (up to 50 each).

The strong feeling of solidarity, the separate group codex and not least the ideological distance of the Jehovah's Witnesses from the "politicals" led to their constituting a closed community, which sharply differentiated them from other prisoner groups. The SS began early to segregate the IBV members within the concentration camps, as far as the camp accommodations and work divisions allowed, in order to prevent the lively missionary activities of the Jehovah's Witnesses and to limit their possibilities of establishing contact with other prisoners.[13] With the Commandant's order of 12/9/1935 the camp leader of the KZ Sachsenburg ordered: "The guards should above all things pay heed, that the 'Bibelforscher' in their free time do not enter into conversation with other prisoners, in order to prevent a spread of the Bibelforscher faith."[14]

1935–36, the SS proceeded to label the prisoners visibly on their clothing according to their entry traits. To that end, different colors — at first not yet standard — were used. In the KZ Sachsenburg the "asocials" received a black patch, the "criminals" a green and the "Bibelforscher" a blue. In the KZ Lichtenburg, the Jehovah's Witnesses wore a blue circle on their chests. Jewish prisoners were likewise marked with circles, though theirs were yellow. For the other prisoner categories, different markings were chosen. In 1938 a unified system of fixed color codes was introduced in all concentration camps. Prisoners now wore a colored triangle on the left side of their chest, below that a black prisoner number on a white rectangle. For the Jehovah's Witnesses "violet" replaced "blue".[15] The political prisoners, who as a stem category had at first remained unlabelled, received the red triangle.

13   In fact, as far as possible an arrangement of the prisoners quarters ("blocks") according to group affiliation in the concentration camps mostly took place anyhow. Since one intended, however, to isolate the Jehovah's Witnesses from the other prisoners, special attention was paid to their separate accommodation. In the provincial factory Moringen (near Göttingen), for example, which served as of October 1933 as the central women's concentration camp for Prussia and to which the first female IBV members were committed in January 1935, there was a separate "Bibelforscher hall" as early as 1936–37. See Deutschland-Berichte der Sozialdemokratischen Partei Deutschlands (Sopade) 1934–1940. Reprinted in six volumes, Salzhausen/Frankfurt a. M. 1980, vol. 4 (1937), p. 713; Barbara Distel "Im Schatten der Helden", in: Dachauer Hefte 3 (1987), p. 21–57, here p. 30.

14   Cited in Pingel, Häftlinge , p. 90.

15   The "Bibelforscher" prisoners of Jewish descent, like other Jews, had to wear under the triangle of their category another, yellow triangle, pointing upwards, so that the two triangles together formed a Star of David. The number of "Jewish Bibelforscher prisoners" (in the SS-files mostly listed as "Bibelforscher, Jew") was quite small.

The classification of the "Bibelforscher" as an independent category[16] apart from the "politicals" (red), the "criminals" (green), the "asocials" (black) and the "homosexuals" (pink) resulted from the desire of the SS to make the Jehovah's Witnesses, who were to be kept separate from the other prisoners, visibly recognizable, and at the same time took into account the actual "special placement" of this group, which differed markedly from the other prisoner categories in its behavior. With the category "Bibelforscher" an assignment was chosen that applied solely and specifically to the members of an ideological community. While Communists and Social Democrats, anarchists and bourgeois democrats, ecclesiastical and Christian resistors of the larger confessions, National Socialists who opposed or had fallen out of favor with the regime (e.g. Otto Straßers of the "Schwarze Front") and discontents who did not view themselves as opponents of the regime ("grumblers and troublemakers") were all commonly marked with the red triangle, the "Bibelforscher" prisoners were provided with an exclusive label. Outside of the Jehovah's Witnesses and a few members of "Bibelforscher" groups that had separated from the IBV (e.g. Freie Bibelforscher-Vereinigung, Menschenfreundliche Versammlung/Engel Jehovas), only members of the Seventh-Day Adventists, whose numbers, however, were very small and in which the SS did not recognize any differences from the "Bibelforscher," wore the purple triangle.[17]

## Particular Object of SS Hatred

The special status of the "Bibelforscher" prisoners within the KZ camp society was rooted in their nearly imperturbable confidence of faith, their community spirit and their courage to profess their beliefs. A report smuggled out of Germany about the conditions in the KZ Sachsenburg, which appeared in May 1937 in the "Deutschland-Berichten" published by the SPD in Prague,

16  Furthermore, there was for the time being still a separate label for "emigrants" (blue) as well as further special categories, some of which were not added until later years (e.g. "special division Wehrmacht"), and classifications that were connected to the stem categories (Jew, "race defiler," "relapser").

17  The number of Seventh-Day Adventists (reformed movement) committed to the KZ is approximately 50. The memorial book published by this denomination reports that twelve people were killed in KZ custody, of those three in Sachsenhausen, two in Mauthausen and one each in Auschwitz, Groß-Rosen and Neuengamme. See Hans Fleschutz, Und folget ihrem Glauben nach! Gedenkbuch für die Blutzeugen der Siebenten-Tags-Adventisten Reformationsbewegung. Zeugnisse der Treue und Standhaftigkeit aus Deutschlands dunklen Tagen. Ed. Internationale Missionsgesellschaft der Siebenten-Tags-Adventisten Reformationsbewegung. Jagsthausen , undated [1967], p. 8 f.

discusses the "peculiarity" of the "Bibelforscher" that caused the SS to treat them as a separate category: "Quite astonishing is the behavior of the Ernsten Bibelforscher. These ... people showed an unshakeable spirit of opposition, they demonstrated a disposition toward martyrdom and were uncompromising like no other group in the camp. From the beginning we political prisoners spread the word among ourselves, not to rebel and to submit to all orders of the camp leadership, as the SS could have made short work of us and were just waiting for us to give them grounds for action. Thus we performed as prescribed the salute, etc. The Ernsten Bibelforscher on the other hand would not be forced under any circumstances. Their Jehovah-beliefs forbade it to them, and they held strictly to that."[18]

The same edition of the "Deutschland-Berichte" reports on the female IBV members detained in the women's concentration camp Moringen: "The old Bibelforscher make a lot of work for the warders. They neither perform the Hitler salute nor do they allow themselves to be deterred from their prayers."[19]

Although the Jehovah's Witnesses otherwise meticulously followed the camp rules and especially conscientiously carried out the tasks that were assigned to them, they were uncompromising when actions were demanded from them which they could not reconcile with their conscience. At the same time very different views prevailed among them on the question of which SS demands a Jehovah's Witness had to refuse. Thus only a few refused the "prescribed deference" to the SS, while the great majority removed their hats and stood at attention. They did not see in the prescribed salutes to the SS guards a behavior that was forbidden to them by their faith, but rather considered this a demand that one by necessity had to comply with and also could without denial of his faith. Nevertheless it was altogether convenient for the Jehovah's Witnesses that the SS had arrived at the opinion that KZ prisoners, as notorious "enemies of the Volk," generally had not earned the "right" to give the "Hitler salute".

Those among the Jehovah's Witnesses who refused the deference to the SS argued that such a show of respect amounted to an homage to the servants of Satan and thus was to be judged from faith out as a most reprehensible "idolatry". In the files of the SS there are numerous references to this resistant attitude, which was pursued free from any tactical calculation. For example, on April 24, 1935 an SS-Oberscharführer recommended to the commandant of the KZ Sachsenburg the punishment of a 36-year-old "Bibelforscher" prisoner with eight days "harsh arrest," as this willfully refused the prescribed deference and with that had given to recognize that "he does not want to submit to the discipline". Even after repeated warnings

18  Deutschland-Berichte , vol. 4 (1937), p. 707.
19  Ibid., p. 714.

the Jehovah's Witness had not found it necessary to stand at attention. As the guard ordered him to do so, he — the report of the SS man noted this with indignation — only answered "cheekily": "As a Jehovah's Witness he didn't have to!"[20] This report caused the camp commandant to draw the attention of the inspectorate of the concentration camps to the insubordinate conduct of the IBV prisoners, whereby he explained: "With the comment, they are Jehovah's Witnesses, they all reject everything military and assert that they do not owe respect to any person, but only to God. They refuse to stand at attention before commanders and guard superiors, to salute, and also to sing the customary songs with the other prisoners when marching in and out of camp."[21]

While this sort of conduct in the pre-war time entailed as a rule harsh beatings and arrests, the "radical" Jehovah's Witnesses in the later years sacrificed their lives for their resistant attitude. The "Bibelforschers" Weiß and Zibold, who served long sentences in the KZ Sachsenhausen, were shot "by personal order of Himmler," according to the testimony of SS-Hauptscharführer Kurt Eccarius, the leader of the camp prison there, "because they did not stand up and salute as the Reichsführer Himmler visited the cell building, but rather remained kneeling and continued the prayer they had begun."[22]

Through their openly demonstrated faith, the "Bibelforscher" became a particular object of SS hatred. Degrading abuses were routine. The SS had a whole arsenal of names that they gave to the "purple triangle" prisoners: "Bible worms," "birds of paradise" and "Sheiks of Jordan" were a few of them. Again and again SS people ridiculed the Jehovah's Witnesses' belief in the omnipotence of God. The journalist and political prisoner Edgar Kupfer-Koberwitz recorded in his notes, secretly prepared in the KZ Dachau, one of these "scenes" between an SS man and a "Bibelforscher": "You with your God! Why doesn't he come down, why doesn't he help you? Because he's an idiot, your God! Because he can't, that piece of shit!" With that he laughed and shook his fist at the sky: "God — God — I am your God, do you understand me, you heavenly fool"?[23] And after these words — for corroboration, so to speak — he dealt the Jehovah's Witness a blow.

Collective resistance actions could have especially harsh consequences, as shown by an example from the KZ Lichtenburg, where female "Bibel-

20  Gedenkstätte Buchenwald, 36–1/2, KZ Sachsenburg, report of 4/24/1935.
21  Gedenkstätte Buchenwald, 36–1/2, Camp Commandant of the concentration camp Sachsenburg, letter of 4/25/1935 to the inspectorate of the KZ.
22  Todeslager Sachsenhausen. Ein Dokumentarbericht vom Sachsenhausen-Prozeß, Berlin 1948, p. 42.
23  Edgar Kupfer-Koberwitz, Die Mächtigen und die Hilflosen. Als Häftling in Dachau. Vol. 1: Wie es begann, Stuttgart 1957, p. 215, see also ibid., p. 243.

forscher" boycotted a "Feierstunde," which was arranged on the occasion of the invasion of the Sudetenland by the Wehrmacht on October 1, 1938 and included a community reception of the "Führer's" address. When the "Bibelforscher" did not appear in the courtyard for the broadcast of Hitler's speech, the SS attempted to beat them out of the hall, which was situated in the top floor. As that did not succeed, the SS people without further ado connected fire hoses to a hydrant, turned the ice-cold water on the women and washed them down the stone steps into the courtyard. The report of a fellow prisoner describes the situation: "A terrible panic arose, women running in utmost fear, human bodies falling, screams of pain, drowned out by the roar and the SS commandos and the onlookers."[24]

Outside the "Bibelforscher" were driven further with sticks. The women, absolutely drenched, had to endure Hitler's speech, standing for over an hour. Afterwards, the SS carried out their threat that the "Bibelforscher" would long feel the consequences of their refusal. All medical treatment was forbidden, the suspension of food was ordered and a writing ban was imposed. The "ringleaders" were committed to dark arrest. The SS also reacted to other refusal actions in the same way.

The SS attempted to break the extraordinary resistance of the "Bibelforscher" with a continuous increase in terror. In 1937 the SS included the Jehovah's Witnesses in the "special division" that was developed in the previous year for "relapsers" (prisoners who were serving their second sentence in a concentration camp). In these penal companies the prisoners were enlisted in the most difficult work and were driven especially hard.

In Dachau and Sachsenhausen the "Bibelforscher" were at the same time sent into the "isolation" installed in both these camps. These were barracks that were separated from the usual camp by a fence. Beyond the heavy burden that lay upon all prisoners of this "special camp," the rules were additionally tightened for the "Bibelforscher" prisoners; further conditions were gradually added for them. These imposed a total mail ban over them in the spring of 1938; that is, the affected "Bibelforscher" prisoners were allowed neither to write nor to receive letters.

Particularly in 1939 and 1940, the SS raged against the Jehovah's Witnesses with a bestial violence. The tortures began on the day of admission — for "new admissions" the SS thought up special "admissions ceremonies". If at the "reception" the Jehovah's Witness, faced with the question placed to all "admissions," as to which type of criminal they were, contradicted the SS men and as answer stated their belief in the Bible and Jesus Christ, they were beaten, and a cross-examination began. Willi Lehmbecker, admitted to

24  Report of Gertrud Geßmann, cited in Hans Maur, Antifaschistische Mahn- und Gedenkstätte Lichtenburg. Ed. Kreismuseum Jessen, Prettin (Elbe) undated, p. 26.

the KZ Sachsenhausen on April 20, 1940, reported: "All questions which were asked me, I attempted to answer biblically. To the question, who is the Führer, they wanted me to answer: Adolf Hitler. But I was silent."[25] After that the Jehovah's Witness was beaten severely.

It was periodically prophesied to the newly committed, that one would see to it that they did not remain Jehovah's Witnesses, whereby the "trials of strength" not seldom led to the most severe mistreatment already on the first day. Alexander Joseph, who was admitted to the KZ Sachsenhausen in September 1939 for listening to foreign radio programs, described one such scene: "A Bibelforscher broke down under the mistreatment by Schubert. He was then asked by an SS man: 'Do you still believe in Jehovah?' When the Bibelforscher answered yes, Schubert kicked him again and asked once more. This repeated itself 4 or 5 times. Finally the Bibelforscher only breathed 'Yes'."[26]

In order to shake the steadfastness of the "Bibelforscher" community, the SS myrmidons picked out individuals again and again, with whom they intended to set an example. Numerous cruelties were directed toward mocking the baptism. From the KZ Sachsenhausen it was reported that SS-Oberscharführer Wilhelm Schubert once ordered the Jehovah's Witnesses who were assigned to the "Garagenbau" commando to "baptize" an old Jewish prisoner, whom he held over a tub of water. In this predicament the "Bibelforscher" were willing to comply with the wish that mocked their faith, but they would not be a party to the mistreatment of the fellow prisoner: "We spread his forehead symbolically with water. Schubert, angered by our resistance, held him fully in the water, and as he let go, the Jewish prisoner fell. Schubert had strangled and drowned him."[27]

In order to force prisoners to break with their "Bibelforscher" beliefs and deny Jehovah, Schubert, Bugdalle, Sorge and other SS myrmidons raged in Sachsenhausen's "isolation" with an indescribable brutality. Their torture arsenal included: running the gauntlet, suffocation of prisoners in the broom closet, insertion of hoses into body cavities, spraying prisoners with a water hose to the heart until the onset of death, and leaving people standing drenched outside in the frost until they froze.

At least once, and according to other statements three or four times, "Bibelforscher" prisoners were suffocated in Sachsenhausen in the beginning

---

25 Personal narrative of Willi Lehmbecker, 4/15/1971.
26 Alexander Joseph, testimony of 11/24/1958 before the superior court in Bonn in the proceedings against Schubert and Sorge (KZ Sachsenhausen), in: KZ-Verbrechen vor deutschen Gerichten. Ed. H. G. van Dam/Ralph Giordano, Frankfurt a. M. 1962, p. 209.
27 Johann Wrobel, testimony of 11/23/1958, ibid., p. 196.

of 1940. To this end the SS closed approximately 25 prisoners in the broom closet. This was very narrow, about one meter wide and three to three and a half meters long, with only one small window up above. The keyholes were stopped up from outside with paper, windows and doors were sealed with blankets. The door was held closed for twelve hours. According to the statements of Paul Wauer, 15 Jehovah's Witnesses did not survive this torture.[28]

In Sachsenhausen in the winter of 1939–1940, which was especially harsh with temperatures of negative 30 degrees Celsius, and in which there were a large number of deaths from general exhaustion, altogether about 130 Jehovah's Witnesses — about every fourth "Bibelforscher" of this camp — lost their lives.[29]

Similarly high death rates are also found in other camps during this time frame. After a military conscription committee appeared in KZ Mauthausen in late February 1940 and, according to reports, approximately 35 Jehovah's Witnesses refused to sign a Wehrpass, they were systematically worked to death in the stone quarry. Of the 143 Jehovah's Witnesses detained in KZ Mauthausen at that time, 52 (according to other statements 53) died in the first quarter of 1940; that is, more than every third.[30]

## Confidence of Faith, Will to Self-assertion and Solidarity Structures

In spite of the terror, the Jehovah's Witnesses within the camps demonstrated a marked will to self-assertion.

On the occasion of "custody review hearings," the SS presented the Jehovah's Witnesses in the concentration camps with a declaration for their signature, in which they should declare their willingness to give up their beliefs.[31] The Jehovah's Witnesses, who also called the questionings, which

28  Bayerisches Hauptstaatsarchiv, OMGUS, Dachauer Kriegsverbrecherprozeß, Mikrofilm 1 a/1, Mr. 182 f., Paul Wauer, testimony of 21. 5. 1945.
29  See Garbe, Zeugen Jehovas, p. 410 f.
30  See Chíne, Mauthausen p. 182; Hans Maršolek, Die Geschichte des Konzentrationslagers Mauthausen. Vienna ²1980, p. 273.
31  The wording of this "statement of obligation" was set by the Reichsführer-SS in late 1938: "Statement. I have realized that the Internationale Bibelforscher-Vereinigung spreads an erroneous teaching and only pursues subversive goals under the cloak of religious activity. Thus I have turned my back on this organization completely and have also freed myself internally from the doctrine of this sect. I hereby declare that I will never again work for the Internationale Bibelforscher-vereinigung. Persons who approach me promoting the heresy of the Bibelforscher, I will immediately report to the authorities."

were carried out at intervals of a few months or sometimes also of one or two years, "loyalty hearings," firmly refused the demand to dismiss their faith as "heresy," although a signature would have placed their release in prospect. In the war years there was yet another reason for the "Bibelforscher" prisoners to refuse the "signature". They knew that — in so far as they were liable for military service — they would have a conscription into the Wehrmacht to reckon with after their release from custody. As it was their firm principle to use no weapons, but refusal to serve was regularly punished with the death sentence in the military courts, they knew that with their signature they were most likely signing their own death warrant. If only for that reason they saw no possibility of obtaining their "freedom" through the "statement of obligation". In the KZ there remained in contrast at least the hope that Jehovah God, to whom they had remained loyal, would lead them out of their affliction and suffering and save them. The group pressure and the dread of giving up the community with the fellow believers, but also the fear of losing the future heavenly reward, held them back. On the few who nevertheless "signed" was hung the stigma of the "deserter" and the "disloyal". Their faith brethren imposed on them the — so named by the Jehovah's Witnesses — "community withdrawal". As they could, however, find re-acceptance into the community of the Jehovah's Witnesses if they named understandable reasons, for which they had not believed themselves able to behave otherwise, and if they expressed their "repentance" through the revocation of their signature, many of those who had signed the declaration decided after a short time to revoke their signature.

Presumably because many of the "Bibelforscher" who finally agreed to the signature, under great difficulties of conscience, frequently remained undecided even afterwards, the Gestapo considered a longer observation period necessary for a review of the prisoner's "credibility" before a release from custody could be ordered. Through the "further remaining in custody," the Reichsführer-SS — as stated in the memoirs of Rudolf Höß — wanted to "make sure that the break had been genuine and convinced."[32]

The number of those who agreed to "renounce," did not revoke their signature during the observation period, which often lasted several months, and finally were actually released from KZ custody, remained altogether very low. They did not amount to more than a few dozen.[33]

Occasionally, especially in the first months of the war, the SS attempted with increased pressure to prompt the Jehovah's Witnesses to give up their refusal attitude and to sign the declaration. Repeatedly the Jehovah's Wit-

---

32 Kommandant in Auschwitz. Autobiographische Aufzeichnungen von Rudolf Höß, with comments and an introduction from Martin Broszat, München 1983, p. 77.
33 See Garbe, Zeugen Jehovas, p. 417.

nesses were called out to "special roll calls," at which "Bibelforscher" prisoners were threatened with the execution of all who did not give up their refusal attitude. At a roll call in the KZ Buchenwald a few days after the war began, the Jehovah's Witnesses were called on by the camp leader, SS-Obersturmbannführer Arthur Rödl, to agree to perform military service. Although guard troops armed with machine guns took position, and according to reports everything looked "as if a mass execution would take place,"[34] no one volunteered. The SS may not have carried out their threat, but the incompliance did carry the consequence of committal to the quarry commando, food deprivation and suspension of any treatment in the hospital barracks.

In the KZ Sachsenhausen an example was set on September 15, 1939; because of his refusal to sign the Wehrpass, the 39-year-old Jehovah's Witness August Dickmann was executed by firing squad on the roll-call square in front of the assembled prisoner workforce. Following this first public execution in the KZ Sachsenhausen the camp commandant Hermann Baranowski directed an address to the "Bibelforscher" prisoners and announced that the same fate would await all of them, if they did not sign the "statement of obligation" and give up their conscientious objection. Although Baranowski ordered those who did not wish to be shot to step forward, this attempt also failed completely. Examples of this sort seemed to produce the opposite effect from what the SS intended with them.

The refusal of the Jehovah's Witnessed to deny their faith comprised the refusal on principle of all actions that were forbidden them by their doctrine. In this respect a new, difficult burden lay ahead for the Jehovah's Witnesses, in that the concentration camps were increasingly included in the manufacture of arms after 1942. Their refusal to produce for the war was regarded by the SS as a refusal to work, on which stood the harshest punishment for KZ prisoners short of the death sentence. When, for example, the production of automatic assault weapons was taken up in the Gustloff works in the camp in Buchenwald in March 1943, the "Bibelforscher" prisoners who were assigned to this employment refused to perform the work. Although the SS imposed numerous "camp punishments," punished the refusers with 25 blows on the "trestle" and transferred a few to the penal company, by far most of the Jehovah's Witnesses would not let themselves be forced to do this work. The tightly organized "Bibelforscher" group in Buchenwald tried with all its strength to avoid the "undermining" of their unity and of their disapproving position toward arms production — even if it is negligible. A statement composed by the Jehovah's Witnesses of Buchenwald in 1945 after the liberation says: "The few who, under the pressure of willing henchmen of the devil, out of their fear of being beaten or killed,

---

34  Moritz Zahnwetzer, KZ Buchenwald. Personal narrative, Kassel 1946, p. 28.

accepted such work, were immediately expelled from the community of this neutral people."[35]

Concerning the refusal of occupation in arms production, the SS in the end had no other choice but to take into account the position of the Jehovah's Witnesses. The refusers were assigned to other commandos, mostly to columns of handworkers working in the camp workshops.

The question, however, of where the line should be drawn in each case in the refusal of "war service," led to passionate arguments among the "Bibelforscher" prisoners — at which the understanding ruled, that the commandments of the Bible forbade the manufacture of weapons and ammunition to a Christian. For the "moderates" only direct participation in the manufacture of war equipment meant for killing could be considered work for the war, while for the "radicals" other activities also constituted support for the conduct of the war, and — in their view — thus were just as much to be refused out of religious reasons. For example there arose just such a conflict when the production of skis, meant for the army units stuck in the Russian winter, was taken up in a workshop in KZ Buchenwald. Willi Töllner, the spokesman of the "Bibelforscher" community in Buchenwald, announced that the Jehovah's Witnesses who were assigned to the workshop also had to refuse this work, as the skis, serving to equip the troops, were war equipment.

The majority of the Jehovah's Witnesses willingly followed this resolution, but a smaller group did not agree with Töllner's assessment. This group argued that one could not kill anybody with skis and it was therefore something different to participate in their manufacture than to produce grenades. When those Jehovah's Witnesses who were assigned to the workshop for ski production and professed the minority opinion did not discontinue working, they were immediately expelled from the Buchenwald "Bibelforscher" community for their conduct, which was judged "unbiblical".

Proceeding from the position that the Jehovah's Witnesses had to establish a united "front against Satan's world," the "Bibelforscher" group in the KZ Buchenwald was strictly hierarchically organized under Töllner's leadership; subordination was demanded of individual members. Under the conditions of a KZ-camp such an interior structure proved to be advantageous. The Buchenwald "Bibelforscher" group succeeded through their collective behavior in remaining relatively firm and also in organizing "underground activities" (secret gatherings, duplication of writings). Toward the excluded

---

35  Statement composed by the Jehovah's Witnesses in Buchenwald after the liberation, printed in: Guido Grünewald, Geschichte der Kriegsdienstverweigerung. Ed. Deutsche Friedensgesellschaft/Vereinigte Kriegsdienstgegner, Essen 1979, pp. 30–33 (32).

minority, however, the nearly 400 Jehovah's Witnesses who sided with Töllner remained strictly cool in their conduct. A situation such as the one in Buchenwald, which existed in the division of the "Bibelforscher" community and continued until the end of the war, did not develop in any other camp. Tensions and arguments over the question of which work should be refused as activity serving the war also existed elsewhere, but did not lead to such an open and permanent break.

Demonstrative actions, such as the refusal to stand for roll calls, were also intensely controversial among the Jehovah's Witnesses. This applied even more to actions whose practical effect was basically directed against themselves. For example, a few believers in Ravensbrück gave up — and later regained, but restricted to 25 words per letter — the writing allowance because they did not want their letters to be given the Führer's portrait as a stamp. A group of about 25 "extremists" decided, referring to the Mosaic law ("None among you shall eat blood" — Leviticus 17:10–16), to give up the consumption of blood sausage and to refuse to receive it at the food distribution.[36] They also publicly announced their resolution in a signed statement.

The majority of the Jehovah's Witnesses imprisoned in concentration camps did not participate in this type of demonstrative action. Certainly nearly all the "Bibelforscher" prisoners — viewed as a whole — firmly refused to work in the arms production through the manufacture of weapons and other war equipment; however, many Jehovah's Witnesses rejected anything more as too "radical". While, for example, "Bibelforscher" in the KZ Ravensbrück were in principle not willing to work in the "Angora breeding" because the wool of the Angora rabbits was used to line pilots' jackets, those imprisoned in the KZ Neuengamme seem to have seen nothing reprehensible in that. Some three years long, fifteen of them worked in the "Angora commando" there. This workplace even became — as the conditions for secret assemblies and the hiding of writings were comparatively good in the isolated commando, whose work force at first consisted exclusively of Jehovah's Witnesses — a center of the "Bibelforscher" resistance in Neuengamme. Since the "Angora commando" fed the SS kitchen's waste to up to 3,800 rabbits, the Jehovah's Witnesses assigned there could also set aside edibles, which they then gave to those members of the faith community who were in urgent need of supplementary nourishment.

Not only arguments over the biblically commanded behavior, but also differing interpretations and predictions could lead to schisms, though mostly only in passing. In mid-1937 there was fractionalization in KZ Sachsenhausen in connection with speculations over the moment of the

---

36 See Margarete Buber-Neumann Als Gefangene bei Stalin und Hitler. Eine Welt im Dunkel, Stuttgart 1958, p. 257 f.

beginning of the decisive battle of "Armageddon". One Jehovah's Witness believed he had, with the help of the Bible, discovered the date on which the Satanic powers would be destroyed and they would be liberated from the concentration camp. Predictions on the disintegration of the Hitler regime and the end of the torture held an understandably large appeal. The evangelical pastor and former Sachsenhausen prisoner Dr. Werner Koch described in a report — which strongly emphasized his rejection of the religious views of the Jehovah's Witnesses — what, according to his memory, took place on the specific day on which the Lord was supposed to "destroy the reign of the Third Reich and of all kingdoms": "Again and again the gazes of the Jehovah's Witnesses turn to the heavens on this day. Full of joyous expectation. There are a few clouds around lunchtime — but nothing happens! In the afternoon their excitement visibly wears out. Dejected they march back into the camp at night under the usual cries and insults of the SS. After the evening roll call one sees how the elders put their heads together and discuss heatedly with one another. On the next morning everything is already clear again: Someone has falsely combined a few numbers out of the Old and New Testaments. A miscalculation is to blame for the fact that the date of the Lord's return was falsely quoted."[37]

Their imperturbable confidence of faith, the strong marked feeling of solidarity and their solid mutual help gave the Jehovah's Witnesses the inner strength to remain to a great extent loyal to their convictions even in the concentration camps. Their community spirit made it possible for them to develop collective strategies of survival, and through that to ease the burden of the camp routine. Moreover the common housing, initially ordered by the SS for the purpose of isolation, also turned out to be very advantageous for the Jehovah's Witnesses in the end. Later attempts to weaken them through scattering strategies could hardly still have an impact.

In the "Bibelforscher" quarters firm solidarity structures developed. For example, the Jehovah's Witnesses formed "parcel communities," as is reported of the "Bibelforscher" community in Neuengamme. If a Jehovah's Witness there received a parcel, they neither kept it to themselves nor did they give it to the block elder for safekeeping (this protection was, as rule, paid for with a share of the parcel). Rather the parcel was immediately handed over to the fellow "Bibelforscher," who weighed it precisely with a scale and distributed the contents evenly amongst the involved "parcel community," who consumed them on the same evening or in the next days. In this way the Jehovah's Witnesses in Neuengamme had "almost every night a little piece of sausage, sometimes a bit of butter or a little

37   Werner Koch, "Sollen wir K. weiter beobachten?" Ein Leben im Widerstand, Stuttgart 1982, p. 219.

blob of marmalade or a small piece of cake."[38] The advantages of parcel communities were obvious. Because the wares were immediately distributed amongst everyone, there was no cause for jealousy and resentment of the "have-nots" against the parcel receivers. A protection against possible theft was unnecessary, and also the rotting of foodstuffs could effectively be obviated.

However, with other prisoner groups in the KZ the Jehovah's Witnesses cultivated no cooperation. They rejected any participation in the camp resistance community carried by the political prisoners. They did not think they could reconcile sabotage and politically motivated actions against the SS with their beliefs. Even in the camp they tried to maintain their "neutrality".

## Special Assignments and Privileged Jobs

Starting in about 1941/1942, that is in the middle of the war, the position of the Jehovah's Witnesses in the concentration camps improved. Whereas before they were, next to the Jews, subjected to the terror of the SS in special measure, now a noticeable relief arose. The general development — that, because of the growing significance of the prisoner labor force since 1942/1943 and the increasing need to recruit functionary prisoners for the camp administration, the chances of survival generally increased for non-Jewish German prisoners in the steadily expanding camps[39] — was amplified in the case of the "Bibelforscher" prisoners because of a few group-specific peculiarities. Through the diligence, reliability and care with which they conscientiously carried out all orders given to them — so long as these did not contradict their religious principles — they had made themselves into desirable workers in the eyes of the SS work leaders. They were regarded as precise, reliable and — an important argument for the SS administration — trustworthy. As a rule the SS did not need to fear manipulation or intrigues directed against them by the "Bibelforscher".

The SS especially learned to treasure one further peculiarity. For religious reasons, the Jehovah's Witnesses rejected escape from the camp. Since they viewed their fate as laid entirely in the hands of God, they felt that escape was rebellion against the divine Providence. In the KZ imprisonment they saw

38  Personal narrative of Richard Rudolph, 9/9/1986; see also Meier, Neuengamme, pp. 31 f.
39  Pingel, Häftlinge, p. 168, proceeds on the assumption that in the last period of the concentration camps around 15 to 20% of all German prisoners were assigned "to relatively secure, privileged jobs".

a test imposed upon them, which it was necessary to withstand. Added to this was their confidence, that Jehovah God would soon erect his kingdom on Earth, open the gates of the camps and prisons and lead them into freedom. Whoever, on the other hand, attempted to escape, expressed with that — or so the majority of the Witnesses saw it — his mistrust of Jehovah.

As no attempts at escape were to be expected from "Bibelforscher" prisoners, they were likely to be assigned outside of the camp to difficult-to-guard work-sites (agriculture, transport, loading and unloading, etc) and to special assignments.[40] In many cases the SS composed such work columns exclusively of Jehovah's Witnesses, particularly since the SS generally aimed at their separation even in work units in order to limit the possibilities of their conversion of fellow prisoners. Gradually it became common for the SS to reduce the number of guards in "Bibelforscher commandos".

Every "Bibelforscher" prisoner who was assigned to work units on agricultural estates in the last years of the war experienced comparatively good conditions. Favored in the first place in the allotment of workers were National Socialist leaders and people who had equivalent connections. For example, 10 female "Bibelforscher" worked as early as early 1942 as house servants, cooking and gardening, on the Hartzwalde estate of Felix Kersten, Himmler's doctor. Lina Heydrich, the widow of the head of the Reichssicherheitshauptamt and mistress of the estate Jungfern-Breschan (Böhmen) was allocated 15 "Bibelforscher" prisoners as workers in February 1944. At times up to 50 people were employed on the estate Comthurey, which served as the country seat for the head of the SS-Wirtschafts-Verwaltungshauptamt Oswald Pohl and, much like Hartzwalde, lay in the immediate vicinity of the KZ Ravensbrück.

On January 6, 1943 the Reichsführer-SS ordered the employment of imprisoned "Bibelforscher" in SS households.[41] Himmler, who dealt with this question personally and with an unusual intensity, perceived in his visits to the estate Hartzwalde the opportunity, in his own words, "to study there the question of the Ernsten Bibelforscher from all angles". On the basis of his "observations" it became clear to Himmler, that a completely different strategy was required in handling the "Bibelforscher question": "Punishments don't work with them at all, as they relate every

40   Jehovah's Witnesses were also given priority in enlistments for the construction of camps not yet surrounded by security systems. See Karl Hüser, Wewelsburg 1933–1945. Kult- und Terrorstätte der SS, Paderborn 1982, pp. 72 ff.
41   RFSS, order of 1/6/1943 (RF/Dr.I 37/43), cited in letter of the head of the Sicherheitspolizei and the SD of 7/15/1943 to the RFSS, printed in: Filip Friedman/Tadeusz Holuj, Oświęcim, Warszawie 1946, pp. 183–186.

punishment enthusiastically. Every punishment is for them a reward in the beyond. Therefore every true Bibelforscher will ... readily accept execution and death. Every dark arrest, every hunger, every freezing is a reward, every punishment, every blow is an advantage with Jehovah."[42]

Himmler, who seems to have understood that one could not break the religious resistance of the activist group of Jehovah's Witnesses serving sentences in the concentration camp even with terror, gave the following instructions: "I ask that we direct the deployment of the male and female Bibelforscher so that they all come into work — in agriculture, for example — that has nothing to do with war and all its high points. One can leave them unattended by the right employment, they will never run away. One can give them independent errands, they will be the best managers and workers."

When in the course of the year 1943 a commando consisting of male "Bibelforscher" prisoners was assigned to agricultural work (turnip and potato cultivation) and also to the construction of a hunting lodge on the Kersten estate Hartzwalde, it was supposed to — as Frank Birk, who belonged to this commando, reported — "be tested for the first time, whether one could put Jehovah's Witnesses to work without guards."[43] Other Jehovah's Witnesses employed on agricultural estates and in a few special Außenkommandos also obtained increasingly larger freedom of movement in the last year of the war. In part the protective custody was even lifted, whereby the released however remained obligated to serve at the same work. Toward the end of the war, even the "Bibelforscher" employed as household help for families of SS leaders actually held the status of "half-released". For example, the "Bibelforscher" employed in the "Führer-houses" in the KZ Auschwitz received special passes that allowed them to move freely outside of the camp during the day and generally during the work time. This arrangement was in the interest of the SS families, because now they could have their shopping and errands done by their servants.

Even for the "Bibelforscher" prisoners who were not assigned to a "special duty" outside the camp, the conditions as a rule visibly improved, even though they remained at the mercy of the SS in the KZ. In the concentration camps numerous Jehovah's Witnesses were employed in "privileged workplaces" and in so-called "positions of trust". These were for those

42  Reichsführer-SS, letter to Müller and Pohl, printed in: Jahrbuch 1974, pp. 196 f. The letter, there undated, could not be archivally located; it is however with great probability to be presumed, that it concerned the order of 1/6/1943 that was mentioned in the letter of 7/15/1943 and was briefly referenced in the content. See also Manfred Gebhard (Ed.), Die Zeugen Jehovahs. Eine Dokumentation über die Wachtturmgesellschaft. License edition, Schwerte (Ruhr) 1971, p. 206.

43  Personal narrative of Franz Birk, 1/31/1971.

concerned quite "sought-after positions". They worked as special craftsmen, as writers for SS officer and as SS "attendants" (barbers, servants and cooks).

While at first the Jehovah's Witnesses rejected as a rule the assumption of "functions" within the "prisoners' self-administration,"[44] a change also arose here in the last years of the war. The "Bibelforscher" prisoners certainly did not pursue such positions and least of all did they participate in the "battle" for supremacy in the "prisoners' self-administration," but they agreed to take appropriate leadership functions, especially in the case of work commandos and barrack communities consisting solely or mostly of "Bibelforscher". This usually involved taking "foreman" and "Kapo" posts; "block elder" functions, however, the Jehovah's Witnesses only very seldom performed.

Prisoners of other groups report that, in general, the conduct of Jehovah's Witnesses in functions was exemplary. The Danish Neuengamme prisoner Lauritz G. Damgaard, who was put under the charge of a Jehovah's Witness in a gardener commando, remembers this very well: "From the Nazi point of view, he was a terrible foreman. From all other viewpoints a first-class foreman and a fantastic person. He didn't hit, he didn't drive us, and he covered up for us both against the SS and against his prisoner superiors, with whom he however had a good relationship."[45] Such individual experiences are supported by the observations of Bruno Bettelheim, psychoanalyst and prisoner of the concentration camps Dachau and Buchenwald, whose report also addresses why the SS nevertheless made "Bibelforscher" Kapos: "When they had become that and the SS people gave them an order, they insisted that the prisoners carried out the work well and in the allotted time. They were certainly the only group of prisoners who never insulted or mistreated the other camp inmates (quite the opposite, they were as a rule quite polite toward their fellow prisoners), but the SS still favored them as Kapos because they were diligent, skillful and reserved."[46]

---

44   The concentration camp Wewelsburg presents an exception, where the Jehovah's Witnesses alone made up the staff during the camp's construction from February to September 1940, and continued to make up the core group and take on numerous functions in the following years, even after the admission of several hundred other German prisoners as well as a few thousand foreigners (mostly Russian prisoners). (See Hüser, Wewelsburg, p. 81). Jehovah's Witnesses were employed in the KZ Wewelsburg as, among other things, camp elders, camp clerks, block elders, SS servants and as Kapos and foremen in several commandos.

45   Personal narrative of Lauritz G. Damgaard, 9/23/1986.

46   Bruno Bettelheim, Aufstand gegen die Masse. Die Chance des Individuums in der modernen Gesellschaft, München 1960, p. 135.

## Mission, Smuggle of Written Works, and Secret Bible Study

The improving material situation of the Jehovah's Witnesses, combined with their access to privileged jobs, formed the basis for an increased continuation of "Bibelforscher" activities even within captivity. Appropriate organizational structures were created. For example, the "Bibelforscher" community in KZ Neuengamme subdivided itself into seven study groups, each of which was directed by a study leader. Each group tried to come together for "book study" at least once a week. For that purpose, copies of the "Wachtturm" were secretly prepared and duplicated with copy paper by a Jehovah's Witness employed as a writer by the SS, and a Bible circulated. For a time it is said that groups were even given a copy of the daily text every morning at roll call.

Even within the concentration camps the Jehovah's Witnesses put all their effort into winning new members for their faith. Numerous fellow prisoners became — often to their regret — objects of conversion attempts. In the scope of a mission campaign carried out in early 1943 in KZ Neuengamme, the camp was divided into zones and special "assault parties" were formed to "process" them: In order to reach the largest possible number of fellow prisoners, small groups of Jehovah's Witnesses went from block to block and gave "witness" to their faith. To this aim multilingual "witness cards" were prepared, which contained a short biblical passage and the offer of a conversation about the hope for the coming kingdom. Lectures were even held, and were translated for the Russian and Polish camp inmates. If a fellow prisoner demonstrated interest, "follow-up visits" were conducted and biblical instruction began.

Even baptisms[47] were performed several times in the camp Neuengamme. The person wishing to be baptized — this is for example reported of a Russian and a young Polish prisoner — was smuggled into the weeding commando, which had to dig drainage ditches. There they slipped as if they were inexperienced. With words like "if you already fell in, then at least dive in properly," the eldest "Bibelforscher" working in the commando then took hold of the baptismal candidate's head and lowered him into the water amongst the howling of the SS guards, who took the whole thing for fun, while the Jehovah's Witnesses, remaining solemn, accompanied the scene with their silent prayers.[48]

The Jehovah's Witnesses also intensified their activities in other concentration camps. In Dachau the Jehovah's Witnesses organized Bible hours

47   The Jehovah's Witnesses practice adult baptism.
48   Interview with Ernst Wauer, televised on SDR III/Südwestfunk Baden-Baden (program "Schaufenster") on 11/14/1982; as well as the personal narratives of Karl Hanl, 11/24/1987 and Richard Rudolph, 9/9/1986.

nearly every night, in Gusen there were baptisms and the "memorial meal" was celebrated by candlelight in a washroom, and in Buchenwald the Jehovah's Witnesses regularly held secret devotions; two hundred and fifty of them celebrated the common "memorial meal" at midnight, and on some days they used a rain barrel for secret baptisms.

The indefatigable missionary urge of the Jehovah's Witnesses did not remain without resonance; in the hopelessness of the KZ-imprisonment their ardently preached message of the coming "kingdom of God" found willing listeners. Prisoners of other groups joined them. Not a few seemed however driven more by the wish to partake in the "blessings" of the "Bibelforscher" community than through an inner acceptance of the "true faith". Mostly it was foreign prisoners, primarily Russians and members of non-political categories, who showed themselves open to the "Bibelforscher" religion.[49] But even prisoners with communist and atheist convictions, who stood in great ideological distance to all religions, were so deeply impressed by the religious confidence and community spirit of the Jehovah's Witnesses, that they felt themselves drawn toward them. A few of them eventually assumed the "Bibelforscher" faith.

The unceasing missionary efforts also did not stop at the guard and SS personnel, whereby this not seldom carried weighty consequences for the "proclaimers of the kingdom": When a "Bibelforscher" employed as a servant in the household of the Buchenwald KZ commandant Karl Koch attempted to share his religious convictions with the commandant's family, Ilse Koch asked her husband to punish the prisoner "because of lapse".[50] At times, however, the Jehovah's Witnesses also met with interest; there are even reports of cases in which SS people secretly read the Bible with them.

The countermeasures of the SS could not have prevented the Jehovah's Witnesses from further spreading their religious teachings even within the concentration camps. The organization of the preaching in some camps came so far that a monthly overview on the "total number of witnesses" was reported to the outside. In this report a distinction was made between the missionary

---

49  Only scattered information is available on the number of conversions. From a "resolution" of May 1945, it can be gathered that among the 230 Sachsenhausen Bibelforscher who formed a marching column at the evacuation of the camp, there were 36 converts to the "Bibelforscher" faith. For the KZ Ravensbrück 70 conversions are reported (Renate Lichtenegger, "Wiens Bibelforscherinnen im Widerstand gegen den Nationalsozialismus 1938–1945". Phil. Diss., Vienna 1984, p. 221, 278); according to other information, 300 young Russian women joined the Jehovah's Witnesses (Gebhard, Zeugen Jehovas, p. 209). In the KZ Mauthausen "a few" are said to have been baptized; for the neighboring camp Gusen it is reported that 5 Poles were baptized (Jahrbuch 1989, p. 133).

50  See Pierre Durand, Die Bestie von Buchenwald. Berlin (Ost) 1985, p. 57.

efforts undertaken toward fellow prisoners and the "total number of witnesses reported to the members of the SS."[51] The Jehovah's Witnesses considered the conversions of other-believers to the "Bibelforscher" beliefs a sign that their God had not turned away from the community, even in the camps, and still looked after the "furtherance of the works of the kingdom".

Now more than ever, opportunities for the production and distribution of writings presented themselves in increased measure. Especially in small commandos comprised exclusively of "Bibelforscher" prisoners and entrusted with "special assignments," for example the "sculptor workshop" in the KZ Buchenwald, illegal writings could be produced and duplicated. The Jehovah's Witnesses even succeeded in constructing a regular courier net between the various camps, at least temporarily. Through it personal letters, "biblical interpretations" and most of all reports on the situation in the KZ were transmitted from the "Bibelforscher" who were assigned to work outside the camp during the day to faith brethren via middle persons, "dead mailboxes," or the like. These smuggled-out texts were duplicated — partly by hand, partly by machine — and sent further by non-imprisoned Jehovah's Witnesses. The "reports" thus obtained then found their way over the "underground movement" back into other camps.

As the "Bibelforscher" groups, which till then had been isolated to a great extent in the individual camps — there had only been a certain flow of information through transfers between the concentration camps — had each developed their own standpoints on various issues, the differing positions collided through the exchange in writings. Thus it happened that doctrinal disputes so to speak now arose between the camps — probably one of the most remarkable occurrences in the history of the Jehovah's Witnesses, which is hardly lacking in curious moments.

## Loyalty of Faith as Resistance

The resistance of the Jehovah's Witnesses directed itself against the prohibition of their association decreed in 1933 and against the fact that religious acknowledgement and, with that, the preaching of the message of the approaching divine kingdom was forbidden them. For them this meant in fact a ban on their faith; they organized and resisted actively against this massive form of state domination. The permanent insubordination of the Jehovah's Witnesses, who were resolved to everything, certainly disturbed the exercise of control by the NS regime, which had intended the unopposed insertion of all the "people's comrades" into the "community of the Volk," however

51  Johannes Rauther, Historical narrative. Typewritten, Calw undated, p. 59.

their intentions and objectives were not directed toward a change of the political relationships. Certainly the Jehovah's Witnesses also contemplated an overthrow, but this should be effected by God and no government created by political powers should take the place of the present ruler, but rather Christ as regent of the divine kingdom. In that sense the opposition of the Jehovah's Witnesses is not to be characterized as a politically motivated resistance.

In their own self-conception the success of their activities did not demonstrate an undermining of the regime, but rather a proof of their religious loyalty. The effort to protect their faith steadfastly, to withstand the "trial" imposed upon them and with that to prove themselves as true Witnesses to their God Jehovah, clearly stood in the foreground in their actions. Through their actions and their refusal behavior, the Jehovah's Witnesses hoped to help the belief in the quick coming of God's kingdom to break through amongst the people. With their resistance they basically did not want to set any sign or "signal" for others, but rather to give "witness". "Resistance" was for them an act of confession.

But their struggle led them with extreme decisiveness and unprecedented courage. For the submission "to a demon" was, for them, synonymous with the forfeit of the "true life". Their own identity did not allow them any self-denial. And the "total state," which demanded the accordance of the whole "body of the Volk" with its "Führer," allowed absolutely no space for people living according to the laws of the "Bibelforscher". With that, the "resistance" became an urgent requirement for the self-respect and self-assertion of the faith community.

Even though the instances of National Socialist persecution undertook manifold efforts to break the Jehovah's Witnesses' spirit of resistance, these plans remained without the desired outcome. Especially the activist group imprisoned in the concentration camps would not be moved to deny the "Bibelforscher" faith and "renounce," neither through isolation and long-term committal in the penal companies nor through continued derision and the most terrible mistreatment. They persistently refused to sign the "statement of commitment," specially designed for the break with the IBV and its "heresy," although by handing over this "declaration" their release from KZ-imprisonment was placed in view. The open and demonstrative attitude, rooted in the strength of faith and willing if necessary to all sacrifices, of the IBV activists, who were not to be put off of their way by anything, amazed the SS often to helplessness. Eugen Kogon reported that in his impression "the SS could not quite cope psychologically with the problem of the Bibelforscher".[52] The "Bibelforscher" union was banned and oppressed,

---

52  Eugen Kogon, Der SS-Staat. Das System der deutschen Konzentrationslager, München [1]11983, p. 266.

but — even through the means to which the regime resorted — it was not possible to break the rebellious and uncompromising behavior of the Jehovah's Witnesses as a whole.

In the end the Reichsführer-SS and supreme ruler over the concentration camps, Heinrich Himmler, realized that the Jehovah's Witnesses — "punishment does not work with them at all" — were not to be dissuaded from their behavior even through continued terror. He drew the conclusion and ordered in 1943 — motivated by the matter-of-fact calculation of the greatest use for the SS and the Reich — that the "Bibelforscher" prisoners from now on would not be enlisted for armaments work, but rather should be used for example in SS households and in farming.

It is not known how many Jehovah's Witnesses were killed in KZ custody. On the basis of the numbers available for individual camps, it is to assume that between approximately 1,100 and 1,200 Jehovah's Witnesses died in the concentration camps,[53] whereby this number also includes foreign "Bibelforscher" prisoners. To estimate their number is difficult; it is known that at least 94 Austrian and 117 Dutch Jehovah's Witnesses died in custody.[54] As however, especially for the East European Jehovah's Witnesses, a higher death rate would be estimated, it can be approximated that the number of foreign victims would amount to about 400. Consequently, one would come to the number of 700 to 800 German IBV members who lost their lives in the concentration camps.

In the reports of former fellow prisoners it becomes clear again and again, how much they were impressed by the steadfastness of the "Bibelforscher," who stood by their religious convictions regardless of the consequences. The Social Democrat Hans Flatterich gave his own opinion in his written memoirs on his time in custody in the KZ Neuengamme: "With what unbelievable firmness these people had to bear the cruelest mistreatments year after year. They, however, did not renounce or betray their idea and attempted even here in the camp again and again to win other prisoners to their idea. I must confess that these people commanded unheard-of respect from me."[55] As their inflexibility however corresponded with an immobility far from any rational considerations, the admiration mixed at times with a lack of understanding and a disapproval. So thought the Buchenwald prisoner and author Ernst Wiechert: "However there lay understandably no example-setting strength in the rigidity of this behavior, because its roots reached

53  See Garbe, Zeugen Jehovas, p. 487.
54  Figures from: Marley Cole, Jehovas Zeugen. Die Neue-Welt-Gesellschaft. Geschichte und Organisation einer Religionsbewegung. Frankfurt a. M. 1956, p. 199; Jahrbuch 1986, p. 133 f.
55  KZ-Gedenkstätte Neuengamme, Ng.2.8., Hans Flatterich, Die Hölle von Neuengamme. Unpublished manuscript, Schleswig undated [1945], p. 16 f.

into too dull a soil. One could respect them all, but one had to pity them."[56]
With one further judgement of a fellow prisoner this contribution should
be settled. Dr. Albert Rohmer, chief doctor at the Medical Faculty of the
University of Strasbourg and prisoner of the KZ Neuengamme, wrote in
his memoirs, published in 1947: "For the SS such men were crazy, but in
Wöbbelin, when there was no more food, our eighty Bibelforscher joined
together to read a prophet-text: These madmen represent the honor of
humanity."[57]

56  Ernst Wiechert, Der Totenwald. Ein Bericht. München undated [1946], p. 151.
57  Albert Rohmer, Herren, "Befreite", Sklaven (translated in part from the report
    first published in France in 1947), in: Christoph Ernst/Ulrike Jensen (Ed.), Als
    letzes starb die Hoffnung. Berichte von Überlebenden aus dem KZ Neuengamme,
    Hamburg 1989, p. 141–145 (143).

Lee Kersten

# W. Macmahon Ball's report
# on the Sachsenhausen concentration camp

## A radio broadcast
## in autumn 1938 on the Australian ABC

The following document was discovered in files of Australian Broadcast
Corporation (ABC) talks scripts in the Australian Archives (Sydney).[1] It is a
report on a visit to the Sachsenhausen concentration camp in the autumn of
1938, dated 22nd October and apparently sent to the ABC for broadcast.about
the beginning of November. The author, William Macmahon Ball, was Seni-
or Lecturer in Political Philosophy and Political Institutions at the University
of Melbourne. At this time he was travelling around Europe, with a letter of
introduction from the German Consul General in Sydney to the Ministry for
Enlightenment and Propaganda in Berlin. Macmahon Ball had visited Germany before, in 1930 and 1931, and had considerable knowledge of the
political and social circumstances in that country.

At the time of the Munich Agreement by which Hitler had forced the
ceding of the Sudeten German territories of Czechoslovakia to Germany,
the Anglo-Saxon world focussed its gaze on Germany, hoping in vain that
peace would be preserved by the concessions made to National Socialist
Germany.by the British appeasement policy. The European crisis of the
autumn of 1938 was being watched in Australia with great interest at the
time of this broadcast. The ABC correspondent in London had been asked
to give daily reports and there were extensive and regular reports and
comment on Germany and German-British relations.[2] Macmahon Ball's
series of talks, "Europe from the inside," described his personal experiences
on the continent of Europe.

---

[1]   The typescript (4 pages) is headed "Concentration Camp" and there is a note
      "copy of talk by Mr Macmahon Ball, dated 22nd October, 1938". Australian
      Archives (NSW): Series Nr: SP 369/2 "William Macmahon Ball; letters from
      overseas".

[2]   See. Lesley Johnson, "Wireless", in: Australians 1938, ed. W. Gammage and P.
      Spearritt, Sydney 1987, pp. 365–371; s. also Ken Inglis, This is The ABC, Mel-
      bourne 1983; Neville Petersen, News not Views. The ABC, the press and politics
      1932–1947, Sydney 1993.

The report on the Sachsenhausen concentration camp was airmailed by Ball to Australia and read on air by an ABC announcer. The broadcast was repeated several times in ABC programmes and may also have been broadcast by the BBC (London).

In an interview in January 1971 William Macmahon Ball, who was by now a very well-known figure in the academic world, spoke about his visit to the concentration camp at Sachsenhausen. He described his trip to Europe, which was partly funded by reports and comment he wrote for the ABC in Sydney and Melbourne and for the BBC London: "I went through Sudetenland with Hitler's army and then was able to go through the lines and spend a little time in Prague, then I had a friend who was a young but influential member of the Nazi party and when I returned to Germany from Prague, I stayed with him in Dresden for a week or two, and he then managed to get me an invitation — I understand it was the first given to any foreigner for some years — to spend a day in Sachsenhausen concentration camp, just near Oranienburg, about 30 miles to the east of Berlin, and I was enormously impressed by the horror, what I considered to be the horror, the overwhelming horror, of the camp, and I did a broadcast on it. I should explain that there was no broadcasting direct then,or rather that I didn't do any direct broadcasting, from London at that time. I wrote an airmail letter and that airmail letter was read by one of the A.B.C. announcers in Melbourne or Sydney, and I did this one on the concentration camp and I believe it was repeated a number of times, and I must say that that experience in 1938 did change my whole attitude to war and peace.

Up till then I had been what you might call a pacifist, not on any absolute religious or philosophical or moral ground but because I believed that any war at that period would inevitably bring far more misery, far more harm than it could possibly do good. They were the days, you may remember, when Mr. Baldwin, the British Prime Minister, kept on saying that the technique of the next war would be to try to kill more women and children more quickly than the enemy, and I was impressed by all this sort of thing. Nevertheless, when I saw the people being overrun by Hitler's army and when I saw the people in that concentration camp, I felt that there were certain human situations when it is inevitable, and because it is inevitable it must be accepted, that human beings would resist. There were certain things, I think, that were unbearable, insufferable, and which it was right and proper to use force to try to protect people from."[3]

3    Interview, conducted by Mrs Hazel de Berg with Williarn Macmahon Ball in January 1971, "Conversations with William Macmahon Ball", Oral History section of the Australian National Library, Canberra, Hazel de Berg Collection, transcript pp. 4 ff.

William Macmahon Ball, born in Melbourne on 29 August 1901, was a student at the University of Melbourne and after graduating became "Research Scholar in Psychology" 1923–1924, then Lecturer in "Psychology, Logic and Ethics" at that university. In the years 1929–1931 he had a "Rockefeller Travelling Fellowship for Political Science" and studied at the London School of Economics, University of London, and made visits to Germany, France and Italy.

From 1932 he was Lecturer in "Modern Political Institutions" at the University of Melbourne and Head of Department. He also taught as an "Extension Lecturer," travelling around the state of Victoria and the suburbs of Melbourne giving talks to interested members of the public. He became well-known to a wide public through his articles for newspapers (particularly for the Melbourne *Herald*). In 1934 he began his long association with the ABC (Australian Broadcasting Commission) for which he wrote many political commentaries.

In the years 1938–1939 he had a Carnegie Travelling Fellowship and went on a study tour to England, Europe and the USA .He had direct experience of the political situation at the time of the Munich Agreement and went through the Sudentenland as the German troops marched into Czechoslovakia.

After the outbreak of war in 1939 he was made "Controller of Short Wave Broadcasting" and so was in charge of news, information and war propaganda in Australian shortwave broadcasts till 1944. After the Ministry of Information took over shortwave broadcasting from the ABC in 1944 Ball chose to stay with the ABC and organised a series of very successful radio debates on political issues. Shortly before the end of the war in the Pacific in August 1945 he returned to the University of Melbourne as Senior Lecturer and Head of the Department of Political Science.

Later in 1945 he was invited to take part in the San Francisco Conference of the United Nations as an Australian delegate. In 1946 he travelled through South East Asia. In 1946/47 he was Minister representing the British Commonwealth at the Allied Conference for Japan. On his return to Melbourne in 1947 he worked for a short time as a specialist for international affairs for Sir Keith Murdoch at the Melbourne *Herald*. In 1949 he became the first Professor of Political Science in the newly established Chair at the University of Melbourne. At this time and for many years to come he made many radio broadcasts He retired in 1968 and died on 26 December 1986.

Alan Rix, editor of Macmahon Ball's diaries for the years 1946/47, describes the experience of the visit to the Sachsenhausen concentration camp as of great significance for Ball. "For the rest of his days his mind retained the scorch-mark of this horror, and part of it he shared with

Australians through his wide ABC radio audience. But what shocked him most was the means by which this unusual visit was made possible: it was arranged by a German whom Ball had known in Australia as a close friend. Returned to Germany, this young man had become a sincere and dedicated Nazi. He was *proud* to be showing his Australian friend the progress and achievements of National Socialism. Ball had been well enough aware that human natures are not all of a piece, that no one is all good or all bad. As an admiring reader of Bertrand Russell he knew 'The Harm that Good Men Do'. But to be shown Sachsenhausen by a dear friend, and to be expected to admire it, gave him a vertiginous view into the ambiguous depths of evil. It was an experience to which he often referred."[4]

The identity of Ball's young German National Socialist friend is at present unknown.[5] Macmahon Ball's report on Sachsenhausen is undoubtedly authentic although there are one or two strange details, for instance Ball's belief that Sachsenhausen is east of Berlin and his reporting that whale meat was served to the prisoners. (The latter detail may have been an acoustic misunderstanding or a wrong translation of the German word for boiled belly of pork 'Wellfleisch'.) The document is yet another proof of how much the world knew about the horrors of National Socialist Germany.

## COPY OF TALK BY MR. W. MACMAHON BALL, dated 22nd October 1938.

### *CONCENTRATION CAMP*

Last Thursday I spent three hours in a Concentration Camp. This was a very interesting experience and I want to write of it with especial care for several reasons. I was told that I was the first foreigner to be allowed in such a camp for some years, and my visit was only made possible by the personal consent of Herr Himmler, the head of the German police; and

4    Alan Rix, William Macmahon Ball 1901–1986 A Memoir, in: Alan Rix (Ed.) Intermittent Diplomat: the Japan and Batavia Diaries of W. Macmahon Ball, Melbourne 1988, p. VII-XIX.

5    After publication of the German version of this article it was discovered that his friend was Karl Heinz Pfeffer, who visited Australia in the early 1930s collecting material for a book subsequently published with the title "Die bürgerliche Gesellschaft in Australien" (Berlin 1935). After the broadcast of Ball's report on Sachsenhausen he wrote to Ball, expressing his hope that they would still be friends while remaining of different opinions. (Information from Mrs J. Ellis, Macmahon Ball's daughter, January 1996).

than only because a German friend of mine gave the fullest assurances that I could be relied upon to give a completely fair and unbiased account of what I saw; that in spite of my being a guest to the Political Police, the S.S. officers who were my hosts. They were not only courteous and hospitable, but put their own car and chaffeur at my disposal for the day. Most important of all, I feel that it is essential in my serious examination of the relations between Germany and Britain today to keep the discussion of such things as Concentration Camps in Germany or British prisons in India in their proper secondary place. Yet there is, of course, a real connection between the Nazi attitude to their political opponents at home and their attitude to democratic nations like Britain wich they feel to be so much under the control of Socialists and Jews. It was mainly because I thought a Concentration Camp might throw some light on the world attitude, as distinct from the domestic policy, of the German Gouvernement, that I wanted to see one. I was not in search of atrocities. I knew that if they did occur, I would not be likely to see them, and if they do not occur, then I would still be without proof of this.

The camp I visited is near Sachsenhausen, a village near the town of Oranienburg about twentyfive miles from Berlin. Pastor Niemoller is perhaps the best known inmate, through there are others there who were very well known in German political life before The National Socialists came to power. As we neared the camp we found S.S. Guards holding their rifles ready, lining the roadside at intervals of about 30 yards. A ring of these man had been thrown around a field in which prisoners were at work chopping wood. Our driver said, perhaps to comfort us, that although this stretch of road could be used by the public the guards were empowered to fire instantly on any car which stopped, without making preliminary investigations. At the outer gate of the camp was another group of armed guards, some with sub-machine guns instead of rifles. These S.S. men are very impressive specimens of the might of the Nazi party. The Brown Shirts — the S.A. — hardly count now as a political force in Germany. All political police work is done by S.S., men of outstanding physique and unquestionable loyalty, disciplined on severe military lines.

Inside the outer gates I found a stretch of neat lawns and trees amongst which the offices and living quarters of the Guards had been built. I was then introduced to the Camp Commandant, and his adjutant than indicated that he was at my service for the morning. I should mention here that my knowledge of the German language, though sufficient for ordinary conversation, is very far from complete, and as I was specially anxious not to misunderstand anything I was told this day, I persuaded a German University man, who speaks perfect English, to go with me as an interpreter. I got him to repeat to me in English every important statement made.

Our guide took us to the inner gates, from where we could see the layout of the camp. It is build in the form of a semi-circle or fan, these main gates being in the centre of the diameter. Above the gates is a concrete watch tower from wich three machine guns on swivels command first the parade ground in front, and than all of the alley ways between the huts, wich are built in straight lines radiating from the central guards house. There are other smaller watch towers round the arc of the semi-circle, so that every spot inside the camp is continuously commanded by a machine gun. Inside the boundary fence there is a path about eight feet wide. If any prisoner puts his feet on this path, he is instantly shot at. On the outer side of the path there are tiers of barbed wire rising to the high wire fence which is electrically charged and flood-lit at night. The scheme is so efficiently planned that it is not surprising that there are only 200 guards for the nine thousand (9,000) prisoners. Last May there were only three thousand (3,000) prisoners at Sachsenhausen, but a big police drive in June and July trebled the members in two months.

The prisoners are classified in accordance with the nature of their offences, and each class wears a different badge and is most of the time separated from the other classes. The Jews have a special badge. The biggest class was made up of those rather vaguely described as "work shy and Anti-Social". I tried hard to find out exactly what this term means. In what precise circumstances was a "work shy" man sent into concentration? What paticular offences were considered anti-social? But at the end of all my questions I could get no clear idea of the nature of this classification.

Second, there are the "political" prisoners, those found guilty of a specific political offence; third, the straight out criminals, those convicted of house-breaking or forgery; fourth, the "Bible students" whose conviction prevent them from giving allegiance to the National Socialist State; and, lastly, a few perverts of various kinds.

When my guide, the adjutant, took me alone to any man at work inside the camp, the prisoner with very quick movements would snatch off his cap, and stand very rigidly to attention, hands and fingers taut and outstretched down his side, and stay like this while we passed. Sometimes the officer would sharply summon a prisoner: "Come here"! The prisoner would run to us as fast as he could and again click to attention. "Why are you here"? The officer would rap out. "Preparing high treason, sir" the answer would come with quick mechanical certainty. "What was your crime?" was the next question. And in several cases the answer came. "Distributing Communist literature, sir". There were, of course, the political prisoners. In one case when the officer asked "What is your crime" the prisoner replied "I don't know, sir". "What," said the officer, "you don't know your crime?" "No, sir". We passed quickly on, and it seemed to me that the officer was faintly annoyed. A little later I asked him how it was that the prisoner did not know his crime. He replied that he had not taken the incident seriously, and that, by looking at the man,s papers he could at once see what his crime was. I nevertheless felt quite certain that this man would have given a clear answer if he had known what answer he was expected to give.

Everything in the prisoners quarters was scrupulously clean and most efficiently hygienic. The were well-built and well ventilated; the bunks looked comfortable; the kitchens and shower rooms were all splendidly planned. I was told that 62 pfennigs per day was spent on each prisoners' food; in comparison with 65 pfennigs spent on the food of each man in a Labour Service Camp. I ate the prisoners lunch, which that day was whale, potatoes and a small portion of fat. I did not find it exactly appetising, but it was well cooked and the whale was not at all bad.

The prisoners' day begins at 5 a.m. After breakfast hard labour begins at 6 and goes till 11.30. Then two hours for roll call, lunch and minor duties. The afternoons' labour is from 1.30 till 5 p.m. I was told that in the evening the men had two to three hours leisure before lights out at 9.

I was told that each prisoner, unless he is under special discipline, may receive money from his family and use it to buy extras from the tuck-shop or tobacco. Smoking is allowed in certain leisure periods, but not inside the huts. Those who do receive money generally share it with their fellows. I saw some German newspapers and there is a lending library of perhaps 2,000 books.

There is also some self-administration by the prisoners. In most of the huts there are no permanent guards during the night. A senior prisoner is entrusted with a key, and if there is any disturbance in his hut, he turns this key in a lock in the wall. This switches on a blue light above the hut with is seen at once by the guards in the watch towers. Then there is a small office where five or six prisoners do the clerical work of keeping prisoner's records; these records being quite distinct from those kept by the political police. The chief clerk in this office is the head prisoner of the camp. We talked with him for some minutes. He was formerly a prominent official of the Social Democratic Party and a member of the Reichstag. He impressed me as a man of intelligence, culture and character.

So far I have been writing only of externals. But the thing wanted most to see was the kind of men in a concentration camp, their and expression, and the relationship between guards and men.

I have never seen before, and never believed it possible to see, a group of men so cowed, so completely deprived of the rudimentary personal dignities that I have always felt belong to human beings. The way in which these men responded to orders was something quite different from the mechanical precision of military discipline; it showed the quick, shrinking nervousness of animals that have been utterly subdued. Of the hundreds of men whom I saw at close quarters, there were perhaps five or six senior prisoners who I was told would soon be released who did not look frightened and cowed. In the eyes of most there was deep misery; when addressed by an officer the misery was mixed with fright, and at least in some cases terror is not too strong a word. In one of the huts a prisoner was ordered to open a cupboard for me to see; he ran to obey the order but, in his exitement, fumbled for an instant with the lock. "Quick"! the officer rapped out. And this the man gave a jump and quiver that shook his body and told his nervous condition quite clearly. In describing the demeanor of these prisoners I am not writing as a psychologist; I am writing as an observer with normal eyesight.

The prisoners differed a great deal in appearance. Many in the "criminal" class had the degenerate look that is sometimes noticed in habitual criminals anywhere in the world. Some of the "work shy and anti-Social class" seemed to me to be well below average intelligence. I think we would class them as morons. There were also some with physical disabilities. I noticed two crippies, and one blind man. But amongst the "political" and the "work-shy" prisoners I saw many faces which I thought showed character, sensitiveness and intelligence. It certainly takes more than average courage to engage in Communist or Socialist activities in Germany today. The officer who took me round and the younger officers I saw in camp, did not in any way look coarse or gross types of men. My own guide, in his manner and appearance, impressed me as being like any good type of officer in the British Army or the London Police Force. He said that neither he nor his comrade relished the job of guarding the Concentration Camp, but it was just one of the jobs that somebody had to do in the interest of the State. He would only be on camp work for perhaps three or six months as it was not the policy of this Gouvernment to keep men permanently on Concentration Camp duties. But this same officer did not think it strange to call up, address, and dismiss prisoners in a manner more peremptory and impersonal than that usually adopted to animals. He saw nothing strange in three men standing facing a wall while they waited outside the camp hospital for medical attention. It was a fresh morning and my university friend and I were glad of our overcoats, but these three men, in their ordinary prison jackets, stood rigidly to attention here in the sharp breeze for at least half an hour — I don't know how much longer — while they awaited medical attention. One of these prisoners was shaking pitifully, and was unable, with the most desperate effort, to get out any coherent answer to the officer's question. Yet apparently the officer thought I would be, if not pleased, at least reassured by my visit to the camp. It is a difference of outlook hard to understand. It was put to me that many of the prisoners had never worked decently or submitted to any discipline in their lives, and that it was hoped that for these the stay in camp would have great educational value. I could not follow this argument, for I saw no training in any trade or profession, nor any other sort af educational work. Since sentences moreover, are indeterminate, I cannot understand when and why a prisoner is released.

My guide was anxious for me to hear the camp singing wich takes place on the huge parade ground after midday roll call. We waited at the main gates while the prisoners marched in. As the last section entered, the gates were closed and armed guards formed in front of it, while the three machine guns were manned in the watch tower above. We stood in the centre of those 9,000 prisoners on parade. Then the choir-master climbed up on to his wooden platform to conduct the singing. No political songs, but German folk songs. I walked among the ranks as they sang. Many did not sing at all; other moved their lips when I looked at them, but thousands lifted their voices loud and clear. And they sang as only Germans can. There were the machine guns watching them, the barbed wire round them, and each man's future quite unknown; but I felt that so long as they could sing like that there must be somewhere deep inside them a faith and a courage that had not been killed.

Lee Kersten

# The Times and the Concentration Camp at Dachau

## December 1933–February 1934: An Unpublished Report

On December 20, 1933 Stanley Simpson, a British journalist living in Munich, sent from Innsbruck, Austria, to Ralph Deakin,[1] then the Imperial and Foreign News Editor of *The Times* in London, an article detailing mistreatment of prisoners in the German concentration camp set up in Dachau in March 1933.[2] At this time the *Times'* Editor, Geoffrey Dawson, who had a particular interest in foreign affairs, was away on Christmas holidays in the country. The article was the subject of at least thirteen letters and memoranda and was set up and corrected in galley-proofs but in the end not published.[3]

1   According to his obituary in *The Times* (20 December 1952) Ralph Deakin was appointed Foreign News Editor of *The Times* in 1921 after serving in the British army in France and then working as a journalist after the end of the First World War in Cologne, Paris, and Berlin.
2   Eamon Dyas, Group Records Manager of News International and so *Times* Archivist, in February 1994 showed me a manila folder with Simpson's letter, the ensuing correspondence and the corrected galley proof of the article.
3   See Sir J(ohn) E. L. Wrench, Geoffrey Dawson and Our Times, London, 1955, p. 312. Dawson was twice Editor of *The Times*: 1912–1919 as Geoffrey Robinson and 1922–1941 as Geoffrey Dawson. In his book *All Souls and Appeasement* (London 1961), A. L. Rowse quotes Lord Northcliffe, the proprietor of *The Times* during the First World War, who described his editor as "by instinct a pro-German." Rowse goes on: "Where this came from is difficult to say. Some of it came from his Cecil Rhodes inheritance; he was deeply and invariably anti-French in prejudice — he had the contempt for the French of all this circle. A very conventional and moral man, regular in his religious observances, he thought them both immoral and weak. Sheer ignorance of Europe was another part of it. He had received his training, like so many of this group, under Milner in South Africa. At Oxford he had read Greats. Without any knowledge of European history, still less of German history, without knowing one word of the language or having the slightest insight into the German mind, he throw all his influence — which was immense — into undermining Versailles and doing the business of the Germans for them" (p. 6).

Simpson sent a letter with the article and also a list of cases of mistreatment of prisoners on 54 days between April 26 and August 19, 1933. He wrote: "I would prefer the article to be anonymous, not only because it might make my position extremely difficult, but, above all because my association could lead to innocent people being tracked down and terribly punished." He wrote further that he was hoping that publication might lead to the establishment of an international commission which would effect a modification of German behavior. He thought that even public knowledge which would be achieved by the article, if published, might have this effect. He wrote that the source of the last part of his manuscript was a Nazi guard who sympathized with the victims, adding that he had only used part of the material and going on to comment: "Although I make allowances for the fact that a wretched business of this sort affects one much more on the spot, I think you will agree that the Dachau story is a particularly wicked and damnable affair, even judged by what I have written above. Many of the victims, men like Götz, Dressel, Stenzer, etc. were not the 'wild' type of communist at all, and were men of high principle respected by their political opponents, for instance the Bavarian People's Party, whose violent anti-Communist principles were wellknown. The Nazis may try to ignore the article or dismiss it with a vague charge of 'Greuel', or they may be brazen enough to deny the facts in detail. In either case, it will not avail." And at the end of the letter he wrote: "I'm sure you will agree that it would be in keeping with best traditions of The Times if it could be the means of putting an end to or even mitigating the suffering of these men, and of saving lives which, if nothing is done, will assuredly be sacrificed."

He asked Deakin to be careful in communications to him; Deakin was to use no names and not to address a letter with his name. Any letter was to be sent not to Munich but to Kufstein in Austria, and even then via Geneva and Innsbruck so that it would not cross German territory. He also warned Deakin about the *New York Times*; if that newspaper was told he wrote the article, then they had also to be warned to be careful: "Will you please impress on them the need for discretion. Their Berlin office is often rather indiscreet over the telephone, and they do not appear to be aware that letters are liable to be opened in Germany."

In a memorandum to Deakin, dated January 3, 1934, the *Times* Deputy Editor, Robin Barrington-Ward[4], wrote that he agreed with Deakin that

4    Robin Barrington-Ward was Deputy Editor of *The Times*, and like many others on the staff an Oxford graduate. He succeeded Geoffrey Dawson as Editor in 1941. In the *Times'* own 1985 bicentennial publication *The Times Past Present Future*, Roy Jenkins writes in his article "The Voice of The Thunderer" on the paper's 200 years of political influence: "Some thought that had he succeeded 10 years earlier he would have avoided the excesses of the late Dawson period" (p. 30).

the matter was serious and advised him to get Norman Ebbott's opinion, and added that if "Simpson is thoroughly trustworthy, and Ebbutt can find no serious flaw, the article will certainly have to be given, probably in company of a leader." Norman Ebbutt had been the *Times'* own correspondent in Berlin since 1927 and had been writing reports warning about Nazi theory and practice for some years. Much of his work was not published in full or in the form that he intended in the paper.

Ebbutt answered in a memorandum dated January 12, 1934 with a hand-written note, "This copy to leader writer," on the first page. He wrote: "I am of the opinion that we should publish it and take the opportunity of challenging Hitler and Goebbels in a leading article. I am fully convinced myself of the substantial accuracy of the details in the article, many of which have been known to me from other (also convincing) sources." Ebbutt sent also some notes to be used by the leader-writer. In the first, labelled "(A) for intro or leader" he suggested among other things that the leader writer point out that the escape of the Communist deputy Hans Beimler had already been reported, with less detail, in Britain and that *The Times* had published other details of the mistreatment of prisoners in other camps. In the notes labelled "(B) for LEADER-WRITER" he suggested that the leader say that the article has appeared not because *The Times* wished "to keep snagging about a particular aspect of German internal policy" but "because it comes from sources we cannot discuss lightly and because it becomes more and more clear that until this matter is cleared up relations between British public opinion and the N.S. regime will be seriously hampered." He advised also that the leader writer mention that "improved camps have been shown to parties of foreign visitors though under conditions rendering a real judgment difficult" and that a letter to *The Times* from General Ian Malcolm had disclosed ill treatment of prisoners in other concentration camps.[5] Ebbutt pressed for *The Times* to use its undoubted influence on behalf of the prisoners in Dachau: "There can be little doubt that a really firm pronouncement by the leaders against the system of maltreatment would stop it." He believed that there would then be no need for a committee of investigation.

On January 15 the Editor of *The Times*, Geoffrey Dawson, returned to London from his Christmas break. A letter from Ralph Deakin to Simpson

5    In the letter published in *The Times* of October 14, 1933 General Malcom wrote about the brutal treatment of Friedrich Ebert's son when he was transferred from the concentration camp at Oranienburg to "Borgenoor" (in fact: Börgermoor). This sort of special case pleading in which both the victim and the letter-writer have well-known names is an example of the *Times'* practice of using readers' letters as a means of influencing public opinion without compromising its policy of avoiding special pleading in its own reports and comments.

then followed, dated January 19, 1934 and sent to Kufstein, in which he reported that there was a problem because the article said nothing about conditions later than August. "This may be inevitable, but you will agree that at this stage, the fact weakens the article considerably." It is likely that Dawson advised sending this letter as he took up again his regular talks with members of the British government. His close connections with the government gave him virtually daily access to its plans and knowledge of its fears. For instance, he wrote in his diary that on January 27, 1934 he visited the Foreign Office "for a talk with Simon and Anthony Eden. I got out of it a copy of their statement of policy on Disarmament and some useful hints about the snags which they foresaw. Hitler was to celebrate his anniversary on Saturday: Mussolini was bursting with a statement of his own: the French government was tottering (over Stavisky) and actually fell in the afternoon."[6]

Simpson had not been to Tyrol and so had not yet had an opportunity to collect Deakin's letter of January 19 when he wrote to him on February 1, 1934 from Munich asking what had become of the article. He wrote again, now from Innsbruck, on

February 5, 1934, (on the letter is a note "Mr. BW" that is, Barrington-Ward) answering the objection about the lack of material more recent than August 1933: "I quite realise that the addition of some more recent facts would improve the article, but I do not think that it is in any way out-of-date, as it stands, making allowance for the abnormal conditions in Germany. The terrorism is so intense and such elaborate precautions taken to keep things secret that it is often weeks before news leaks out from the camp, and more weeks before it can be tested and confirmed." He wrote that in fact he had information up to September but had stopped earlier in his article to protect his informants.

Now more than six weeks had elapsed since he had sent his letter and the article, and on February 12, 1934 Simpson wrote again to Deakin urging that the article be published in *The Times*. He wrote that he was now supplying some additional information from November.

The article was set up and edited with corrections in the galley proofs, headed "Times Dachau Camp Await Release — Headings to Come — Three Proofs to Mr.Deakin — Not to be Sent to the Services or Elsewhere." The text contained a reference to October, so the article was still under review and was changed to include an October example after receipt of Simpson's letter of February 12. In his article there are various details about the treatment of Jews in the camp, but these are not given greater stress than other instance of brutal treatment, as for instance of Communists.[7]

6   Wrench, Geoffrey Dawson, p. 314.
7   The murder of four Jews immediately on the takeover of the camp by the SS is also mentioned in Martin Gilbert, The Holocaust, Glasgow 1987, pp. 36 f.

The article set up consisted of about 3,500 words in 27 paragraphs, and the cuts indicated in the corrected copy amount to about 500 words. These cuts indicated on the galley proofs, mostly concern details about the camp, but some cuts probably were dictated by political jugdments, as for instance the cutting of two references to foreigners in Germany (to Austrians, Czechs, and Poles) and of a reported speech meade by the first SS Commandant to prisoners saying they would be detained for at least five years. The final paragraph was deleted, perhaps on the basis of the general principle in journalism that stories are often shortened by cutting from the end of the report, but it is at least as likely that this paragraph was cut because it contains opinion rather than fact; namely, that the Nazi leaders from Hitler downwards had a moral responsibility for the brutality in the camp because they had preached that political murder, however brutal, was a deed of heroism. The cuts made in the article also removed some description of the physical details of the camp, but none of the cuts in the story, apart from one reference to a possible suicide, the two to foreigners, and the final moral jugdment, removed completely any topic mentioned by Simpson. It described the physical layout of the camp and the prisoners' accommodation, the daily outines, the division of the prisoners into various companies, including one exclusively for Jews, and details of beatings, torture, deaths, and successful and unsuccessful attempts to escape.

In the file of memoranda and correspondance there is a memorandum dated February 13, 1934 from Barrington-Ward to Deakin: "The Editor is now inclined to feel that was appeared in the 'New Statesman and Nation' really disposes of this article."[8] There is also a letter dated February 13, 1934 from Deakin to Simpson in which Deakin says he is writing following a telephone message: "It is in all the circumstances difficult to explain our point of view, but it seems best to let you know of this decision without

---

8    This is a reference to an article on the concentration camp at Sonnenburg which had appeared in *The New Statesman* on January 20, 1934. This edition, *The New Statesman* reported in its January 27 edition, sold out. The reason for this may have been a special article by J. Maynard Keynes on gold. The article in *The New Statesman* followed immediately after J. M.Keynes' article and took up nearly two columns on pages 77 f. It was headed: "The Terror Continues Sonnenburg Concentration Camp" and in the introduction the editor (Kingsley Martin since 1931) wrote: "The impression that the Nazi Terror has now ceased appears to have gained ground in this country, thanks to the efforts of the German Ministry of Propaganda and of sympathisers here. In fact it continues unabated, though with increased secrecy. As an important additional evidence of this, we print the following translation of part of a report (covering the events of several months) which recently found its way out of Sonnenburg Concentration Camp. The statement has been compared and found to tally in detail with the experiences of others who were present at the time."

further delay." And then there is a note dated february 15, 1945 from R(alph) D(eakin) to Barrington-Ward asking for two guineas (that is, £ 10-10-0) for Simpson with a copy to the Contributors' Department to be dated February 13. Deakin says in this note that Simpson had done a substantial amount of work and should be paid for it even though the article would not be published.

The matter was still not quite settled apparently, as in late February, after Simpson had been paid for his work, there is yet another communication advising against publication. The advice came from Deputy Editor Barrington-Ward's acquaintance, William Teeling[9], whose story on unemployment in Austria was published in *The Times* on January 9, and whose three-part article on traveling around Germany appeared in the paper on February 20, 21, and 22 under his name, an unusual circumstance in *The Times*, which had a policy of anonymity for most contributors and virtually all its journalists. Teeling's opinion was probably asked because he had visited the camp at Dachau in October 1933.[10] A letter in the file, dated February 24, 1934 from Teeling in London to Deakin commented at length on an enclosed article (evidently Simpson's). He wrote that *The Times* was respected in Berlin. "But it is felt in Berlin, and even admitted to me by Canadian and other press people living there that the correspondents seem to hate the whole Nazi regime. After all in two months or a little more we will have Oberammergau and then the youth hostels will too be filled with walking English people. Isn't it a pity to stress these atrocities, when things seem a bit more friendly?"

He wrote further that in October 1933 Jewish bankers insisted on his seeing Dachau. "The majority of the prisoners are Communists — large numbers of them unconvicted murderers in last year's street fights. All pretty tough men, they hate this regime. If they go away they will write anything against it. The kitchens were good — the food no worse than at Oranienburg and just about the same as a labour camp." Then he went on to say that "there was a loudspeaker relaying across the whole camp cheerful music." He reported that there were also skating prisoners, and "Herr Himmler visited the camp while I was there. As he walked about I watched ordinary

9 William Teeling was probably asked for an opinion by Barrington-Ward, maybe after the editor's decision not to publish. Perhaps there was still some debate about that decision. Teeling is mentioned as a critic of Nazi Germany in Angela Schwarz's article "Der Zauber der Normalität. Britische Besucher und das 'soziale' Experiment des Nationalsozialismus", in: German Life and Letters, Vol. 46 (1993), Nr. 4, p. 116.

10 For instance, the *History of* the Times volume which deals with the expulsion of Norman Ebbutt from Germany in August 1937 and his subsequent illness, which prevented him from working again as a journalist, doesn't mention his name.

prisoners walk up to him, salute and then put their grievances. I would also add that our Consul General in Cologne told me he went into every case officially for atrocities and never found a real one." He believed "their oriental exaggeration had got the better of them. And some Jewish rabbis assured me these atrocities if there were any were now completely over." Towards the end Teeling's letter reaches a crescendo and reveals perhaps more clearly his prejudices or maybe just his concern about what seemed to him "an article oozing with harmful possibilities and full of calculated propaganda, carefully leaving out sides that are extremely well-run i.e. the play grounds, shops, dormitories, heating, hospital etc." The popularity of camps in England at the time and the positive stories about labour camps in Germany may have dulled the perceptions of visitors to the concentration camps too.[11]

On February 27, 1934 Deakin replied: "It hardly seems to me that Oberammergau and English youths filling the youth hostels are relevant to the question of Dachau, but I quite see your point."

The newspapers in London were engaged in a circulation war at this time, which may have something to do with the decision not to publish Simpson's longer than usual, detailed, and some months old story. In this period *The Times* did publish a great deal of material that was critical of the government in Germany. There are a number of brief reports about events in Germany which reflect a country in which freedom and democratic processes are threatened. *The Times'* method was to juxtapose stories rather than to comment on them, so that the news itself could lead readers to make their own judgments by comparing information offered. The excesses of Nazi propaganda tended to strengthen the wish to be restrained in report and comment by providing an example of unbiased media discourse.

This unpublished article and the correspondence related to it are interesting primarily for what they add to the history of the concentration camp at Dachau and also as part of the history of British caution in dealing with the government in Germany. It is also part of the history of the involvement of the British press in the conduct of foreign affairs, particularly of *The Times* as a semi-official journal of record. The expectation that the paper would be read not only by decision-makers in Britain but also in Germany possibly made the editor extremely cautions. In this case the report was probably in fact rejected, not only for political reasons but also because the news was not recent and the topic of concentration camp mistreatment of prisoners had already recently been covered in the *New Statesman and Nation's* January 20 report on Sonnenburg. The falling sales of newspapers had led to a newspaper war in Britain and a wish to avoid publishing news

11   Angela Schwarz gives examples of such enthusiasm in her article.

that might appear to be stale, or long rather than short articles, was perhaps really a factor in the decision not to publish.[12] It is likely that it was seen as more productive of change for the better to concentrate on publishing report and comment on the mistreatment of people who were famous and likely to be innocent, including in this latter category the churchmen who were involved in conflict in Germany. Perhaps the hope of a diminution of Nazi arrests now that their government had been in office for over a year also made the publication of the long report seem unnecessarily confrontational to those in the editorial office in London, at a distance from the reality of the situation in Germany. However, the two reporters in Germany, Ebbutt and Simpson, believed the article should be published in London in the hope of achieving some lessening of brutality in Germany. Deakin, who had worked as a journalist in Germany, was apparently still in favor of publication even while passing on the negative comments of his editor, Dawson, who acted as Foreign Editor above Deakin whenever it suited him. Barrington-Ward's initial advice to publish seems to have been modified not only by Dawson but also by the advice of his acquaintance William Teeling.

At this time such articles were a rarity. Most *Times* reporting about Germany appeared at this time in the form of brief reports, sometimes highlighted by irony; sometimes reports were significant for what they hinted at rather than what they said outright. There were also longish stories on the question of German rearmament and international debt and the divisions in the Lutheran Church between "German Christians" and their opponents and brief reports on the treatment of the priests arrested for criticizing the regime or on the closing of 600 newspapers in Germany in 1933. There is evidence of the *Times'* wish not to criticize the Germans too much, to hold the ammunition perhaps until Anthony Eden had visited Berlin for talks in February 1934, and maybe to concentrate on defending as well as possible people who were seen to be clearly innocent, for example the Bulgarians cleared in the Reichstag fire trial but still in detention. The letters to *The Times,* normally appearing on the same page as the leaders, often constituted a discourse with the paper about serious matters, and quite often were sent by a member of the House of Lords. These letters sometimes gave more details about a person or event than a brief *Times* report had given. On January 23, 1934 a letter about concentration camps was published, written by Dawson's immediate predecessor as editor (1919–1922), Wickham Steed. In this letter, which appeared in the prominent position of top of the page, middle column, he protested about the Nazi treatment of the journalist Carl von Ossietzky.

12  Frank McDonough, "The Times, Norman Ebbut [sic] and the Nazis", in: Journal of Contemporary History 27 (1992), pp. 407–424; here p. 411.

There were a number of leaders in the period January-February-March 1934 on German affairs, including fourth leaders which were intended to be humorous. There was one, for instance, on the need to be recognizably English in Germany especially if one was of "non-Aryan appearance," achievable perhaps by carrying *The Times* and/or wearing an English hat. Other fourth leaders dealt with the Nazi salute, the gift of Hitler's *My Fight to* all couples marrying in Germany, the banning of comic postcards in Munich because they were seen as deleterious to the national image, beer in Munich, and the banning of the golliwog because the toy was identified with the wrong music and the wrong skin color. There were also serious leaders about Austrian-German relations, the Reichstag fire trial and the continuing detention of people acquitted in it, about disarmament and unemployment.

Readers of *The Times,* and probably especially those in government circles, could be expected to read the paper daily and to read the news and comment about Germany and Austria, whether contained in short reports, longer articles, leaders, or readers' letters. They were aware of the discourse patterns of their times: that reports, comment, and leaders, and in the case of *The Times* the readers' letters, were to be read as a whole and between the lines too.

In this correspondence from *The Times* archives something of the way decisions were reached, modified, and revoked can be seen. There is no direct word in it from Geoffrey Dawson, who finally recommended against publication. This may be because he communicated directly and not by letter or memorandum or perhaps because letters, etc., were not kept or were subsequently lost. It is possible that this article was published elsewhere in a journal less conscious of its responsibility to the government. It hasn't been possible to find such a publication, and perhaps Simpson, having been paid ten guineas by *The Times,* didn't try to find another publisher for information now many months old.

Jürgen Zarusky

# "That is not the American Way of Fighting"

## The Shooting of Captured SS-Men During the Liberation of Dachau

In the afternoon of April 29, 1945, a Sunday, American soldiers liberated the concentration camp Dachau, where about 32,000 prisoners from all over Europe were incarcerated at that moment. The arrival of the Americans brought freedom to the prisoners, the deliverance from hunger, typhus and the dreaded plans of extermination by the SS.[1] Though the capture of the camp by the Americans was not accomplished without some combat, they had no losses, and it took place rather quickly. However, many of the SS-men still in the camp were killed, part of them after they had surrendered. "These killings are a very sensitive issue — outside of Germany because of the shadow they cast on the reputation of the liberators, and within Germany due to their potential and actual use by apologetic circles to retroactively justify Nazi atrocities and pseudo-exonerate German perpetrators," states Harold Marcuse.[2] The existing accounts of the events are in many respects contradictory and unclear.

*Memoirs, Propaganda, Research*

The shooting of the overpowered SS-guards is mentioned in a whole series of memoirs of prisoners. This subject is only a marginal aspect of the over-whelming events of the liberation in the memoirs of the concentration camp survivors. Yet in the right-radical polemic against the Dachau camp

---

1    The most recent detailed account of the liberation by Klaus-Dietmar Henke, Die amerikanische Besetzung Deutschlands, München 1995, pp. 862–931. Regarding the rumors of extermination and plans, ibid., p. 915 ff.

2    Harold Marcuse, Nazi crimes and identity in West-Germany. Collective memories of the Dachau concentration camp, 1945–1990 (Diss), Ann Arbor, Mich. 1992, p. 88.

memorial, it occupies a central role.[3] Since there is hardly any historical event which compresses the true character of the Third Reich and the political-moral justification of the allied victory over the nationalsocialist Germany as the liberation of the concentration camps, those who are nationalistic and neonazi-motivated pseudohistorians are anxious to distort the events. Depending on disposition and the degree of political extremism, these authors try to effect the impression that war crimes are a general and evenly widespread occurrence of the Second World War in order to relativize the condemnation of Nationalsocialism. Or they virtually turn the spear around and proclaim the American soldiers as "US-Killers" who organized a massacre of several hundred defenseless SS and members of the Wehrmacht and thus "demonstrated the wretchedness (Erbämlichkeit) of the American 'crusaders'".[4] The former SS-Untersturmführer Erich Kernmayer, alias Erich Kern, was the first representative of the right-extreme scene who took up this topic. He presented the witness testimony of a Hans Linberger, who survived a shooting action by American soldiers, in several publications.[5] Kern implanted this testimony in a description that meant to play down the conditions in the concentration camps and discredit the prisoners. For this purpose, he used a one-sided and misleading selection of citations, mostly from the books of Edgar Kupfer-Koberwitz and Nerin Gun,[6] which resulted in the image of the prisoners of Dachau as a band of Communists and brutal criminals who terrorized their fellow prisoners and who altogether lived relatively well.[7] Once the Neo-nazi packaging of the testimony of Linberger, in which Kern had wrapped it, is removed, one must, however, take it quite seriously as it withstands a critical examination.

---

3   Cf. in general, Barbara Distel, Diffamierung als Methode. Erfahrungen an der Gedenkstätte des ehemaligen Konzentrationslagers Dachau, in: Wolfgang Benz (Hrsg.), Rechtsextremismus in der Bundesrepublik. Voraussetzungen, Zusammenhänge, Wirkungen, aktualisierte Neuausgabe, Frankfurt a.M., 1989, pp. 189–201, about the liberation, especially pp. 193–197.

4   Quoted by Distel, p. 194, loc. cit.

5   Erich Kern, Verbrechen am deutschen Volk. Eine Dokumentation alliierter Grausamkeiten, Göttingen, 1964, pp. 314–316. The same, Meineid gegen Deutscvhland. Eine Dokumentation über politischen Betrug, Preußisch Oldendorf, 1971, pp. 243–247. In the following, reference will be made to the last-cited publication. Regarding Erich Kern, see Astrid Lange, Was die Rechten lesen: fünfzig rechtsextreme Zeitschriften. Ziele, Inhalte, Taktik, München 1993, p. 152.

6   Edgar Kupfer-Koberwitz, Die Mächtigen und die Hilflosen. Als Häftling in Dachau, 2 vols., Stuttgart 1957 and 1960; Nerin E. Gun, The Hours Of the Americans, Velbert, 1968, (first published under the title, The Day of the Americans, New York, 1966)

7   Kern, Meineid, p. 233 ff. and p. 310 ff.

The propagandistic and unscientifically motivated use of sources by the right-extremist authors is revealed itself, among other things, in that they regard as a matter of course that all SS-men found in the Dachau camp were shot, though the testimony of Linberger, especially, contradicts this. Thus, Alfred Schickel, active in the grey zone between conservatism and right-extremism, stated in 1981 that the real significance of the statement of the U.S. High Command that about 300 SS-men were put out of action at the capture of the camp can be gathered from a photo that he saw in the National Archives in Washington. "It shows three German soldiers standing with raised arms in front of a wall, amidst a mass of corpses, and in front, two American soldiers loading their guns, evidently about to 'put out of action' the still standing soldiers".[8] The picture, which, incidentally, had already been published in 1964, actually shows quite unmistakably the scene of an execution, and the official caption that it involves men who feign death after American soldiers fired a volley at the fleeing SS-men, is not very convincing, considering the wall the men stand in front of.[9] Schickel's method, to conclude a total event from a snap shot is, however, more than questionable and clarifies that what is taking place here is more a search for confirmation of prejudices than for a factual reconstruction of historical events.

When, in 1986, the former army colonel and army doctor Howard A. Buechner published his book "Dachau, The Hour of the Avenger," it seemed, however, to present a definite confirmation of the systematic massacre by American soldiers of the guard detachment in the Dachau camp. Buechner represents the double authority as an eye witness and as a member of the liberating forces. Briefly, Buechner told the following story: Deeply shocked when confronted by the cruelties committed by the SS, a burning rage erupted among the soldiers of the 157th infantry regiment who captured the camp. The 1977 deceased 1st lieutenant Jack Bushyhead — a Cherokee Indian — supposedly collected 346 German guards in a yard of the SS-garrison, after having seen the concentration camp and the crematorium, and had them shot by a machine gun. Survivors were reputedly liquidated by prisoners armed with pistols. Altogether, 480 Germans supposedly have been shot by U.S. soldiers, 40 presumedly were the victims of revenge acts by

8   Alfred Schickel, Zeitgeschichte am Scheideweg. Anspruch und Mängel westdeut-
    scher Zeitgeschichte, Würzburg 1981, p. 20 f.
9   The first publication of the in the meantime often duplicated photo known to me,
    in Rodney G. Minott, The Fortress That Never Was. The Myth of Hitler's Bavarian
    Stronghold, New York a.o. 1964, picture section. Reproduction of the photos
    with the official caption in Andrew Mollo, Dachau, in After The Battle, Number
    27: Dachau, (London 1980), pp. 1–19, here p. 15.

prisoners.[10] Buechner refers to his own observations and the interpretation of a series of photos, among them the above mentioned picture. They had to be made just prior to his arrival.[11]

Buechner's book was received by the German right-extremist circles shortly after its publication and interpreted by Ingrid Weckert, in the periodical "Deutschland in Geschichte und Gegenwart" as "indubitable confirmation" of an American massacre, while nevertheless rejecting Buechner's description of the gruesome conditions in the concentration camp Dachau.[12] Similar to Weckert, an American, publishing under the pseudonym "John Cobden," also strives to play down the conditions in the concentration camp and, citing Buechner, to depict the liberation as a great massacre.[13]

Among serious historians, Harold Marcuse in his dissertation of 1992, and Klaus-Dietmar Henke in his 1995 book about the American occupation of Germany were the first to deal with the events in detail.[14] Though Henke indicates a strictly skeptical attitude in regard to Buechner and registers doubts both about the number of 480 executions and also regarding Jack Bushyhead as the main culprit, his description still depends strongly on Buechner, due to the lack of relevant sources. Similarly, this applies to Marcuse's research.

Now, new material came recently to the archive of the KZ-Gedenkstätte Dachau that enables one to depict these events in detail, and, especially, to scrutinize the description by Buechner more thoroughly. It concerns the copies of an investigation by the Assistant Inspector General of the 7th Army, Joseph M. Whitaker, who by order of the Headquarters of the 7th Army from May 2, 1945, on the next day already initiated a meticulous investigation of the events at the liberation of the concentration camp Dachau,[15] and

---

10   Howard A. Buechner, Dachau. The Hour of the Avenger, Metairie, Louisiana,1989 (first edition 1986), pp. 84–107.

11   Ibid., p. 102.

12   Ingrid Weckert, Dachau — Tag der Rache, in: Deutschland in Geschichte und Gegenwart, 35 (1987) H. 2, pp. 14–20.

13   John Cobden, Dachau, Reality and Myth, Newport Beach 1994.

14   Marcuse, Nazi Crimes, pp. 87–95; Henke, Amerikanische Besetzung, pp. 920–928; Robert H. Abzug, Inside the Vicious Heart. Americans and the Liberation of Nazi Concentration Camps, New York a.o. 1985, p. 92, also mentions already the shooting of prisoners.

15   The documents consist of over 160 pages and contain a reference with recommendations for further proceedings, the conclusion of the investigation, the transcription of Whitaker's interrogations (altogether 960 questions directed at 38 witnesses under oath), a statement of the Headquarters of the 7th Army, as well as a report of the commander of the 1st battalion of the 222nd infantry regiment of the 42nd infantry division. The originals of the sources are in the National Archives in Washington and were released in the summer of 1992.

also a collection of sources assembled by John H. Linden, for the purpose of documenting the role of his father, General Henning Linden, in liberating the concentration camp Dachau.[16]

## The Initial Situation

The final months of Dachau were the worst. The camp was extremely overcrowded due to the continuous arrivals of transports evacuating the camps near the front. These transports resulted in a large number of fatalities. Most of the survivors arrived near death from exhaustion, undernourished and physically completely broken down. The hygienic conditions and the food situation were catastrophic. A typhus epidemic broke out in December 1944. Over 15,000 prisoners died due to sickness, undernourishment and by assault of the SS from the end of 1944 to the liberation. This is nearly half of the total of the fatalities of the Dachau camp. Cremation of the corpses was no longer possible. The bodies were piled up in the mortuaries and around the crematorium. There were over 32,000 prisoners in the camp at the end of April 1945. Hope of imminent liberation and fear of extermination by the SS or an evacuation of the camp caused the most diverse rumors and resulted in an atmosphere of the highest nervous tension. Actually, a mass murder of the prisoners was at least considered. The various evacuation transports, especially the death march put into action on April 26th, precipitated a high number of casualties.[17]

The disintegration of the Nazi regime resulted both in more brutalization and also in a feverish search by individual leading figures for options to avoid the visible collapse. The attempts by Heinrich Himmler to use the Jews in his power as "bargaining chips" is the most characteristic example.[18] In this context belong also the modest achievements of the International Red

---

16  The material assembled by Linden is of the most varied origin. Partly, it derives from the estate of his father, and contains, among others, newspaper items, personal testimonies, correspondence and copies from archives. The background of Linden's efforts regarding documentation is an old quarrel between the 42nd and 45th division of the 7th army about which of them should have the credit for the liberation of Dachau. Cf. Henke, Amerikanische Besetzung, pp. 916 u. 918 ff.

17  Henke, Amerikanische Besetzung, p. 867 ff.; Barbara Distel, Der 29. April 1945. Die Befreiung des Konzentrationslagers Dachau, in: Dachauer Hefte, 1 (1985), pp. 3–11; regarding the evacuation marches, Henke, ibid., pp. 898–913; Andreas Wagner, Todesmarsch. Die Räumung und Teilräumung der Konzentrationslager Dachau, Kaufering und Mühldorf Ende April 1945, Ingolstadt 1995.

18  Yehuda Bauer, Freikauf von Juden? Die Verhandlungen zwischen dem national-sozialistischen Deutschland und jüdischen Repräsentanten 1933–1945, Frankfurt a.M. 1996, p. 376 ff.

Cross in its efforts to gain access to the concentration camps. On March 12, 1945, Carl Jacob Burckhardt, the president of the International Red Cross, received the consent, after consultations with the Chief of the Reich Main Security Office (Reichssicherheitshauptamt), Kaltenbrunner, that delegates of his organization would gain access to the concentration camps, provided they were ready to stay there until the end of the war.[19] Due to this agreement, the Swiss delegate of the Red Cross, Victor Maurer, who was stationed at the Red Cross base in Uffing near the Staffelsee (Staffel lake), about 70 kilometers from Dachau, was directed to proceed to the camp.[20] Maurer brought five trucks with food packages, which were unloaded by prisoners.[21] Maurer stayed in the camp according to agreement. He stayed for the night in a barrack outside the prison camp.

During the first night that Maurer stayed in the camp, a railroad transport with prisoners from Buchenwald arrived. This transport, of at least 4,480 but probably 4,800 prisoners, had left Buchenwald already on April 7th. The time for travel was estimated as 24 hours and supplied with food accordingly: according to the testimony of the SS-Untersturmführer Hans Mehrbach, in charge of the train, a handful of cooked potatoes, 500 gram bread, 50 gram sausage and 25 gram margarine per person. Actually, the train was nearly for 21 days on the way and Mehrbach could only once, on the twelfth day, obtain further supplies in the form of 3000 breads

19  Report of the International Red Cross on its activities during the Second World War (September 1, 1939–June 30, 1947). Volume I:General Activities. Geneva 1948, p. 620: Hans Haug, Menschlichkeit für alle. Die Weltbewegung des Roten Kreuzes und des Roten Halbmondes, Bern, Stuttgart 2001, p. 69: Werner Rings, Advokaten das Feindes. Das Abenteuer der politischen Neutralität, Wien/Düsseldorf 1966, pp. 122–124.

20  The Work of the IRC for Civilian Detainees in German Concentration Camps from 1939 to 1945. Geneva 1975, p. 121 ff. (reproduced in the forms of extracts in the material from Linden); Marcus J. Smith, The Harrowing of Hell. Dachau, Albuquerque 1972, pp. 256 ff. The 1975 published version of Mauerer's report diverges in some formulations and details from the one of Smith. A detailed, however somewhat freely spruced up and inaccurate regarding dates, as well as based on uncertain sources, description of the Red Cross Commission, presented Christian Bernadac. La Libération des Camps. Le Dernier Jour de Notre Mort, Paris 1995, pp. 645–649.

21  Arthur Haulot, Lagertagebuch Januar 1943–Juni 1945, in: Dachauer Hefte 1 (1985), pp. 129–203: here p. 192. According to the testimony of Haulot, who met Maurer personally, these food packages were intended for "the people of the West". The Dutch prisoner Floris B. Bakels noted in his diary on April 27th "the French get packages again. In fact why not we?" Floris B. Bakels, Nacht und Nebel. Der Bericht eines holländischen Christen aus deutschen Gefängnissen und Konzentrationslagern, Frankfurt a.M. 1979, p. 338. According to Bernadac, Libération, p. 648, Maurer arrived with seven trucks at the camp.

and 3000 little bits of cheese.[22] On April 22nd, when the train stopped in
Nammering near Passau, the prisoners received additional food for the
second time — the result of a food collection of the parish priest of Aicha
vorm Wald, Johann Bergmann. Mehrbach deliberately did not mention
this in his testimony before American interrogators, for in Nammering not
only were prisoners who died during the transport cremated, but a large
number of prisoners were shot. Altogether nearly 800 corpses were cremated
or buried there.[23] According to Johann Bergmann's testimony, the train
left Nammering on April 22nd with 3,100 prisoners. That "Mehrbach
brought them safe and sound to Dachau," as was told to the priest later, is,
however, anything but correct. The train was parked at a rail siding within
the confines of the SS-garrison in the night from April 27th to the 28th.
The presumed scarcely 800 survivors were taken to the camp. More than
2,300 corpses remained.[24]

According to a report by the American journalist Marguerite Higgins,
who entered the camp as the first reporter, the prisoners in the camp had
refused an order of the SS to unload the corpses.[25] This is entirely within
the scope of the possible, for the SS displayed signs of disintegration already
for a number of days. On April 23rd, the outside work detachments no
longer left the camp.[26] During the following days quite a number of the
commanding SS-officers took off.[27] The last camp commander, appointed
in November 1943, SS-Obersturmbannführer Eduard Weiter, left the camp
on April 26th. He shot himself in the castle Itter, a Dachau satellite camp
in Tyrol, on May 6th.[28] It is not quite clear who assumed the command of
Dachau after Weiter took off. There are, however, clues that for a period
of two to three days Martin Weil, who had already been camp commander
from September 1942 to November 1943 took over the command. According to Günther Kimmel, Weiß had been ordered back to Dachau shortly
before the end of the war, "presumably to give a hand to the commandant

22  IfZ-Archiv, Nürnberger Dokumente, NO 2192, testimony Hans Mehrbach.
23  The Death Train from Buchenwald. Eye Witness Report of Johann Bergmann,
    former parish priest of Aicha vorm Wald, Passauer Neue Presse, 19 April 1955,
    reprinted in: Buchenwald. Mahnung und Verpflichtung. Dokumente und Berich-
    te. Forth, completely new edited edition, Berlin 1983, pp. 503–505.
24  Pierre C. T. Verheye, The Train Ride into Hell. Unpublished manuscript. The
    author thanks Mr. Verheye, Tucson, Arizona, for important references about the
    train transport from Buchenwald.
25  Hermann Weiß, Dachau und die Internationale Öffentlichkeit, Reaktion auf die
    Befreiung des Lagers, in: Dachauer Hefte 1 (1985), pp. 12–38, here p. 27.
26  Distel, Befreiung (liberation), p. 6.
27  IfZ-Archiv, Nürnberger Dokumente, NO 1253, testimony Visintainer.
28  Johannes Tuchel, Die Kommandanten des Konzentrationslager Dachau, in: Dach-
    auer Hefte 10 (1994), Täter und Opfer, pp. 69–90, here p. 88 ff.

and to stop irregularities".[29] Kupfer-Koberwitz confirms the presence of Weiß on April 23, 1945.[30] On April 28th, SS-Standartenführer Kurt Becher arrived at Dachau and engaged in a discussion with the camp commandant. Becher maintained later that he could no longer remember the name of the man. However, it stated with a "W" and it was a lieutenant colonel of the SS, thus an Obersturmbannführer. This is exactly the rank that Weiß had then.[31] It is, therefore, to be assumed that Weiß was Becher's partner in the discussion. Becher informed that the concentration camp was to be handed over through a negotiator. He could refer regarding this to an order by Ernst Kaltenbrunner, the chief of the Reichssicherheitshauptamt, who was near Linz and to whom Himmler had delegated his functions in the South-German region shortly before.[32] Though Kaltenbrunner had described a surrender as obsolete, considering the war situation, in a telephone conversation with Becher on the same day, Becher, however, succeeded to get Kaltenbrunner's consent for it. Becher told Weiß, who had stated that he did not believe in the possibility of an orderly surrender, he definitely didn't have to execute the surrender personally.[33]

It seems that Weiß took off — he was arrested by the Americans in Mühldorf on May 2nd[34] — and entrusted the just 23-year-old Untersturmführer Heinrich Wicker, who was stationed in Dachau since the turn of the year 1944/45, the surrender of the camp.[35] On April 29th, when the arrival of the American troops was just a question of hours, Wicker also wanted to take off with his men. Victor Maurer tried his best to deter him from that. The Red Cross delegate was afraid of assaults by the unguarded CC-prisoners against the local population and the spread of the typhus epidemic.

29 Günther Kimmel, Das Konzentrationslager Dachau. Eine Studie zu den national-sozialistischen Gewaltverbrechen, in: Martin Broszat/Elke Fröhlich (Hrsg.), Bayern in der NS-Zeit, Bd. 2: Herrschaft und Gesellschaft im Konflikt, München u.a. 1979, pp. 349–413, hier p. 373.

30 Edgar Kupfer-Koberwitz, Dachauer Tagebücher. Die Aufzeichnungen des Häftlings 24814, München 1997, p. 432.

31 Tuchel, Die Kommandanten, p. 87.

32 Peter Black, Ernst Kaltenbrunner. Vasall Himmlers: Eine SS-Karriere, Paderborn u.a. 1991, p. 271 ff.

33 IfZ-Archiv. Eichmann-trial, Beweisdokument 827, witness evidence by Kurt Becher, pp. 3–5.

34 Tuchel, Die Kommandanten, p. 88. Condemned to death in the first large Dachau-trial, Weiß was executed in Landsberg on May 26, 1946.

35 The Work of the IRCS, p. 122 ff. Maurer incorrectly spells the name 'Wickert'. The biographical date about Wickert are based on a friendly information of the Deutsche Dienststelle, Berlin, from May 13, 1997. The identity of Heinrich Wicker with the one mentioned by Maurer as 'Wickert' is confirmed by the comparison of a picture on the list of missed personnel with the pictures of the meeting of Maurer and Eicker with General Linden.

He succeeded to persuade Wicker to stay and to come to the following agreement: The guard towers were to remain occupied to keep the prisoners under control and to prevent them from fleeing. Companies not engaged in guard duty were to assemble unarmed in a yard,[36] the entire garrison were to retain the right to withdraw to their own lines.[37] Since the Americans were already so close in the night from Saturday to Sunday that the sound of battle could be heard, most of the officers, rank and file and employees had fled the SS-garrison.[38] When Maurer arrived at the prison camp Sunday morning about 10.30 am, he found the guard towers manned. A white flag fluttered from one of the towers.

*Shock and Irrational Reactions (Kurzschlussreaktionen)*

On the same morning, the 3rd battalion of the 157th infantry regiment of the 45th infantry division of the U.S. army received the order to occupy the camp Dachau. The battalion commander, Felix S. Sparks, designated the I-company to execute the order and personally took over the command. Shortly before noon, the Americans, coming from the west, reached the SS-compound.[39] This consisted by no means of only the concentration camp; actually the camp comprised only a small part in terms of area. The SS-training camp on Dachau represented "a central military base for soldierly and ideological education of the SS-rank and file".[40] Dachau was the garrison of the executive school (Führerschule) of the SS-Economic- and Management Service, the technical armament educational school, the medical service school of the Waffen-SS and other educational institutions. In addition, there were numerous administrative offices and the location of large economic enterprises of the SS. There were 224 structures in the SS part of the compound alone.[41] In the east it was bounded by the small canalized creek Würm which at the same time formed the western boundary of the prisoners' camp. This was shaped in the form of a rectangle with the measurements of 583 times 278 meters.[42] The entrance to the entire camp

36  It is not quite clear which yard was meant; probably the one behind the main building of the prison camp.
37  The Work of the ICRC, pp. 122 f.
38  In January 1945, the guard detachment comprised 3544 men and 62 women; cf. the compilation of the IfZ Fa 183, Bl.8.
39  Henke, Amerikanische Besetzung, p. 917.
40  Sybille Steinbacher, Dachau — die Stadt und das Konzentrationslager in der NS-Zeit: die Untersuchung einer Nachbarschaft, Frankfurt a.M. u.a. 1993, p. 90.
41  Ibid.
42  Klaus Drobisch/Günther Wieland, Das System der NS-Konzentrationslager 1933–1939, Berlin 1995, p. 271.

complex was about one kilometer west of the prisoners' camp and was not visible from there.[43]

Nevertheless, the Americans were immediately and without warning confronted by the extreme horrors of the concentration camp universe: On the access road to the entrance of the SS-camp there stood the train that had arrived from Buchenwald one and a half days before — a long train with 39 wagons[44] — and in most of them there were corpses, the emaciated bodies of dead prisoners. Some lay shot next to the tracks. The scene was described in the following way in an informational bulletin for officers of the 42nd division: "In these stinking cars were seen the bodies of these people prisoners too weak even to get out. A few tried, and they made a bloody heap in the door of one of the cars. They had been machine gunned by the SS. A little girl was in that car. In another car, sitting on the bodies of his comrades, his face contorted with pain frozen by death, was the body of one who completed the amputation of his gangrenous leg with own hands and covered the stump with paper. Underneath was one with a crushed skull (...) Close by was one who had been beaten until his entrails protruded from his back. But most of them had simply died in the attitudes of absolute exhaustion that only starving men can assume."[45] This sight distressed the U.S. soldiers profoundly: "Combat veterans wept, stared with sullen moveless faces, and anger sharpened their already edgy nerves."[46] The whisper slogan "Take no prisoners here" made its rounds and found evidently general assent.[47]

43  Cf. the camp plan by Paul Berben, Dachau 1933–1945. The Official History. London 1975, p. 271, as well as the large-format printed aerial picture in Mollo, Dachau, p. 6 ff.

44  Verheye, Train Ride.

45  Cited in Weiß, Internationale Öffentlichkeit, p. 20 ff. Pictures of the train a.o. in: Abzug, Vicious Heart, p. 90; München — 'Hauptstadt der Bewegung', hrsg. von Münchner Stadtmuseum, München 1993, p. 244; Antony Penrase (ed.), Lee Miller's War Photographer and Correspondent with the Allies in Europe 1944–1945, London 1992, p. 182 ff; Gun, Stunde Bildteil 1.

46  Abzug, Vicious Heart, p. 90; further proof for the mood in Whitaker, Interrogation protocol 50 (in this protocol the question and reply number is always referred to). GI's who came to the camp shortly after liberation were also deeply shocked at the sight of the train. Cf. Dan P. Daugherty, My Recollection of Dachau, in 45th Division News, February 1997. Copy in the archive of KZ-Gedenkstätte Dachau. Similarly, Holger Hagen, 'Im schlimmsten Alptraum meines Lebens'. Die Eindrücke des ehemaligen US-Leutnants Holger Hagen vom kurz zuvor befreiten Konzentrationslager Dachau, in: Süddeutsche Zeitung/Dachauer Neueste: 50th anniversary of the liberation of Dachau. Special edition, May 1995, p. 14ff; Chuck Ferree, Dachau Liberation, http://remember.org/dachlib.html (The author thanks Margret Chatwin, Munich, for the transmission of this testimony).

47  Whitaker, Interrogation protocol 177, 856 ff., 884 ff.; Buechner, Avenger, p. XXIX.

The Americans encountered the first SS-men at about the end of the train or a little further on. Four men approached the GI's with folded hands on their heads and surrendered to lieutenant W., the commander of the I-company. He ordered them to enter an empty wagon of the train of corpses and shot them down with his pistol. The prisoners — or at least some of them — were not dead, actually. Cries of pain and moaning could be heard from the car. The Private P. entered the car and finished off the men who were lying on the floor with eight or nine shots. "Well, I don't know who suggested it," replied the soldier, clearly agitated, to the corresponding question of the deputy inspector general Whitaker, "but they were all hollering [the wounded are evidently meant] and taking on and I never like to see anybody suffer, and I had one brother killed by them and one lost his leg, so I didn't like to see them suffer."[48]

When advancing further, the American soldiers faced the military hospital buildings that stood in the immediate vicinity of the entrance. At least one hundred Germans, among them also a few women, were taken out of the hospital to the road.[49] Two GI's checked if the patients who remained in the beds were actually unable to walk.[50] In the meantime, the SS-men were separated from the other prisoners, by order of the commander of the battalion. A Polish prisoner who identified the SS-men, who had exchanged their uniforms for other clothing, helped with that. He mistreated them and punched and kicked them.[51]

The Pole was evidently assigned to work in the nearby heating plant.[52] While the rest of the prisoners stood near the hospital under guard, the segregated SS-men were led to a yard that was divided from the hospital complex by a wall and was not visible from there; it evidently belonged to the power station. The information about their number varies significantly. At the interrogations by Whitaker, estimates between 50 and 125 were given, with the majority ranging from 50 to 75.[53] Kern alleges to "about forty men".[54]

---

48  Whitaker, Interrogation protocol 813–829, 854 ff., 867–875. 915–942, quotation 940 ["Well, I don't know who suggested it, but they were all hollering and taking on and I never like to see anybody suffer, and I had one brother killed by them and one lost his leg, so I didn't like to see them suffer."]

49  Ibid., pp. 50, 378.

50  Ibid., pp. 221. Cf. th. description of Kern, Meineid, p. 245.

51  Whitaker, Interrogation protocol 242, 261, 285. On a picture published by Gun, Bildteil 2, Mollo, p. 15, and Buechner, p. 114, one can see two men in prison uniform who berate a knocked down SS-man. One of them holds a shovel in his hand.

52  Weiß, Internationale Öffentlichkeit, p. 24.

53  Whitaker, Interrogation protocol 56, 163, 222, 258, 349, 378.

54  Kern, Meineid, p. 245.

In the yard, where the coal was stored, the SS-men were lined up a-gainst the wall. The officer of the company requested a machine gun. Ac-cording to some witnesses, the prisoners moved towards the U.S. soldiers from the flanks when the machine gun was placed and made ready to fire.[55] Another witness, however, testifies that the SS-men just stood there. The company commander had said "get ready to shoot them," someone else had called "fire", and then the shooting had started.[56] According to the first version, the commander started the firing with his pistol when the prisoners started to approach the Americans, and called "let them have it". The machine gunner C. testified to this, and further stated that Lieutenant W. had wanted to fire the machine gun himself, however, could not get to it on account of the movement among the SS-men.[57]

The machine gunner declared that he fired about 30 to 50 shots in three rounds. Three or four other Americans also fired at the captured SS men, among them Lieutenant Bushyhead, who was armed with a carbine.[58] The ones hit, fell to the ground, and the uninjured let themselves also fall. Only some SS-men remained standing with raised arms.[59] "Everything happened so fast, and they were all driven there together, and everything was over. It seemed like a kind of dream to me," thus described Lieutenant Bushyhead this event.[60] The shooting lasted only a few seconds.[61] But GI's made preparations to continue it. In the meantime, two SS-men tried to commit suicide by cutting their carotid arteries.[62] It is possible that the interruption of the shooting was caused by the jamming of the machine gun, which the gunner C. tried to repair.[63] Linberger ascribes it to the appearance of drunken CC-inmates who "had armed themselves with shovels to kill a man by the name of Weiß".[64] This statement corresponds

55  Ibid. 50 ff., 73, 194, 237.
56  Ibid. 231–233.
57  Ibid. 342–344.
58  Ibid. 192 ff.,233. Whitaker spells "Busheyhead".
59  This scene is captured in the above described photo: cf. also the testimony Linberger's in Kern, Meineid, p. 245 ff.
60  Whitaker, Interrogation protocol 173.
61  Ibid. 378.
62  Ibid. 104 and Linberger in Kern, Meineid, p. 246. According to Linberger, a man with a red-cross-arm band throw razor blades to the survivors of the shooting and urged them to commit suicide. The wife of a Dr. Müller had in desperation during the shooting action poisoned herself and her two children. The death of a woman and two children is also confirmed by a GI, questioned by Whitaker, who undertook a futile rescue attempt with the help of a German doctor; Whitaker, Interrogation protocol 115.
63  Ibid. 345.
64  This could have meant the former camp commander Martin Weiß, who, howev-er, at that moment, was no longer in Dachau.

with an often published photo, among others also in Buechner, in which two CC-inmates can be seen who threaten and insult a man lying on the ground. One of them has evidently a shovel in his hands. In the background, the SS-men lying at the wall, as well as an American are visible.[65] It cannot be established from the available sources if the prisoners actually killed the man. One indication that points to this, however, is that Whitaker found among others the corpse of a man with a broken skull when he inspected the coal yard on May 3rd.[66] According to a report of the "Associated Press" of May 1, 1945, the corpses of two Germans "slain by a Pole and a Czech, who had worked in the engine room" lay in front of the power station.[67]

The events in the coal yard lasted in any case only a few minutes before Colonel Sparks appeared on the scene and ordered, evidently very angry, to cease the firing.[68] Sparks, who had been positioned about 100 to 200 meters on the other side of the wall, ran immediately to the coal yard where he heard the shooting.[69] "When I went over there there were" testified one of his aides, "I should say about seventyfive or so lying on the ground. It looked like they were pretty badly wounded. Then, somebody gave the order for them to get up and most of them got up."[70] The survivors were brought to the old town of Dachau where they were kept first in the hall of the Hörhammer Inn together with other prisoners of war.[71] A witness, who a short time later was at the coal yard, saw there 15 or 16 dead or wounded Germans lying at the wall. He recognized that a few were still alive from their slight movements. The witness in question is Howard Buechner, the author of the book "Dachau. The Hour of the Avenger".[72]

Howard Buechner's Constructions

Buechner's description, published in 1986, differs quite substantially from his witness testimony on May 5, 1945. He describes the scene in his book the following way: When he and his companions arrived at the hospital buildings, they had heard machine gun salvos and pistol shots. Because of curiousness, he had walked towards the noise, looked around the corner

---

65  Buechner, Avenger, p. 114.
66  Whitaker investigation documents, inspector's exhibit.
67  Weiß, Internationale Öffentlichkeit, p. 24.
68  Ibid., pp. 345, 50, 234 ff., 269, 281.
69  Ibid., pp. 393 ff.
70  Ibid., p. 378.
71  Linberger in Kern, Meineid, p. 246.
72  Whitaker, Interrogation protocol 363–374 (testimony Buechner). The spelling in Whitaker — Howard E. Buchner — is incorrect, correctly, Howard A. Buechner.

of a wall and caught sight of Lieutenant Bushyhead, who stood on a kind
of shed next to a machine gun, operated by one or two soldiers. A second
machine gun was placed on the ground. A number of marksmen also stood
around. About 350 SS-men lay at the wall. Prisoners armed with pistols had
killed the survivors. Some of the survivors, however, had been carried away
on stretchers by German hospital personnel. He had offered his help to the
German doctors, but they had rejected it. When he questioned Lieutenant
Bushyhead why he had done that, he replied: "Doc, have you been to the
crematorium? Have you seen the gas chamber? Have you seen the boxcars?
Have you seen the little people?"[73] In Buechner's portrayal, Bushyhead
becomes the avenger of the tortured concentration camp victims. Since Colonel
Sparks as well as the commander of company I, Lieutenant W., had left the
camp already, Bushyhead suddenly became the only officer present. "He could
no longer reject the role which fate had fashioned for him and for which he
seems to be predestined."[74]

But it was not fate that had assigned the role of the "avenger" to Lt.
Bushyhead, but Howard Buechner. And this is not by far the only distortion
which his book contains. The most important ones are quickly enumerated:

1. At the time of the shooting in the coal yard, the Americans had not
reached the concentration camp yet. It took place, therefore, not after the
capture of the entire camp, as stated by Buechner, but rather during its
initial stage, immediately after the encounter with the train with the corpses.

2. Lt. Bushyhead was by no means the only officer present. Contrary to
Buechner's description, the SS-sector and the camp were, indeed, not yet taken.
Both the head of company I and Col. Sparks were in the close vicinity of the
hospital.

3. Lt. Bushyhead does not have the leading role in the execution action
that Buechner assigns to him. Ringleader was the head of the company.
According to his own testimony, Bushyhead shot at the SS-men with his
own carbine.[75] The investigation files clearly indicate only one machine
gun, operated by gunner C. Buechner himself states in his book that he
thought that a second machine gun was placed on the roof of a shed, but
did not insist that his impression was correct.[76]

4. Buechner's description that three or four prisoners had systematically
finished the execution with 45-revolvers, is more than doubtful. The only
proof for this are the otherwise unreliable memories of Buechner. Neither
in the interrogations nor in Linberger one can find a clue for his statement.

---

73  Buechner, Avenger, p. 86 ff.
74  Ibid., p. 91 ff.
75  Whitaker, Interrogation protocol 192 ff.
76  Buechner, Avenger 87.

Apart from the ones employed in the heating plant, there were no prisoners in this part of the SS-sector. The alleged appearance of armed prisoners is, however, of considerable significance in Buechner's justification of his own role, as evident from the following point.

5. That doctors from the hospital took away wounded, as described by Buechner, is confirmed by US-soldiers who testified that Col. Sparks had ordered German doctors to take care of the wounded.[77] Contrary to the assertions in his book, that he had offered the German doctors his help; Buechner, however, declared during his interrogation as a witness on May 5, 1945, he did not know if any help for the wounded Germans had been requested.[78] He himself had neither examined the wounded nor rendered any medical help.[79] Buechner writes about the interrogation in his book that he was questioned why he had not stopped the execution and had not rendered medical help. He had replied that as an unarmed medical officer he was unable to restrain the halfcrazed prisoners who had liquidated the survivors. In addition, he pointed to the rejection of his help by the German doctors. The investigating officer had accepted this explanation and had exonerated him from any suspicion.[80] There is nothing of that in the interrogation protocol. There is no mention of an ongoing execution action for that reason alone that Buechner had testified in May 1945 that he had arrived at the location after the event. The alleged appearance of armed prisoners is obviously a belated invention by Buechner in order to justify his lack of help. The German doctors are also not mentioned in Buechner's interrogation. And by no means did the investigator consider Buechner's behavior blameless. On the contrary: He recommended initiating court martial proceedings against him for dereliction of duty.[81]

6. According to Buechner's "Avenger"-description, the number of casualties amounted to 346, more than 20-fold of what ensued from other data. Linberger stated: "At this action, about twelve nameless were left on the ground."[82] Whitaker found 17 corpses in German uniforms, most of them belonging to the SS, during his inspection of the coal yard.[83] Buechner himself stated during his interrogation that he had seen 15 or 16 dead or wounded Germans. But in his book he claims "to have seen about 350 dead soldiers".[84]

---

77  Whitaker, Interrogation protocol 384, 397, 378 ff.

78  Ibid. 374.

79  Ibid. 371.

80  Buechner Avenger, p. 118 f.

81  Examination sources Whitaker, routing slip from June 8, 1945.

82  Linberger in Kern, Meineid, p. 246; Weckert, who evaluates Buechner's description as confirmation of Kern's publication, and who cites Linberger in detail, suppresses his numbers.

83  Examination sources Whitaker. Inspector's report.

84  Buechner, Avenger, p. 86.

The contradiction reveals itself when one inspects more closely how Buechner arrives at his figures. He calls this procedure "an analysis".[85] While the 7th Army announced that about 350 soldiers and guards were overpowered at the liberation of Dachau,[86] Buechner starts with a total number of 560 SS-men present in Dachau. This number is based on the official morning roll-call and was to have been claimed by a First Lt. Heinrich Skodzensky, when he tried, together with the Swiss Red Cross delegate, and in the presence of Pat O'Leary, the head of the International prisoners' committee, to surrender the camp.[87] Buechner cites the publications of E. Gun and Andrew Mollo.[88] Henke rates Gun's memories as "not always reliable, of course"[89] — a rather too restrained judgment, for the book of the sensational journalist actually is full of errors.[90] According to Gun, the mentioned 1st Lieutenant Heinrich Skodzensky was entrusted with the administration of the camp during the last days of April.[91] The delegate of the Red Cross, Viktor Maurer, on the other hand, names the Untersturmführer Wicker as responsible for the concentration camp.[92] Upon inquiry, the competent authority, the "Deutsche Dienststelle" in Berlin, was not able to find any SS-officer active in Dachau by the name Skodzensky, or similar.[93] The alleged numbers of prisoners given by the so-called Skodzensky cannot in any case, as Buechner does it, be given equal weight with the information of the official morning roll-call.[94] They are in regard to the prisoners demonstrably wrong. There were 32,325 prisoners in the camp, not 30,000;

85  Ibid., pp. 95–99

86  Report of April 30, 1945, Archive of the KZ-Gedenkstätte Dachau 16.486; Henke, Amerikanische Besetzung, p. 920.

87  Buechner, Avenger, p. 291.

88  Gun, Stunde, p. 57; Mollo, Dachau, p. 13.

89  Henke, Amerikanische Besetzung, p. 921.

90  Some references may illustrate this: The name of the prisoner who fled the camp and tried to contact with the Americans, was Kurt Riemer, not Reiner, as Gun, p. 53, writes; the former commander of Dachau, Martin Weiß, never became "General Inspector of all camp". — Gun, p. 54 — Inspector of the concentration camps, as the correct title was called, was since 1939 Richard Glücks; for the liberation of Dachau not two battalions of the US Army were engaged, but substantially only one company; that the "1st Battalion of the 45th Division advanced over an open tract from the East", and there met fierce resistance from the combined SS, is also erroneous (Gun p. 56); no tanks were employed during the liberation (ibid.)

91  Ibid., p. 54. In the German edition of Gun's Book, however, only the initial S. appears, while in the American edition the full name is mentioned; Gun, The Day, p. 60.

92  The Work of the ICRC for Civil Detainees, p. 122.

93  Information from the Deutsche Dienststelle, Berlin, from May 13, 1997.

94  Buechner, Avenger, p. 96.

among them 4,260 infirmary patients, not 2,340 as is stated by Gun.[95] The episode described by Gun appears already in a biography of Pat O'Leary that had appeared ten years before Gun's work though with noticeable differences. According to this book, when the Prisoners' Committee approached the Americans, an SSlieutenant stepped forward and saluted with "Heil Hitler," intending to make a declaration. The general commotion, however, drowned his voice.[96] Therefore, one should better not rely on the numbers given by Gun. Buechner, however, accepts them as facts. He cites in his "analysis" diverse facts regarding the killing of SS-men in Dachau in a quite rash manner, without examining them closely, or at least scrutinizing whether they may not overlap other facts; he adds them up, plainly and simply, to arrive finally at a total sum of 560. There remain 346 men to be charged to the account of the "Avenger".[97]

Confident of the authenticity of Buechner's eyewitness report, Klaus-Dietmar Henke assigned him considerable space in his description of the liberation of Dachau, and labeled the events described by Buechner as the "probably [...] worst war crime of the US-Army during the occupation of Germany 1944/45," though he expresses definite reservations regarding the other description by Buechner.[98] Buechner's "recollections" are — as made evident by the investigative report of Whitaker, which was not yet available to Henke — a subsequent construction, however, that does not conform to the facts.

95  Gun, Stunde, p. 57; Concentration Camp Dachau 1933–1945 [Catalog of the Gedenkstätte]. Dachau 1978, p. 193 [Reports of the morning roll-call of April 29, 1945].

96  Vincent Brome, L'histoire de Pat O'Leary, Paris 1957, p. 237. The name of the SS-officer is not given.

97  Buechner adds the following numbers: 122 camp guards were supposedly shot on the spot, according to army photographer George Stevens Jr., 40 were supposedly killed by camp inmates, a corporal with the nickname Birdeye would have shot 12, 346 were presumed executed by Lt. Bushyhead, additionally 30 were killed in action and 10 escaped SS-men; Buechner, Avenger, p. 99. The report of 122 [camp guard] is evidently a total number, which Buechner, however, does not accept as such because he assumes that SS-guards were not only shot on the spot, but were also executed after the complete occupation of the camp. His description, according to which a corporal by the name Birdeye had fired at the collected prisoners, is also incorrect (p. 98 ff.). In the investigation of Whitaker no such incident is mentioned anywhere. According to Buechner, Colonel Sparks intervened personally. In fact, Sparks admitted to Henke that a headless reaction of a corporal of his battalion had lead to the killing of twelve prisoners of war, however, he states as the place of the incident the wall of the yard in which the execution took place; cf. Henke, Amerikanische Besetzung, p. 922. As can be ascertained from the files of the investigation, there was indeed a corporal with the name 'Birdeye' present at the execution in the coal yard, however, he was not the machine gunner.

98  Henke, Amerikanische Besetzung, pp. 922–924.

*The Capture of the Concentration Camp*

While the soldiers of the 157th Infantry Regiment moved towards the actual concentration camp through the SS-facilities and encountered shooting or fleeing SS-men occasionally, a small detachment, led by Brigadier General Henning Linden of the 42nd US-Division (also called Rainbow Division), arrived. Linden actually wanted to direct a battalion of the 222nd Infantry Regiment towards Munich.[99] The Belgian war reporter Paul Levy testifies that he directed Linden's attention to the nearby concentration camp when he arrived in Dachau.[100] Linden and his company started on their way to the concentration camp, together with Levy and his driver and the photographer Raphael Algoet, where, as Levy knew, his friend Albert Haulot was imprisoned. This group also encountered the train with the dead. But they did not penetrate deeper into the SS-area and swung to the right directly to the prison camp. At some distance from the entrance, a civilian with a Red Cross armband and a white flag, an SS-officer of a lieutenant rank, and an SS-man approached them. "These three people were a Swiss Red Cross representative and two SS troopers who said they were the camp commander and the assistant camp commander and that they had come into the camp on the night of the 28th to take over from the regular camp personnel for the purpose of turning the camp over to the advancing Americans," says Linden's report from May 2, 1945.[101] Wicker told the Americans that he had just arrived from the Eastern front,[102] evidently, lest he be made responsible for the conditions in the concentration camp, and also lest he be held as someone who had fought the US-Army, a circumstance of significance considering the furious indignation about the shooting of American prisoners of war at Malmedy in December 1944.[103] Actually, he had been stationed in Dachau since the beginning of the year, as previously mentioned. Wicker further stated that the still present SS was surrendering. They do not belong to the camp, but had replaced the SS that had fled to prevent a break-out of the "half-crazed and dangerous prisoners". In the middle of this declaration, the group came suddenly under fire and had to look for cover.[104]

99   1st Lieutenant William Cowling. Report on Surrender of the German Concentration Camp Dachau, 2 May 1945, in Material Linden, B4.
100  Paul Levy to Sol Feingold, October 27, 1992, Material Linden C 4.6.
101  Report on Surrender of Dachau Concentration Camp, Material Linden B.3.
102  42 Infantry Division, 222 Infantry Regiment, History of Operations, April 1945. Copy in the archive of the KZ–Gedenkstätte Dachau 20.838.
103  Cf. Henke, Amerikanische Besetzung, pp. 825–828.
104  Paul Levy, Déjà un an! Le 29 avril 1945, 17 h. 20 nous libérations ... Dachau. Newspaper report without reference to the place and date of publication [29.4.1946] in material Linden 8.5; the same, Nous pénétriona — neuf dans le camp de Dachau, La Cité Nouvelle, 29. 4. 1946. Material Linden B 6; Report Linden; Report Cowling.

Linden states that he accepted the offer of surrender,[105] however, there was an episode in between that he does not mention: according to Maurer, he and his companions were brought to the railway train in order to make photos for the press.[106] There actually exists a photo that shows Wicker — he appears overbearing and unmoved on it — and his companions together with Maurer and American soldiers at the train with the corpses.[107] According to Maurer, he had met a Major Every after that and informed him of the plan to surrender the camp, and had asked him to transmit his proposal to the General. Then, the group drove back to the camp, where some Americans were already there.[108] Maurer's statement is quite compatible with the report of Col. Sparks of the 45th Infantry Division, who wrote that after the arrival at the prison camp, he saw three jeeps of the 42nd Division getting there.[109] Thus, for Sparks and his men the impression must have been created that they were the first arrivals at the concentration camp, while Linden and his companions, on their part, first encountered Maurer and Wicker, who wanted to surrender the camp. Perhaps because they came under fire, and the General then called for reinforcement,[110] and also because they wanted to confront the arrogantly acting Wicker[111] with the just discovered horrors of the train full of corpses, Linden's group probably did not immediately advance to the prison camp. The long-lasting argument between the 42nd and 45th US-Division regarding the question of which earned the glory of reaching the concentration camp Dachau first and liberating it,[112] turns out to be meaningless upon closer examination, unless one intended to apply the doubtless unsuitable standards of modern sports competition to this event.

Spark's men had already overpowered some guard tower guards at the time of the return of Linden's group from the train.[113] This did not take place without some shooting, which Maurer also mentioned.[114] At the

105 Report Linden.
106 The Work of the ICRC, p. 123.
107 Material Linden B 9.6. Cf. also the photo of the meeting of Linden, Maurer and Wicker B.9.3
108 The Work of the ICRC, p. 123.
109 Felix L. Sparks, Dachau and its Liberation, cited in Buechner, Avenger pp. 60–68, here p. 65.
110 Report Cowling.
111 Levy, Paul Levy, Déjà un an! and Nous pénétrions. The same to Sol Feingold, 27. 10. 92 in Material Linden C 4.5. Levy writes that he also had functioned as interpreter and comments at the same time that he felt the remark of Wicker that the prisoners were dangerous and crazy as especially infamous and insulting.
112 Cf. Henke, Amerikanische Besetzung, p. 918 ff., who leans towards Spark's version. Cf. also the material Linden to this.
113 Sparks, Dachau and its Liberation in Buechner, p. 64.
114 The Work of the ICRC, p. 123.

same time, the appearance of the Americans had aroused the entire camp. Kupfer-Koberwitz, who lay wounded in the infirmary, noted: "Everyone starts to move — the sick leave their beds, the nearly well and the personnel run to the block street, jump out of the windows, climb over the wooden walls. Everyone runs to the roll-call place. One hears the yelling and cheers of hooray from afar to here." And Arthur Haulot made a note: "The entire camp pushes its way to the fence. The SS-men rounded up on the other side are publicly jeered at. If they fell into our hands, we would tear them to pieces. The masses howl with joy. Only a few hours later, when darkness descends, it becomes possible to clear the entrance."[115] The situation threatened to get out of hand. Prisoners started to enter the Jourhaus, and the Americans had to use all their efforts to prevent a mass break-out and to restore orderly conditions to some degree.[116] It seems to have come to a serious confrontation between Sparks and Linden, who met at the camp gate, and according to Sparks, because the general sought entrance to the camp for the reporter Marguerite Higgins, who had accompanied him. This contradicted the order not to let anyone into the camp prior to the arrival of special relief teams.[117] The reporter and her companion, Sergeant Peter Furst, nevertheless busied themselves at the gate, climbed over the fence-gate and were received enthusiastically by the prisoners.[118]

The joy of liberation was marred by the death of prisoners. Three prisoners, made careless by the excitement, made contact with the electrified barbed wire fence and were electrocuted.[119] Shots were still fired from at least one guard tower, too. A Polish prisoner was said to be fatally wounded then.[120] According to another version, the guards shot only over the heads of the prisoners to prevent a break-out. The Pole ended up at the electrified fence at that occasion and was electrocuted, however, the prisoners believed that he had been shot.[121] Regardless, the white flag on the towers and the shooting contradicted each other.

In this tense situation, the prisoners directed the attention of the US soldiers to the guard tower B, North of the Jourhaus, still occupied by SS-men.[122]

115 Haulot, Lagertagebuch, p. 193.
116 Copies of photos in material Linden, B 9.4 and B 9.12-15.
117 Sparks, Dachau, p. 65.
118 Sparks, Dachau, p. 65; excerpts from Marguerite Higgins: News is a Singular Thing in material Linden C 12 (a not very reliable, somewhat egocentric description); Haulot, Lagertagebuch, p. 193.
119 Linden, Report; Cowling, Report; Bernadac, Libération, p. 658.
120 Berben, Dachau, p. 192; Levy, Nous libérations.
121 Bernadac, Libérations, 664. The version comes from a former prisoner whom Bernadac cites under the pseudonyme "Joseph". He was supposed to have been a collaborator of the Deuxieme Bureau, the French Secret Service.
122 Whitaker, Interrogation protocol 416, 577.

The Americans approached the tower in two groups from left and right of the Würm canal. Shots were fired at the approaching Americans from there.[123] Sergeant W. arrived first at the tower, positioned himself next to the entrance and fired one burst into it, whereupon enemy personnel came out, still armed with their pistols. According to the testimony of the sergeant, these SS-men formed two rows only reluctantly,[124] and the last remaining guard in the tower seemed to have refused to come out and was forced with blows to do so.[125]

The depositions regarding the subsequent course of events are contradictory. Sergeant W. stated that one of the prisoners was likely to have made a false move; suddenly, there were shots from somewhere; he threw himself to the ground and, because he felt himself threatened, shot in the directions of the prisoners. The other Americans on that location also had fired from both sides of the canal.[126] This version of the events is confirmed by the Polish prisoner Marion Okrutnik,[127] however, the answers of the sergeant to the insistent questions of the investigator remained strangely vague so that one cannot avoid the impression, when reading the interrogation protocol, that one deals with excuses. This impression is strengthened by other testimonies. Thus, T/5 John B. reported, the prisoners, i.e. the members of the tower troop, were placed in rows along the canal. The last remaining SS-man in the tower, however, came down only, hesitantly "and as he came down one of the GI's pushed him to the rear of the other prisoners. As he got closer he still kept pushing him and pushed him right into the water. I guess as he went in he grabbed and pulled some more in. That must have been about two men, and after they fell in GI's on the other side opened up. At the same time GI's on this side opened up on them, too. They shot them all down."[128] This version of the events is substantially confirmed by various reports of prisoners. The Dutchman Floris B. Bakels writes in his memoirs: "I limped through the narrow passage between two blocks towards the fences, the ditch, the electrified barbed wire and the guard towers and saw there a robot from another world standing: pot helmet covered with branches, cartridge belt wound around the body, hand-grenade under the belt, a big machine pistol, high brown boots. I called: 'Are you American?' He turned around towards me: 'Yeah'. Then he turned again towards the guard tower

---

123 Whitaker, Interrogation protocol 512, 616.
124 Whitaker, Interrogation protocol 577.
125 Whitaker, Interrogation protocol 464, 469 ff. 516.
126 Whitaker, Interrogation protocol 577 ff.
127 Whitaker, Interrogation protocol 401.
128 Whitaker, Interrogation protocol 516. Cf. also the testimony of Corporal John V. "[...] they were pushed into the river and the guns or small arms weapons opened up." Ibid. 482.

with the white flag. A Mof [German] tumbled down and out, with raised hands. The American tore his insignias off, turned him around and ordered him to run away. When the Mof ran away, the American shot him dead as a doornail."[129] The Austrian priest Johannes Steinbock recounts similarly: "We run around, there we see already five SS-men shot dead at the guard tower B outside block 18. High on the tower the machine gun still projects towards the camp, on the outside flutters a white cloth. The prisoners who observed it tell that the men came down, the Americans had frisked them, something was said (it probably dealt with the possession of some kind of weapons). Suddenly, one of the Americans drew, hardly noticeable, his machine pistol and by a small move of the finger, the five lay dead on the ground. We looked for the reason for the further shots. On the other side of the camp wall, near the gate to the Plantage, we saw eight SS-men lying shot on the ground. They had been taken away from the towers; why they had been put against the wall, I could not learn. The dead remained lying for days, until the various commissions, political and military visitors arrived."[130] The questions, which remained unanswered for Steinbock, is very likely settled by the testimony of the Private R. who was questioned by Whitaker. He stated that he had seen how GI's walked a group of German prisoners, about eight or nine, along the canal, when a large group of prisoners, perhaps 200, coming from all sides and climbing over the fence began to attack the prisoners, shouting "SS, SS". Yells and shots could be heard.[131] It appears that the Americans were not, or not the only ones, doing the shooting: "I just hear also that excited prisoners tore the machine pistols from the hands of the soldiers and shot SS-men, who stood with raised hands behind the electrified wire fence," remarked Kupfer-Koberwitz in his diary.[132]

There is "considerable confusion" about the events of guard tower B, wrote the investigating officer Whitaker in his report,[133] summarizing, how-

---

129 Bakels, Nacht und Nebel. Der Bericht eines holländischen Christen aus deutschen Gefängnissen und Konzentrationslagern, Frankfurt a.M. 1979, p. 340.

130 Steinbock, Das Ende, p. 35. A similar second hand description by Kupfer-Koberwitz, Dachauer Tagebücher, p. 447; further: Johannes Neuhäusler, Wie war das in Dachau. Ein Versuch, der Wahrheit näher zu kommen, München n.d., p. 67 ff.; Bernadac, Libération, p. 658 (Georges Villiers). Summary execution mentioned by Haulot, Lagertagebuch 193 and Nico Rost, Goethe in Dachau, Frankfurt a.M. 1983, p. 244.

131 Whitaker, Interrogation protocol 843–851. The presence of Russian prisoners is also confirmed by the Corporal H.; ibid. 681. The Alsatian clergyman FranÁois Goldschmitt reports that the attack of a single prisoner on one of the captured SS-men initiated the shooting. François Goldschmitt, Die letzten Tage von Dachau, Sarreguemines 1947, p. 40.

132 Kupfer-Koberwitz, Dachauer Tagebücher, p. 449.

133 Investigation report Whitaker.

ever: "The whole incident smacks of execution, similar to other incidents described in this report."[134] The memories of former prisoners corroborate this impression.

The number of killed guards of guard tower B amounts with considerable certainty to 17. This number is summarized in a report of the commanding officer of the 1st Battalion, 222nd Infantry Regiment of the 42nd (Rainbow) Division, summoned by General Linden. The author, Lt. Col. F. tried, however, to depict the shooting as a consequence of combat actions.[135] Inspector Whitaker found six corpses lying at the guard tower when visiting the camp.[136] Three prisoners were alleged to be pushed into the canal and shot. Together with the eight corpses mentioned by Steinbock, the total number is arrived at. Members of the 42nd and 45th Division participated at the shootings[137]; in addition, an undetermined numbers of prisoners seem to have been involved in the entire incident.

Roughly at the same time as these events, Maurer finally succeeded in submitting the offer of surrender to General Linden, who accepted it.[138] Maurer's report has an irritating quality regarding this point, for, according to his own statement, the Americans had, after all, already occupied the camp. The planned orderly surrender without a fight had failed. The retreat of the guard company to their own lines was already out of question. This aspect of the surrender conditions was in any case unrealistic from the very start. Yet, it would be wrong to maintain that Maurer's mission had been a failure. Thanks to his intervention the camp remained under guard until the arrival of the Americans and the escape of thousands of prisoners with unforeseeable consequences was prevented. The US-Army in cooperation with the International Prisoners' Committee continued the quarantine nearly seamlessly.[139]

The fate of SS-Untersturmführer Heinrich Wicker is unclear. Is he identical with the young SS-lieutenant about whom Pat O'Leary, alias Albert Guerisse, the President of the International Prisoners' Committee reported

134 Investigation regort Whitaker, No. 18.
135 Impression of the Dachau Concentration Camp, Report to the Commanding General of the 42nd Infantry Division from May 6, 1945, Exhibit from the investigating files of Whitaker.
136 Inspector's exhibit. Cf. the photo in Mollo, Dachau, p. 13, ibid. also a photo of the recovery of the corpse of an SS-man from the canal. The photographer Lee Miller took a picture of a corpse of a SS-man floating in the canal; Lee Miller's War, p. 184.
137 Whitaker, Interrogation report 742.
138 The Work of the ICRC, p. 123, Smith, Dachau, p. 259.
139 Cf. Wolfgang Benz, Between Liberation and the Return Home. The Dachau International Prisoner's Committee and the Administration of the Camp in May and June 1945, this volume pp. 41–65.

and who got the name "Heinrich Skodzensky" from later authors? He is alleged to have been ordered by an American major onto his jeep and taken away after he had tried to deliver an explanation. His corpse is supposed to have been found with a shot in the head in a distance of five hundred meters. But, the O'Leary biographer Brome, in certain details not quite precise, says that the SS-lieutenant had awaited the arrival of the Americans at or near the camp.[140] Heinrich Wicker's fate is in any case considered as unexplained by the "German Competent Authority" (Dienststelle) responsible for ascertaining the civil status of people until today. His family received the last sign of life from him in January 1945 from the infirmary in Dachau.[141]

It is certain, however, that, shocked by the confrontation with the conditions in the camp, further excesses were committed by American soldiers. "They could not understand that we were in such good mood," reported the former Dutch prisoner Carel Steensma about the Americans. He observed how they came out of the barracks white as a sheet, and how some had to vomit. Steensma also witnessed the shooting of a young SS-man. It is not clear if this incident took place at the guard tower B or if it dealt with another occurrence. Steensma saw how five or six young SS-men came out of the tower. "I talked with one of them, he was 17, inducted only a few weeks ago, he showed me his pay-book. While I talked to him, an American soldier shot him, his blood splattered on me. I was besides myself. I yelled at the American 'How dare you, you fucking son of a bitch'. I thought of the mother of this youth. What had he done? Nothing. 14 days in uniform and sent onto the tower."[142]

Buechner mentions in his book a testimony of the military chaplain Leland L. Loy in which he describes how a soldier of the 42nd Division, who had completely lost control of himself, shot a German just taken prisoner from closest range.[143]

Prisoners also committed acts of revenge on SS-men, Kapos, or prisoners who had collaborated with the SS. The Polish prisoner Walenty L. told Whitaker that after the shootings at the guard tower B, four fleeing SS-men had been stopped and killed by prisoners.[144] According to estimates of the 42nd Division, at least 25, perhaps up to 50 SS-men were killed by

140 Brome, Histoire, p. 237.

141 Information from the Deutsche Dienststelle, Berlin, May 13, 1997.

142 Holzhaider, Hans, Und am Ende war das Leben. Konzentrationslager Dachau, Häftling Nr. 103050: Die Geschichte eine befreiten Holländers, in: Süddeutsche Zeitung Nr. 99, April 29–May 1, 1995, p. 3.

143 Buechner, Avenger, p. 75.

144 Whitaker, Interrogation protocol 402. Cf. ibid. 108. It is not clear if this deals with the same incident.

prisoners during the first 24 hours of the liberation.[145] Individual reprisals took yet place several days after the liberation. Thus a carbine was snatched from a soldier of the L-Company of the 157th Infantry Regiment, who was assigned to guard duty on May 2nd, by prisoners, supposedly Russians. These killed two persons, who were accused of being SS-men, with it.[146] And Marcus J. Smith, a military physician, observed the next day how prisoners hit SS-collaborators for hours in the presence of American soldiers.[147] American newspapers treated acts of revenge by prisoners briefly and altogether sympathetically.[148]

## Conclusions

"Stories about Dachau are so varied that no one will ever know exactly what happened on the day of liberation," so writes Howard A.Buechner.[149] It would be certainly presumptuous to intend to maintain the opposite. The reconstruction of a historical event can always be only an approximation of the authenticity, but especially when one deals with quickly moving events that take place on a spacious and vast terrain, with a great number of people participating, as was the case here. This, however, is no justification for inaccuracy or arbitrariness. On the contrary: There are different degrees of completeness and precision of personal recollection as well as of the historical representation. Buechner dealt both with his personal recollections and his historical sources carelessly, for whatever motives. In his book, the capture of Dachau camp by the Americans appears only as a great massacre that not a single SSman survived. This version is untrue. Admittedly, there was the disposition among the GI's not to take prisoners. Lieutenant M. of the 157th Infantry Regiment testified to this among others, who at the same time made it clear: "However, we did take prisoners."[150]

The numbers mentioned in Buechner are incorrect; his description regarding the course of events is in large parts distorted and confused. A systematic execution of SS-prisoners in connection with the liberation of the camp, as described by Buechner, did not take place.

145 Henke, Amerikanische Besetzung, p. 927. Kupfer-Koberwitz, however, reports only two acts of lynching of a Capo and a room elder (Stubenältester), and generally states: "Excesses hardly occurred [...]", Kupfer-Koberwitz, Dachauer Tagebücher, p. 448.
146 Whitaker, Intertogation protocol 35–38, 749–779.
147 Smith, Dachau, pp. 132 ff.
148 Weiß, Internationale Öffentlichkeit, p. 24, 28 and 31.
149 Buechner, Avenger, p. 95.
150 Whitaker, Interrogation protocol 884; according to Marcuse, Nazi crimes, p. 90, about 160 persons were taken prisoner.

Yet it is a fact that, as a result of the shock among the liberators by their encounter with the train full of corpses at the entrance of the SS-domain and the conditions in the concentration camp, American soldiers shot SS-men taken prisoner. Four SS-men were shot by the commanding officer of the I-Company of the 157th Infantry Regiment together with a private at the train. In the coal yard, 16 German prisoners were also shot at the initiative of the commanding officer of the company; one was killed by prisoners working in the power station, most likely with the acquiescence of the present Americans. During the seizure of the concentration camp, the entire company of guard tower B, comprising 17 men, was killed in two evidently successive actions, shortly apart, after they had surrendered. A group of prisoners who had climbed over the camp fence participated in this action in a way that cannot be precisely ascertained. Another SS-man was shot by an GI in the area of the Jourhaus, according to the testimony of the Chaplain Loy. The number of SSmen, confirmed to some extent, who were killed by Americans contrary to international law during the liberation of the concentration camp amounts, therefore, to 39. Possibly the 17-year old recruit, whose killing is reported by Carel Steensma, is to be added. He could have, however, been included among the guard tower B company. The question of whether the shot SS-lieutenant, about whom Pat O'Leary reports, is the Untersturmführer Heinrich Wicker cannot be definitely clarified. It is possible that additional shootings of captured SS-men took place, however there are no clues to an especially high number of unrecorded cases; thus the total number could hardly have been greater than 50.

Though there were considerations among officers on the spot to cover up the events by removal of the corpses,[151] it evidently did not happen. This is demonstrated by the testimony of Johann Steinbock about the dead at the guard tower B, and from the concurrence of various testimonies, and Whitaker's findings regarding the coal yard on May 2nd.

It is to be recorded that the killings by US-soldiers involved excesses of individuals of small groups that did not result from orders of superiors. The shootings at the coal yard were stopped by Col. Sparks. Already on May 2nd, an official inquiry of the events in Dachau was initiated by the Inspector General of the Seventh Army and his deputy, respectively. On June 8th, Whitaker's report, derived from extensive and thorough investigations, was on hand. The Assistant Inspector General recommended the court martial proceedings for murder against the commanding officer of I-Company, Lieutenant Bushyhead, the Private P. on account of the shootings at the railroad train and in the coal yard and against Sergeant W. because of the

---

151 Henke, Amerikanische Besetzung, p. 920 ff.

shooting of the guard detail of guard tower B. He recommended proceedings against Lieutenant D., who had ordered the placement of the machine gun in the coal yard, without participation in the subsequent events, and, for dereliction of duty, against military doctor Howard Buechner, who failed to provide medical help for the wounded he discovered there. The superior of the soldier, with whose gun prisoners shot two alleged SS-men, was to be reprimanded for failure to initiate an official inquiry.[152] A comment of the Headquarters of the Seventh Army under General Alexander Patch indicates, however, that higher echelons were striving to play down the charges. Only the conclusions about the shootings directly at the train were approved. The events in the coal yard and at the guard tower B were interpreted as the prevention of an attempted escape of the prisoners or as a combat action, respectively, i.e. the general accepted the interpretations of the principal accused. The head of the investigation was criticized for having conducted a biased inquiry, and that he lacked comprehension of small unit combat action and of the unbalancing effects of the horrors and shock of Dachau on combat troops already fatigued with more than 30 days continuous combat action.

A new investigation was recommended in the statement.[153] It is evidently false, as presented by Buechner,[154] that General Patton, the Military Governor of Bavaria, had personally burned the records of the investigation. The available documents are, however, derived exclusively from departments of the Seventh Army. Buechner possibly mixes up the investigation of the shootings with proceedings that General Linden tried to initiate against Sparks regarding their clash at the camp gate.[155] That Whitaker did not raise any accusations against Sparks supports this assumption. However, it is a fact that no American proceedings regarding the killings in Dachau ever took place.[156]

The shootings of prisoners during the capture of the Dachau camp undoubtedly cast a shadow on the US-Army. These deeds did nothing to contribute to the liberation of the concentration camp. They violated inter-

152 Report Whitaker from Jun. 8, 1945.
153 Headquarters Seventh Army, Memorandum from June 18, 1945. Investigation material.
154 Buechner, Avenger, p. 119.
155 Cf. Spark's own description in Buechner, Avenger, p. 67 ff. and Carlo D'Este, A Genius for War. A Life of General George S. Patton, London 1945, p. 741 ff. Here there is only a general reference of proceedings against Sparks and some of his soldiers, that was oppressed by Patton in recognition of Spark's soldierly qualities. The disputes between Sparks and General Linden are given as background, the shootings are not mentioned.
156 Henke, Amerikanische Besetzung, p. 925, Fn. 762.

national norms and just as well American laws.[157] The officers and soldiers who participated in the shootings forgot themselves and acted as judges and avengers. Overwhelmed by the sudden confrontation with a hitherto unimaginable horror, they saw the SS-uniform as proof of guilt.

A special tragedy of the event — and simultaneously a sad lesson about the inappropriateness of self-administered justice — is due to the fact that the camp-SS had left already when the Americans arrived and had been replaced by other units. These also would probably have left, had not the delegate of the Red Cross, Maurer, persuaded the acting camp commandant Wicker to remain.

The reactions of the prisoners, as well of the Americans, to the shootings were quite disparate. Only a minority of both groups allowed their lust for revenge to provoke them to violence. Many observers were shocked and depressed by the events. Lieutenant D., one of the witnesses interrogated by Whitaker, expressed it thus: "You would not have to come here to do that. That is not the American way of fighting."[158]

---

157 Contrariwise, the Third Reich issued orders for the systematic killings of prisoners of war when the Soviet Union was attacked. One of the execution sites was the SS-shooting range of the Dachau Garrison in the vicinity of Hebertshausen, where about 4000 Soviet prisoners of war were shot. Cf. also Reinhard Otto: "Vernichten oder Ausnutzen?" Aussonderung und Arbeitseinsatz sowjetischer Kriegsgefangener im Reichsgebiet in den Jahren 1941/42. Diss. phil., Paderborn 1996.
158 Whitaker, Interrogation protocol 299.

Florian Freund

# The Mauthausen Trial

## About the American Military Trial in Dachau in the Spring of 1946

*Introduction*

Although research about the complexity of KZ Mauthausen/Gusen depended significantly on the files of the Allied, German and Austrian courts during the last years, the trials themselves were, until now, never a research subject.[1] This, in general, may be due to the meager research into the history of Concentration Camp Mauthausen/Gusen, which then indicated a need to reconstruct the history of the Camp system that would not only encompass the dual camp Mauthausen/Gusen, but also its 40 sub-camps. The trials had been held in Germany and in Austria and records for research are no longer easily accessible. Also it is no longer possible through the court proceedings to give an overview about all the criminal matters that took place in Mauthausen/Gusen.[2] In what follows I limit myself to the most important aspects of the trial that was held in Dachau by the American Military Court known as "USA versus Altfuldisch et. al.",[3] which went under the name of "The Mauthausen Concentration Camp Case" or as "Parent-Mauthausen-Case" and was given file number "Case No.000.50.5".[4] This trial took place in

1 Florian Freund, About the condition of the research on the sub-Camps of Mauthausen, in: Nouvelles recherches sur l'univers concentrationnaire et d'extermination Nazi (Textes reunis et publies sous la direction de Jacques Bariety). Revue d'Allemagne et des pays de langue allemande, tome 17, numero 2, Avril–Juin 1995, pp. 275–282; Bertrand Perz, Das Konzentrationslager Mauthausen in der historischen Forschung, in: Nouvelles recherches sur l'univers concentrationnaire et d'extermination Nazi (= Textes reunis et publies sous la direction de Jacques Bariety). Revue d'Allemagne pays de langue allemande, tome 27, numero 2, Avril–Juin 1995, pp. 265–274.

2 This article was made possible through a Melzer-Fellowship at the U.S. Holocaust Memorial Museum during the summer of 1997.

3 Hans Altfuldisch had been the 2nd Commander of the Protective Detention Camp and was the first accused based on alphabetical order.

4 The files of the Mauthausen-Main-Case as well as the other trials are in the National archives in Washington, NARA RG 338.

Dachau from 29 March until 31 May 1946 before the American "General Military Government Court" with 61 men before it who had been accused of war crimes. What did the American troops find when they liberated such camps? Captain Timothy C. Brennan, Commanding Officer of one such unit which, on 6 May 1945, liberated sub-Camp Ebensee, the last one of the National-Socialistic concentration camps, wrote:[5] "When I arrived at the camp, there were 400 bodies in the crematory waiting to be burned and more in the barracks that had not been collected. Insofar as the inmates were concerned, most of them were animals. They had been treated as animals for so long that they became animals. They would fight like dogs over a piece of bread and would readily kill for a few potato peelings."[6]

Neither Captain Brennan nor the troops of the Allies were prepared for the scope of the crimes they found. Since its establishment in 1938 until 1940 and until the liberation of dual camp Mauthausen/Gusen, which was located in the vicinity of Linz in Upper Austria, a destruction camp with a quarry had developed into a complex net of deadly camps to force tens of thousands of prisoners into forced labor.[7] The establishment of the destruction camp in the "occupied territories," dual camp Mauthausen/Gusen held a special place among concentration camps: It would be the "Killing camp" of the Third *Reich*. The death rate of the prisoners in Mauthausen/Gusen, until the end of 1942, was the highest among all concentration camps of the German Reich. At the beginning of 1940 8,200 prisoners were incarcerated in Mauthausen/Gusen. During that year 8,114 prisoners died but at the end of that year the number of prisoners had increased to 15,900 because of ever newly arriving transports.[8]

The function of Mauthausen/Gusen as a "Killing camp" was officially established at the start of 1941 in that it would be the only camp in the "camp stage II" so listed; it would be the type of camp set aside for the so-called "most difficult, incorrigible" prisoners who should not have any chance at all of surviving.[9] Concentration Camp Mauthausen/Gusen, because of its function within the Concentration Camp System during the years 1940/41, can be looked upon as the forerunner of the destruction camps; it established the "division of labor-professionally and assembly line destruc-

---

5    About the history of KZ Ebensee read: Florian Freund, "Arbeitslager Zement". Das Konzentrationslager Ebensee und die Raketenrüstung, Wien 1989.

6    Translation from a copy of a letter from Timothy Brennan to his wife on 15 May 1945. Owned by author.

7    About the history of Mauthausen see: Hans Marsalek, Die Geschichte des Konzentrationslagers Mauthausen. Dokumentation, Wien/Linz 31995.

8    See Marsalek, Mauthausen, pp. 109 ff., 145 ff.

9    Decree by the head of Sipo and the SD of 1. 1. 1941 IMT PS 1063, reprinted in: Marsalek, Mauthausen, p. 33.

tion".[10] After most of the smaller sub-camps had been evacuated by the SS and the large number of left over prisoners had been placed in the overcrowded camps that would be liberated by the American troops it became obvious to the prisoners of Mauthausen/Gusen and its sub-camps, that those responsible for all this should be punished. The built-up rage and aggression expressed itself next in spontaneous lynch-actions against especially brutal Kapos and other hated prisoner functionaries. Such acts of revenge were most prevalent in Ebensee and Gusen, where over 50 people were killed by raging ex-prisoners.[11] That need to punish expressed itself also in the first attempts to secure evidentiary documents.

For example a few days before the liberation, and under great risks to their lives, the prisoners hid the Death Books of Mauthausen and Ebensee.[12] The guards knew that they had committed crimes and tried to destroy as much evidence as possible and kill as many as possible of the witnesses as long as they were still in control of the camps. The Allies had also given a warning to all guard units which basically dealt with prisoners-of-war. In leaflets thrown from airplanes the Allies threatened all "Commanders and Guard Units," "as well as [...] members of the Gestapo and all such other persons, independent of the character of their service and their rank in whose power prisoners-of-war of the Allies had been entrusted"[13]: "The three governments declare that all those persons will be held responsible for the safety and well being of the prisoners-of-war of the Allies in whose power they were entrusted [...]. Every person who arbitrarily treated prisoners-of-war of the Allies badly and is found guilty of this or who permits such bad treatment, whether it is during the fighting, or during transportation to the rear, in camp, in military hospital, in prison or any other such place, will be unsparingly hunted down and punished. The three governments want you to take notice of the following: this responsibility is unconditional and deals with all circumstances; nobody will be able to avoid this by trying to shove this responsibility onto other authorities or persons."[14]

10  See Florian Freund, Technisierung des Tötens: Mauthausen im historischen Kontext, in: Rudolf G. Ardelt/Christian Gerbel (Hrsg.), Österreichischer Zeitgeschichtetag 1995. Österreich — 50 Jahre Zweite Republik, 22.–24. Mai 1995 in Linz, Innsbruck/Wien 1996, pp. 209–213.

11  See Marsalek, Mauthausen, p. 38; Freund, Arbeitslager Zement, p. 420.

12  Engineer Hans Martin hid the death books of the garrison doctor of Mauthausen and later turned them over to the Americans. Marsalek, Mauthausen, p. 330. In Ebensee Drahomir Barta, with the help of other prisoners, hid the death books of the camp. Freund, Arbeitslager Zement, p. 418.

13  Leaflet, thrown out over Ebensee on 23. 4. 45, Private archive of Drahomir Barta, Prague. Reprinted in: Florian Freund, Arbeitslager Zement, p. 405; Hans Marsalek, Mauthausen, p. 327.

14  Ibid.

By the end of the war the Allies had not yet developed a single approach as to how they were going to prosecute which crimes and by what statute. Also the structure of a judicial investigation and prosecution apparatus had not been created.[15] Though by the end of 1943 there already existed the "United Nations War Crimes Commission," and since the middle of 1944 there also existed the first investigatory authorities within the common British-American Headquarters, a "Court of Inquiry" and furthermore there existed a "War Crimes Branch" at the "Judge Advocate European Theater of Operations United States Army".[16]

This group, as well as a series of other units, investigated, first of all, any crimes against Allied troops. Only in December 1944 did they establish the area of responsibilities that described all war crimes and was independent of the nationality of the victim.[17] In order to be most efficient in the executions of the investigations they ordered the establishment of 19 "War Crimes Investigating Teams" whose actual activities were really implemented after the end of the war. About ten days after the liberation of the camps there were already "War Crimes Investigating Teams" in Mauthausen, Gusen, Steyr, and Ebensee. There were numerous recorded statements by surviving prisoners which established the basis for future investigations and the later accusations in the Dachauer Mauthausen Trials.[18] The liberated prisoners gave the Team the most important documents they possessed: the secured Death Books. They also confiscated a whole series of other original documents.[19] Presumably a French Commission arrived in Ebensee a few days after the liberation and began their own investigative work.[20]

The 11th Armored Division of the 3rd US Army liberated Jack H. Taylor from Mauthausen. He had been an American secret agent who, through his report about conditions in Mauthausen, and supplementing the recorded statements of surviving prisoners, added considerably to the information about criminal activities in Mauthausen/Gusen.[21]

15  The nearest to it is by: Robert Sigel, Im Interesse der Gerechtigkeit. Die Dachauer Kriegsverbrecherprozesse 1945–1948, Frankfurt a. M./New York 1992, pp. 16 ff.
16  See ibid., pp. 15 ff.
17  Ibid., pp. 17 f.
18  See Organization Order No. 270, 24. 4. 1945, National Archives Record Administration (NARA) RG 338, Records of U.S. Army Europe (USAREUR), War Crimes Branch, War Crimes Files ("Cases not Tried"), 1945–1959, Box 534, Case 000-50-69.
19  See Marsalek, Mauthausen, p. 330; Freund, Arbeitslager Zement, p. 435. "War Crime Investigating Team 6827" was active in Ebensee.
20  Letter from Drahomir Barta to Hermann Langbein, dated 10. 12. 1979, see: Freund, Arbeitslager Zement, p. 435.
21  Florian Freund/Bertrand Perz/Karl Stuhlpfarrer, Einleitung zur Dokomentation: Der Bericht des US-Geheimagenten Jack H. Taylor über das Konzentrationslager Mauthausen, in: Zeitgeschichte 22 (1995), Volume 9/10, pp. 318–341.

The interest shown by the Allies in the information they had received stimulated many of the prisoners to cooperate with them fully to insure that the culprits would receive just punishment. Typical of that sort of thing was the letter by Simon Wiesenthal which he sent on May 25th, 1945, to the Commander of the Mauthausen Camp, Richard R. Seibe, and which in his case became the start of a life-long involvement in finding Nazi criminals: "I spent many years in thirteen concentration camps, including Mauthausen. I was liberated from it on May 5th, 1945, by American armed forces and as of this moment I am still here. I would very much like to assist the American Authorities in their efforts to make the Nazi criminals be held responsible for their actions and because of that I make the following statement: ... In as much as all members of my family and my other close relatives were murdered by the Nazi criminals I would like to make myself available to the American Authorities who have been given the assignment to investigate Nazi criminality. Although I am a Polish citizen I do have the feeling that the crimes of these men is so monstrous that no efforts should be shunned to arrest them".[22]

Wiesenthal, as well as numerous other surviving prisoners, worked intensively together with the Allied persecution authorities on these cases to make it possible that these war criminals would receive just punishments.

The principle of punishment for war crimes — criminal acts in concentration camps were clearly in that category[23] — was very clear to the Allies, the procedural instructions for the Americen court proceedings had already been released in different directives during the summer and fall of 1945 and on 30.11.1945 had been assembled into "Military Government Regulations". These procedures were also to be implemented in the Mauthausen Concentration Camp Case[24] and anticipated establishment of "General Military Government Courts" in which these trials were to be heard. These courts were to consist of not fewer than five American officers of whom the highest ranking officer was to be the presiding officer.[25] In cases where the Court was required to impose the death sentence it had to do so with a two-thirds vote; otherwise a simple majority of the officers would be sufficient.

---

22  Copy of letter from Simon Wiesenthal to U.S. Camp Commander, Camp Mauthausen, dated 25. 5. 1945, NARA RG 388, ("Cases not tried"), Box 534, Case 000-50-69. On some of the attached lists Wiesenthal names 91 suspected SS-men and gives solid, but brief, information about their criminal activities in Galicia and KZ Plaszow.

23  Holger Lessing, Der erste Dachauer Prozess (1945/46), Baden-Baden 1993, pp. 53ff.

24  Ibid., p. 66; also look at: Sigel, Im Interesse der Gerechtigkeit, pp. 28 ff., 35; Lessing, Der erste Dachauer Prozess, p. 70.

25  Lessing, Der erste Dachauer Prozess, pp. 67 f.

The right to a defense was safeguarded in that the accused was allowed to select his own defense counsel provided that the court had not excluded him. In a case where the death penalty was being demanded, and if the accused had not availed himself of his own defense counsel the court was obligated to appoint an officer of the Allied Forces as his defense counsel.[26]

The crimes would be charged as violations of international rights and as a charge against the "Common Design," and also of the common cause.[27] The sharing in a main proceeding and the supporting subsequent trials would make it possible to proceed against hundreds of suspects. The case "USA vs. Weiss et al.," the first Dachauer trial (against the offenders of Concentration Camp Dachau), which had already gotten started on 15. 11. 1945, was looked upon as the model trial for judicially correct actions to be carried out in subsequent trials on mass criminal activities in Concentration Camps Buchenwald, Flossenburg, Mauthausen, Nordhausen and Muhldorf. The establishment of the main proceedings would serve as the format for the proceedings yet to follow.[28]

In the cases of the trials against the offenders of Concentration Camp Mauthausen they first had to have a model trial — the parent Mauthausen Concentration Camp Case — from which proceedings the other trials about the criminal activities in Concentration Camp Mauthausen/Gusen could make use.

## The Accused

In the Mauthausen Concentration Camp Case 61 men had been accused among whom were 42 Germans and 12 Austrians, three from Czechoslovakia, two from Yugoslavia, one Rumanian and one Hungarian. 55 of them had been members of the Waffen-SS,some of whom had already been turned over to the SS by the German Army between 1944 and 1945.[29] Two of the accused had been civilians, three others had been former prisoners. At their sentencing their average age was 38.4 years.

The most prominent one of the accused certainly was the former area leader of the Upper Danube, August Eigruber, who on 29 March 1938, a few days after the "Anschluss" of Austria, in a speech in Gmunden had proudly

26  Ibid., p. 70; Sigel, Im Interesse der Gerechtigkeit, p. 35.
27  Ibid., p. 29.
28  Ibid.
29  The nearest to it is by: Bertrand Perz, Wehrmacht und KZ-Bewachung, in: Mittelweg 36, Zeitschrift des Hamburger Instituts für Sozialforschung, 4 (1995), pp. 69–82; ders., Wehrmachtsangehörige als KZ-Bewacher, in: Walter Manoschek (Hrsg.), Die Wehrmacht im Rassenkrieg. Vernichtungskrieg hinter der Front, Wien 1996, pp. 168–181.

proclaimed: "We, Upper Austrians, will be receiving another special recognition for our accomplishments during the time of the struggle. [...] We will be getting a concentration camp to house the people's traitors from all over Austria."[30] Camp Commander Franz Ziereis was not one of the accused because he had died on May 25th, 1945, during an escape attempt when he was fatally wounded.[31] However, Hans Altfuldisch was one of the accused who had been one of the camp commanders whose last command, towards the end of the war, had been as Second Camp Commander of Mauthausen. Julius Ludolf was the only Camp Commander of the 40 sub-camps of Mauthausen/Gusen who had been accused because he had been the Camp Commander of the Concentration Camps Loibl-Pass, Gross-Raming and Melk.[32] Another six of the accused had belonged to the commanders staff of Mauthausen. Succeeding each other as adjutants to Camp Commander Ziereis were Viktor Zoller and Adolf Zutter.[33] At times Josef Medermeyer had been one of the Roll Call Chiefs in Mauthausen and had also served as the Detail Chief of Arrests within the Camp ("Bunker").[34] Josef Rieger and Andreas Trumm had also been Roll Call Chiefs and towards the end had also been Chiefs of the Worker Readiness Unit. Karl Struller had held a leading function in the administrative office of the Commanders' Headquarters. Others who can be listed as part of the administration were Heinrich Eisenhofer who had been in charge of the prisoners' personal belongings division,[35] Hans Hebenscheid who had been in charge of the kitchen supply facilities and Willy Eckert, Head of the Laundry.[36] Otto Striegel, who held the rank of Sergeant-Major, was in charge of the kitchen and the store room in Concentration Camp Melk.[37]

30  Bollwerk Salzkammergut, Volkischer Beobachter, Wiener Ausgabe, 29. 3. 1938, in: "Anschluss" 1938. Eine Dokumentation, ed. by Dokumentationsarchiv des österreichischen Widerstandes, Wien 1988, p. 514.

31  See Marsalek, Mauthausen, p. 185.

32  About the activities of Ludolf in KZ Melk see: Bertrand Perz, Projekt Quarz. Steyr-Daimler-Puch und das Konzentrationslager Melk, Wien 1990.

33  See Marsalek, Mauthausen, p. 185.

34  See ibid., p. 288.

35  In the files he is often also listed as Hans Eisenhofer. See Deputy Judge Advocate's Office, 7708 War Crimes Group, Headquarters European Command, United States vs. Hans AltPuldisch et al., Case No. 000.50.5. Reviews and Recommendations ofthe Deputy Judge Advocate for War Crimes, o. O., 30. April 1947, p. 26. (Henceforth cited as "Reviews and Recommendations"). In Marsalek's work Eisenhofer has the first name of Franz. Marsalek, Mauthausen, p. 186.

36  Head of the Administration was SS-Captain Xaver Strauss, had been sentenced to life imprisonment in a successive Dachauer Mauthausen Trial but soon thereafter was pardoned and released from prison. See Marsalek, Mauthausen, p. 186. 37 Perz, Projekt Quarz, p. 328.

37  Ibid., p. 328.

Four of the accused, Hans Diehl, Werner Grahn, Josef Leeb and Wilhelm Muller, held subordinate positions in the "political division" which was part of the formal GESTAPO and was much feared by the prisoners. This division dealt with all personal matters of all prisoners and also looked into state and criminal charges and performed interrogations.[38]

There were another six accused who had been very important to the survival of the prisoners especially as it related to the importance of the medical sector:[39] Dr. Eduard Krebsbach, garrison doctor of Mauthausen from July 1941 until August 1943, Dr. Waldemar Wolter, also garrison doctor from August 1944 until May 1945; Dr. Friedrich Entress, Camp doctor from October 1943 until July 1944; dentists Dr. Wilhelm Henkel and Dr. Walter Hohler and druggist of Concentration Camp Mauthausen Master Erich Wasicky; the camp doctor of Concentration Camp Ebensee, Dr. Willi Jobst, and the subordinate first-aid man Gustav Kreindl.[40]

Eight of the accused had held positions of Block leaders or Work Detail leaders in Concentration Camps Mauthausen/Gusen, Steyr, Gunskirchen, Hinterbruhl, Ebensee, Linz and Melk. They were: Heinrich Haeger, Franz Huber, Panl Kaiser, Hermann Pribill, Hans Spatzenegger, Erich Miesner, Emil Muller, and Rudolf Mynzak.

Except for Eigruber all the others mentioned above often had direct contact with the prisoners because of their functions in Concentration Camp Mauthausen/Gusen and the sub-camps, even within the "Protective Detention Camp" of the actual detention area. The outside area of the camp was guarded by "Guard Units" who were not allowed to enter the "Protective Detention Camp" and because of that had basically far less direct contact with prisoners. Even so there were 19 guards among the accused who had served in Mauthausen, Eisenerz, Red-Zipf, Gusen, Linz, Modling, Ebensee, Wiener Neudorf, Steyr and Loibl-Pass.[41] The guard units were commanded by Company Chiefs and of those August Blei was one of the accused.

Among the accused there were also four employees of the "German Earth and Stoneworks GmbH" (DEST), a company that was owned by the

---

38  Head of the political division was SS-Captain Karl Schulz(e), was sentenced in 1967 in the BRD to 15 years of imprisonment. At the end of the war the political division consisted of 31 SS-members, 12 of them had been born of women from that area around Mauthausen and their sons had been raised there; Marsalek, Mauthausen, p. 186.

39  See ibid., pp. 173 ff.; Freund, Arbeitslager Zement, pp. 293ff.

40  Nearest to Jobst and Kreindl look at: ibid., pp. 295 ff.

41  These were the ones: Stefan Barczay, Karl Billmann, Willy Brunning, Michael Cserny, Ludwig Dorr, Heinrich Fitschok, Heinrich Giese, Herbert Grzybowski, Paul Gutzlaff, Franz Kautny, Kurt Keilwitz, Kasper Klimowitsch, Viktor Korger, Ferdinand Lappert, Wilhelm Mack, Josef Mayer, Theophil Priebel, Adolf Rutka, Thomas Sigmund.

SS and which was responsible for the stone quarries in Mauthausen and Gusen. One of them, Leopold Trauner, had remained a civilian during the whole time of the war while the others, Johannes Grimm, Anton Kaufmann and Otto Drabek, had been employees of the DEST since 1941 and had performed their duties in the uniform of the SS with an appropriate rank since 1942. Among the accused of the Parent Mauthausen Concentration Camp Case were also three prisoner functionaries: Willi Frey, who had been a Senior Block Prisoner, Kapo, and firefighter in Mauthausen, Rudolf Fiegl, Disinfection and Stone Quarry Kapo in Gusen, and Sick Bay Kapo of Hinterbruhl, Georg Gossl.

Vinzenz Nohel, the only one of the accused to fall completely outside of the framework in some respects, was listed in the American files as "Fireman at Castle Hartheim". Evidently he was the only one the American investigators were able to apprehend with whom they were able to draw a direct connection from Concentration Camp Mauthausen/Gusen to the "Euthanasia" institution Hartheim.

Inasmuch as the American Authorities, at the time of the preferring of charges, already had arrested many suspects of the criminal enterprise Mauthausen/Gusen one must ask the question by what criteria the accused had been selected for the first Mauthausen proceeding. It is clear from the above mentioned list of the accused that the prosecuting authorities tried to establish, as well as possible, a complete picture in order to clearly understand what had taken place in the camp system of Mauthausen/Gusen by accusing suspects of each and every command structure of all the known sub-camps.

In fact the 61 accused are only a small number of the larger number of suspects. At least 350 to 400 people worked in the headquarters of Concentration Camp Mauthausen/Gusen or as camp commander of one of the sub-camps. All-in-all about 50 SS-doctors worked inside the Mauthausen/Gusen facility. Their behavior vis-a-vis the prisoners had varied considerably.[42] In February 1942 there were a total of 1,270 guards whose number increased to 9,800 by March 1945 and this growth corresponded to the number of prisoners; to this number the 66 SS-female wardens should be added.[43] Hundreds of Block Senior Prisoners or Kapos who had been selected by the SS from among the ranks of the prisoners so that they could rule over the prisoners, lived to see the liberation. Many of them had

---

42  Look also at: Marsalek, Mauthausen, pp. 173 ff.; Freund, Arbeitslager Zement, pp. 293 ff.

43  Copy of a letter dated 12. 2. 1940 to Camp Commander of Concentration Camp Mauthausen, Archiv des Museum Mauthausen (AMM) P 6/9; Marsalek, Mauthausen, pp. 183 f.

committed crimes while in those positions. An unknown number among the thousands of civilians had direct daily contacts with prisoners on the work site. Their behavior, as reported by surviving prisoners, was often not much different than that of the SS; however, some of them had shown their sympathy and solidarity with the prosoners.[44]


## The Accusation

The charge of particulars was used as the standard for all the accused and was based on "Violation of the Laws and Usages of War". This same standard was also used for all the accused but emphasized their individual particulars: "Hans Altfuldisch (then followed the names of the other 60 accused), German citizen, or persons, who together with other German citizens had a common plan to kill people, beat them, torture them, starve them, abuse them and humiliate them. This happened within or near Concentration Camp Mauthausen, the Castle of Hartheim, within or near the sub-camps of Mauthausen, which were Ebensee, Gross-Ramig, Gunskirchen, Gusen, Hinterbruhl, Lambach, Linz, Loiblpass, Melk, Schwechat, St. Georgen, St. Lambert, St. Valentine, Steyr, Vienna, Wiener-Neudorf. All of these camps were located in Austria at different points in time between January 1st, 1942, and May 15th, 1945. Of their own free will they cooperated illegally and voluntarily, helped, encouraged and fostered success in the oppression of Poles, Frenchmen, Greeks, Yugoslavians, citizens of the Soviet Union, Norwegians, Danes, Belgians, citizens of The Netherlands, citizens of the Great Duchy of Luxembourg, Turks, citizens of Great Britain, people without citizenship, Czechoslovakians, Chinese, citizens of the United States of America and German criminal or 'political' elements. The oppressed ones had been taken from their homes and incarcerated by the German Reich and among them were members of the armed forces of those nations who had found themselves at war with the then German Reich. At that time they had served their countries as soldiers and then become disarmed prisoners-of-war under the care of the former German Reich. They were killed, were beaten, were tortured, were starved, were abused and were humiliated. The exact number and names of these people is unknown but they run well into the thousands."[45]

The accusation of having committed crimes "in pursuance of a common design," and also "in persecuting a common project" and to have participated

44   See Freund, Arbeitslager Zement, p. 260 ff.; Perz, Projekt Quarz, pp. 393 ff.
45   Charge Sheet, 7. 3. 1946, NARA RG 338, Records of U.S. Army Commands, 1942, Records of Headquarters, US Army Europe (USAREUR), War Crimes Branch, War Crimes Case Files ("Cases Tried"), 1945–1959, Box 334.

in it, would make it possible to judge those criminals in absentia which, because of the nature of the crimes it was difficult to ascribe each individual to a particular crime. Most of the witnesses and the evidence had been destroyed by the suspects themselves. Through the construction of the "Common Design" approach the accusers wanted to make it clear that "it was not just the singular acts of individual concentration camp henchmens' criminal activities but the establishment of the concentration camp system was itself a criminal enterprise".[46] The concept "Common Design" was defined "as the agreement of two or more persons to commit an unlawful act"[47] and does not mean to conspire to an act (Conspiracy).

As had already been shown in the "Parent Dachau Concentration Camp Case" the accusers had to show proof that here had been a system that had reigned with absolute power and had violated the laws and customs of war ("Laws and Usages of War") and that the prisoners had been treated as had been described. In addition they had to give proof that each of the accused had a clear understanding that he knew what was to happen to the prisoners and they had to prove, in each and every case, his place within the administration, that he had been involved in those functions within the organization of the camps and through his behavior and activities he had supported them.[48] If an accused had been involved in such criminal acts as was understood from the above he would be considered guilty and his punishment would then depend on the kind of activities he had been involved in and also its intensities. In this connection the Review Authority would emphasize that "the crime charged is the violation of the laws and usages of war and the manner in which it was accomplished was by participation in a common design to perform certain illegal and unlawful acts as an incident of aiding in the Mauthausen Concentration Camp operation".[49]

The chronological reduction of the charge of particulars from January 1942 until May 15th, 1945, (later on this was corrected to read May 5th, 1945) can be understood by the fact that an American Military Court's charge of particulars about the violation of the laws and usages of war could only begin as of the date that the USA had entered the European war. Even so, insofar as it related to the general criminal character of Concentration Camp Mauthausen/Gusen the events prior to 1942 could be discussod before the Court.[50] The nationality of the victim had meaning only in the

---

46  Sigel, Im Interesse der Gerechtigkeit, p. 42.
47  Ibid., p. 43.
48  Ibid., p. 44. See Lessing, Der erste Dachauer Prozess, p. 103 ff.
49  Review and Recommendations, p. 14.
50  About a legal discussion about the timely limitation of the accusations see: Sigel, Im Interesse der Gerechtigkeit, pp. 46 ff.; Lessing, Der erste Dachauer Prozess, p. 86.

sense that criminal acts against Germans could not be taken into account because those acts could not be looked upon as War Crimes.[51]

Through the 154 evidentiary documents that had been presented and through the 200 eyewitness accounts (including the statements of the accused) the charge of particulars was able to paint a very clear picture of the murderous system within Concentration Camp Mauthausen/Gusen. With the help of some precise examples that had occurred between 1942 and 1945, as described by some of the eyewitnesses, the systematic mistreatments of incoming prisoners could be shown.[52] In addition there were catastrophic conditions for the prisoners which dealt with their clothing and housing, facts that the Review Authorities, because of the trial protocols and the evidentiary documents, had combined in the following manner: "The number of inmates of camp Mauthausen increased from 70,000 in September 1944 to 92,000 by the middle of March 1945. In Mauthausen proper there were 25 barracks, each of which contained 70 three-tiered bunks. On April 1st, 1945, there were 400 occupants in each barrack, which later grew to 600. Each bunk had one only blanket.[53] "In 1942 the bodily weakened inmates received about 900 calories each day. In some cases they only received turnips the entire winter. The average worker sometimes received only 1,000 to 1,500 calories per day."[54]

After numerous arbitrary operations in Gusen, medical attempts with diets and hormone preparations were also mentioned. Conditions in the "Russian Camp" in Mauthausen, which served as the hospital in the spring of 1943 and had 9,000 patients crammed within it, were discussed. The trial showed evidence that, in fact, every means of killing had been used in Mauthausen; "For example prisoners were murdered with poisoned gasses, through injections into their hearts, prisoners would be driven into the electrically charged fence, were subjected to genital brutalization, were buried alive and had red-hot pokers driven into their necks."[55]

The system of "Working them to Death" in the stone quarry was also analyzed as was the practice of massive killings by means of injections. The murders in the gas chamber of Mauthausen and in the autos equipped with gassing apparatus that traveled between Mauthausen and Gusen was also a thematic subject. The covering-up of the real causes of death in the death books which had been brought to the court as evidence in the charge of particulars as testified to mostly by Engineer Ernst Martin from Inns-

---

51  See Sigel, Im Interesse der Gerechtigkeit, p. 30.
52  It was thus summarized in General Statement of Evidence. Review and Recommendations, p. 5.
53  Ibid, p. 6.
54  Ibid.
55  Ibid., p. 7.

bruck: the accused Martin gave testimony that on April 23rd, 1945, the death book documents of Mauthausen indicated about 72,000 cases of death having been recorded. In cases where the killings had been done by means of gas or through injections into the heart, the files would list them as death due to illnesses. In some cases there are notes in the files that the victim had been shot "by decree of the authority of military court". The information for these entries was provided by the political division and consisted of such information as "executed by military court order," "hung by order of the Reichsführer," or "shot by order of the SD". In those cases where the prisoner had been shot they listed on the note "shot in trying to escape".[56] The defense unintentionally showed weakness in their approach to the discrepancies between the norms and the measures taken. They relied on the fact that official nutritional standards had existed. The truth was that these standards had existed but had not been adhered to. The defense meant to say that these nutritional standards had not been adhered to only at the end of the war because of transportation problems due to Allied bombings. In fact the bombings had a great effect on the nutrition of the prisoners as their rations sank even lower than their former meager level. In addition, according to the defense, they had made some effort to order accommodations and medicines from Berlin but they had received none. The mistreatment of prisoners was forbidden by the regulations then in existence, the defense argued, and this ban had been on paper since the beginning. Everything, according to the defense, that had taken place in Mauthausen/Gusen had been the responsibility of Ziereis. He had been the only one who had given such orders. In addition Mauthausen had been inspected by Berlin but nothing had been ordered changed regarding the conditions in Mauthausen/Gusen.[57]

Based on the overwhelming evidence about how the Mauthausen/Gusen System functioned the Court noted in a "Special Finding" the following to be the case: "The Court finds that the circumstances, the conditions and the entire composition of Concentration Camp Mauthausen together with the individuals and all its subcamps was of such a criminal scope that each member of the military or of the Civil Service who served there, whether as a member of the Waffen-SS, the general-SS, a guard or civilian were guilty and were responsible for the criminal activities ... The Court has determined that each member of the military or of the Civil Service, or as a guard or civilian employee of Concentration Camp Mauthausen itself or any of its subcamps, either as leader or employee or had been present or who resided within Concentration Camp Mauthausen or in the sub-camps during the

56  Review and Recommendations, p. 9.
57  Look also at the summary, ibid., pp. 10 f.

entire time of the existence of the camps had, without any doubt, known of the criminal acts performed there ... The Court has determined that the irrefutable documentary information about death through shooting, by means of poisoned gasses, by hanging, planned hunger and additional detestable means of killing, through the conscious arrangement and planning by the officials of the 'Reich' in Concentration Camp Mauthausen and its sub-camps or the higher Nazi hierarchy and all those involved who knew about this, even those who had been political, criminal or military prisoners ... Therefore this Court declares: Every serviceman whether of the military or the Civil Service, or member of the Waffen-SS or the general-SS, or guard or civilian employee, who had been active in whatever form possible or who had been stationed there, or who had been active in whatever form of business of Concentration Camp Mauthausen or in one of its sub-camps is guilty and needs to be punished for having participated in criminal acts against well-known laws, customs and the dealings of civilized nations according to the letter and spirit of the tradition of war."[58]

On the basis of the described legal situation the charge of particulars had to make clear in which way, and to what degree, the accused had been involved. August Eigruber was presumably not in the chain of command structure of Concentration Camp Mauthausen,[59] as the defense was trying to point out, except where it pertained to the reduction of rations for sick patients during the fall of 1944 as witnesses had pointed out and for which he was held responsible. For these matters he was the responsible party in that he served in the function of District Leader and, at the same time, was the leader of the nutrition office in Upper Donau District. In his capacity as District Leader he also leased Castle Hartheim to the Reich. A group of witnesses attested that he ordered a number of executions which he attended and had them demonstrate to him some executions that were done on a newly constructed folding gallows. In this testimony the witnesses described Eigruber as a typical giver of orders which, as he himself admitted, had visited Mauthausen about ten or fifteen times but while there had not "dirtied" his hands.

Hans Altfuldisch, who towards the end had been the second Camp Commander of the Protective Custody Camp in Mauthausen, was shown by the aforementioned witnesses to have never beaten any prisoners but had always been present when the murder of certain groups, such as Allied prisoners of war, took place. He frequently joined in the executions although

58  Records of the Trial USA vs. Altfuldisch et al. pp. 3509 f., NARA RG 338, Records of U.S. Army Command, 1942, Records of Headquarters, US Army Europe (USAREUR), War Crimes Branch, War Crimes Case Files ("Cases Tried"), 1945–1959, Box 334 (henceforth cited as "Records").

59  Records, p. 1526. The following is summarized from: Review and Recommendations pp. 18–78 and from the Trial records.

during the firing of bullets into the base of the necks of prisoners he, himself, would not participate but at least be present. Shortly before the liberation Altfuldisch had ordered gassings to take place in the gas chamber of Mauthausen. Altfuldisch, who held the rank of a 1st Lieutenant in the SS and was also the second Protective Custody Leader, thus held a relatively high rank on the basis of his function as Commander. Still, that did not make him shrink from murder, and he did participate in some murders himself.

The accusations against the remaining accused of the Headquarters Staff read in a similar vein. The adjutants of Camp Commander Ziereis, Viktor Zoller and Adolf Zutter, were accused of having ordered executions to take place, to have prisoners arrested inside the camp, have them incarcerated within the "Bunker," ordered the deaths of slow working prisoners, supervised the gassings of prisoners and to have murdered in February, 1945, recaptured, escaped Soviet prisoners of war. The charges against Struller, Trumm, Rieger and Niedermayer were comparable to the others except for function and detail, and in this charge of particulars against them described them as having tortured prisoners until they died.

Julius Ludolf had also been a Camp Commander (his last command had been in Melk) but he, himself, committed excessive torture.[60] He murdered prisoners mostly by beating them to death and he gave the order to murder prisoners by means of injections or hanging. Ludolf had been a 2nd Lieutenant as had Heinrich Eisenhofer. As can be seen from witness statements he had obviously made a career of it all with his demonstrated gruesome acts and had been promoted from Sergeant-Major to 2nd Lieutenant. The witnesses also accused the others of excessive gruesome acts although they were part of the administrative group; they were: SS-men Eckert, Hegenscheid and Striegel who were accused of excessive torture that led to the deaths of prisoners; they participated in firing squad executions and participated in murder in the stone quarry at Wiener Graben, etc.

The accused Block Leaders and Work Detail Leaders, all of whom held the ranks of Sergeant-Majors, Corporals, Senior Lance-Corporals and Junior Sergeants were charged with the usual offenses of mistreatments, beatings and shootings of prisoners and not for the fact that they did not have the power to give orders. Franz Huber and Paul Kaiser were charged with having shot weakened prisoners during the evacuation march from Hinterbrühl to Mauthausen, and on the march from Mauthausen to Gunskirchen. The members of the political division were charged with having tortured prisoners during interrogations and murdering them afterwards and having cooperated in executions. Especially numerous were the many charges against the eight accused who were employed in the medical

60  The nearest to it see: Perz, Projekt Quarz, pp. 230 ff.

area. They spanned from autopsies to deadly iniections into the hearts, to being part of executions, to participation and execution of gassings. Both dentists Walter Hohler and Wilhelm Henkel were basically charged for their role in the removal of gold teeth from already dead or murdered prisoners.

The accusations against the guards resembled the charges that were filed by the witnesses. Nearly all of them were accused of, or acceded to, having shot prisoners while "trying to escape". In addition there were the frequent mistreatments of prisoners that resulted in their deaths. One of the guards, Willy Brunning, was additionally accused of the shootings of bodily weakened prisoners during the evacuation march from Modling to Mauthausen during April 1945. A point in the accusation against the Company Commander August Blei described again a person who did not shrink from giving orders. The charge against co-workers of DEST were similar to the ones that were filed against the Block and Work Detail Leaders. The witnesses described the stereo-typical forms of mistreatments. Also very grave were the statements against the three accused Kapos. They were accused of having assisted in the gassings, the deadly injections and the "beating-to-death" of fellow prisoners.

## The Defense of the Accused

At the start of the Court proceedings all the accused pled not guilty — except Eigruber, who claimed not to understand the charge of particulars.[61] The accused were given the opportunity to give statements on their own behalf. All of them made use of this opportunity except for Altfuldisch, Entress, Krebsbach, Niedermayer, Rieger, Trumm and Spatzenegger.

During the interrogations, shortly after they had been imprisoned, the accused had, without exception, incriminated themselves mutually. However, in their imprisonment they developed a common line of defense: They retracted their confessions and without exception quarreled about what they had stated before and denied every accusation from their fellow accusers. Nearly all of them fell back on the fact that as soldiers they had followed orders. However, this was legally irrelevant because it had been stated at the beginning of this trial that the illegal character of the criminal orders had been understood by every one of them and that these orders were in contradiction to national and international laws.[62]

---

61   Records 2215. The following defense strategy of the accused is summarized from: Review and Recommendations and the Trial Records.
62   See Sigel, Im Interesse der Gerechtigkeit, p. 34; Lessing, Der erste Dachauer Prozess, p. 222. The order by a superior was not a reason for excluding punishment but could be a reason for mitigating circumstances.

Most of the accused claimed to have submitted requests for transfers because they had found the conditions in Concentration Camp Mauthausen to have been unbearable. These first confessions about the criminal conditions in Concentration Camp Mauthausen stood in noticeable contradiction to other statements by these men in which they stated never to have seen any mistreatments or to have heard about murders having taken place. All accused denied having given orders or having been responsible for issuing them. Eigruber stated that he had visited Concentration Camp Mauthausen perhaps ten or fifteen times but he did not have any control over the distribution of food rations nor had he ever given an order to execute someone. His posts as "Gauleiter," "Reichsstatthalter" and "Reichsverteidigungskommissar" had not given him any jurisdiction over Mauthausen. Zoller, the adjutant to Camp Commander Ziereis also lied about ever having given any orders and maintained that no one in his presence had dared to even touch a prisoner as mistreatment of prisoners had been forbidden. Yet Zoller admitted to having known about the gassings and the liquidations of the Soviet commissars; but he maintained that this political decision had been made in Berlin. He, himself, had sat in his office all day long.

Julius Ludolf, Camp Commander of Concentration Camp Melk, maintained that he never fired a single shot during the entire war. He allowed that he had slapped prisoners lightly and had never seen a riding crop in Melk. This was a typical argument because the accused claimed, without exception, that they had never mistreated prisoners but did admit that they had seen mistreatments taking place and had slapped prisoners with an empty hand. A number of the accused tried to defend themselves by claiming not to have been at the place where these things had happened. For example, Rudolf Mynzak, who had also been charged by his fellow accused, maintained that he had served only in the stone quarry in Wiener Graben. August Blei lied about having been in charge of that Work Detail on the day when prisoners in the punishment detail had been shot. Others claimed to have been on leave just then, such as, for example, druggist Erich Wasicky who lied about being present in camp in the fall of 1942 at the time when 260 Czechoslovakians had been gassed. The accused who had served as guards would, without exception, only admit to "shot trying to escape" when the charge of particulars could be documented through an SS-document. They, too, argued that they had not been in a particular location where things had happened, and denied ever having been in this or that Work Detail.

Vinzenz Nohel was the only accused who openly described to the Court what his work had been while in the "Euthanasia" institution at Hartheim. He, who had assisted in the murder of tens of thousands of presumably mentally ill patients, hoped that he could remain alive by simulating mental illness. One of the investigative commissions that had been appointed by the Court did decide that although he had a "subnormal mentality" he could be held fully responsible for his acts.

## The Verdict

On May 13th, 1946, the Court assembled for the last time and pronounced the verdict: All the accused were found guilty of having violated the Laws and Usages of War. 58 of the accused were sentenced to death by hanging, three of the accused, Michael Cserny, Panl Gutzlaff and Josef Meyer, were sentenced to life imprisonment. Admittedly no means of appeal existed towards the verdict although the convicted prisoners had the opportunity to request a review, a "Petition of Review".[63] All of them took advantage of this right. With that they set in motion a review of the verdict through the "Review Board" whose recommendations could be made known to the American Supreme Commander in Europe. An officer appointed by him would be required to review the verdict once again.

As the result of this, numerous review requests and clemency pleas were filed by the accused, their attorneys, their relatives as well as friends and people in public life.[64] On April 30th, 1947, almost a year after the verdict, the "Review Board" presented its recommendations. In that presentation they described legal problems, corrected them, and confirmed the verdict; however, the scope of punishment for a few of the accused would be reduced: "The review of the entire court protocol had not shown any errors or any omissions that would have unjustly added to the burden of the accused. It was determined that the evidence was more than judicially sufficient for the Court to have come to this verdict. Because of that it is being recommended that the judicial court verdicts of all the accused are hereby confirmed and that the sentence of death by hanging of the accused Altfuldisch (then follow the names of the other 53 accused) and that their execution is hereby ordered to proceed, that the sentence of death by hanging of the accused Billmann, Doerr, Grzybowski and Mack are hereby confirmed but are hereby ordered to be changed into lifelong imprisonment and their writs of execution are hereby deleted and that the sentence to lifelong imprisonment of the accused Cserny, Gutzlaff and Mayer are hereby confirmed and that their writs of execution are hereby deleted."[65]

63    The nearest to it see: "Review"-Proceedings by Sigel, Im Interesse der Gerechtigkeit, pp. 61 ff.

64    The petitions are the greatest part of the Post-Trial-Records. NARA RG 338 Records of U.S. Army Commands, 1942, Records of Headquarters, US Army Europe (USAREUR), War Crimes Branch, War Crimes Case Files ("Cases Tried"), 1945–1959, Box 346–357.

65    Review and Recommendations, pp. 78 f.

The Supreme Commander of the American Armed Forces, in the person of General Clay, reviewed these recommendations and changed the death sentences of Heinrich Giese, Viktor Korger, Ferdinand Lappert, Adolf Rutka and Walter Hohler to lifelong imprisonment. On May 27th and May 28th, 1947, all those who had been sentenced to death were hung in "War Criminal Prison No. 1".[66] Otto Striegel, who had received a temporary delay, in order for him to present new evidence, was executed on June 19th, 1947.[67]

Generally the last words of the convicts showed that they did not comprehend their guilt and were deeply convinced that they had fought for Germany as soldiers and were now dying for their "country". Altfuldisch called out: "I die for Germany. May God protect members of my family."[68] Heinrich Fitschock, who originally came from Croatia, said: "I have done my duty like any American soldier. Now I have been accused of something that I did not do. I die innocently but like a soldier for his country. Long live Croatia, long live greater Germany."[69] Just before being executed Eigruber called out: "God protect Germany, God protect my family, God protect my children. I consider it an honor to be hung by the most brutal victors. Long live Germany."[70] Diehl sang the German National Anthem and called out at the end: "Long live Germany". August Blei also called out: "I die for Germany. Long live Germany." Ludolf revealed a national way of thinking when he called out: "We Germans have to die so that other countries can live".[71] When he was standing on the gallows' platform Otto Striegel cried out: "I am not a war criminal but revenge and hatred against Jews will never come to an end because they are guilty of the suffering and misery here in Landsberg. I greet my poor country. God protect my wife and children. Now carry out the order the Jews have given you."[72] A conflicting mixture from remorse and insight was shown by Willy Eckert: "The Lord will protect

---

66 Report of Execution on 27 May 1947, 3. 6. 1947, Office of the ProvostMarshal,FirstMilitary District, NARA RG 338, Box 350; Report of Execution on 28 May 1947, Office of the Provost Marshal, First Military District, NARA RG 338, Box 350.

67 Report of Execution of 19 June 1947, 23. 6. 1947. Headquarters First Military District, NARA RG 338, Box 350.

68 Last words of Altfuldisch, War Criminal Prison Landsberg, 28. 5. 1947, NARA RG 338, Box 350.

69 Last words of Fitschock War Criminal Prison Landsberg, 28. 5. 1947, NARA RG 338, Box 350.

70 Last words of Eigruber, War Criminal Prison Landsberg, 28. 5. 1947, NARA RG 338, Box 350.

71 Last words of Ludolf, War Criminal Prison Landsberg, 28. 5 1947, NARA RG 338, Box 349.

72 Last words of Striegel, War Criminal Prison Landsberg, 28. 5. 1947, NARA RG 338, Box 349.

my children and give the German people the opportunity to rise up again as a peace loving people. I thank the kind Americans who, at all times, treated me well and especially so Major Denson. I hope that the world will find peace. I die as a German for his country."[73]

Stefan Barczay was the only one who showed remorse: "The good Lord will forgive me."[74] Those who had been sentenced to lifelong imprisonment started a real campaign in 1947/48 to be released. In the files one finds numerous representations which, because of the Cold War then starting, did not fail to make their mark. All those who were incarcerated in the War Crimes Prison at Landsberg were released between March 1950 and November 1951.

---

73  Last words of Eckert, War Criminal Prison Lamdsberg, 28. 5. 1947, NARA RG 338, Box 350.
74  Last words of Barczay, War Criminal Prison Landsberg, NARA RG 338, Box 350.

Wolfgang Benz

# The Omnipresence
# of the Concentration Camps

## Satellite Camps in the
## National Socialist Concentration Camp System

If we take the formally correct definition of a concentration camp, which
is based on its administrative subordination to the Reichsführer-SS and its
central administration by the Inspectorate of the Concentration Camps in
Oranienburg and the SS Economic and Administrative Main Office
(WVHA) in Berlin, then in 1944 there were at least 25 concentration camps
situated within National Socialist territory.[1] This figure, however, does
not take into account the sites that functioned solely as murder and extermination camps, such as Chelmno (Kulmhof), Belzec, Sobibor, Treblinka
(the remains of which had in part already been covered over by 1943). It also
does not consider the countless numbers of prison and terror sites that were
not defined as concentration camps and which fell under the jurisdiction
of various authorities: the forced labor camps for Jews, the work education
camps, the police detention camps in the occupied areas, the "special camps"
(such as Hinzert[2]), the sites that served multiple functions (such as the

---

1    See the provisional list of concentration camps and their satellite commandos as
      well as other prison sites under the control of the Reichsführer SS in Germany
      and the German occupied territories (1933–1945), published by Internationa-
      len Suchdienst Arolsen 1969; list of concentration camps and their satellite com-
      mandos according to §42, paragraph 2 BEG, in: Bundesgesetzblatt I (1977), p.
      1786–1852 (revisions and additions to the list in: BGBl. I, 1982, p. 1571–1579);
      Gudrun Schwarz, Die nationalsozialistischen Lager, Frankfurt a. M. 1990 (soft
      cover 1996).
2    A hut camp that was erected near Hinzert in Hunsrück in 1938 for the Siegfried
      Line workers, and in 1939 was under the control of the Todt Organisation, was
      used as a "re-education camp for police prisoners," and in 1940 as an "SS special
      camp". It was by then managed by the Inspectorate of the Concentration Camps,
      but was not placed under the SS Economic and Administrative Main Office until
      May 1942. Hinzert was de facto a concentration camp and functioned primarily
      as a transit camp. See Marcel Engel, Andréo Hohengarten, Hinzert. Das Sonder-
      lager im Hunsrück 1939–1945, Luxembourg 1983.

complex of 15 camps in Emsland[3] on the border to the Netherlands), the "youth protection camps," the ghettos, the "gypsy resting area" (such as Marzahn near Berlin[4]), or the mobile SS building and railway construction units. These prison sites, in which for the most part the same living conditions prevailed as in the official concentration camps, were not a part of the concentration camp system that was founded with the establishment of Dachau in March 1933 and which came to an end with the liberation of Mauthausen on May 5, 1945 and its satellite camp, Ebensee, on the following afternoon.

Before the terror was systemized and perfected, and prior to and following the establishment of Dachau, there was a first generation of prisoner and torture sites, which gave meaning to the term "concentration camp" and lent to it in German daily vocabulary, the association of murder and manslaughter, ruthless despotism, desperate powerlessness and extreme humiliation. Under the control of the SA and SS, police and other state and local authorities, these sites were the notorious "wild concentration camps" in Kemna, Oranienburg, Eutin, at the Heuberg military training grounds in Württemberg, in Hohenstein in Sachsen, in Fuhlsbüttel in Hamburg, on the Lichtenburg mountain, on the Oberen Kuhberg mountain in Ulm, and at any number of areas in Berlin and on locations throughout Germany. These early concentration camps disappeared quickly, some already by 1933, most by 1934; the last ones closed down in 1937. In their place emerged an ordered landscape of persecution, at first on established locations: Dachau (March 1933), Sachsenhausen (July 1936), Buchenwald (July 1937). In May 1938, Flossenbürg was added and in May 1939 the Ravensbrück women's concentration camp was established on the site where the Lichtenburg camp (Prettin/Torgau district) had been until then. In August 1938, following the annexation of Austria, a concentration camp with particularly rough living conditions ("camp level III") was established at Mauthausen near Linz, close to a granite deposit. After the war began, the purpose of the camps changed: in addition to isolation, oppression, humiliation

3   The Emsland camps were prison sites with changing functions, where political opponents, prisoners of the judiciary and prisoners of war were incarcerated. In addition people convicted by military courts of being "unworthy of serving in the military" were also imprisoned there. The living conditions were not any different than in the concentration camps.

4   In Marzahn on the outskirts of Berlin Sinti and Roma from Berlin and the surrounding areas were detained. The camps served as a transit camp. Most of the prisoners were deported to Auschwitz. In spite of this, Marzahn was not accnowledged as a concentration camp by German restitution law. See Wolfgang Benz, Das Lager Marzahn: Nationalsozialistische Verfolgung der Sinti und Roma und ihre anhaltende Diskriminierung, in: Wolfgang Benz, Feindbild und Vorurteil. Beiträge über Ausgrenzung und Verfolgung, Munich 1996, pp. 139–169.

and torture, the exploitation of the prisoner labor for the war effort became an additional component of the persecution in the camps. The number of main and satellite camps grew rapidly during the war years in accordance with the need for slave labor.

With the outbreak of war in 1939, not only did the persecution of supposed, potential and real opponents of the regime increase. The "Principles of Internal State Security during the War," which was promulgated by the head of the Security Police on September 3, makes reference to excessive arrests and "brutal liquidation".[5] The camps also assumed new political and economic functions.

In late 1941 in the occupied areas, a new group of prisoners, people who had engaged in resistance against the occupying rulers and who were arrested as part of the "Nacht und Nebel Erlass"[6] (Cloak and Dagger Decree), were sent to the concentration camps on the territory of the German Reich. Approximately 7,000 prisoners fell into this category in 1944. Most of them were imprisoned in Groß-Rosen and Natzweiler-Struthof. By the fall of 1941 there was also a special area in most the camps for Soviet prisoners of war who had been handed over from the Wehrmacht to the SS as laborers. From the outbreak of war until March 1942, the number of camp prisoners rose from 25,000 to almost 100,000.

Buchenwald and Sachsenhausen were heavily overcrowded, which had an impact on the living conditions in the camp and took its toll on the prisoners. The mortality rate rose. For this reason and in expectation of a rise in the number of "protective custody cases," new concentration camps were set up in the winter of 1939-40, among them Auschwitz, Neuengamme, Groß-Rosen and Stutthof. Some of them were designed to fulfill a specific purpose, for example as a transit camp to serve the needs of Nazi population policies. As of 1941, "work re-education camps" were established, primarily for the temporarily incarceration of foreign civilian workers who were to be punished for such misdemeanors as refusing to work.[7]

The functional change of the camps during the phase of the war is characterized by the fact that the treatment of prisoners was not foremost determined by terror. The role of prisoners as part of a labor force became increasingly important because the civilian labor force in the armaments industry was deficient and required replacements. Recruitment and forced enlistment of both male and female workers in the occupied areas was only partially able to satisfy the need for workers and in the long run

5   See Martin Broszat, Nationalsozialistische Konzentrationslager, 1933–1945, in: Martin Broszat/Hans-Adolf Jacobsen/Helmut Krausnick, Anatomie des SS Staates, vol. 2, Olten/Freiburg i. B. 1965, pp. 104 f.
6   "Nacht und Nebel Erlass", Nuremberg document PS 1733.
7   See Broszat, Nationalsozialistische Konzentrationslager, p. 121.

proved insufficient. Himmler's decision to divide the camps into categories at the beginning of 1941 was also made in consideration of labor needs and operations. (Camp level I for prisoners in need of special handling or who were "capable of improvement": Dachau, Sachsenhausen, Auschwitz I; Camp level II for severe criminals: Buchenwald, Flossenbürg, Neuengamme; Camp level III for prisoners "with little hope of being disciplined": Mauthausen).

The last phase in the history of the concentration camps began in 1942 and is characterized by prisoner slave labor. It was during this phase which culminated in 1944 that the concentration camp system was extended through the establishment of satellite camps in areas with industrial plants into a comprehensive network. The functional change of the camps in the last phase of the war becomes recognizable through a number of bureaucratic changes: For one, the SS Economic and Administrative Main Office was established on February 1, 1942 through the linking of two main departments: "Household and Construction" and "Administration and Economy";[8] Secondly, the position of the Inspectorate of Concentration Camps (which had previously been under the SS Leadership Head Office) was integrated into the SS Economic and Administrative Main Office (WVHA)on March 16, 1942.[9] The office headquarters continued to be situated in Oranienburg, but it now functioned under the name "Amtsgruppe D-Konzentrationslager." With these changes the concentration camp system became the central arsenal for cheap labor in which countless agencies — the independent concentration camps and their subordinate branches, the satellite camps — were spread out across the country.

The 25 concentration camps of 1944 together had a total of over 1,200 satellite camps. These were both external and auxiliary commandos that in some cases were established at quite a distance from the main camp and which provided labor for SS factories and state enterprises, later for the armaments industry. The concentrations camps with their satellite and auxiliary camps spread like mushrooms over National Socialist Germany and ultimately Europe. Satellite camps developed into independent camp complexes, as was the case, for example, with Groß-Rosen in Silesia, which was established in August 1940 as a commando of Sachsenhausen and on May 1, 1941 became independent. Ultimately Groß-Rosen administrated more than 100 satellite camps of its own, in lower Silesia and the Lusatia, in "Reichgau Sudentenland" and in "Reichsgau Wartheland." Female prisoners made up half of the camp population.

---

8    Order of the Reichsführer SS of Jan. 19, 1942, in: Walter Naasner, SS-Wirtschaft und SS-Verwaltung, Düsseldorf 1998, p. 225.
9    Broszat, Nationalsozialistische Konzentrationslager, pp. 132 f.

Mauthausen and Flossenbürg were built near the granite deposits by Groß-Rosen, southwest of Breslau, so that the mines could be worked by prisoner slave labor on behalf of the SS "Deutsche Erd- und Steinwerke" company (German earth and stone works). The auxiliary camps became a reservoir of labor for armaments companies such as Krupp and Siemens and many other smaller firms. With the help of prisoners from the Dyhernfurth auxiliary camp, IG-Farben produced in its sister company, "Anorgana," the poisonous gas Tabun. In Peterswaldau Jewish women assembled fuses in a branch of the Nuremberg company Diehl. Oskar Schindler's last production plant, Brünnlitz in "Sudentenland," was an exception in the Groß-Rosen complex. At other sites straw sacks were produced for the Wehrmacht, radio parts for the electric company Lorenz, munitions crates, tank tracks and airplane parts were produced for other companies. Four auxiliary camps were set up on the eastern border ("Unternehmen Bartold") to build military constructions: in late fall 1944 female prisoners were evacuated from Auschwitz and forced to dig out trenches. In the Eulen mountains, a number of auxiliary camps were combined to form the "Riese" complex. Seven women's camps in Sudentenland were administrated together as the "SS special commando Trautenau." Most the female forced laborers were put to work in the textile branch.

The Groß-Rosen camp cosmos exemplifies the complete evolution of National Socialist terror in its linking of persecution, exploitation and extermination. The number of Jews in Groß-Rosen was particularly high because the work camps of the "Organisation Schmelt" were eventually integrated into the concentration camp complex and because in 1944 when there was a great need for laborers, Hungarian women from Auschwitz were deported to the Groß-Rosen area. A total of 120,000 prisoners suffered in the Groß-Rosen camp complex; at least 40,000 are estimated to have died there.[10]

Under orders of the SS, the satellite camps of the concentration camps served many masters and many functions, but their biggest service was to the war effort of the Nazi regime. As slave laborers for the airplane industry, for weapons and ammunitions factories and their suppliers, for equipment factories, military uniform tailors, soldiers' boot-makers — prisoners were set to work in all branches of the war industry. Concentration camp prisoners slaved away in the satellite camps which in their organization, method and terror were no different than the main camps. They worked for big industry, for the commercial middle class, for research facilities, for agriculture, for local authorities, for public institutions and for businesses of the SS.

---

10  See Isabell Sprenger, Groß-Rosen. Ein Konzentrationslager in Schlesien, Cologne 1996.

The SS had a considerably large need for labor in their own enterprises.[11] The SS company "Deutsche Erd- und Steinwerke GmbH" which was founded on the concept of exploiting slave labor in quarries, clay and gravel pits, brick factories and building material works, became especially active beginning in 1938 in the Flossenbürg, Mauthausen, Natzweiler, Sachsenhausen and Neuengammer camps, as well as at other sites. With the establishment of the "Klinker penal commando" in late summer 1938, the world's largest brick works was constructed. It was erected not far from the main camp of Sachsenhausen in Oranienburg. The "Deutsche Erd- und Steinwerke" produced the bricks needed to realize Albert Speer's new design of Berlin. In 1941 the construction of the stone processing plant began, but in the end the granite was not cut there to be used in future Nazi monumental buildings. Instead prisoners were involved in the recycling of raw materials for the armaments industry. The penal commando made up of Jews, Sinti and Roma, homosexuals, Jehovah's Witnesses and other prisoner groups, worked under particularly severe conditions. In 1941 it was renamed the "Klinker works satellite camp," but the miserable conditions did not improve. The mortality rate in the clay pits was especially high.

The "Deutschen Ausrüstungswerke GmbH" (which was founded as a company of the SS in May 1939) produced furnishings in concentration camps and other nearby areas as well. It produced furniture for housing and offices and for people who had resettled or were bombed out of their homes. It also provided wood houses, temporary accommodations in concrete prefabricated constructions and household equipment. There were also textile companies, weaving mills, wicker works and shoemakers. The SS exploited the labor of prisoners for still other purposes, such as to change the nourishing habits of the German people as part of the "life reform" movement. That was one of Heinrich Himmler's obsessions as was the medicinal herbs garden in the Dachau main camp. Later, in other camps, plantations were established where prisoners were also sent to work. The Dachau plantations developed into an SS enterprise which was called "Deutsche Versuchsanstalt für Ernährung und Verpflegung GmbH" (German research institute for nutrition and food, Ltd.) which ran agricultural production centers at various locations (including one near the Ravensbrück women's concentration camp), which were in part farmed by prisoners.

A satellite camp of Sachsenhausen had the task in late 1938 of putting back into operation a shut-down brick factory that was located on the outskirts of Hamburg. By April 1940 it had developed into one of the largest con-

---

11   Enno Georg, Die wirtschaftlichen Unternehmungen der SS, Stuttgart 1963; Walter Naasner, SS-Wirtschaft und SS-Verwaltung. Das SS-Wirtschafts-Verwaltungshauptamt und die unter seiner Dienstaufsicht stehenden wirtschaftlichen Unternehmungen, Düsseldorf 1998.

centration camps of the National Socialist state, exploiting a labor force of more than 100,000 prisoners. In the end, Neuengamme had more than 80 satellite camps of its own spread out over all of northern Germany. The most southern camp was located in the Harz mountains, the most northern on the Danish border, the most western on the British channel Island Alderney (a mobile building brigade was in operation there, which was run for a period of time by Neuengamme) and the farthest eastern camp was on the Baltic Sea peninsula Darß, where a commando made up of 50 Jehovah's Witnesses was put to work cutting reeds. The reeds were then used in an SS reed mat wickerwork factory in the Ravensbrück women's camp. The Neuengamme brick factory was bought and modernized by the SS company "Deutsche Erd- und Steinwerke", and converted into an industrial complex that functioned in cooperation with the city of Hamburg. Using slave labor it first produced clinker bricks for the mammoth Nazi buildings, and later temporary accommodations for people who had been bombed out of their homes. Its satellite camps worked to serve all kinds of armaments production purposes, ranging from the construction of underground airplane factories to repairs on damaged railway lines.

The history of the Neuengamme concentration camp ended with a singular tragedy: a ship on the Lübeck bay carrying "evacuated" prisoners sunk. On May 3, 1945, 7,000 prisoners drowned in the Baltic Sea.[12]

The Mittelbau Dora concentration camp grew out of a satellite commando of Buchenwald near Nordhausen in Thuringia that had been established on August 27, 1943. By October 28, 1943 it had acquired the status of an independent concentration camp and ultimately was in charge of 32 satellite commandos, four SS building brigades and three SS railroad construction brigades. The name Mittelbau-Dora is associated with the underground manufacturing of "V" weapons. It is not well-known, however, that women and children were integrated into the forced labor system and made up a considerable portion of the 10,000 prisoners who died in the camp (the total camp population ranged between 50,000 and 60,000 prisoners).[13]

Only a few concentration camps remained without subordinate branches, among them Bergen-Belsen, Warsaw, Niederhagen (Wewelsburg), and Arbeitsdorf in Fallersleben, an area which today is part of Wolfsburg. The camp "Arbeitsdorf" only existed from April to October 1942. The camp at Wewelsburg was a special case as was the Warsaw camp, which

12  Hermann Kaienburg, Das Konzentrationslager Neuengamme 1938–1945, Bonn 1997.

13  See Angela Fiedermann/Torsten Hess/Markus Jaeger, Das Konzentrationslager Mittelbau-Dora. Ein historischer Abriß, Bad Münstereifel 1993; Manfred Boremann, Geheimprojekt Mittelbau: vom zentralen Öllager des Deutschen Reiches zur größten Raketenfabrik im Zweiten Weltkrieg, Munich 1994.

had been erected solely for the purpose of removing the ruins of the ghetto following the uprising. In reversal of the usual genesis of a main camp, it was first run from July 1943 to April 1944 as an independent camp and later became a satellite camp of the Lublin-Majdanek concentration camp.

Dachau lead all the concentration camps in its number of satellite camps. Almost 200 auxiliary camps were opened during the war, a few others were established earlier, like the commandos in Munich, St. Gilgen in Salzburg and St. Wolfgang in upper Austria, where prisoners were forced to build country houses for SS leaders and the Dachau camp commandant, Loritz.[14] In Halfing in Upper Bavaria, prisoners worked on the villa of Oswald Pohl, the head of the SS Economic and Administrative Main Office (WVHA).

The more than 1,200 camps that existed in towns and cities throughout the territory under National Socialist rule, in which hundreds of thousands of prisoners were used as forced laborers and regularly marched to and from their work site, were, like the industry that used prisoners as slaves, an integral part of German daily life.

The population had to have been aware of these camps and their inmates. The work and suffering of the forced laborers was for the most part not concealed. When prisoners dug out entrenchments for the Friesland Wall in the north, or the Bartold Line in the east of the Reich territory; when they cleared out the ruins in the large German cities following an air raid attack; when they built underground factories for German construction companies under the direction of the Todt Organization, it was impossible for them to go unnoticed.

A few examples should serve to illustrate the problems involved in the perception of camp prisoners by the local populations and their interaction with them in daily life: From August 21 to December 13, 1944, a satellite commando of Buchenwald in Ahrthal near Dernau was put to work building V-2 rockets in the tunnels of a deserted pre-1914 railway project. All traces of the original 180 men, mostly Belgians, Italians, French and Russians, were lost by mid-December 1944 when the underground production site was closed.[15] From August 27 until October 31, 1944 there existed in Walldorf near Frankurt am Main a satellite camp of the Natzweiler-Struthof concentration camp, in which 1,700 Jewish women from Hungary worked under miserable conditions on the construction of a runway for the Rhine-Main airport. The women arrived on August 22 from Auschwitz on a freight train following requests for labor from the Todt Organization. They

---

14  Klaus Drobisch/Günther Wieland, System der NS-Konzentrationslager 1933–1939, Berlin 1993, p. 276.
15  Report in the General-Anzeiger Bonn, January 27, 1999: "Von den KZ-Häftlingen fehlt jede Spur".

were put up in barracks on the grounds of a former chicken farm. The women worked for the construction company Züblin, unloading railroad cars, digging out ditches and leveling the taxiway. By mid-November the "airport work camp" was closed and the prisoners were transferred to Ravensbrück. The company Züblin paid the SS Economic and Administrative Main Office (WVHA) four Reich mark per workday and worker and provided the prisoners with a minimum amount of food. Nourishment and clothing were insufficient in every way: "We were sent to Ravensbrück in November in the same summer dress that we had worn upon arrival in August from Auschwitz. In order not to freeze to death we laid sacks of cement over our bodies, from which many got rashes and sores. Most of us didn't have shoes anymore, they were also replaced by cement paper sacks even though that was punished with beatings."[16]

One day the order came for pregnant women to make themselves known. They were going to be sent to a recuperation home, it was said. After the 34 women were deported, those who remained behind found out from a very young SS man who was emotionally distraught by what he had seen, that they had been driven away naked by train in October in rain and snow and that he later heard that the women were shot along the way.[17]

In August 1944, about 2,200 prisoners from Auschwitz arrived in Vaihingen an der Enz. They were imprisoned in "KZ Wiesengrund," a satellite camp of Natzweiler-Struthof, and given construction work to do. The prisoners describe the civilian population as cold and hostile, especially when the train arrived in Bietigheim: "They had us walk through the narrow streets of the town, driven on by the butts of rifles, much to the delight of the population, which was mostly women and children. From the comments that we overheard we could gather what the population had been told about us: we were incorrigible criminals who were to sent to work on farms."[18] But there were some residents who were aware of the true nature and situation of the prisoners. The diary entry of the Vaihingen newspaper publisher from August 13, 1944 makes this clear: "Even around here these days we were given an impression of the merciless and nasty treatment. An entire transport of Jews was driven away in four cattle cars to the construction site of the local works, where they are forced to live crowded together in a barracks camp fenced in by barbed wire. On the day of

16  Susanne Farkas, letter from September 14, 1978, in: Magistrat der Stadt Mörfelden-Walldorf (ed.), Nichts und niemand wird vergessen. Zur Geschichte des KZ-Außenlagers Natzweiler-Struthof in Walldorf, Mörfelden-Walldorf 1996, p. 20.
17  Statement of Helena Halperin, ibid., pp. 14 f.
18  Bernd Martin, Das Konzentrationslager "Wiesengrund", in: Schriftenreihe der Stadt Vaihingen an der Enz, Beiträge zur Geschichte, Kultur und Landschaftskunde, vol. 4, Vaihingen an der Enz 1985, pp. 141 f.

their arrival it was unbearably hot and the Jews stood so close together in the cattle cars that they couldn't move. Even the local resident here who is known to be a Jew-hater had sympathy for these poor people."[19]

A satellite commando of Neuengamme was established near Kaltenkirchen (in the Segeberg district in Schleswig-Holstein) in August 1944 and had the task of building take-off and landing runways for the Me 262 fighter planes. The work capacity of 500 men was pushed to its ultimate limits, with 10 to 11 hour workdays and a three-hour march to and from the camp.

On occasion prisoners were also put to work in the "Wald- und Gartenstadt". The residents there became witnesses to their treatment: "One Sunday morning, while the people were having breakfast, terrible screaming could be heard outside. When the witnesses went outside, they saw how, right in front of the house next door, a prisoner was beaten to death with the butt of a rifle by the guards."[20]

From July 1943 until the beginning of April 1945 circa 150 prisoners were assigned from Buchenwald to work as construction workers in Kassel in district IX (Kassel and Kurhessen) for the Higher SS and Police Leaders. A former restaurant named "Druseltal" that had been rented by the SS served as a satellite camp and the commando took its name. A former Dutch prisoner, Alfred Frederik Groeneveld, reports on contact to the Kassel residents: "It was a strange feeling. Civilians were on their way to work, either by foot or by bicycle. The streetcar, Line 3, drove by and the passengers looked motionless out of the window. They had apparently already gotten used to the emaciated prisoners that stumbled through the area in zebra clothing and wooden shoes. Various passersby greeted the guards with a sympathetic smile while others just looked straight ahead as if they consciously didn't want to see the column."[21] Groeneveld, who was sent to Buchenwald in April 1941 along with other men from the Dutch resistance, also describes a very different reaction from the Weimar population as the prisoners were marched from the train station through the streets of Weimar in running tempo, driven onward by raging SS men and dogs. In Weimar civilians called out "dirty Jew" and "traitor" and even the women threw horse dung. "In Kassel the people just didn't react. It was as if the people just didn't want to know! They looked towards us as little as possible as if they were trying in advance to repress the memory."[22]

19  Ibid., p. 146.
20  Gerhard Hoch, Hauptort der Verbannung. Das KZ-Außenkommando Kaltenkirchen, Bad Segeberg 1981, p. 44.
21  Alfred F. Groeneveld, Im Außenkommando Kassel des KZ Buchenwald. Ein Bericht, Kassel 1991 (= Nationalsozialismus in Nordhessen. Schriften zur regionalen Zeitgeschichte, No. 13), S. 31.
22  Ibid.

It is possible that the different reactions — fanaticism in Weimar, apathy in Kassel — had to do with the developing war situation or with the effect of propaganda on the Weimar population. The scale of reactions to concentration camp prisoners was large, ranging from angry rejection to quiet sympathy and even modest help for the captives. Perceiving the prisoners and the conditions under which they lived and worked was inevitable and could not be avoided, not even by looking away.

The situation in the Buchenwald satellite camp at the Annener cast steel factory in Witten was typical of the working conditions of the prisoners. As was the case in countless other factories, concentration camp prisoners were integrated in 1944 into the workforce of the steel and iron industry in the Rühr area as the last reserve. The 700 men who, guarded by 30 SS men, were sent on a transport from Buchenwald to Witten on September 16, 1944, were in part selected as skilled workers (including 256 lathe operators, metal workers, electric welders), but some were selected without any regard for their work experience, knowledge or physical suitability. They worked in two rotating shifts of six days each in a manufacturing hall that was carefully guarded against escapes by the SS and overseen by the foremen and bosses of the steel works. A Polish prisoner observed the following: "Once a soviet prisoner that I knew from sight didn't meet the obligatory production norm. The boss ... brought an armed SS man to the prisoner who then began to beat the prisoner on the head and wherever else he could with a leather whip from which wire shown from the middle. The beating lasted a long time. The beaten prisoner fell to the ground and the SS man kept on beating and kicking him. Following this maltreatment he left. I don't know how it happened, whether it was on purpose or unconscious, but in any case after the SS man and the boss had gone, the prisoner crawled on top of a furnace ... and was killed by an electrical current."[23]

Although there are many reports from prisoners on their daily life in concentration camps, references in the memories of the German civilian population are few. People were determined not to see what might burden them, they didn't want to be affected by the sight of a miserable figure, and hence chose not to recognize the reality. "When we exited the train the civilian population disappeared from the train station," writes Ladislaus Ervin-Deutsch, who arrived in Kaufering at dawn on a day in June 1944 on a transport of 1,500 deported Hungarian Jews. "Behind the train station a peaceful, small town was just waking up. The war had not left any traces here yet. Perhaps the residents of Kaufering had not yet seen people deported

23   Manfred Grieger/Klaus Völkel, Das Außenlager "Annener Gußstahlwerk" (AGW) des Konzentrationslagers Buchenwald September 1944–April 1945, Essen 1997, p. 45.

for forced labor. As we passed by they collected the bed coverings that they had been airing out and shut the windows. The people on the streets pressed themselves against the walls of the buildings. We were the outcasts of the civilian world. We now had more contact to our guards than to the indifferent and occasionally curious on-looking citizens."[24]

The lodgings were not usually as successful in sealing prisoners off from the civilian world as the perpetrators had intended although this was later offered as an explanation for the population's failure to acknowledge the prisoners' existence. At work sites contact between the bosses, foremen and other civilians and the forced laborers could not be avoided. Ella Lingens, who was transferred from Auschwitz to Dachau in December, worked in the women's satellite camp "Agfa-Camera-Werke" in the east of Munich. She reported on her lodgings there: "Late at night we arrived at a large not yet completed new building built in the style of Viennese council houses that the DAF [German Workers' Front] had planned as residential homes for workers and where, for the most part, civilians lived. In one part with a courtyard that had been provisionally separated by barbed wire, 300 Polish and 200 Dutch women and a few Yugoslavians, Belgians and besides myself, one other German women were put up. There was also the commandant, his deputy and about ten female guards who were managed by a kind of head guard and a few old men from the factory security service ... In the courtyard there still stood a quite old barrack with a large kitchen and a spacious dining hall. All in all I had the feeling of having returned to civilization. The fence was not electrical but just barbed wire; the street car passed nearby; we walked along the streets of East Munich on our way to work in the factory or to get potatoes, once we even went far into the city to roll home a barrel of beer that the company had donated for Christmas."[25]

Passersby who during their daily routine encountered concentration camp prisoners were not all indifferent. Some took an interest or took sides. Siegfried van den Bergh, who was sent by way of Westerbork and Theresienstadt to Auschwitz and who from there was deported in October 1944 to the satellite camp Gleiwitz I, worked in a commando outside of the camp: "While unloading the truck of coal I was often beaten to the ground by an SS man or Kapo because he wasn't satisfied with my tempo. I fell between the rails of the adjacent tracks. Sometimes the German citizens watched. I heard them say to the SS guard: 'I don't understand why you

24   Ladislaus Ervin-Deutsch, About Those woh Survived and Those who Died. From Auschwitz to Labour Camp III in Kaufering, in: Benz/Distel (ed.), Dachau and the Nazi Terror 1933–1945, Vol. I, pp. 75–118.

25   Ella Lingens, Als Ärztin in Auschwitz and Dachau, in: Dachauer Hefte 4 (1988), p. 29.

don't beat them to death, the dirty Jews!' Encouraged, the SS man hurled another piece of wood or coal at my head."[26]

There were, of course, also people who responded with sympathy and who offered aid. Solly Ganor, a Lithuanian-Jewish prisoner in Utting am Ammersee in the Kaufering Camp X was in the kitchen commando with two other boys and had the task of loading food at an inn. The inn-keeper gave them a loaf of bread and promised a bowl of soup next time, thereby winning the trust of the young prisoner. He then asked her for a few cigarettes so that he might bribe the Kapo and save his father's life. "'Don't give me that!' she said before she saw the tears in my eyes and realized that I had told the truth. 'My God, what are they doing to you in that camp?' she exclaimed. 'I thought that was a work camp and that every one was treated decently.' This time it was me who was shocked. How could the Germans still believe the propaganda after all that which has happened around them? 'Oh sure it is a work camp' I said and looked directly into her eyes. 'They are working us to death. We do hard labor twelve hours a day on empty stomachs. They are starving us. In a few months we will all be dead, even the youngest and the strongest.' She took a start as if I had personally insulted her. Suddenly I realized what immense danger I had put myself in. If she was a Nazi — and that was all too possible — then I was doomed. I broke out in a cold sweat. She must have noticed my panic because she told me not to worry. But if I wanted to stay alive, she added, I should stop spreading around those sort of things."[27]

When National Socialist rule came to an end, there were at least 700,000 people imprisoned and used as forced labor. (The total number of concentration camp prisoners for the period from 1933 to 1945 comes to between 2,5 and 3,5 million; approximately 450,000 prisoners did not survive their imprisonment). The majority of prisoners lived and suffered in the satellite camps, sites that have not yet been given the attention they deserve by research.[28] Many have been forgotten except in the memories of the former prisoners. In the recollections of most local contemporaries they often remain marginal; memories are vague and defensive, and offer little information on the existence of the many camps. On the other hand, a rising interest in the concrete historical remains of National Socialist terror

26  Siegfried van den Bergh, Der Kronprinz von Mandelstein. Überleben in Westerbork, Theresienstadt und Auschwitz, Frankfurt a. M. 1996, p. 101.

27  Solly Ganor, Das andere Leben. Kindheit im Holocaust, Frankfurt a. M. 1997, p. 183.

28  On current research, see Ulrich Herbert/Karin Orth/Christoph Dieckmann (eds.), Die nationalsozialistischen Konzentrationslager. Entwicklung und Struktur, Göttingen 1998.

at a number of sites has emerged out of history projects and among people actively involved in preserving the history. But that does not provide a complete picture since the local initiatives which find expression in difficult-to-obtain informational brochures and documentary exhibits are not a part of the general historical record. The concentration camp as omnipresent persecution exists in the collective memory solely in connection with the main camps. The subordinate branches, which are often perceived as a blemish on the personal surroundings, are as a consequence often played down by local dignitaries who deny the historical truth by arguing that the local sites were not "concentration camps" but "merely work camps".

Why are the local branches of the larger concentration camps which were spread across Germany and the occupied territories so important? The satellite camps convey the deeper nature of the tyranny, which emerged not as a central Moloch but with ubiquitous manifestations. The satellite camps also provide insight into the morphology and genesis of the concentration camp system and, because they often entailed close contact between prisoners and civilian populations, provide information on the interactions and relations between the camp cosmos and the civilian world. The civilian population's knowledge and awareness of the camps, its reaction to the terror and violence in the immediate personal surroundings is easier to ascertain on the basis of the satellite camps than from other manifestations of National Socialist rule. For this reason the satellite camps also play an important role in the efforts of memorial work, which strives to present and convey the history of local events.

Thomas Rahe

# Jewish Orphans in the Concentration Camp Bergen-Belsen

With her book "The Century of the Child", published in 1900, which in Germany alone went through 15 editions prior to the First World War, the Swedish pedagogue and women's rights campaigner Ellen Key made an emphatic plea for the recognition of the genuine rights of the child. This plea was just as much a call for showing respect towards the individuality and autonomy of the child as well as a prophecy that the new century indeed could and would be an age of the child and its rights and, hence, one of more humanity.[1] Looking back, this century hardly presents itself however as a "Century of the Child" in the sense of humanitarian progress. Instead, even viewed from a universal historical perspective, with the murder of 1.2 million Jewish children in the Holocaust a low point in the history of childhood, in how a civilisation deals with its children, was reached. Jewish children were very much a preferred target within the genocide of the European Jews in the extermination camps, and in the concentration camps the children were also forced to line up for role call and exposed in the same degree to cold and hunger, sickness, violence and death as their fellow adult prisoners.

It is difficult to face the suffering of these children. This is especially the case for a group about whom little is known, namely Jewish children who were imprisoned as orphans in National Socialist concentration camps. Their fate especially touches and frightens probably because it also evokes in us the primal anxiety that seizes us whenever we are faced with the absolute helplessness of being on our own.

Given the fanatical will to exterminate displayed by the National Socialist regime, why there were any orphans at all amongst the prisoners in the con-

---

1    Ellen Key, The Century of the Child, Berlin 1902 (Swedish first edition: Stockholm 1900). A critical appreciation (also as to the problematic role played by eugenics in the thought of E. Key) is offered by Claudia Schmölders, "Das Jahrhundert des Kindes". Über einen Bestseller von Ellen Key aus dem Jahr 1900 ["The Century of the Child". On A Best-Seller of Ellen Key from the Year 1900], in: Schmölders (Hrsg.), Deutsche Kinder. Siebzehn biographische Porträts, Berlin 1997, p. 350–368.

centration camps, for what reasons and through which channels were they first of all able to evade extermination and end up in a concentration camp and what were their chances for survival there — these queries shall be presented in the following by taking the concentration camp Bergen-Belsen as an example. This requires, first of all, a short sketch of the particular structure and the evolution of this camp, which was assigned a very specific function in the overall system of National Socialist concentration camps.[2]

The concentration camp Bergen-Belsen was set up in early 1943 as an "Aufenthaltslager" ["reception camp"] for specific groups of Jewish prisoners who were to be exchanged for Germans interned in Western countries. This purpose determined the selection of the Jewish prisoners (as a rule entire families), who were, for the moment at least, exempt from extermination and deported to Bergen-Belsen: nationals from enemy or neutral states, holders of Palestine certificates, representatives from important Jewish institutions etc. The hope to become part of an exchange programme and so to be ultimately released was, however, to be fulfilled for only a few prisoners. Unlike in almost all other concentration camps, the Jewish prisoners in Bergen-Belsen were not subjected to live under generally valid camp orders, but instead, in accordance with the view held by the SS as to their differing legal status and national heritage, they lived spread out in several section camps, at first strictly separated from one another, each with its own different conditions. The largest of these section camps was the "Star Camp" (named so because the prisoners there — mainly Dutch Jews — were forced to wear the star of David). Next to this camp there existed, amongst others, a "Neutral Camp" for Jewish prisoners who were nationals of neutral states, a "Special Camp" for Polish Jews and a "Hungarian Camp", from which a total of 1,683 Hungarian Jews were released to Switzerland in the second half of 1944. Apart from the strictly separated "Prisoner Camp", at first exclusively Jewish prisoners lived in Bergen-Belsen. A change in this social structure, but above all a disastrous worsening of living conditions began to take place from the end of 1944 onwards as an increasing number of prisoners from other camps were brought to Bergen-Belsen on the "evacuation transports", giving rise to the creation of new camp complexes. Prisoner numbers increased dramatically (at the beginning of December 1944: ca. 15,000, 1. 2. 1945: 22,000, 1. 3. 1945: 41,520), and so the living conditions worsened drastically once more. If at the beginning living conditions were

2    Cf. on the following, Eberhard Kolb, Geschichte des "Aufenthaltlagers" Bergen-Belsen 1943–1945 [The History of the "Reception Camp" Bergen-Belsen 1943–1945], Hannover 1962; Kolb, Bergen-Belsen. Vom "Aufenthalslager" zum Konzentrationslager 1943–1945 [Bergen-Belsen. From "Reception Camp" to Concentration Camp 1943–1945], 5th edition, reworked and extended, Göttingen 1996.

somewhat better as in other concentration camps — the prisoners designated for exchange were not to be able to report on the true state of the camps in foreign countries — from the beginning of 1945 onwards they reached, after they had already continually worsened in the course of 1944, an unsurpassable low: more than 18,000 prisoners died in March 1945 alone in Bergen-Belsen from hunger, thirst and epidemics, while the SS undertook no serious measures to relieve the situation. The total number of victims at Bergen-Belsen is estimated to be 50,000.

Bergen-Belsen was hence a camp characterised by a confusing diversity of conditions and social structures as well as the extreme worsening in the prisoners' living conditions, starting as a "Vorzugslager" ["privileged persons camp"] for hostages and ending as a chaotic death camp. All this also had grave effects on the number and fate of the children imprisoned at Bergen-Belsen in general and the orphans in particular.[3]

According to the definition given by the SS, prisoners under the age of 15 were considered to be children and they were accommodated with their mothers in one of the women's barracks. Given the fact that shortly before liberation the SS succeeded in almost completely destroying the records at Bergen-Belsen, including the prisoner personnel index, no precise statistical data on the overall number of children among the prisoners at Bergen-Belsen can be established. Following conservative estimations and considering the numerous prisoner transports which also affected children (release or exchange actions, evacuation transports to and from Bergen-Belsen, transfer to other camps, etc.), it is nevertheless possible to assume a figure of some 3,000 children who were imprisoned at Bergen-Belsen at various points for various lengths of time.

The majority of these children were brought to Bergen-Belsen together with their parents or at least one parent. At first these were Jewish prisoners who were considered to be candidates for the planned exchange actions. However, even in these initial groups of Jewish prisoners, who reached the "Aufenthaltslager" Bergen-Belsen from summer 1943 onwards, there were occasionally orphans. The concept of "orphan" is not to be understood as a biological or legal term in this context, but as a social one. It was perfectly

3   On the children in Bergen-Belsen in general, see Thomas Rahe, Aus 'rassischen' Gründen verfolgte Kinder im Konzentrationslager Bergen-Belsen. Eine erste Skizze [Children persecuted on 'racial' grounds in the concentration camp Bergen-Belsen. A first sketch], in Edgar Bamberger/Annegret Ehmann (Hrsg.), Kinder und Jugendliche als Opfer des Holocaust, Heidelberg 1995, p. 129–143; Rahe, 'Ich wußte nicht einmal, daß ich schwanger war'. Geburten im KZ Bergen-Belsen ['I didn't even know I was pregnant'. Births in the concentration camp Bergen-Belsen], in: Claus Füllberg-Stolberg et. al. (Hrsg.), Frauen in Konzentrationslagern. Bergen-Belsen — Ravensbrück, Bremen 1994, p. 147–155.

possible that the parents of a Jewish child deported alone to Bergen-Belsen were still alive — whether in hiding or in one of the countless other National Socialist camps. Decisive for the situation of such a Jewish child was, however, that it had to live as a prisoner in Bergen-Belsen without the social and emotional support of its parents.

The Jewish orphans deported to Bergen-Belsen from July 1943 till around August/September 1944 were children who, in the view of the SS and the Foreign Office, appeared to qualify for an exchange with German nationals abroad and were hence considered to be valuable hostages. The reasons for this could be very different. 12 Jewish orphans reached Bergen-Belsen on 26 July 1944 on a transport from the transit camp Drancy because their French fathers were German prisoners of war. Beforehand they all had lived in various Jewish children's homes. A smaller proportion of these were only children, a larger proportion were siblings, such as in the case of the eleven-year-old Maurice Przemyslanyski, who was brought to Bergen-Belsen with his seven-year-old sister and five-year-old brother.[4] That at least ten of these French-Jewish orphans survived Bergen-Belsen clearly shows the special situation there, one which meant for these children an essentially higher chance of survival as in the majority of the National Socialist camps. For most of the other Jewish orphans sent to the "Star Camp" at Bergen-Belsen, familial connections to Western foreign countries was the reason for their deportation there. For them this camp meant the end of a journey characterised by persecution and the despairing efforts of their relatives to save their lives, such as in the case of the siblings Georg and Ursula Levy, born in Lippstadt in September 1930 and May 1935, respectively.[5] Their father was deported to the Sachsenhausen concentration camp in connection with the pogrom of November 1938 and died there shortly afterwards as a result of the maltreatment he had suffered.

Following this, their mother desperately sought to organise the emigration of the children to the USA through contact with her sister living in Chicago. As this however proved impossible, she decided to send her children to the Netherlands, where she believed they would be safe. There they

---

4   See transport list from 26. 7. 1944 a.Drancy (Archive Beith Lohamei Haghetaot, Dutch Archive Section: Dossier Josef Weiss Nr. 317, Nachlaß J. Weiss; copies in the Archive of the Bergen-Belsen Memorial); cf. also Serge Klarsfeld, French Children of the Holocaust. A Memorial. New York/London 1996, p. 367 f. and Mo Is [= Maurice Przemyslanyski], U.B.B. Unforgettable Bergen-Belsen, Montreal 1994.

5   Cf. for the following interview conducted by the author with Ursula Levy, 17. 6. 1991 (Archive of the Bergen-Belsen Memorial); Interview with George Mueller (previously Levy), 14. 7. 1995 (Shoah Visual History Foundation, copy in the Archive of the Bergen-Belsen Memorial).

were admitted to a Catholic children's home. Although they were baptised and those in charge at the home used all means to ensure their safety, this could not hinder their arrest and deportation to the camp Vught. However, the director of the home was able to convince the SS with the help of forged papers that the uncle living in Chicago was in fact their father, so that their apparently real father would be an American citizen. This was to prove life-saving for both the children: instead of being sent to the extermination camps in the East, they were brought to the transit camp Westerbork and finally, in January 1944, to Bergen-Belsen, where both survived.

A considerable number of Jewish children who landed in Bergen-Belsen as orphans came to the "Aufenthaltslager" with fake biographical dates in their papers. On the basis of these fake details they then also appeared — in so far they are preserved — in the transport and prisoner lists, so that in many cases they can only be identified as orphans at all with the help of later reports or interviews with survivors. For example, in the prisoner lists, kept under the orders of the SS by the "Jewish elder" in the "Star Camp", Josef Weiss, beside the name of the married couple Josef and Frederika Melkman there is also that of a child registered as theirs, Abraham A. Melkman, born in July 1941. In fact, this child was not a son of Josef and Frederika Melkman but an only child with a quite different name whom they had taken charge of shortly before their arrival in Bergen-Belsen and then presented as their own.[6]

There were a greater number of orphans, even if not immediately recognisable as such from the preserved name lists, in the "Special Camp" for Polish Jews and in the "Hungarian Camp", here in particular in the so-called Kasztner Group. Confronted with the threat of deportation and mass death in the ghettos, to Polish Jews who had learnt about the possibility of being transported to an "exchange camp", from where there was hence some prospect for release, Bergen-Belsen must have appeared as the last chance for saving their own lives and those of their relatives.

However, for this to become possible they required proof, based on identity papers, of "justified admittance" to the "Exchange Camp" Bergen-Belsen — a strong motivation for faking passports and other personal papers. Above all nationality, seen as having a decisive significance for the possible inclusion in an exchange transport, was the object of forgeries. But there were also complete forgeries of identity papers, leading to changing

6    Cf. Nachlaß Josef Weiss (as in note 4): "Judentransport aus den Niederlanden-Lager Westerbork am 15. Februar 1944" ["Jewish Transport from the Dutch camp Westerbork on 15 February 1944"]; statement made by Dr. Joseph Michman (formerly Melkman), Jerusalem, to the author, 10. 3. 1991 (Archive of the Bergen-Belsen Memorial).

names, dates of birth etc. "Anyone who could afford to pay," remembers Simcha Korngold, deported to the "Special Camp" at Bergen-Belsen, "was added to an artificially formed family which was sometimes made up of forty members. Demand was large. Whoever paid was added as son, son-in-law, daughter-in-law, child or grandchild. Everyone was told to firmly fix in their head their new name and to remember which family they belonged to."[7] Another recollection on the "Special Camp" tells of the evacuation transports arriving at Bergen-Belsen from the end of 1944 onwards: "Amongst the arrivals were some 'lucky devils' who found their relatives and friends again or heard something about their closest friends and relatives. I remember the 8-year-old Halinka, who we all thought to be an orphan [...] and who had recognised her mother in the dirty, stripped rags. A hysterical scream from the girl and a wild look from the women. The truth was not allowed to be let out because Halinka had forged papers issued under another name."[8]

As Hungary was at first spared German occupation, it was the target destination for principally Polish and Slovak Jews who fled there from National Socialist persecution. However, because they often possessed no residency permit, they lived there illegally or with forged identity papers. Children who had lost their parents, mainly in Poland, also belonged to these refugees. As, after the German occupation of Hungary and the deportation of Hungarian Jews to the extermination camps had begun, negotiations between the SS and the leadership of the Hungarian Zionists took place — negotiations which gave at least a few hundred Jews from Hungary a chance to get out — the Hungarian Zionists consciously included these Polish-Jewish orphans in the rescue operation. In the preserved name lists of the 1,683 Jews who came to Bergen-Belsen at the beginning of July 1944 as the so-called Kasztner Group and from here, as a small group in August, a larger one in December 1944, were then released to Switzerland, a mere three adult prisoners are identified as Poles.[9] All Polish-Jewish orphans who came to Bergen-Belsen as part of the Kasztner Group were hence

---

7   Recollection reported by Simcha Korngold in Abraham Shulman, The Case of Hotel Polski. An account of one of the most enigmatic episodes of World War II, New York, p. 59.

8   Mina Tomkiewicz, Tam sie tez zylo, Sussex 1984 (German trans. in the Archive of the Bergen-Belsen Memorial), p. 36 of the German translation.

9   There are several name lists with the corresponding biographical dates for the Kasztner Group, some diverging from each other, others supplementing one another: Yad Vashem: M 20/176, M 20/46; Archives of the American Jewish Joint Distribution Committee/American Jewish Archives: Saly Mayer Papers, SM 24; Nachlaß A. Speter, Tel Aviv; Sammlung Dr. D. Hermann, Tel Aviv (copies in the Archive of the Bergen-Belsen Memorial).

given a new "Hungarian identity". That these children were in fact Polish-Jewish orphans cannot be gathered from the name lists (in this regard objectively false), but rather only emerges through the relevant recollections, such as those noted down by Miriam Buck when she was still in Switzerland in 1945. Under the chapter title "Polish Orphans" her recollections state: "We have very many orphans in our camp. Their parents had been murdered only because they were Jews and the children were frequently witnesses of the execution. [...] They stick together, form a caste and keep much to themselves. They accept everything you give them, clothes, soap, food. Their thanks is mechanical though, for they have lost the belief in human goodness and feel the abyss that even here, in an internment camp, separates them from others. [...] It is their memories that poisons life for them, even more as the present. Alek, the youngest, around four years old, is probably the only one who tells everyone with unbroken trust that the Germans are looking after his toys in Warsaw until he returns home. He was still too young when his parents were murdered, he is now still too young to know what murder means. He says with a radiating smile that he has already had three mothers, and thank God he does not know how much less three are than one. [...] Some who are older are full of hate. Their hate is universal, it is directed against everyone who has more, everyone who has suffered less. They thirst for revenge, murder is their longing, justice is not enough for them. Others have had their sensitivity blunted, they only want to eat their fill, are satisfied when they receive another blanket and imagine freedom to be a clean-sheeted bed."[10]

Given this background it may appear almost cynical to characterise their situation in Bergen-Belsen as "privileged". At the same time, in quite a decisive point, their fate was different from that of most of the other prisoners (also within Bergen-Belsen): between the middle of August and release at the beginning of December 1944 a total of 3 prisoners died in the Hungarian camp, meaning that almost the entire Kasztner Group, and hence the Jewish orphans belonging to it, survived and were released from Bergen-Belsen before the mass deaths caused by hunger and disease took place.[11]

And yet, it is not always possible to clarify the identity of Jewish orphans and so also the reason for their deportation to Bergen-Belsen. Such a case is that of the young Albertico from Saloniki, about whom Marietta Duschnitz, who herself came to Bergen-Belsen with her parents as a 15 year old, wrote in early 1945: "They called him Alberto or sometimes Albertico, this small, parentless Greek boy, but nobody knew who he was. They didn't even

---

10   Miriam Buck's recollection (Yad Vashem 03/1098), p. 8 f.
11   Statement given by Eva Speter, Tel Aviv, to the author on 27. 10. 1994 (Archive of the Bergen-Belsen Memorial).

know his exact age, we thought he was about five or six, maybe seven years of age. [...] All he could tell this group, who sat in a livestock car and waited to be sent to an unknown place in Germany, was the word Albertico. He was brought there by a German SS-man at the last minute before the train departed, with nothing more than the clothes he wore. After a long discussion it was decided that he was to be looked after in turns, every woman was to care for him for a week or maybe for even two. But after a few weeks they felt that this decision would never work. The women who had their own children had more than enough to do in camp life and were really in no position to care for another child belonging to someone else. So Albertico was given to some older people without children and they gave him food, put him to bed in the evening and sometimes washed his shirt, his socks and his underwear. But that was all they did for him and in the middle of a barrack full of people this small orphan was terribly alone."[12]

As little is known about Albertico's further fate as about that of the sisters Inge and Stefanie Mandel, born in Dresden in December 1930 and June 1933, respectively. In September 1943 they were brought without any relatives to Bergen-Belsen from the Dutch transit camp Westerbork. Marietta Duschnitz also described the situation of the sisters in her notes about the children in Bergen-Belsen: "They had already been in the camp for some time, more than half a year, and in these months they had struggled through admirably. That is Inge had struggled through, for the 10-year-old Stefie was nothing other than a spoilt child who shrugged off all that was uncomfortable and sad and left all the concerns to her only three year older sister. Inge was in contrast in all she did a fully-grown person. The work involved in keeping things clean and in order as well as in procuring the little bit of food which one got in the camp posed great problems for adults. But Inge filled this task with a dogged sense of duty. She fought hard for her place at the stove or in the food lines, she obtained milk for Stefie and gained a place at the wash room. It was her misfortune that with 13 she looked like 17, for in addition to her own work she was also sent to work in the barracks, although she was still well under the age required to work. But Inge's greatest task was Stefie. [...] When she came home crying with hands and feet aching from the cold after standing for a long time at roll call, Inge, forgetting her own aching limbs, was immediately ready to rub her sister's hands, to take off her shoes and to bring her to bed with

---

12  Marietta D. Moskin (formerly Duschnitz), "Albertico" (unpublished text in English, unpaged, copy in the Archive of the Bergen-Belsen Memorial). Marietta Moskin wrote this text and some other stories about younger fellow prisoners in the internment camp at Biberach prior to liberation, to where she had been transferred from Bergen-Belsen in January 1945. (Statements made to the author on 11. 7. 1994 and 27. 9. 1994).

comforting kisses. Inge herself had nobody to whom she could have poured out her own grief."[13]

The transport with which Inge and Stefie Mandel arrived at Bergen-Belsen was actually planned for Theresienstadt (where the Mandel sisters suspected their parents to be), but was then redirected to Bergen-Belsen. In January 1944 this group was then indeed transported to Theresienstadt as originally planned. Around twenty prisoners from this group remained however in Bergen-Belsen for no recognisable reason — amongst them the Mandel sisters — and were sent instead on a transport on the 24. 5. 1944. "It was one of the few times that I saw Inge cry. [...] I believe she had some evil premonition without knowing exactly what it was. As she said goodbye to me she gave me an exercise book. 'Keep this for me' she requested, 'it's my diary and I don't think that I can keep it! You'll give it back to me when the war is over and we meet again in freedom!'"[14] There was to be no such reunion for the Mandel sisters: the transport with which they left Bergen-Belsen in May 1944 went to Auschwitz, where their trace vanishes.[15]

From the end of 1944 onwards there was an increasing number of Jewish children who first became orphans in Bergen-Belsen through the death of their parents. How traumatic this was for the children affected, not the least due to the circumstances of the deaths, is depicted by the Dutch woman Renata Laqueur: "For days a little girl sat at the bed of its mother. The little one was hideously dirty, the clothes torn, her hair lice-ridden, eyes gummed up with nits, her legs puffed up through oedema. And yet she sat there, forced the critically ill mother to eat pieces of lukewarm pieces of turnips, till she suddenly gobbled down the bites with a greedy but guilty look. The mother had shoved the blankets aside, they were pressing too much against the swollen legs. Like white, glassy columns they lay on the grey blankets swarming with lice. The shawl wrapped around the head had slipped and revealed her short cropped, sticky hair. The child cried and went away to get something edible. 'Mother', she said as she was going, 'mother, I'll find some gruel for you.' The women, once a well-known beauty from the Amsterdam Jewish quarter, did not answer. Her small, thick hand hung out of the wooden bunk, water dripped from her swollen fingers and formed wet stains on the ground. When the girl came back the mother was dead. The little one sat there petrified for a long time on the bed. Finally she spread the blanket over the dead mother and straightened

---

13  Marietta D. Moskin, "Stefie and Inge" (unpublished text written in German, unpaged, copy in the Archive of the Bergen-Belsen Memorial). This text was also written in the internment camp Biberbach in early 1945.
14  Ibid.
15  Cf. Nachlaß J. Weiss (as in note 4).

the headscarf. With the red beaker of gruel in her hand she went away. Now she was alone. The father had died of camp fever. The corpse was left lying during the night and it was first collected on the next morning, for although the crematorium was working at full capacity it could not cope with the work that 'keeps coming up'. The mattress in the bunk was turned over and the floor cleaned. During the whole night water had dripped out of the hand."[16]

The children suddenly orphaned now had to be provided for by someone else and this task often fell to the older siblings. "I am not capable of depicting", writes Schlomo Samson looking back, himself much involved in looking after the children at Westerbork and Bergen-Belsen, "how children aged between 12-14 kept their families alive, especially when both parents were dead. It is really unbelievable — I'll never forget it. I know of families where a 12 to 13-year-old girl looked after her five younger brothers and sisters till liberation and brought them back safe and sound to Holland."[17]

And yet, not all children were old enough or had the strength to look after their siblings so that they, just like the only children who had become orphans, had to rely on being looked after by the women from their barrack — children up to the age of 14 years were as a rule housed in the women's barracks at Bergen-Belsen.

One striking example for this is to be found in the report given by Lin Jaldati, a childhood friend of Anne Frank: "On the plank bed across from us lay a mother with three children, Marianne Asscher. Her husband, who had worked in the diamond trade in Holland, was forced on a transport with two children over fourteen years, all three died. Marianne was already sick when she arrived at our block. She was particularly worried about her youngest child, a girl of almost two years. She was born in Westerbork, could not yet sit up, reacted only with large sad eyes and whimpered softly to herself. Now and than the mother gave her a little milk powder that she had brought with her from the family camp and small pieces of bread that she chewed soft beforehand. It was a mystery to us how this little creature still managed to live. Jannie, myself and a Frau Schwarz, who herself had a six-year-old girl with her, we looked after both of the other Asscher children: Bram was about eleven and Jopie around seven years old. First of all we snipped off their hair outside and then carefully scratched away the lice from their scalp every second day and cooled their heads with snow or

---

16  Renate Laqueur, Bergen-Belsen Tagebuch 1944/1945 [Bergen-Belsen Diary 1944/1945], Hannover 1983, p. 97 f. (supplement summer 1946).
17  Schlomo Samson, Zwischen Finsternis und Licht. 50 Jahre nach Bergen-Belsen. Erinnerungen eines Leipziger Juden [Between Darkness and Light. 50 Years after Bergen-Belsen. Recollections of a Leipzig Jew], Jerusalem 1995, p. 273.

puddle water. Marianne Asscher had already had a high fever for days, one morning she lay in agony. Soon after she died. We laid her in one of our blankets and six of us carried her to the large grave. Just as we wanted to break gently to Bram and Jopie that their mother was dead, a Kapo came into our barrack with a list and called out: 'One dead, Marianne Asscher.' For the boys this was terrible. I took Brammetje in my arms and tried to console him. Jannie put Jopie on her lap, he cried till he feel asleep. The baby also had fever, dried out skin and bones struggled against death. Then we also had to lay this tiny little thing in the grave. Brammetje and Jopie were desperate. We looked after them like our own children and were able to drag them along till we were set free."[18]

On 16. 9. 1944 the last transport from Westerbork reached Bergen-Belsen with a total of 279 prisoners. In the transport surveys that have survived is a separate list with the heading "Group 'Unknown Children'", which notes a total of 50 children.[19] They carried signs, tied around their necks with shoelaces, with the inscription "Unknown Child" and the suspected name. Like the other prisoners in this transport, these children were brought to Bergen-Belsen in freight cars and had been on their way for two days and three nights.[20] Almost all the names and dates of birth on the transport list of these "unknown children" from the Netherlands are marked by question marks. "Unknown girl, supposedly Rothe? Ellen? 29. 1. 39?" it says, or: "Unknown boy, Jossje?, ca. 2 years".[21] According to these uncertain details, 35 of these children were younger than 6 years old; for the oldest child November 1933 is given as date of birth, for the youngest 24. 12. 1943.

But who were these orphans and why were they deported to Bergen-Belsen? The first part of the question can be answered relatively easily using the reports of former prisoners. These children had obviously "dived under", they were namely children who had been hidden with non-Jewish Dutch by their Jewish parents or Jewish organisations, eventually though discovered and deported to Westerbork. Before diving under they were mostly provided with a new identity, that is with new names, dates of birth etc., and the accompanying forged papers, thus explaining the missing names and dates of birth or the question marks added to these details on the transport list.

18  Lin Jaldati/Eberhard Rebling, Sag nie, du gehst den letzten Weg. Erinnerungen [Never say you're taking the last path. Recollections], Berlin 1986, p. 423 f.
19  Cf. "Transport aus Lager Westerbork am 13. 9. 44. Übersicht" (Rijksinstitut voor Oorlogsdocumentatie, Amsterdam: C [64] 312); cf. for the following also Daphne Meijer, Unbekannte Kinder. De laatste trein uit Westerbork [Unknown Children. The Last Train from Westerbork], in: Kinderen in kamp Westerbork (= Westerbork Cahiers 2), Assen/Hooghalen 1994, p. 86–103.
20  Cf. S.Samson, p. 325.
21  See note 19.

In earlier such cases of Jewish children who had hidden in the Netherlands but were then discovered, they were deported from Westerbork to
one of the extermination camps.[22] For the group brought to Bergen-Belsen
there must have therefore been a specific reason why these orphans were
dealt with differently. That photos of these 50 "unknown children" were
hung up at Westerbork and the prisoners ordered to tell the camp command
more about these children, indicates this specific reason, namely the uncertainty about the identity of these children.[23] In contrast to earlier cases of
Jewish children apprehended in hide-outs, this group proved to be a problem
for the SS because doubts arose as to the *Jewish* identity of these children.
These doubts had obviously emerged at Westerbork, where Hanni and
Joschua Birnbaum, a Jewish couple from Berlin who had been at Westerbork
with their six children since the end of 1939, were ordered by the camp
commandant to look after the Jewish orphans, for whom an "orphanage"
had been erected.[24]

The orphans were not excluded from the weekly transports which left
here for Auschwitz and Sobibor. And yet, in individual cases, the Birnbaums
were again and again able to get orphans, already designated for "transport
to the East", struck from the transport list, whether through false certifica-
tions from the Jewish camp doctors or by being able to obtain papers which
showed that a child was only of "half-Jewish" extraction.

In this context we need to consider what S. Samson describes in his recollections: "Amongst the children there were some who did not look 'Jewish'
at all and others whose names had no Jewish sound. Hanni Birnbaum [...]
had a brillant idea. She went to Obersturmführer Gemmeker [SS First Lieutenant, camp commandant at Westerbork] and asked him, as if she were
completely amazed — why had so many non-Jewish children been brought
to the camp and so to the orphanage. Gemmeker was astonished, wanted to
be in no way responsible for having sent Aryan children to Auschwitz. He
asked Hanni Birnbaum to draw up a list of these children and immediately
ordered that they were not permitted to be sent on a transport until their

---

22   Cf. the recollections of Julie Bial de Vries (Spitz), who occasionally worked in the
     Westerbork "orphanage" and experienced such a transport of orphans for "work
     deployment in the East", the youngest of whom was one year old (Beit Lohamei
     Haghetaot 296/24/01).

23   Cf. recollections of Rudolf Martin Cheim (YIVO Institute, New York: RG 804),
     p. 4. Here Chiem cites approvingly an anonymous newspaper report on Westerbork
     published after 1945.

24   Cf. on the following "Erinnerungen geschrieben von Joschua Herschel Birnbaum"
     ["Recollections written by Joschua Herschel Birnbaum"] (unpublished report,
     copy in Archive of the Bergen-Belsen Memorial); Willy Lindwer, Kamp van
     Hoop en Wanhoop. Getugen van Westerbork, 1939–1945, Amsterdam 1990,
     p. 101–109.

descent had been established. [...] The research into the descent of these children was naturally difficult. It was difficult to obtain the documentation and the various directive offices were overburdened. The children remained in Westerbork for a long time."[25]

That this group of, still at this point in time, "unknown children" was transferred to Bergen-Belsen in September 1944 was not only due to a directive issued by the Reichssicherheitshauptamt [Reich Security Main Office] to extensively dismantle the Westerbork camp, but rather also corresponded to the criteria for the transport of selected groups of Jewish prisoners to Bergen-Belsen. The first transport of Jewish prisoners to the "Exchange Camp Bergen-Belsen" — Polish Jews with papers stating nationality from mainly South American states — was brought to Bergen-Belsen so as to have their identity documentation intensely reviewed.

In February 1944 the Birnbaum family was brought from Westerbork to Bergen-Belsen, where in September 1944, directly after the arrival of the "unknown children", they were once more charged by the camp commandant to set up an "orphanage" for these children based on the model of Westerbork. For this purpose a separated barrack section, previously used as a depot for corpses, was initially made available.

The "unknown children" remained, however, barely two months in the care of the Birnbaum family at Bergen-Belsen. On 17. 11. 1944 they were sent on a transport to Theresienstadt. As a comparison between the transport lists from September 1944 and November 1944 (from Bergen-Belsen to Theresienstadt) shows, the review of their descent had hardly produced any further information about the identity of these children.[26] For the children affected this did not prove to be a disadvantage, but rather protection, since, in addition, the Dutch resistance in Amsterdam had spread rumours to the effect that these children were not Jewish, rumours which also reached the Gestapo.[27]

Even if the precise reason for the transport of these children from Bergen-Belsen to Theresienstadt can no longer be reconstructed using the available documentation, it can, however, be interpreted as an attempt to raise the chances of survival for these "unknown children" till the final clarification of their identity, for Theresienstadt was considered, even more so than Bergen-Belsen, to be a "Vorzugslager" ["camp for privileged persons"]. As Bergen-Belsen evolved more and more into a death camp from the end of 1944 and a large proportion of these children were already sick (with typhoid) as they were transferred to Theresienstadt, but also given the fact that almost

25  S. Samson, p. 374 f.
26  Cf. Name list "Transport 17. 11. 1944" (Nachlaß J.Weiss, as in note 4)
27  Cf. D.Meijer, p. 92 f.

all of the children from this group were ultimately liberated at Theresienstadt, such an interpretation can indeed be considered plausible.[28]

Even after the transport of the "unknown children" the "orphanage"
looked after by the Birnbaums in the Star Camp at Bergen-Belsen remained,
for here, from the end of 1944, more and more children became orphans
following the death of their parents. In so far as nobody else adopted them,
they were handed over to the "orphan barrack", where at the beginning of
April 1945 over 50 Jewish orphans lived. Together with the other prisoners
earmarked for exchange, they were then forced to leave Bergen-Belsen shortly
before liberation with a train transport but were finally liberated at Tröbitz.

Even the intensive efforts of the Birnbaums in looking after the Jewish
children entrusted to them at the "orphanage" could not hinder that some of
them died in Bergen-Belsen.[29] That Hanni and Joschua Birnbaum nevertheless did not give up was also due to their Jewish religiousness, which they
practised in accordance with Orthodox values and also sought to convey
to "their" Jewish orphans. What kind of impression this left on the children is explained by Lisette van Vlijmen, who had belonged to the group
of "unknown children": "Probably one of the reasons why I always wanted
to go to Israel was because we heard at the camp 'Next Year in Jerusalem'
from the family Birnbaum. Every evening a prayer was spoken with this
text and every evening we repeated it. This left a deep impression. It really
became an obsession. I just had to go there."[30]

Even at the end of March 1945, as Bergen-Belsen had long since become
a death camp and the corpses were already piling up between the barracks,
the Birnbaums organised a traditional Seder evening at the start of the
Passover celebrations for the children in the "orphanage". "The second
part of the Seder", so noted the deputy "Jewish Elder" at Bergen-Belsen,
Josef Weiss, shortly after liberation, "was just as solemn as the first, the
songs were sung by the children. I have never heard them sung as beautifully
as from these children's voices. To finish we sang together 'Leschanah haba
biruschalajim' [Next Year in Jerusalem]. Moved, we left the children's home
to return to 'reality'. I accompanied my wife and our son to their barracks,
then I went to the office to draw up together with my staff the usual daily

---

28  Cf. Resi Weglein, Als Krankenschwester im KZ Theresienstadt. Erinnerungen
    einer Ulmer Jüdin [A Nurse in Theresienstadt. Recollections of a Ulmer Jew],
    Stuttgart 1988, p. 75; H. G. Adler, Theresienstadt 1941–1945. Das Anlitz einer
    Zwangsgesmeinschaft [Theresienstadt 1941–1945. The Face of a Forced
    Community], 2nd improved and supplemented edition, Tübingen 1960, p. 564;
    Erinnerungen Joschua H. Birnbaum, p. 17.
29  Cf. Interview with Sonni Schey-Birnbaum, 1989 (Archive of the Bergen-Belsen
    Memorial).
30  Quoted in D. Meijer, p. 93 f.

name list of those who had died in the entire camp. Today it was '596', from these ca. 500 Jews."[31]

A further group of Jewish orphans was formed by those children who had come to Bergen-Belsen on evacuation transports or similar means since the end of 1944. As there are very few name lists for the evacuation transports — due to the destruction of documentation by the SS — it is hardly possible to ascertain how many Jewish children landed at Bergen-Belsen already as orphans in the course of such transports, and who, in contrast to the Jewish children in the section of Bergen-Belsen characterised as the "Aufenthaltslager", never had the status of "exchange prisoners" and were put in the so-called Large Women's Camp that had newly come into being at the end of 1944.

A few biographical examples allow us to nevertheless show the paths by which these children came to Bergen-Belsen. Eva Katz, born in 1936, was deported with her mother from Budapest in March 1944 after the German occupation of Hungary, but lost contact with her during the transport to Ravensbrück — she was presumably shot by the guard troops. There she found though many "substitute mothers" who looked after her till she — presumably in February/March 1944 — came to Bergen-Belsen on a large evacuation transport, where she was freed on the 15 April 1945.[32]

Quite different is the story of Renée Gross and her deaf sister Hertha, born in December 1933 and May 1937 in Bratislava, respectively.[33] Their parents brought them to a farm close to the Moravian border to hide them from persecution. As their parents were deported to Auschwitz at the beginning of 1944, the payments for both of the sisters ceased, forcing them to leave their hide-out and return to Bratislava. There they found shelter at night in a small mattress factory, but were forced to spend the days on the streets, where they were recognised by acquaintances of their parents. After about three weeks, in which they lived merely on bread and water, they saw no other alternative but to go to the Slovak Police and request to be sent on the same transport as their parents. Handed-over to the Gestapo by the Slovak Police, the Gross sisters were first brought to the collection camp at Sered and from there presumably directly to Bergen-Belsen at the end of 1944.

31   Joseph Weiss, Report on Bergen-Belsen from 11. 1. 44 till 10. 4. 45, written on 7. 6. 45 in Tröbitz (Rijksinstituut voor Oorlogsdocumentatie C [II] 09), p. 11.

32   Cf. Night of Remembrance. 50th Anniversary of the Destruction of the Hungarian Jewish Community, ed. by Yeshiva Gedolah, Los Angeles 1994 (without page numbers).

33   For the following see Interview RH-NIJK 4/14/83 (Jerome Riker International Study of Organized Persecution of Children, Sands Point, New York).

Like Eva Katz, Fredzia Lichtensztajn came as a nine-year-old lonly child to Bergen-Belsen.[34] Whereas her mother and two brothers were deported to Treblinka, she initially remained with her father at the hard labour camp Petrikau (Piotrkov) and was finally brought to Bergen-Belsen without her father (presumably via the hard labour camp Tschenstochau) in the winter of 1944/45, where like Eva Katz she found "substitute mothers".

What may seem as implausible at a first glance — the enlistment of a child to hard labour and subsequent deportation to a concentration camp — was however no isolated case. In other concentration camps there were also other Jewish children who had been used as forced labourers and then — whether as part of an evacuation or a punishment transport — sent to a concentration camp. "Yesterday another Russian transport is supposed to have arrived", notes for instance Edgar Kupfer-Koberwitz in his Dachau diary, "many of them children, barefoot, some of whom were just six to eight years of age. — Till now our youngest Russian was nine years old."[35]

Finally, a further clearly identifiable group of Jewish orphans at Bergen-Belsen were the children of the so-called "diamonds".[36] In May 1944 Dutch-Jewish diamond traders and cutters — who with their family members a totalled 213 persons — were transferred from Westerbork to Bergen-Belsen, the objective being to set up a "diamond polish workshop" through which urgently required foreign currency was to flow into the German Reich. They were therefore housed in their own special barrack and relieved of labour duties. At the same however, the "diamonds" were viewed as hostages and were put under pressure to hand-over their allegedly hidden raw diamonds. As the interrogations and threats achieved nothing, it was decided to send the diamonds on a punishment transport. On 4 December 1944 the men were transported to Sachsenhausen; on the following day the women and children were to be transported. Contrary to the original plans to also transport the children from Bergen-Belsen — on the prisoner list recorded by the deputy "Jewish Elder" of the Star Camp the transport date behind the names of the children and their mothers was given as 5 December 1944 — it was decided at short notice to leave the diamond children at Bergen-Belsen.

Rachel Sacksioni-Levee, who (falsely) passed herself off as a diamond and was sent with the other women in this group from Bergen-Belsen to hard labour at Helmstedt-Beendorf, an external subsidiary camp to Neu-engamme, reports: "On the morning of 5 December the women and chil-

---

34 For the following see interview of the author with Rena Quint, 3. 6. 1997 (Archive of the Bergen-Belsen Memorial).

35 Edger Kupfer-Koberwitz, Dachauer Tagebücher. Die Aufzeichnungen des Häftlings 24814 [Dachau Diary. Notes of Prisoner 24814], Munich 1997, p. 187.

36 For the following E.Kolb, Geschichte des "Aufenthaltsagers", p. 117–121; Report from Rudolf Martin Cheim, p. 23–25.

dren were to be sent on the transport. The children were then lined up separately at the camp; the women were to walk, the children were to be brought with cars to the station. We thus marched out of the camp, and the children remained with the others. As we passed a garage, the mothers were called aside and somebody came and said to them: 'I've got something to tell you. The children aren't going. You're going to a labour camp to work, the children are staying here at Bergen-Belsen, but you'll see each other again later.' You can imagine the atmosphere that arose. They cried out: 'Just shoot them dead.' They were half mad from worry. It defies description. We were forced to continue to walk, and the mothers were brought to the station on carts. As we arrived there they were already sitting in the freight cars which stood ready for us."[37]

The sudden nature of this decision — whose background is yet to be explained — to leave the diamond children in Bergen-Belsen after all had as one consequence among many that nothing had been planned for the housing and care of these children, so that they — completely frightened through the unexpected and brutal separation from their mothers — were first of all left to look after themselves in a garage outside the camp complex. On the evening of 5 December 1944 Abel Herzberg noted in his Bergen-Belsen diary: "Beyond the camp gates, in the garage, the little ones sit together. They have been given some white bread. Isn't that touching? Some of the elder children are looking after them. Just now camp blankets were picked up here for the children. Oh, poor H. with his sweet snotty nose, six years old! The children know nothing. We know what's going to happen. I won't write it down. Perhaps after the war."[38]

The fear indirectly expressed by Herzberg, that certain death awaited these children, did not however come true. Rather they were separately housed first of all in the Star Camp and then in the Large Women's Camp, where several Jewish women, who had been brought to Bergen-Belsen from Auschwitz a few days beforehand, looked after them with the approval of the SS.

Amongst the total of 56 diamond children whose parents were transported from Bergen-Belsen on 4 and 5 December 1944 were ten youths over the age of 14; the youngest of these children was born in the transit camp Westerbork in November 1943.[39] In accordance with their age, these

37  Verklaring van Rachel Sacksioni-Levee [19. 6. 1947], opgenomen door [...] het Rijksinstituut voor Oorlogsdocumentatie (Herinneringscentrum Kamp Westerbork: 7778-01), p. 6.

38  Abel Herzberg, Zweistromland. Tagebuch aus Bergen-Belsen [Between Two Streams. Diary from Bergen-Belsen], Wittingen 1997, p. 197.

39  Cf. "Transport List for the Departing Transport of 5.December 1944", (Nachlaß J. Weiss, as in footnote 4).

children were allocated to two different barracks in the Large Women's Camp so that in some cases siblings were housed separately from one another, but could be with one another during the day.[40]

Even when it is considered that the death toll amongst children at Bergen-Belsen was overall less than that of adults, it is nevertheless remarkable that almost all of the diamond children survived Bergen-Belsen; there is no information on the fate of only two children from this group, and only two more diamond children died at Bergen-Belsen in the week following liberation as a result of their imprisonment.

This is probably due to in the first instance to the Jewish women — amongst them a doctor and several nurses — who looked after these children courageously, showed a great deal of skill in dealing with the SS, acquired additional food rations, medicine etc. and understood how to protect in particular the younger children from the SS.[41]

With both of these barracks for the children and youths a second "orphanage" now arose — in addition to the one looked after by the Birnbaum couple in the Star Camp — in which, besides the diamond children, an increasing number of Jewish children who came to Bergen-Belsen on evacuation transports ended up. These were children from Poland, the Soviet Union and other Eastern European states, about whose number and fate hardly anything precise is known, however, due to the destruction of sources by the SS. The recollections written after the liberation of Bergen-Belsen also provide no clear information on the number and origin of the children housed in the "orphanage" of the Large Women's Camp.[42] The most reliable details are probably contained in a letter written by the English military rabbi, Issac Levy, on 26 April 1945, where he speaks of 100 liberated children from the "orphanage" at Bergen-Belsen, 85 of whom were of Jewish descent.[43]

40   Cf. Osher M. Lehmann, Faith at the Brink. An Autobiography of the Formative Years, New York 1996, p. 150.
41   Interview with Hadassah Rosensaft, 18. 5. 1981 (Center for Oral History, University of Connecticut); Interview with Luba Frederik (formerly Tryszynska), 18. 8. 1980 (Holocaust Memorial Museum, Miami); Hadassah Bimko-Rosensaft, The Children of Belsen, in: Belsen. Published by Irgun Sheerit Hapleta Me Haezor Habriti, Tel Aviv 1957, p. 98–108; O. Lehmann, Faith at the Brink, p. 147 ff.
42   The numbers fluctuate between 101 (so the number given by H.Rosensaft in her interview from 18. 5. 1981 (see note 41) and 300 (as given by Derrick Sington. Die Tore öffnen sich [The Gates Opened], Hamburg 1948, p. 149 f.)
43   Public Record Office, London: WO 309/424.

Robert Sigel

# Clemency Pleas and General Pardons

## War Criminals in the American Zone of Occupation

"Munich, 29. 1. 46
General McNarney!
I have just read in the press about the three pardons for the hangmen from Dachau granted by General Lieutenant Truscott. [!] Please allow me, Herr General, an unhappy mother, whose son was arrested as a political opponent in 1933 and brought to Dachau and who is without a [!] sign of life from him for all these years, do not, Herr General, confirm the pardon. Free us from this sort of person. Already for twelve years I have been ashamed to be a German, as a work-shy, stateless swindler was placed at the head of the German Reich. And his supporters, who have brought so much misfortune upon the people, are to be pardoned? Please, Herr General, do not do it. [...]"[1]

This letter to the Commander-in-Chief of the American Forces in Europe, General McNarney, refers to the so-called "Order on Review" from 24 January 1946, in which a series of judgements from the first large concentration camp trial, the Main Trial for Dachau Concentration Camp, were amended. From 40 accused, 36 were condemned to death on 13 December 1946 at this trial, the remaining four had received prison sentences; after both reviews of the judgements handed down, 28 death sentences finally remained, all others were commuted to prison sentences.[2]

The reviewing authority within the American Military jurisdiction possessed the right to repeal guilty verdicts, to amend, revoke, or reduce sentences and to order new trials. An acquittal however could not be revoked. An increase in the sentence handed down was only possible in rare, precisely

1   USA versus Martin Gottfried Weiss et al., Nov. 15, 1945–Dec. 13, 1945, Post-trial Records, Roll 5, Target 39, Nr. 000918-000919, BayHstA Munich, OMGUS Dachau War Criminal Trials, Microfilm 1/5.
2   On the war criminal trials in the American Zone of Occupation, the so-called Dachau Trials, see: Robert Sigel, Im Interesse der Gerechtigkeit. Die Dachauer Kriegsverbrecherprozesse 1945–1948 [In the Interests of Justice. The Dachau War Criminal Trials 1945–1948], Frankfurt a. M./New York 1992.

defined cases; such an increase never eventuated within the entire area of American war criminal trials.

The sentences so reviewed, confirmed or amended were from then on legally valid. Death sentences were, however, subjected to a second review before they, after their confirmation by the Commander-in-Chief of the American Forces in Europe, became valid. This second reviewing authority — the confirming authority — possessed the same powers as the first.

Responsible for the review was not a court however, but rather the so-called review boards that were incorporated into the section of the US Army responsible for the prosecution of war criminals.

As the Federal Supreme Court in the USA had refused to accept jurisdiction for the war criminal trials in the US Zone of Occupation, after the military courts and the two review authorities had handed down their decisions, clemency pleas remained the last opportunity to hinder an execution of sentence, to slip out of the noose.

Whereas review applications were lodged by the lawyers as a rule, pleas for reprieve could be handed in by the accused themselves or their relatives. In contrast to the review applications, the focus of argumentation for clemency pleas lay less in the area of evidence as in mitigating personal circumstances. An analysis of the numerous clemency pleas shows that most follow a set pattern in which specific set pieces keep recurring.

The common opening stereotype is the protestation by the applicant not to have voluntary served duty in the concentration camp, but rather to have been delegated there against their will. So writes Anton Endres, SS-Obersharführer [SS-Staff Sergeant], condemned to death on 13. 12. 1945 in the Main Trial for Dachau Concentration Camp: "I have never been a member of the NSDAP or one of its organisations. My joining the Waffen-SS, too, did not follow from my own initiative, rather I was called up to the Waffen-SS for service in Dachau at the beginning of the war in 1939."[3]

Similar is the argumentation in the clemency plea made for Baptist Eichelsdorfer, condemned to death at the same trial: "My husband, who never belonged to either the NSDAP or the SS, was reposted from the Wehrmacht due to illness in the autumn of 1944 and given command of Camp No. 7 and later Camp No. 4."[4]

Further examples could be given; transfer requests which were allegedly rejected are mentioned, an inner disapproval with which the unwanted

---

3  USA versus Martin Gottfried Weiss et al., Nov. 15, 1945–Dec. 13, 1945, Post-trial Records, Roll 5, Target 8, Nr. 000131-000132, BayHStA Munich, OMGUS Dachau War Criminal Trials, Microfilm 1/5.

4  USA versus Martin Gottfried Weiss et al., Nov. 15, 1945–Dec.13, 1945, Posttrial Records, Roll 5, Target 6, Nr. 000084, BayHStA Munich, OMGUS Dachau War Criminal Trials, Microfilm 1/5.

duty in the concentration camp was grudgingly carried out is depicted, etc.

Another often recurring topos in the clemency pleas is how unemployment, poverty and adverse social conditions are cited as reasons for joining the SS. Typical in this regard are the clemency pleas for Josef Jarolin and Josef Filleböck, both condemned to death on 13. 12. 1945; the clemency pleas were submitted by their wives: "Only due to a long period of unemployment did he go to the SS, for he had to care for his parents and in part also for his siblings. He was always of the conviction that a man should earn an honest living."[5] "I've been married to my husband for 19 years. In this time, in which we also had to go through grave economic distress as a result of 4 years of unemployment suffered by my husband, we had in him the best imaginable family father devoted to our well-being."[6]

The argument presented in the clemency pleas, to have become an SS-man against one's will or due to social distress, sought to refute the accusation of "common design" in the joint participation in a criminal plan — the running of a concentration camp; frequently this argument was followed by the appeal to the necessity of obeying orders: "I implore once again to make allowances for the fact that he did all that genuinely incriminates him only in executing his duty as a soldier".[7] "Never thought that a soldier who was forced to carry out commands would be condemned to death. [...] Believe me, Herr General, if I had refused to carry out the orders given by Zill, I myself would have been condemned to death, ruthlessly and without mercy from one of the feared and notorious SS and Police Courts on the grounds of refusal to obey orders or some similar paragraph."[8]

The next level of exonerating oneself from guilt is the assertion of never having been guilty of personal maltreatment, even going so far as claiming to have helped the prisoners, of having done good for them. So states the clemency plea for Fritz Degelow, condemned to death at the first Dachau trial: "Also during the march-off of one section of the prisoners from Dachau — from 26 to 29. 4 — I alone hindered a far greater disaster by halting the

5   USA versus Martin Gottfried Weiss et al., Nov 15, 1945–Dec.13, 1945, Posttrial Records, Roll 5, Target 12, Nr. 000245, BayHStA Munich, OMGUS Dachau War Criminal Trials, Microfilm 1/5.

6   USA versus Martin Gottfried Weiss et al., Nov. 15, 1945–Dec. 13, 1945, Posttrial Records, Roll 5, Target 9, Nr. 000150, BayHStA Munich, OMGUS Dachau War Criminal Trials, Microfilm 1/5.

7   Clemency plea for Josef Jarolin, USA versus Martin Gottfried Weiss et al., Nov. 15, 1945–Dec. 13, 1945, Posttrial Records, Roll 5, Target 12, Nr. 000245, BayHStA Munich, OMGUS Dachau War Criminal Trials, Microfilm 1/5.

8   Clemency plea Simon Kiern, USA versus Gottfried Martin Weiss et al., Nov. 15, 1945–Dec. 13, 1945, Posttrial Records, Roll 5, target 14, Nr. 000308-000309, BayHStA Munich, OMGUS Dachau War Criminal Trials, Microfilm 1/5.

march on 28. 4., by ordering the distribution of the rest of the existing provisions and the transfer of prisoners to the American troops."[9] In another plea: "In both camps he constantly tried to create better conditions for the prisoners and he was successful in gaining many improvements and relief."[10] Or: "My reprimanding of the prisoners was though only with an open hand [...] it only ensued so as to prevent an even graver punishment."[11]

Similar examples, sometimes with the naming of witnesses, are to be found throughout almost all of the pleas.

After seeking to lessen their guilt, as a rule a reference to the private situation follows: reprieve for the sake of the children, the wife, the parents, either for material or idealistic reasons: "I am married, have 3 children, 3, 5 and 7 years of age: together with my wife, who is not in the best state of health, farm a 20 Tagwerk large agricultural property."[12] "I have a wife and 3 children who have lost their flat and possessions through the war."[13] "Therefore I request — also in consideration of my suffering family in Waltershausen / Thuringia, a wife, 2 children and 2 grandchildren — a just verdict."[14] "My parents are honourable and respected working people. I have to provide for a wife with a small child and in part for my parents."[15] "Herr General, in the name of my three children — they are 2, 3 and 5 years of age — I plead you to spare my husband's life. [...] spare me and my children the disgrace of having the husband and father executed."[16] "I do not know how I am

9   USA versus Martin Gottfried Weiss et al., Nov 15, 1945–Dec. 13, 1945, Posttrial Records, Roll 5, Target 4, Nr. 000063, BayHStA Munich, OMGUS Dachau War Criminal Trials, Microfilm 1/5.

10  Clemency plea Baptist Eichelsdorfer, USA versus Martin Gottfried Weiss et al., Nov. 15, 1945–Dec. 13, 1945, Posttrial Records, Roll 5, Target 6, Nr. 000084, BayHStA Munich, OMGUS Dachau War Criminal Trials, Microfilm 1/5.

11  Clemency plea Alfred Kramer, USA versus Martin Gottfried Weiss et al., Nov. 15, 1945–Dec. 13, 1945, Posttrial Records, Roll 5, Target 17, Nr. 000372, BayHStA Munich, OMGUS Dachau War Criminal Trials, Microfilm 1/5.

12  Clemency plea Anton Endres, USA versus Martin Gottfried Weiss et al., Nov. 15, 1945–Dec. 13, 1945, Posttrial Records, Roll 5, Target 8, Nr. 000131, BayHStA Munich, OMGUS Dachau War Criminal Trials, Microfilm 1/5.

13  Clemency plea Alfred Kramer, USA versus Martin Gottfried Weiss et al., Nov. 15, 1945–Dec. 13, 1945, Posttrial Records, Roll 5, Target 17, Nr. 000372, BayHStA Munich, OMGUS Dachau War Criminal Trials, Microfilm 1/5.

14  Clemency plea Fritz Degelow, USA versus Martin Gottfried Weiss et al., Nov. 15, 1945–Dec. 13, 1945, Posttrial Records, Roll 5, Target 4, Nr. 000063, BayHStA Munich, OMGUS Dachau War Criminal Trials, Microfilm 1/5.

15  Clemency plea Leonhard Eichberger, USA versus Martin Gottfried Weiss et al., Nov. 15, 1945–Dec. 13, 1945, Posttrial Records, Roll 5, Target 5, Nr. 000078, BayHStA Munich, OMGUS Dachau War Criminal Trials, Microfilm 1/5.

16  Clemency plea Dr. Hans Eisele, USA versus Martin Gottfried Weiss et al., Nov. 15, 1945–Dec. 13, 1945, Posttrial Records, Roll 5, Target 7, Nr. 000124, BayHStA Munich, OMGUS Dachau War Criminal Trials, Microfilm 1/5.

going to explain the humiliating death by the noose if my plea is rejected, especially since my children only have the best memories of their father."[17]

A last argument was frequently added to the request for mercy repeated at the end of every plea by the applicants, one that was to indicate a change in attitude: "For these reasons I request that the death sentence [...] be changed into a corresponding prison sentence so as to give me the opportunity [...] of being able to become a useful member in a new German democracy."[18] "Give me freedom! [...] Long live democracy!"[19] "I would like to help somewhere in Europe to clear away the war damage caused by the National Socialist government."[20] "I swear on all that I cherish that my husband, whom you shall spare through my hopeful plea, shall only serve one resolution for the rest of his life, to prove himself worthy of the mercy shown to him."[21]

Even when consideration is given to the occasion for and the objective pursued by these pleas, when consideration is given to the fact that it was literally a matter of life or death for the supplicants, an odd image nevertheless arises out of these clemency pleas, one in which the concentration camp thugs ultimately become victims, who, apolitical, joined the SS because of economic hardship, then sought to evade duty in the concentration camps, and as this failed, took it upon themselves to improve the living conditions of the prisoners. And if they once did anything wrong, it only happened because they were ordered to do so. All devoted and caring family fathers, imbued with the resolve to become active for a better, democratic world in the future.

Is this image only the expression of an understandable manoeuvre to save their own life, or, after all, the self-image of culprits convinced of their own innocence?

An investigation into the effectiveness of the clemency pleas shows that these seldom brought about the desired results. The number of commuted sentences in both review instances, by no means small, is as a rule not to be

---

17  Clemency plea Dr. Fritz Hintermayer, USA versus Martin Gottfried Weiss et al., Nov. 15, 1945–Dec. 13, 1945, Posttrial Records, Roll 5, Target 11, Nr. 000215, BayHStA Munich, OMGUS Dachau War Criminal Trials, Microfilm 1/5

18  Clemency plea Anton Endres, USA versus Martin Gottfried Weiss et al., Nov. 15, 1945–Dec. 13, 1945, Posttrial Records, Roll 5, Target 8, Nr. 000132, BayHStA Munich, OMGUS Dachau War Criminal Trials, Microfilm 1/5

19  Clemency plea Simon Kiern, USA versus Martin Gottfried Weiss et al., Nov. 15, 1945–Dec. 13, 1945, Posttrial Records, Roll 5, Target 14, Nr. 000310, BayHStA Munich, OMGUS Dachau War Criminal Trials, Microfilm 1/5

20  Clemency plea Alfred Kramer, USA versus Martin Gottfried Weiss et al., Nov. 15, 1945–Dec. 13, 1945, Posttrial Records, Roll 5, Target 17, Nr. 000372, BayHStA Munich, OMGUS Dachau War Criminal Trials, Microfilm 1/5

21  Clemency plea Josef Jarolin, USA versus Martin Gottfried Weiss et al., Nov. 15, 1945–Dec. 13, 1945, Posttrial Records, Roll 5, Target 12, Nr. 000246, BayHStA Munich, OMGUS Dachau War Criminal Trials, Microfilm 1/5

put down to the pleas themselves, but rather resulted from a revision of the trial, the evidence, the witness statements and the sentencing.

That nevertheless a series of pardons were granted, from which hundreds owed the alteration of their death sentences into prison sentences or a reduction in their prison sentences, was, on the one hand, the result of a changed political situation and, on the other, due to a public that increasingly expressed its rejection of the war criminal trials.

The break up of the anti-Hitler coalition and the beginning of the Cold War created a situation in which West Germany advanced from vanquished enemy to a much sought-after partner. The founding of the Federal Republic and, later, rearmament completed this process. This was complemented and reinforced by a sometimes hysterical anti-Communism in the USA.

The broadening rejection of the trials by the German public had differing motives: ignorance about the American trial system, errors, contradictions and, at times, no small lack of deficiencies in the trials as well as in the pre-trial investigations. These serious reservations converged with the fundamental rejection of juridical prosecution of National Socialist war criminals or the playing down and denial of these crimes in general.

All these motives converged; the pressure on the USA came from many sources: the press, the churches, the federal government, prisoner assistance associations, lawyers, etc.

Centre and co-ordination point for all activities was the so-called Heidelberger Documentation Archive.

The Heidelberger Documentation Archive was an informal amalgamation founded by the Heidelberg Law Professor Eduard Wahl, who held a seat in the federal parliament for the CDU from 1949 to 1969. Wahl had taken part in the IG Farben trial in Nuremberg as defence lawyer. Up to 30 persons gathered at the meetings he initiated, amongst them more than a dozen lawyers who were engaged in war criminal trials in all three Western zones as defence lawyers, as well as numerous law academics, high-ranking representatives from the Catholic and Protestant churches, civil servants from the Federal Justice Ministry and, occasionally, from the Federal Chancellery or the Foreign Office. The meetings served to exchange information as well as to discuss, to plan and to co-ordinate the actions to be undertaken by a singular or numerous participating groups and persons. The available set of instruments for such action encompassed diverse possibilities for exerting influence. These ranged from contact and talks with the American authorities through to the call for press intervention or for the engagement of German politicians.

The last trial before an American military court was concluded in 1948, since the pressure had grown on the USA to revise the judgements passed at Dachau and Nuremberg by reopening the trials — as often as possible in German courts — or by granting an amnesty.

The war criminal trials now became a war criminal problem, an international problem between two states, the USA and the Federal Republic of Germany. While the responsible American authorities continued to insist on the legal validity of the sentences, and therefore rejected a reopening of the trials, they were however basically willing to attain a solution to the war criminal problem by granting general pardons.

This became clear in talks between members of the Heidelberg Documentation Archive and the American High Commissioner McCloy. Participants for the German side were the President of the Celle-Hanover High Court, Dr. von Hodenberg, the aforementioned initiator of the Heidelberg circle, Professor Wahl, his Heidelberg colleague, Professor Geiler, and the Munich Law Professor E. Kaufmann. Hodenberg's report on these talks states:

"McCloy expressed that he, in contrast to Churchill, had fought very hard for fair play in the issue of the war criminals. [...] He rejected a general review and revision of the sentences. In individual cases pleas for review based on new evidence will be dealt with by his department. He is not opposed to parole proceedings. [...] The talks did not take a particularly favourable course and suffered greatly from the lack of time available. McCloy was again and again reminded by his staff of the other tasks he had.

As for the discussion about carrying out the death sentences, McCloy explained that this question is undergoing serious review. At the moment all executions have been stopped. Towards the end of the talks the tension was relieved somewhat as McCloy himself proposed talks with his legal advisor McLain and expressed his willingness to receive proposals from the Heidelberg circle, of which he knows."[22]

Talks with McLain already took place in December, and further talks were held in January and February 1950.

McLain made it clear "that he (regards) it as wrong when the German side only always touches on the principles of the trials and the legal maxims"[23]; and, clearer still: "attacks upon the soundness of judgements shall be fundamentally excluded [from the pleas for pardon] so that the idea of the war criminal trials remains fundamentally affirmed. Nevertheless, in individual cases it is not to be excluded that new evidence is to be accepted and the opinion underlying the judgement passed also be gone into."[24]

22  Federal Archive Koblenz, Bestand Zentrale Rechtsschutzstelle, B 305, Nr.140, Bd. 1, Report on the meeting of the "Documentation Archive Heidelbeg" on 21. Jan. 1950.

23  Federal Archive Koblenz, Bestand Zentrale Rechtsschutzstelle, B 305, Nr. 140, Bd. 1, Report on the meeting of the "Documentation Archive Heidelberg" on 21. Jan. 1950.

24  Federal Archive Koblenz, Bestand Zentrale Rechtsschutzstelle, B 305, Nr.140, Bd. 1, Report Prof. Dr. E. Wahl, Heidelberg Documentation Archive from 6. 11. 50.

The issue at hand was to develop practical procedures for solving the question. Parole proceedings could be one way.

Release on parole — on word of honour — is not actually defined as an act of mercy. It merely allows the sentenced person to spend a specific part of their prison sentence outside the prison under the supervision of a responsible official. Any offence against the parole conditions meant the possible annulment of release and the return to prison.

However, de facto parole was a means — together with further aspects such as good conduct, social hardships, age and health — to create an instrument for a merciful remission of sentence, an instrument for clarifying a problem that was in truth much more a political than a legal one.

The Federal government could also thoroughly approve of such a solution; through the circle around the Heidelberg Documentation Archive it attempted to win over the German public for this solution. At a meeting in Heidelberg on 29 November 1950 the Head of the Federal Justice Ministry Department, Rotberg, declared: "It is not practically possible to push through a general reopening of proceedings in the some 400 cases. This is neither technically nor politically feasible. We must thus in some way meet in the middle. The release must not always be based on the concession that the released person is innocent. What matters is to achieve a release as soon as possible."[25]

In 1949 a Modification Board was set up by the Supreme Command of the US Army that was to once again review the judgments passed by the American Military Court in Dachau. Pursuing the same objective, in 1950 McCloy installed an Advisory Board on Clemency for War Criminals convicted at Nuremberg. For both boards clemency pleas were to be submitted and these were to serve the board members as a basis for their review. At the so-called Landsberg hearings the convicted and their defence lawyers were also given the opportunity to deliver their pleas verbally. This procedure for the boards was positively received by the Heidelberg Documentation Archive. In confidential minutes from a meeting held on 25 November 1950 it is stated: "The defence lawyers advised to give the modification board more time to get going before we undertake new steps. The meeting agreed to this view. If the proceedings or the results shall turn out to be unfavourable, the Heidelberg circle, on the basis of corresponding notification from the defence lawyers, is to approach General Hardy prior to the next meeting and to prompt approaches by the Federal government."[26]

25  Federal Archive Koblenz, Bestand Zentrale Rechtsschutzstelle, B 305, Nr. 140, Bd. 1, Report on the participation in the meeting of the Documentation Archive Heidelberg on 25. 11. 1950.
26  Federal Archive Koblenz, Bestand Zentrale Rechtsschutzstelle, B 305, Nr. 140, Bd. 1, Notes taken about the talks of 25 November 1950 in Heidelbeg.

Two months later, on 31 January 1951, High-Commissioner McCloy, responsible for the convicted at Nuremberg, and General Handy, as Supreme Commander of the US troops in Europe responsible for those convicted by the American Military Courts in the so-called Dachau trials, issued a comprehensive amnesty:

from the 89 Landsberg prisoners convicted at the Nuremberg trials, 79 were reprieved by an act of mercy; the five confirmed sentences included the death sentences given to Paul Blobel, Werner Braune, Erich Naumann and Otto Ohlendorf, main culprits in the murders carried out by the SS-Einsatztruppen, as well as Oswald Pohl, Chief of the SS Wirtschafts- und Verwaltungshauptamt [SS Economic and Administrative Main Office] that had been responsible for the concentration camps. As for the pardons granted by General Handy, only two of the thirteen death sentences were confirmed: those given to Hans Schmidt, deputy camp commandant at Buchenwald, and Georg Schallmair, member of the camp command at the Mühldorf concentration camp.

Even after this large amnesty the practice of pardoning continued. On 1 November 1951 there were still 480 persons convicted in war criminal trials in Landsberg:

- 432 from the Dachau trials, amongst them 5 women,
- 48 from the Nuremberg trials, amongst them 1 woman, 3 Field Marshalls, 16 Wehrmacht Generals.

In order to resolve the still existing war criminal problem, all three western powers worked together with the Federal government; war criminals convicted by British and French courts were also still in prisons at Werl, Wittlich and Neuwied.

In 1953 three Mixed Parole and Clemency Boards were set up, one each for the areas of former zones of occupation, in which, besides representatives from the respective custody authorities, a German delegate was also included. These Clemency Boards were explicitly defined as temporary — Interim Mixed Parole and Clemency Boards; they were to give way to a single board of the same name that would be set up upon annulment of the occupation status.

The boards had the right to pronounce recommendations for granting pardons or release on parole; applications for pardons could be submitted by the convicted, their relatives and the defence lawyers. The criteria for a pardon included not just legal aspects such as possible irregularities in sentencing, but personal circumstances were also of importance. The definitions were laid down in an order issued jointly by the US High-Commission and the European Headquarters of the US Army on 4 September 1953:

"7. In deciding whether a pardon or release on parole is to be recommended, the board, in so far as these come into consideration, must review, amongst other aspects, the following issues:

a) the kind of offence or offences for which the applicant was convicted, as well as any previous convictions;
b) every considerable irregularity between a sentence in relation to others sentences for the same offence;
c) behaviour, attitude and work performance during imprisonment;
d) circumstances which are of importance for the social reintegration and the probability of successful social conformity of the applicant;
e) age, physical and intellectual constitution of the applicant;
f) prospects of the applicant for employment and the possibility of securing a livelihood which guarantee that they do not become a burden to society, further the living situation of their family."[27]

Despite the willingness of all involved to reach a swift solution, a settlement was dragged out due to the resistance of sections of the public in the USA. On 11 August 1955 the Joint Mixed Clemency Board, comprising of one representative each from the USA, Great Britain and France, as well as three representatives from the Federal Republic of Germany, began its work. At this point of time there were still

17 war criminals in French custody in the prison at Wittlich,
2 female war criminals in French custody in the prison at Neuwied,
26 war criminals in British custody in the prison at Werl,
49 war criminals in American custody in the prison at Landsberg,
201 war criminals under American parole supervision.

Whereas France and Great Britain now released their prisoners relatively swiftly, the USA still insisted, at least formally, upon a review decision for each individual case. The conditions for formulating the submissions were to be exactly maintained, a significant say in the matter was granted to the prison director, who was to pass judgement on whether the convicted person "had proven by their behaviour that they regret the offence or offences for which they have been convicted".

So, despite considerable pressure exerted by the German Federal government, it was not until summer 1958 that the last convicted war criminal was set free and could leave Landsberg.

---

27 Excerpt from the Gazette of the Allied High Comission for Germany Nr. 107, from 4. September 1953. American Zone, Office of the United States High Comission for Germany and Headquarters of the Commander-in-Chief of the United States Army in Europe; Directive concerning the Interim Mixed Parole and Clemency Board. Federal Archive Koblenz, Bestand Zentrale Rechtsschutzstelle, B 305, Nr. 53.

Johannes Tuchel

# The Commandants
# of the Dachau Concentration Camp

Although there is still no satisfactory monograph on the Dachau concentration camp within the overall context of the National Socialist apparatus of persecution, in the meantime the wealth of literature dealing with this camp cannot be overlooked. Certain themes however, such as the significance and the function of the SS in Dachau, have till now only been initially investigated. This is also the case with the biographies of the commandants of this concentration camp.

The group biography by Tom Segev on the commandants of the concentration camps, in which a number of Dachau commandants are also portrayed, commits itself to a psycho-historical approach and presents the sum of a number of individual biographies, the analysis of which brings out the common features of a "process of gradual hardening".[1] The personnel policy pursued by Himmler and the SS did not, however, stand at the centre of his work. Elsewhere I have investigated this personnel policy of the "Reichsführers SS" and, above all, that of the Inspector-in-Chief for the Concentration Camps and leader of the SS-Totenkopfverbände [Order of the Death's Head], Theodor Eicke, during the reorganisation of the concentration camps in 1934/35[2] and pointed out that the decisions made in this period were without any fundamental personnel concept.[3]

Using the example of the commandants of the Dachau concentration camp, in the following I will not just look into their biographies, but also

---

1   Tom Segev, The Commanders of the Nazi Concentration Camps. Diss. Univ. Boston 1977. The German edition, published under the title "Die Soldaten des Bösen. Zur Geschichte der KZ-Kommandanten" (Reinbeck 1992), of the reworked English version, "Soldiers of Evil. The Commandants of the Nazi Concentration Camps" (New York 1988), does not go beyond the results of the 1977 dissertation, indeed, in addition, it contains a number of poor retranslations back into German and false dates.

2   Johannes Tuchel, Konzentrationslager. Organisationsgeschichte und Funktion der "Inspektion der Konzentrationslager" 1934–1938 [Concentration Camps. Organisational History and Function of the "Inspectorate for Concentration Camps" 1934–1938], Boppard 1991, pp. 160 ff.

3   Ibid., p. 165.

into the circumstances of their recruitment and whether they were able to meet the expectations raised by the SS leadership.[4] This can however only be a first survey and not a conclusive presentation.

Already in January 1933 the empty works premises at Dachau was under discussion as a camp site for voluntary or compulsory labour; the exact reasons for the decision leading to the erection of a concentration camp in Dachau are still not fully known.[5] One decisive factor though was that since 1926 the entire premises were in the possession of the Bavarian State and administered by the Dachau Taxation Office. A week prior to the press conference held on 20 March 1933 where Heinrich Himmler announced the opening of the concentration camp in Dachau, and so hence just four days after his appointment as Munich Police President, the Political Police (at the time still Dept. IV of the Munich Police Headquarters under the commissary direction of Reinhard Heydrich) became active.

The "Chronicle of the Whole SS Camp Grounds at Dachau," written with great detail and factual knowledge, says in this regard: "On 13 March 1933 a Commission from the Political Police turned up at the local administration to examine whether the works premises would not be suitable for accommodating protective custody prisoners. All sections of the grounds were inspected and, following the proposal of the architect Dinkel, part of the former munitions section was found to be suitable. In view of the urgency, the necessary measures were immediately discussed and it was decided that on the 14. 3. 33 50 men from the work camp Planegg were to be assigned to carry out these measures. The repair work on the lighting wires and water mains was already begun on the night of the 13.–14. 3. 33. The work was so carried out that the first protective custody prisoners, around 120 men, ... and the necessary guard squads could be accommodated within the next eight days. In this short time the erection of the concentration camp Dachau was considered and the necessary measures for this also

4   A parallel study on the commandants at the Flossenbürg concentration camp has appeared in: Helge Grabitz/Klaus Bästlein/Johannes Tuchel (Hrsg.), Die Normalität des Verbrechens [The Normality of Crime], Berlin 1994, pp. 201 ff.

5   On the early history of Dachau in general see Hans-Günter Richardi, Schule der Gewalt. Das Konzentrationslager Dachau 1933–1934 [School of Violence. The Concentration Camp Dachau 1933–1934], München 1983, Günter Kimmel, Das Konzentrationslager Dachau [The Concentration Camp Dachau], and Lothar Gruchmann, Die bayerische Justiz im politischen Machtkampf 1933/34. Ihr Scheitern bei der Strafverfolgung von Mordfällen in Dachau [The Bavarian Judiciary in the Political Power Struggle 1933/34. Its Failure in the Criminal Prosecution of Murder Cases in Dachau], both in: Martin Broszat/Elke Fröhlich (Hrsg.), Bayern in der NS-Zeit, Band II, Herrschaft und Gesellschaft im Konflikt, München 1979. The following is based on my earlier presentation (see footnote 2), pp. 123 ff.

dealt with ... The work was so carried out that already within 8 days another 540 protective custody prisoners could be accommodated. Through extensions to the rest of the buildings it was possible in the shortest time to securely accommodate 2,700 protective custody prisoners."[6] The 2nd Police Group under the command of Police Captain Schlemmer assumed guard duty on 21 March 1933; the first prisoners arrived at Dachau on 22 March 1933. On 2 April 1933, just one day after his appointment as Political Police Commander, Himmler notified the command of the police force: "The concentration camp Dachau is to be immediately placed under the control of the leader of the Political Auxiliary Police. This change is to be undertaken in amity between the leader of the Political Auxiliary Police and the command of the Police Force."[7] In this way Himmler had transferred one of his executive functions to the area of his authority as Reichsführer SS. The Political Auxiliary Police was at this time legally an organisation with governmental tasks, factually, however, it was a National Socialist party formation, namely the SS, obeying only the commands of Himmler as Reichsführer SS.

However, in the course of the following weeks, units from the state police were required to remain in Dachau because the SS was yet to be adequately trained as a guard squad. First only 60 and then 100, later more than 200 SS "Auxiliary Police" were trained in Dachau. The final handing over of the entire camp to the SS proceeded on 30 May 1933. Police Chief Schlemmer left the camp on 11 April. The training of the SS men, which dragged on till the late summer, was subsequently taken over by the Police Captain Winkler, who had already worked together with the first "camp commandant," SS-Sturmhauptführer [SS-Captain] Hilmar Wäckerle.[8]

Hilmar Wäckerle was born on 24 November 1899 in Forchheim (Upper Franconia).[9] He joined the Bavarian Cadet Corps in 1913, served from 1917 till the end of the war in the 2nd Bavarian Infantry Regiment, was promoted to sergeant in 1918 and wounded in the same year while serving at the front.[10] In 1919 he caught up on and completed his schooling, joined the Freikorps Weilheim, after that the 2nd Bavarian Gunner Regiment and finally the Freikorps Oberland. Between 1921 and 1924 he studied agriculture at the

6   Federal Archive Koblenz (in the following BAK), R 2/28350. The chronicle, dated 1. March 1938 and obviously drawn up in the Verwaltungsamt SS [SS Administrative Office], is a detailed description of the building development at the Dachau site.

7   Dachau Archive, 16. 103.

8   Ibid.

9   See for the following the Berlin Document Center (BDC), SS-Officers Personnel File (in the following SSO) Hilmar Wäckerle.

10  On this phase in Wäckerle's life see Segev, Soldaten, pp. 81 ff., with extremely speculative elements.

Technical University in Munich and completed his studies in farming.[11]
Joining the NSDAP for the first time in 1922, he belonged to the so-called
"Blutordensträgern" ["Blood Order Bearers"]. On 1 May 1931 he once again
joined the NSDAP, after his SS admission had already gone ahead on 1 March
1931.[12] At this time Wäckerle worked as an estate steward in Kempten. In
October 1931 he was promoted to SS-Scharführer [SS-Sergeant] and in
Unterkürnach charged "with the raising and administering of the SS Troop
1/I/29 Buchenberg".[13] Already in February 1932 he was promoted to SS-
Truppführer [SS-Troop Commander] and in July 1932 proposed as SS-Sturm-
führer [SS-Master Sergeant] in the SS-Sturmbann [SS-Battalion] Kempten.
Himmler promoted him to this rank in August 1932 and at the same time
appointed him as "adjutant of the I. Sturmbann in the 29. SS-Standarte [SS-
Standard]".[14] Within this section he was promoted in February 1933 to SS-
Sturmhauptführer and came to Dachau on 29 March 1933 as member of the
Auxiliary Police.[15] Wäckerle was a protégé of the SS-Oberführer [SS-Briga-
dier General] Erasmus Freiherr von Malsen-Ponikau, at this point of time
leader of the SS Section Munich, who delivered a warlike address in front of
the prisoners in Dachau at the end of March 1933.[16] Already in April 1933
Wäckerle signed as "camp commandant," on 30 May he also took over
command of the SS Guard Troops and responsibility for the "guard and
security duties at the concentration camp Dachau"[17] from Police Captain
Winkler. Wäckerle's appointment as commandant was due to his position
as the highest-ranking SS commander at the camp.

Wäckerle only remained camp commandant till the end of June 1933.
Under his command a series of murders took place which were investigated
by the State Prosecution Munich II.[18] These investigations found "Special

11  Segev's note (ibid., p. 84) that Heinrich Himmler was a fellow student of Wäckerle
     in Munich suggests a connection that in fact did not exist. Wäckerle began his
     studies in the summer semester of 1921, Himmler already completed his in July
     1922. An acquaintance between the two is not very likely at this stage.
12  Segev dates without evidence the joining of the party in 1925. BDC, SSO Wäckerle,
     clearly shows he joined in 1931.
13  BDC, SSO Wäckerle. Communication of the 29.SS-Standarte from 22. 10. 1931.
14  BDC, SSO Wäckerle, Promotion and Appointment from 25. 8. 1932.
15  BDC, SSO Wäckerle, Muster Roll Excerpt from 1. 2. 1934.
16  Segev's assertion about Wäckerle, that "Hitler chose him in February 1933 to be
     the first commandant of the concentration camp Dachau", is pure fantasy.
17  Dachau Archive, 16. 101/1.
18  Documents on this in BA, R 22/1167, BA, Slg. Schumacher/329, IMT, Bd.XXVI,
     pp. 172 ff., Dok. PS 642 ff. as well as in the Dachau Archive, passim. There is no
     need to go into great detail as to the facts here, for, besides Martin Broszat, Natio-
     nalsozialistische Konzentrationslager [National Socialist Concentration Camps],
     in: Hans Buchheim et. al., Anatomie des SS-Staates, Freiburg 1965, pp. 46 ff. and

Regulations" issued by Wäckerle for those "persons accommodated in the collection camp Dachau," which, among other things, subjected the prisoners to military law and provided for a "camp court" under the chair of the camp commandant whose powers were to go so far as to even include the imposition of the death penalty.[19] In the course of the investigations Himmler saw himself forced to relieve Wäckerle of his post as camp commandant and to appoint Theodor Eicke, later Inspector-in-Chief for the Concentration Camps, to this position.

Wäckerle was transferred from Dachau to Stuttgart as Stabsführer [Staff Chief] for the SS Section X, command of which was taken over by Erasmus von Malsen-Ponikau at the end of 1933. Malsen-Ponikau proposed Wäckerle's promotion to SS-Sturmbannführer [SS-Major] in February 1934, and Himmler pronounced this on 1 March 1934.[20] In May 1934, in the course of erecting the "Political Squad" of the SS, from which later the SS-Verfügungstruppe (SS-VT) [SS-Special Service Troops] was to develop, Wäckerle went as company commander to Ellwangen.[21] He advanced his career in the SS-VT: from September 1936 he was Obersturmbannführer [Lieutenant Colonel], after he had taken over command of the 1st Sturmbann of the SS-Standarte "Germania" in Hamburg-Veddel early in the year. In May 1940 he took part in the German invasion of the Netherlands and from May/June 1940 commanded the Standarte (later regiment) "Westland" in the Waffen-SS. On 21 August 1940 he was promoted to Standard Colonel and fell in battle on 2 July 1941 east of Lwów/Lemberg.

Theodor Eicke, born on 17 October 1892 in Hampont/Alsace as the eleventh child of a station-master, became the second camp commandant.[22]

Shlomo Aronson, Reinhard Heydrich und die Frühgeschichte von Gestapo und SD [Reinhard Heydrich and the Early History of the Gestapo and SD], Stuttgart 1971, pp. 104 ff., above all Gruchmann, Die bayerische Justiz, pp. 415 ff. and Richardi, Schule der Gewalt, pp. 88 ff. offer detailed analyses.

19   State Archive Nuremberg, War Crime Trials, Prosecution Documents, PS 1216: "For those persons accomodated in Dachau the following special regulations are enacted."

20   BDC, SSO Wäckerle, Promotion from 1. March 1934.

21   BDC, SSO Wäckerle, Vita from 6. June 1934.

22   For the biography and personality of Theodor Eicke see, besides his personal files in the Berlin Document Center, Charles W. Sydnor, Soldiers of Destruction. The SS Death's Head Division 1933–1945, Princeton 1977; Rudolf Höß, Kommandant in Auschwitz [Commandant in Auschwitz], ed. from Martin Broszat, München 1978, pp. 55 ff.; Heinz Höhne, Der Orden unter dem Totenkopf [The Order of the Death's Head], München 1979, pp. 188 f.; Klaus Drobisch, Theodor Eicke — Verkörperung des KZ-Systems [Theodor Eicke — Embodiment of the Concentration Camp System], in: Helmut Bock (Hrsg.), Sturz ins Dritte Reich. Historische Miniaturen und Portraits 1933/1935, Leipzig/Jena/Berlin (Ost) 1983, pp. 283 ff., as well as Tuchel, Konzentrationslager, pp. 128 ff.

He left secondary school without completing examinations in 1909 to become a professional soldier and to sign up for service as a volunteer with the 23rd Bavarian Infantry Regiment in Landau/Palatinate. Eicke pursued an administrative career in the army. In 1913 he became paymaster candidate, he married in 1914; as active army paymaster he came to the 2nd Bavarian Infantry-Art. Regiment, 1918 to a reserve M.G. Company of the Second Army Corps. Demobilised in 1919, Eicke moved with his family to Thuringia. Here he began studies at the College of Technology at Ilmenau, which he discontinued shortly afterwards to begin an "informative activity" with the police administration. There he was dismissed after two months due to anti-Republic activity. Subsequently he went to the Police Academy in Cottbus from where he "graduated with a grade 2 mark after completing the inspector's examination". After the exam Eicke was unemployed for a period. After failed attempts to find a position in the police he joined the Commercial Administration of the Badischen Anilin- und Sodafabriken (BASF) on 1 February 1923 in Ludwigshafen, to where he had moved in 1922. Employed in the works' security service he rose there, according to his own account, to "deputy director of the security service" with an income of 550 Reichsmark.

Eicke only became active in the NSDAP and the SA in 1928, transferred to the SS in 1930 and set up SS formations in Ludwigshafen and its surrounding areas. In November 1931 he took over the command of the 10th SS-Standarte. Here Eicke commanded around 290, a year later around 1,000 SS-men. In summer 1931 Eicke was commissioned by the Palatinate Gauleiter Joseph Bürckel, with whom he was later to come into serious conflict, to produce explosives and he was subsequently arrested in March 1932. On 15 July 1932 he was sentenced to two years in prison, but a day later, under the pretence of bad health, he was granted leave for six weeks. Shortly before the end of this leave, at the beginning of September 1932, Eicke received an order from Himmler, obviously impressed by Eicke's abilities, not to enter his prison sentence, but rather to flee to Italy. In October 1932 Eicke, in the meantime promoted to SS-Oberführer, took over the direction of the NS Refugee Camp Malcesine at Lake Garda. From Italy he attentively followed the intrigues going on in the Rhine Palatinate. On 16 February 1933 he returned to Germany and came into conflict with Bürckel, who had him arrested on 21 March 1933. After a two-day hunger strike Eicke was admitted to the Psychiatric Clinic of the Würzburg University. Himmler had him struck from the SS lists and refused to comply with Eicke's repeated request to be released from "protective custody". On 22 April 1933 Eicke's doctor, Dr. Werner Heyde, lecturer for psychiatry and neurology and after 1939 a leading figure in the murder action "T 4" on invalids and the frail, wrote to Himmler and attested Eicke had "no signs whatever of mental illness or brain problems".[23] On 2 June 1933 Himmler replied: "Personally I am convinced that Eicke has suffered wrongly at the hands of the Palatinate Gau, nevertheless I cannot change and rearrange the situation from one day to the next. I willingly give my consent for Eicke's release from the clinic at Whitsun, but I request you to persuade Eicke to stay low for the rest of his stay in Ludwigshafen and not to again cause the trouble and discord he started during his last stay in Ludwigshafen and which ultimately lead to his arrest. I intend to use Eicke in some position, possibly even in a position of state, he just cannot make it too difficult and impossible for me."[24]

Himmler could appoint Eicke to the Dachau camp in early summer 1933 because he knew of his devotion and organisational talent, but also of his stubbornness and brutality. Himmler was fully aware of who he released from the psychiatric clinic and placed at the head of the Dachau concentration camp; he knew the nature of a man who, starting from Dachau, was to develop the system of German concentration camps.

Shortly after Eicke officially arrived at Dachau on 26 June 1933, a large number of Social Democrats were committed to the camp.[25] Eicke quickly got down to establishing the first measures. On 26 July 1933 he requested from Himmler through the SS Group South, which was now put under his control as commander for special tasks, the promotion of two subcommanders: "I require both ranks urgently so as to uphold the authority absolutely needed here."[26] On 4 August Himmler, together with the SA-Staff Chief Ernst Röhm, inspected the camp for the first time since the start of Eicke's command and took part in the official unveiling of a Horst Wessel monument.[27] Under Eicke's command the brutality in the Dachau camp did not cease. Through the camp rules, which are still to be dealt with, Eicke ensured, however, that the number of murders not planned by the camp leadership decreased. Most of all the murders covered up as suicide were now also hushed up more carefully by Himmler. For example, as Franz Stenzer was allegedly shot trying to escape from Dachau on 22 August 1933, Himmler already reported this to Frank and Siebert a day later.[28] In the murder of Alfred Fruth, whose alleged escape from Dachau was reported in the press, Eicke was supposedly even personally involved.[29] The alleged escape re-

---

23  BDC, SSO Eicke.

24  Ibid.

25  Cf. Richardi, Schule der Gewalt, p. 167.

26  BDC, Eicke.

27  Vossische Zeitung, 6. August 1933, evening edition. Cf. also the depiction given by Richardi, Schule der Gewalt, pp. 179 ff.

28  See Gruchmann, Die bayerische Justiz, p. 422. The trial against those who had carried out the shooting was abandoned in December 1933.

29  Cf. the detailed presentation given by Richardi, Schule der Gewalt, p. 187.

ported in the press was to cover up the bloody deed. From 1 October 1933 the "disciplinary and punishment regulations for the prison camp",[30] although oriented on Wäckerle's "special regulations" far more detailed, and the "service regulations for the escort guards and sentries"[31] came into force. Whereas Reichsstatthalter [Reich Governor] von Epp tried to reduce the number of prisoners, a new series of murders took place in Dachau around 17 October.[32] On this day the camp command allegedly discovered the passing of secret messages in Dachau which were to spread "atrocity propaganda" in Czechoslovakia. Wilhelm Franz and Dr. Delwin Katz, suspected by Eicke of initiating the messages, were murdered the same day by the guard squad; their death was covered up as suicide.

In January 1934, together with members of the Reich Executive of the NSDAP, Himmler visited the camp. He was so satisfied with this inspection that, while still at the camp, he promoted the deputy guard squad commander, SS-Truppenführer Max Koegel, to SS-Sturmführer, backdated to 1 January 1934.[33] Eicke was also rewarded: on 30 January 1934 he was promoted to SS-Brigadeführer [SS-Major General] and shortly afterwards received the right of promotion to Section Commander.[34] Within a few months Eicke had succeeded in erecting the facade of a "model" concentration camp which, in its mixture of Prussian parade ground drills, senseless harassment and calculated brutality, was to shape the image of the Dachau concentration camp.

In May 1934 Eicke received the order from Himmler to dismantle smaller SA concentration camps and to reorganise some of them after the model of Dachau. At the end of May 1934 he arrived at the concentration camp Lichtenburg near Prettin on the Elbe: "Upon the orders of the Staff Chief of the Secret State Police Berlin, Reichsführer SS Himmler, I have taken over responsible command in the concentration camp Lichtenburg on the 29.5.34 in the capacity of Inspector-in-Chief for Concentration Camps."[35]

30  Incomplete copy in IMT, Vol. XXVI, PS 778, § 1–5 are missing.

31  § 6 for these regulations in IMT, Vol. XXVI, PS 778. Complete in BA, R22/1167, fol. 62 ff.

32  Cf. for this Gruchmann, Die bayerische Justiz, pp. 423 ff.; Richardi, Schule der Gewalt, pp. 204 ff. as well as the contemporary reports of Fritz Ecker, Die Hölle Dachau [The Hell that is Dachau], in: Konzentrationslager. Ein Appell an das Gewissen der Welt, Prague 1934, pp. 13 ff.; Wenzel Rubner, Dachau im Sommer 1933 [Dachau in Summer 1933], ibid., pp. 54 ff. as well as the anonymous depiction "Als Jude in Dachau" [As a Jew in Dachau], ibid., pp. 77 f.

33  Max Koegel, later commandant at Ravensbrück, Lublin and Flossenbürg.

34  Both in BDC, Eicke. Also worthy of mention in this context is that Eicke received his certificate of appointment to commandant of Dachau dated only from 9 March 1934. Possibly the right to promotion became effective on this date.

35  Facsimile in Klaus Drobisch, Konzentrationslager im Schloß Lichtenberg [Concentration Camp in Lichtenberg Palace], Cottbus 1987, p. 29.

On 21 June 1934 Eicke requested Curt Wittje, Chief of the SS Office, to formally record this reorganisation order in writing: "Furthermore, I request to be relieved of my duty as commandant of the concentration camp Dachau and to be affiliated to Staff of the RFSS with the section description = Inspectorate of the Concentration Camps RFSS. Please allow me to retain my aide, SS-Truppenführer Weibrecht from K.L.D. [concentration camp Dachau], as Weibrecht is an indispensable support for me."[36]

Taking effect on 4 July 1934 Eicke was appointed to "Inspector-in-Chief for Concentration Camps" and "Commander of the SS Guard Units".[37] In the summer months of 1934 Eicke then re-organised the concentration camps Esterwegen in Emsland and Sachsenburg near Chemnitz and dismantled the concentration camp at Oranienburg that had existed since March 1933 in a shut-down brewery.[38]

During the elimination of the SA at the end of June 1934 Eicke, coming from Lichtenburg via Berlin, arrived at Dachau on 30 June 1934. On that afternoon Gustav Ritter von Kahr, whom Hitler had not forgiven for "breaking his word" during the Hitler Putsch on the night of 8–9 November 1923, was committed to Dachau. Eicke awaited him at camp headquarters; Kahr was shot dead on this very day in Dachau.[39] Overall, between 30 June and 2 July 1934, 17 persons were murdered by the SS in Dachau (not just in the camp itself, but also in its surroundings).[40]

At midday on 1 July Hitler, once again in Berlin, decided to have Röhm killed after intense persuasion by Himmler and Göring. By telephone Hitler ordered Eicke, waiting for the call in the Bavarian Interior Ministry, to carry out the murder; Röhm was however to be given the opportunity to commit suicide beforehand. Together with Michael Lippert and the SS-Gruppenführer [SS-Major General] Heinrich Schmauser Eicke went to Stadelheim and demanded access to Röhm. The prison director refused and became embroiled in a loud and heated discussion with Eicke. Only after Eicke had spoken with the Bavarian Justice Minister Hans Frank on the telephone and directly referred to the "Führer's order" was he given access to Röhm. Lippert later reported: "The director refused at the beginning and referred to an order from Ritter von Epp that nobody was permitted access to the

---

36   BDC, SSO Eicke. Communication from 21 June 1934 to Wittje.
37   BDC Personal file Theodor Eicke, personal list.
38   For more detail on this see Tuchel, Konzentrationslager, pp. 184 ff.
39   For more detail see Kimmel, Das Konzentrationslager Dachau, p. 365.
40   A precise listng of those murdered in ibid., p. 366. Besides SA commanders and some civilians, four prisoners also belonged to the dead. See also Richardi, Schule der Gewalt, pp. 235 ff., who deals with the murders in detail, but not with evidence in all cases.

prisoners. As the discussion became quite heated, I left the room and waited in the corridor. After some time Eicke came and ordered me to come with him. We went up one or more sets of stairs and came to the cell where Röhm was. Whether Eicke or a prison officer opened the cell I can no longer say. Eicke entered the cell first and I followed him. Röhm sat in the cell, and Eicke now told him that he has come by order of the Führer, who lets him know that he has forfeited his life with his immoral way of life and his treasonable plans, but he gives him the possibility to draw the consequences, whereby Eicke laid a loaded pistol on the table. As far as I can recall Eicke gave Röhm a deadline of 20 or 30 minutes. Eicke and I then left the cell and Eicke ordered me to station myself in a side corridor that lead to the wing housing Röhm's cell and to prevent any disturbance that could occur during the deadline given to Röhm."[41]

There are differing accounts on the further course of Röhm's murder: the exact sequence of events can probably no longer be reconstructed. In the trial of 1953 Lippert incriminated Eicke, who had fallen in 1943, and accused him alone of having shot Röhm. There are, however, many pieces of circumstantial evidence which indicate that this was merely a lie to cover himself and that both Lippert and Eicke fired the fatal shots at Röhm after he decided against suicide. After the murder of Röhm, Eicke travelled back to Dachau, where he presumably ordered on the same evening the murder of four SA commanders and remained there a few days till he returned to Lichtenburg on 4 July at the latest.

Responsibility for the Dachau camp thus now lay with Michael Lippert as commander of the Guard Company Dachau and Günter Tamaschke, since May 1934 commander of the protective custody camp. The new commandant for Dachau was decided upon by Himmler personally, and once again he made a personnel decision by which he did not appoint an "experienced" camp commander, but rather a high-ranking SS-commander who had become untenable in his current position: on 6 October 1934 the SS-Oberführer Dr. Alexander Reiner was "commissioned with the command of the concentration camp Dachau".[42] Reiner, who came to the Danzig SS as Standarten dentist in February 1932, had enjoyed a rapid rise under the protection of the SS-Brigadeführer Werner Lorenz and on 12 March 1934 was promoted by Himmler to SS-Oberführer and commander of the SS-Section XXVI (Danzig). As Lorenz took on a new position and the SS-Brigadeführer Erich von dem Bach-Zelewiski assumed the command of the Regional Section Northeast, serious tension between him and Reiner arose. Reiner, who had almost lost his dental praxis through financial losses incurred while setting

41   BAK, NL 263/47. Notes by Michael Lippert on 15 May 1952.
42   BDC, SSO Reiner.

up the Danzig SS, was interested in becoming the commander of the Danzig Police Force as Lieutenant Colonel in May 1934. Von dem Bach-Zelewiski wrote him a sharp letter, later approved by Himmler: "I regard it as my duty to draw your attention to the fact that I do not consider the tenure of such a post compatible with the goals and interests of the SS. As this post deals not with the military regional police but merely the traffic police, it is incomprehensible to me why you could have any interest whatsoever in such an office. As you have become Standartenführer in such a short time and then immediately afterwards Oberführer, and so given special distinction by the Reichsführer SS, I must demand of you not to pursue any other interests but those in the service of the formation and building up of the SS, so that this section will also become a sharp instrument in the hand of the Reichsführer within the whole SS."[43] At the same time, an internal SS investigation began into Reiner's methods in setting up the Danzig SS, in the course of which a climate became clear that belongs somewhere between an adventure novel, frontier problematic and sheer corruption.

Already in the run up to this investigation Himmler must have decided to transfer Reiner. On 6 October 1934 he commissioned Reiner, who neither possessed extensive military experience nor had had anything to do with the police or concentration camps, with the command of the Dachau concentration camp.[44] Reiner received notification of his transfer on 15 October and requested leave till 24 October "to see to personal affairs". On October 19 the Danzig Gauleiter Albert Forster congratulated him: "Dear Pg. Dr Reiner! After I found out that the Reichsführer SS has appointed you commandant of the concentration camp Dachau, I would not want to miss the opportunity to express my congratulations to you on this honourable appointment, one which best expresses the trust the Reichsführer places in you."[45] Forster's congratulations came too late however. The investigation into Reiner's activities had proceeded and he received only a short notice in reply to his leave request: "Leave granted. Not commandant Dachau, rather command RFSS. After leave ends report to Munich."[46] As Reiner reported for duty in Munich he was to make himself available to the SS-court. Forster himself travelled from Danzig to Munich to testify on behalf of Reiner. Nevertheless, not all the accusations raised against him could be overlooked. Customs and mores had caught on under Reiner's charge in Danzig which were not in keeping with Himmler's ideals for the SS order.

---

43  Ibid., Communication from 14 May 1934.
44  Ibid.
45  Ibid.
46  Ibid.

The proceedings ended for Reiner with a "strict reprimand" from Himmler: "You have not fulfilled your duties in relation to the supervision of the units under your charge and the use of the budget in a way expected of a SS Section Commander."[47] Seldom has the attempted bribery of the League of Nations commissioner, some members of the Danzig Senate, the use of SS-men for not quite transparent private purposes and intensive black market trade with the support of corrupt Polish customs officers been more nobly described as here. Himmler no longer wanted to entrust the concentration camp Dachau to this man. He transferred Reiner to his native Saxony and appointed him commandant of the concentration camp Sachsenburg at the beginning of November 1934.

Dachau was to receive a new commandant first in December 1934, the SS-Oberführer Heinrich Deubel.[48] Deubel was born on 19 February 1890 in Ortenburg/Lower Bavaria. After completing basic primary and secondary school he went to the non-commissioned officers' school at Fürstenfeldbruck in 1906 and from 1909 was a professional soldier with the 16th Bavarian Infantry Regiment. In July 1916 he fell into British captivity at the Somme, from which he was first released in November 1918. He returned to Passau, served some time with various units and was released as a Lieutenant with the Iron Cross I. and Iron Cross II from the army after 12 years of service on 6 December 1919. As a "temporary volunteer" he took part in the Kapp Putsch. In May 1920 he joined the Reich Customs Administration at the Main Customs Office in Passau, was in the same year Customs Operating Assistant and passed through a normal career in the customs services (1922 Customs Assistant, 1924 Customs Secretary). He married in 1927. After previously being a member in the German-National (völkisch) Schutz- und Trutzbund organisation, Heinrich Deubel was one of the founding members of the Passau NSDAP. During the banning of the NSDAP he belonged to a substitute organisation and rejoined the party with the NSDAP-Nr. 14178 in August 1925. Deubel was a member of the SS from August 1926 (as Scharführer) with the Nr. 186 and so belonged to the longest serving SS-commanders. From 30 October 1928 onwards he commanded the SS-Standarte VI (Lower Bavaria) and was promoted a month later to Sturmbannführer. Even for the SS, to jump four ranks was an usual promotion. From 1 February 1931 Deubel commanded the Brigade East Bavaria as Standartenführer [Colonel], afterwards the 31. SS-Standarte in Straubing. In 1933 Deubel commanded the "Frontier Guards," comprising of around 200 SS-men, in Bavaria, after which he returned for a short period to the customs services. From 22 October 1934 he was Staff Chief at the SS collection point

47  Ibid.
48  On Deubel see BDC, SSO Deubel and Segev, Soldiers, pp. 155 ff. and Kimmel, Das Konzentrationslager Dachau, p. 368.

Dachau, where at this time the first SS formations were undergoing military training. Deubel was tied to Himmler, who had already helped him out of personal difficulties in summer 1933, by a close and intimate relationship of mutual trust.[49] Himmler appointed Deubel to SS-Oberführer on 9 November 1934, the highest rank he was to attain. Himmler appeared to believe that the professional soldier Deubel, who possessed a similar career path as Eicke, was capable of commanding the concentration camp Dachau. However, his appointment as commandant of the concentration camp Dachau followed mainly because, after the fiasco with Alexander Reiner, Himmler had no other high-ranking SS-commander at his disposal in the Dachau area. It is out of the question to speak of a long-term personnel policy in this case.

When Deubel took command of Dachau the camp had around 1,700 prisoners. In the course of 1935 2,111 prisoners were committed, but many also released, so that the number had only increased to around 2,300 prisoners by the beginning of 1936. The constant increase in prisoner numbers first took place in the phase of camp extension, from 1936/37 onwards.

Under Deubel a somewhat less gruesome period in the history of the camp began in comparison to the preceding phases of terror. Deubel tried to improve the prisoners' living conditions somewhat.[50] Not only his proposal to enable an "unrepenting communist" sitting in protective custody in Dachau to undertake a trip to Scandinavia with the NS travel organisation "Kraft durch Freude" ["Strength through Joy"] led to Deubel being considered as "almost too good-natured" in Eicke's eyes. Also contributing to the relative security of the prisoners was how SS-Standartenführer d'Angelo was, in Eicke's view, "as commander of the protective custody camp not only soft as butter, but also completely without any interest for this area of service"[51] and, furthermore, very open to the more comfortable side of life.

Deubel was relieved of his post in Dachau at the end of March 1936 and appointed as commandant of the concentration camp Columbiahaus in Berlin. Here he was sent on "compulsory leave" on 22 September 1936: "An investigation against me was opened because I had allegedly handed over a copy of camp regulations to an English journalist and, furthermore, the grave register for the camp cemetery at Dachau is supposed to have been lost during my period of service there."[52]

Officially Deubel retired from the service area of Inspectorate for Concentration Camps on 31 March 1937 and returned to the customs service.

49   Cf. Deubel's expression of gratitude in BAK, NS 19/1719.
50   Cf. amongst others Kimmel, Das Konzentrationslager Dachau, p. 368.
51   BDC, SSO d'Angelo. Communication by Eicke from 28 May 1936.
52   Statement given by Deubel before the Camp Verdict Chamber Regensburg, undated [1948].

In 1939 he became Chief Customs Inspector, 1941 District Customs Commissioner. In the same year he was company commander of a Genesenden-kompanie (reconvalescent company) as a Lieutenant Colonel z.V. (at disposal), followed by an engagement in France as a commander in the Customs Frontier Guards. From 1945 to 1948 he was imprisoned; investigation proceedings launched by the State Prosecution Munich II against him for participation in crimes committed in Dachau did not lead to any charges being laid. Heinrich Deubel died on 2 October 1962 in Dingolfing.

Deubel's successor at Dachau, Loritz, had both of Deubel's closest assistants, protective custody commander d'Angelo and the Staff Chief for the Commandant, SS-Standartenführer Walter Gerlach, removed from Dachau within a few weeks. Already in 1936 Loritz initiated disciplinary proceedings against d'Angelo and these ended with his removal from concentration camp duty.[53] Walter Gerlach requested of his own accord a transfer to the General-SS, a request camp commandant Loritz supported in submissions to Eicke on 14 July 1936: "Standartenführer Gerlach is no longer entirely happy here. He had not just tolerated the previous course of events in Dachau, but also knew of a lot more that was going on. On the basis of my observations, today I even incline to the view that Standartenführer Gerlach was just as responsible for the mess which ruled here [this refers to the, in the view of the SS, lax and relative humane period of camp command under commandant Deubel] as the Commandant was, for he certainly knew about what was going on but never queried it. If I had accepted the advice he has given me till now, I certainly would also have attracted attention long before. After he noticed that I do not set great store in this advice and take care of my own work, he sees himself as being superfluous here."[54]

Theodor Eicke agreed to the submission and handed it on to the Personnel Chief of the SS on 31 July 1936. At the same time he gave a résumé of the era of Deubel in Dachau: "I approve the request simply on the grounds that SS-Standartenführer Gerlach had previously been assigned as a support to the work-shy SS-Oberführer Deubel, whereas now, due to the activity of the new camp commandant, SS-Oberführer Loritz, he has indeed become superfluous."[55]

---

53   Cf. the detailed proceedings in BDC, SSO d'Angelo. Here one can speak of a "classic" SS intrigue. Loritz received a report from the Darmstadt Gestapo on 20 April 1936, according to which a former concentration camp prisoner had been "on good terms" with d'Angelo. Loritz sent the report to Eicke on the same day; four days later the desired result was attained: Eicke relieved d'Angelo of his duties and notified him that disciplinary proceedings were to be opened.

54   BDC, SSO Walter Gerlach.

55   Ibid.

Loritz was the first commandant of Dachau who had gained his experience in other concentration camps.[56] Hans Loritz was born on 21 December 1895 as the son of a civil servant in Augsburg. He attended elementary school for eight years and then completed a bakery and pastry-cook apprenticeship. He undertook his journeyman's travels till 1914, amongst others places he was in Innsbruck, Vienna, Budapest and Berlin, and in the same year he joined the 17th Bavarian Infantry Regiment as a volunteer. After training as an airman he was sent into combat with the Bomb Squadron of the Supreme Army Command, and after being shot down, whereby he was severely wounded, he was taken prisoner in France in July 1918. After his release in February 1920 he entered the police and later communal service in Augsburg in early 1921. He joined the NSDAP in August, the SS in September 1930. Promoted to Untersturmführer [Second Lieutenant] in November 1931 and to Hauptsturmführer in April 1932, he built up the SS in Augsburg. From August 1932 he was SS-Sturmbannführer and was decisively involved in the National Socialist seizure of power in Augsburg in March 1933. As commander of the 29th SS-Standarte he was at the same time "Special Frontier Commissar" for the area between Bayrischzell and Lindau in 1933 and on 15 July 1933 he was promoted to SS-Obersturmbannführer. After vehement conflict with his superior, SS-Brigadenführer Rodenbächer, he received a severe reprimand from Himmler in November 1933 and was transferred on 15 December 1933 as Commander with special tasks to the Regional Section South, relieved of the command of the 29th SS-Standarte and ordered to serve in Dachau. In the "Hilfswerk" [relief organisation] Dachau he was then commissioned with the command of the Austrian SS-men. He worked closely with Eicke and lodged many applications to be taken on in camp duty. From 9 July 1934 he was commandant at the Esterwegen camp and reorganised it completely in line with Eicke's conception.

To the prominent political prisoners held at Esterwegen at this time belonged the journalist and Noble Peace Prize winner Carl von Ossietzky, the former members of the Reichstag Theodor Neubauer, Julius Leber and Bernhard Bästlein, the lawyer Hans Litten and trade union leader Fritz Husemann. The high proportion of criminal prisoners or those prisoners defamed as "professional criminals" in Esterwegen was stressed by Eicke in an almost emphatic judgement of Hans Loritz written in summer 1935: "Loritz runs the concentration camp Esterwegen to my great satisfaction. Of all Ger-

56   For the following see BDC, SSO Loritz. Further, also Segev, Soldiers, pp. 161 ff. and Segev, Soldaten, p. 194, however with many speculative elements and misleading details. For instance, Loritz was not "commandant of the guard squad" at Dachau in 1933, rather commander of the Austrian SS-men in the Dachau camp.

man concentration camps this one is to the most difficult to command as it really does hold criminals, lies completely isolated in the countryside and is surrounded by a civil population with reactionary attitudes. Esterwegen stood variously under the command of the SS, the police and the SA, and had, till SS-Staf. Loritz took over as camp commandant, unreliable guard squads and incapable commanders. Within a short period Loritz has not only built up a disciplined SS Guard Squad but also a model prison camp."[57]

This high praise from Eicke was cynical to the highest degree, for the reality in the camp was completely different. In spring and summer 1935 the ill-treatment of prisoners during their enforced labour on the moor or in the camp not only increased, but between March and May 1935 five prisoners were murdered, and these were mostly covered up as "shot while trying to escape". In the camp itself, after a "violent assault," the "Jewish protective custody inmate" Wolf Willi Baron was shot by SS-guard Börger on 2 March 1935. The murder of the 61-year-old miners' leader Fritz Husemann on 5 April 1935 was then covered up as an "escape attempt". On 3 May a guard shot dead the prisoner Röhrs, who had just arrived at the camp, on 8 May the prisoner Willi Ohl — also during an alleged escape attempt. The temporary end to this series of murders was the shooting of the prisoner Agranoff, characterised as a "professional criminal," on 31 May 1935. Even the Reich Justice Ministry began to pay attention to the events taking place in Esterwegen.

These murders had just as little negative effect on the career of the Standartenführer Hans Loritz as the report presented by the League of Nations Commissioner C. J. Burckhardt in August 1934, who due to the treatment of Ossietzky had complained to Heydrich. On 15 September 1935 Himmler promoted Hans Loritz to SS-Oberführer and appointed him as successor to Deubel as commandant of Dachau in April 1936. Under Hans Loritz and his Protective Custody Camp Commander Jakob Weiseborn, later commandant at Flossenbürg, there followed the enlargement of the Dachau camp and a permanent worsening of prisoners' living conditions.[58] The "Chronicle of the whole SS Camp Complex in Dachau" glossed this over as: "The merging of different existing concentration camps and their moving to Dachau demanded a complete reorganisation of the prison camp. The possible capacity of the camp had been till now 2,700 prisoners, whereas after the merger around 6,000 prisoners had to be accommodated here."[59]

57  BDC, SSO Loritz, assessment from 31 July 1935.
58  Cf. Klaus Drobisch/Günther Wieland, System der NS-Konzentrationslager 1933–1939 [The System of the NS Concentration Camps 1933–1939], Berlin 1993, p. 271.
59  BAK, R2/28350.

When Dachau was cleared for a couple of months in summer 1939 and served as training ground for the later SS-Totenkopfdivision, Loritz was appointed as commander of the SS Section Graz on 1 July 1939. The thesis of Rudolf Höß, that Loritz was dismissed from Dachau on the grounds of too harsh a treatment of the prisoners,[60] appears to be more like an apology and belated wishful thinking and cannot be brought into line with the reality of the concentration camps. For only a few months later, at the end of March 1940, Loritz took up duty as commandant of Sachsenhausen till he was transferred at the beginning of 1942 to the position of Higher SS and Police Commander for Norway in Oslo, responsible as "commander for the concentration camps to be erected in Norway". This, too, was not, as Höß asserted, the result of too harsh a treatment of prisoners in Sachsenhausen, but rather due to the estimation held by the Inspectorate for the Concentration Camps that Loritz possessed the necessary firmness for setting up a network of concentration camps in Norway. There he was active in various duties till the end of the war. He committed suicide on 31 January 1946 at the internment camp Neumünster. What is conspicuous in Loritz's career is the fact that his last promotion to Oberführer occurred in 1935. Certainly, existing sources show many recommendations for promotion up until 1944, in the end, however, Loritz retained his old rank till the end of the Third Reich.

The new commandant of Dachau was Alex Piorkowski, born on 11 October 1904 in Bremen.[61] Piorkowski, a trained mechanic and during the twenties active as a travelling salesman, joined the NSDAP and the SA in 1929, where he stayed till his move to the SS on 1 June 1931. He was active in setting up the Bremen SS and enjoyed rapid promotion.[62] On 20 July 1935 he was commissioned with the command of the 88. SS-Standarte (Bremen), on 30 January 1936 he was promoted to Sturmbannführer. On 20 September 1936 he was transferred in the same post to the 61. SS-Standarte (Allenstein) and released from his duties there on 19 September 1936 for health reasons. After a long break he was Protective Custody Camp commander at Lichtenburg from February till July/August 1938 and was then transferred in the same post to Dachau. In February 1940 at the latest he took over duty as commandant at Dachau.

During this time responsibility fell to Piorkowski not just for the steady worsening of the prisoners' living conditions, but also the mass murder of

60 Höß (note 22), p. 173.
61 For the following, BDC, SSO Piorkowski as well as the Dachau Archive, trial files in the case of USA vs. Alex Piorkowski et.al. Case Nr. 000-50-2-23.
62 8. 1. 1932 SS-Hauptscharführer [SS-Technical Sergeant], 20. 4. 1933 Untersturmführer [SS-Second Lieutenant], 9. 9. 1934 Obersturmführer [SS-First Lieutenant], 20. 4. 1935 Hauptsturmführer [SS-Captain].

the Soviet prisoners of war, the selection for the "invalid transportations" to Hartheim and the escalating brutality of the SS-commanders and sub-commanders towards the prisoners in the camp.[63] Within the framework of the large-scale personnel exchange amongst the concentration camp commandants planned for autumn 1942, Piorkowski, who was often ill for longer periods, was to be "deployed in the Fürsorge- und Gesundheitswesen [Community and Health Services] by SS-Brigadenführer Dr. Haertel".[64] Himmler decided differently; a SS judicial proceeding — obviously on suspicion of corruption — was to be brought against Piorkowski.[65] However, the investigations did not lead to such proceedings; with the casting off of his rank Piorkowski was to be transferred to the SS-Nachrichten-Ausbildungs- und Ersatzregiment [SS-Intelligence Training and Reserve Regiment] in Nuremberg for training as a radio operator in July 1943. Himmler however no longer wanted to even grant him this. Due to "lack of suitability" Piorkowski was dismissed from the SS.[66] Why Himmler shortly afterwards revised this decision and dismissed Piorkowski on 31 August 1943 "due to being unfit for duty to the Waffen-SS" and, at the same time, "effective from the same day from the SS" is not discernible from the available sources.[67] Alex Piorkowski was interned in 1945, condemned to death by an American court in Dachau on 17 January 1947 and executed on 22 October 1948 in Landsberg.[68]

Successor to Piorkowski was to be Anton Kaindl, up until this point Chief of the Office D IV (Administration) in the "Inspectorate for the Concentration Camps" in Oranienburg, since March 1942 under the term "Office Group D" integrated into the SS-Wirtschafts-Verwaltungshauptamt [SS-Economic and Administrative Main Office].[69] Presumably to spare Kaindl the move to Dachau he became commandant of the concentration camp Sachsenhausen, and instead the commandant initially designated for Sachsenhausen, SS-Sturmbannführer Martin Weiss, was transferred to Dachau. At this point in time Weiss was commandant of the concentration camp Neuengamme in Hamburg.

63   Cf. the diverse inmate reports in the Dachau Archive.
64   State Archive Nuremberg, War Crimes Trials, Document NO 1994. Communication from Pohl to Himmler on 28 July 1942.
65   Ibid. Communication from Rudolf Brandt to Pohl on 23 August 1942.
66   BDC, SSO Piorkowski. Communication from the Personnel Office on 28. 9. 1943.
67   BDC, SSO Piorkowski. Decree given by Himmler on 28. 9. 1943, back-dated to 31. 5. 1943.
68   On the trial proceedings see the detailed account from Robert Sigel, Im Interesse der Gerechtigkeit. Die Dachauer Kriegsverbrecherprozesse 1945–1948 [In the Interests of Justice. The Dachau War Criminal Trials 1945–1948], Frankfurt a.M./ New York 1992, p. 83 ff.
69   Communication from Pohl on 28 July 1942 (note 64).

Martin Weiss was born on 3 June 1905 in Weiden in the Upper Palatinate.[70] After attending a mechanical engineering school he worked as an intern at the Iron and Steel Works Weiherhammer and till 1928 at the Upper Palatinate Electrical Company. Subsequently he studied at the College of Technology in Bad Frankenhausen, where he worked for a year as an assistant after completing his engineering exams. In April 1932 Weiss became unemployed and joined the SS in the same month, in August 1932 the NSDAP. His unemployment came to an end when he joined the Auxiliary Police in Weiden in March 1933 and came to Dachau on 11 April 1933. In the following years Weiss was active here as camp engineer, he became a SS-Obersturmführer in 1937.[71] For an SS-man, prisoner reports depict him as an obliging SS-commander during the early phase of the camp: "He did not tolerate that the guard squads maltreated us when we worked. When a guard once aimed a rifle at me, he threw him out of the workshop on the spot. In his rage he went after him with his pistol. From then on he made sure that the guard squads remained outside the workshop."[72] From 1 April 1938 Weiss was Loritz's aide, was promoted to SS-Hauptsturmführer on 30 January 1939 and was also aide to Piorkowski till he, after the unexpected death of SS-Sturmbannführer Walter Eisfeld in April 1940, became commandant of the Neuengamme camp, which in these months was developed into a camp in its own right. Hermann Kaienburg notes on this period: "He [Weiss] obviously kept himself more at a distance from what took place in the camp than Eisfeld, but ensured just as well that the terror system functioned efficiently."[73] In April 1942 Weiss was commandant of the concentration camp "Arbeitsdorf" ["Work Village"] in Wolfsburg for a short time, returned however to Neuengamme. Weiss became commandant of Dachau on 1 September 1942, after he was to have actually assumed this position in Sachsenhausen.

At Dachau Weiss attempted to put into practice some of the orders for improving the work capacity of the prisoners given by the SS-Wirtschafts-Verwaltungshauptamt. He forbid the immediate punishment of prisoners,

70   On Martin Weiss see BDC, SSO Weiss.
71   In 1934 alone Weiss was promoted five times: 10. 2. 1934 SS-Sturmmann [SS-Private], 20. 4. 1934 SS-Rottenführer [SS-Private First Class], 15. 5. 1934 SS-Unterscharführer [SS-Corporal], 15. 7. 1934 SS-Scharführer [SS-Sergeant], 15. 10. 1934 SS-Oberscharführer [SS-Staff Sergeant], 20. 3. 1935 SS-Hauptscharführer [SS-Technical Sergeant], 20. 4. 1936 SS-Untersturmführer [SS-Second Lieutenant], 12. 9. 1937 SS-Obersturmführer [SS-First Lieutenant].
72   Karl Röder, Nachtwache. 10 Jahre KZ Dachau und Flossenbürg [Night Watch. 10 Years Dachau and Flossenbürg], Wien 1985, p. 271. Röder also reports however that Weiss was supposedly actively involved in the murders of Jewish prisoners in 1940.
73   Cf. Hermann Kaienburg, "Vernichtung durch Arbeit". Der Fall Neuengamme ["Annihiliation through Work". The Case Neuengamme], Bonn 1990, p. 153.

brought the excesses of the camp SS, obviously still prevalent under Piorkowski, to an end and forbid arbitrary terror. He attempted to raise the "efficiency" of the camp. The prisoners' living conditions under the regime of forced labour and the insufficient rations of food continued to worsen however. Weiss' period of commandatuer is still characterised by further murders, "invalid transportations," medical experiments and the criminal handling of prisoners.

Martin Weiss became commandant of the camp Lublin-Majdanek in November 1943. His predecessor there, Hermann Florstedt, was relieved of his post due to corruption. Here, too, Weiss attempted to reduce the senseless terror in order to preserve the working capability of the prisoners. Many thousands of prisoners from various concentration camps, who were no longer capable of working, were none the less accommodated at Majdanek during the winter of 1943/44 in the Fields III and IV in horse stable barracks without any medical assistance. Almost all of them died. From the Inspectorate of the Concentration Camps, SS-Gruppenführer Glücks, Weiss received almost hymnal praise: "Weiss is one of my best commandants, he also possesses very good character qualities. His duty performance is well above the average. His manner is soldierly; he is hard towards himself. Ideologically he is as an old SS-commander steadfast."[74] On 30 January 1944 Weiss was promoted to SS-Obersturmbannführer and from May 1944 onwards deployed as Office Chief for special tasks in the Office Group D of the SS-Wirtschafts-Verwaltungshauptamts. In the view of the SS, Weiss had proven so worthwhile in four concentration camps (Dachau, Neuengamme, Arbeitsdorf, Lublin) that he was promoted to the Central Administration of the Concentration Camps at Oranienburg and was henceforth always charged with special tasks. He was always sent where the predecessor had failed. In November 1944 Weiss was transferred to Mühldorf, where he was obviously to take over command in the coordination of a large forced labour project.[75] Martin

---

74  BDC, SSO Weiss. Personnel application and assessment from 8. 12. 1943.

75  Symptomatic of the poor state of research into the lives and careers of the Dachau commandants is the fact that in her comprehensive study on Kaufering and Mühldorf Edith Raim does not mention Weiss at all or deal with his activities at Mühldorf. Cf. Edith Raim, Die Dachauer KZ-Außenkommandos Kaufering und Mühldorf. Rüstungsbauten und Zwangsarbeit im letzten Kriegsjahr 1944/45 [The Dachau Subsidiary Camps Kaufering and Mühldorf. Armament Works and Forced Labour in the Last Year of the War 1944/45], Landsberg 1992. In his 1946 interrogation Weiss himself explained, he was "technical representative operating between the Oranienburg Office Group [D] and the OT Association for building construction in Mühldorf" (Dachau Archive 6574). The deployment of a high-ranking office chief for special tasks from the SS-Wirtschafts-Verwaltungshauptamts must have been somewhat more comprehensive, so that Weiss' statement has to be viewed sceptically.

Weiss was arrested in Mühldorf on 2 May 1945, sentenced to death by an American military court on 13 December 1945 and executed on 28 May 1946 in Landsberg. His own estimation of his time as commandant at Dachau given during the trial, was just as positive as it was unrealistic: "Dachau was a good camp."[76]

Eduard Weiter became the last commandant of Dachau on 1 November 1943.[77] Weiter was born on 18 July 1889 in Eschwege. After attending elementary school and a three-year course at a commercial college, Weiter took up a paymaster (administration) career and served with the Bavarian Army and the Reich Army for twelve years, from October 1909 to October 1920. In October 1920 Weiter transferred to the Bavarian State Police, where he entered service first as Police Accounts Secretary, then as Police Inspector and from 1933 as Head Paymaster of the State Police. On 1 April 1935 he was promoted to Captain in the State Police and made commander of the Innendienst [Office Duty] with the State Police in Ludwigshafen. In 1936 Weiter joined the Examiner's Department belonging to the SS Administration Chief and was taken on in the SS with the rank of SS-Hauptsturmführer. He first applied for entry to the NSDAP in January 1937. In September 1938 Weiter, at the time director of the Main Accounts of the SS-Verfügungstruppe, was promoted to SS-Sturmbannführer. During 1939 and 1940 Weiter was first administrative director of the SS-Standarte "Deutschland," later the SS-Standarte "Westland" and the SS-Standarte "Nordland". In April 1941 he came to Dachau as director of the substitute unit of the SS Administrative Services, where he was promoted to Obersturmbannführer in the same year. In November 1943 the administration expert Weiter, who till than had had nothing to do with concentration camps, was appointed commandant of Dachau. In Dachau he continued to limit himself to administrative activities and left the camp in the hands of the Protective Custody Camp Commander Michael Redwitz and other SS-commanders. He never appeared before the prisoners; only a few reports about him exist.

The Dachau of winter 1944/45 at Dachau occurred during Weiter's time as commandant. There is no evidence to suggest that he did anything to improve the prisoners' living conditions. As increasing numbers of prisoners from other concentration camps arrived in Dachau the situation worsened. On 26 April 1945 Weiter left the camp with a prisoner transport. He reached Schloß Itter, an external command post of Dachau, where he shot himself on 6 May 1945.[78]

76 Quoted following Sigel, Im Interesse der Gerechtigkeit, p. 55. Sigel gives a detailed presentation of the trial against Weiss. [Weiss' original statement made in English].

77 For Weiter see BDC, SSO Weiter and Segev, Soldaten, pp. 162 ff.

78 Cf. Barbara Distel, Die Befreiung des KZ Dachau [The Liberation of the Concentration Camp Dachau], in: Dachauer Hefte 1 (1985), p. 7.

If one were to offer a résumé of the appointments to commandant for the concentration camp at Dachau, one comes to the following considerations:

1. Dachau was not only one of the earliest but also one of the most important concentration camps. This is reflected in the fact that in comparison to the other concentration camps relatively high-ranking SS-commanders were appointed as commandants.

2. The social profiles of the commandants do not deviate from those of the commandants of other concentration camps. Most possessed basic secondary schooling; five of the seven commandants had served in the First World War; of these, four were professional soldiers, one a volunteer. Two commandants, Piorkowski (1904) and Weiss (1905), were too young to serve in the war. Two commandants, Eicke and Weiter, had taken up careers in the administrative services of the army; all those who served during the World War remained soldiers after 1918 and joined a Freikorp unit.

3. A systematic personnel policy pursued by the SS for the concentration camp Dachau or in the area covered by the Inspectorate for the Concentration Camps cannot be discerned. The commandants of the camp were only in part appointed due to their "qualifications," i.e. on the basis of their experience in other concentration camps. Only Loritz, Piorkowski and Weiss were experienced SS-commanders in concentration camps. Whereas under Loritz and Piorkowski the prisoners were subjected to senseless terror and the excesses of the SS Unterführer, Weiss at least attempted in part to maintain the prisoners' capacity to work, in line with the objectives set by the SS-Wirtschafts-Verwaltungshauptamts.

4. In the view of the SS, only two of the commandants at Dachau, Eicke and Weiss, qualified themselves for "higher tasks" through their time spent in Dachau. Eicke developed in Dachau the concentration camp model that was to be later transposed to all camps throughout the Reich; after his time at Dachau and Lublin Weiss was appointed to the position of Office Chief with special tasks in the Office Group D of the SS-Wirtschafts-Verwaltungshauptamts. A further commandant, Hans Loritz, was later appointed commandant in Sachsenhausen and responsible for Norwegian camps.

5. Three of the seven commandants from Dachau were relieved of their posts. The first commandant, Wäckerle, had to go because the judiciary wanted to open an investigation against him. The third commandant, Deubel, was forced to leave the duty area of Inspectorate for the Concentration Camps because he appeared to be "too soft" and, finally, Alex Piorkowski was relieved of his post because he was involved in a corruption affair. A further designated commandant, Alexander Reiner, could not even assume his post at Dachau due to incidents in Danzig.

6. The last commandant of the Dachau camp, Eduard Weiter, was only given the post because Weiss was urgently needed in Lublin to clear up the miserable state of affairs left there by his predecessor, who had been handed over to an SS-court. Weiter had no experience whatsoever in the concentration camps; he was obviously hopelessly overtaxed by the tasks facing a concentration camp commandant in the last two years of the war.

7. During the war at the latest it can be seen that the claims raised by the National Socialist "Elite Order," the SS, corresponded in no way with the reality prevailing in Dachau. Improvisation and incompetence dominated; precisely this had a disastrous effect upon the prisoners' situation. The improvisation and incompetence of the SS-commanders in Dachau must be seen however as a further element in the terror that was characteristic of the National Socialist terror regime. The thesis however, that the commandants of the concentration camp were selected for their position on the basis of rational criteria and possessed in the eyes of the SS specific "qualifications" for meeting the task at hand, cannot be maintained for Dachau.

Christa Schikorra

# Prostitution of Female Concentration Camp Prisoners as Slave Labor

## On the Situation of "Asocial" Prisoners in the Ravensbrück Women's Concentration Camp[1]

Work in the brothels of the concentration camps for men was regarded by the SS as one work commando among many, in which prisoners of the women's concentration camps were exploited.[2] Slave labor as a prostitute in the concentration camps brothels touches in many respects on taboos and assumptions that are closely linked to structures of prejudice. Both in reports of prisoners who survived as well as in research on concentration camps, work in the concentration camp brothel is often not acknowledged as slave labor. The assumption that prisoners volunteered to work in these commandos plays a significant role here. These women are generally referred to as prostitutes. The view of them as concentration camp prisoners is often lost or disappears behind this label, which in turn functions as a characterization of the women rather than of their slave labor. To address these women as prostitutes rather than as prisoners who worked in forced prostitution in concentration camp brothel commandos reinforces the structures of prejudice developed from the construct of "asociality" (asocial behavior): the assumption here is that a woman who worked in this commando was already a prostitute when she was free or that she belongs in the category

---

1   The essay is based on a revised chapter of the author's dissertation: Christa Schikorra, *Kontinuitäten der Ausgrenzung – "Asoziale" Häftlinge im Frauen-Konzentrationslager Ravenbrück,* Berlin 2000.
2   Christa Schulz, Weibliche Häftlinge aus Ravensbrück in Bordellen der Männer Konzentrationslager, in: Claus Füllberg-Stolberg/ Martina Jung/ Renate Riebe/ Martina Scheitenberger (eds.), *Frauen in Konzentrationslagern.* Bergen-Belsen, Ravensbrück, Bremen 1994, p. 135–146. There were also brothels for the Wehrmacht and SS, and for foreign and forced laborers as well. See Christa Paul, *Zwangsprostitution. Staatlich errichtete Bordelle im Nationalsozialismus,* Berlin 1994.

of "asocial" persons. Embedded in this causal connection is also a reference to the assumed "inferiority" of the person in question.

It was recorded for the Ravensbrück women's concentration camp that beginning in 1942, when the first brothels in the concentration camps of Mauthausen and Gusen[3] were established, prisoners were chosen and "prepared" for this work. Ravensbrück, as the central concentration camp for women in the German Reich, took on an important role in the "provision" of female prisoners for these commandos.[4] The first women were "recruited" for work in the brothels with the promise that they would be released after six months. According to reports from prisoners, a noticeably large number of prisoners with black triangles[5] registered themselves and it was assumed that they had previously worked as prostitutes before they were sent to the concentration camp. Nanda Herbermann,[6] who until March 1943 was the first barrack senior, later block elder for Block 2, the "prostitute block, the most notorious in the entire camp," notes further that "about every three months requests came for between eight and ten prisoners, mostly from my block, to work for the brothel of the concentration camp for men at Mauthausen, as well as for other men's camps."[7]

3    Prisoners from the Ravensbrück women's concentration camp worked in brothels, referred to as "special buildings" (Sonderbau), in the concentration camps of Buchenwald, Dachau, Dora-Mittelbau, Flossenbürg, Gusen, Mauthausen, Neuengamme and Sachsenhausen. It has been documented that brothels for the SS concentration camp guards existed in Buchenwald, Mittelbau-Dora and Neuengamme. See Christa Paul, *Zwangsprostitution*, p. 26 and p. 106 and Kerstin Engelhardt, Frauen im Konzentrationslager Dachau, in: *Dachauer Hefte* 14 (1998), pp. 218–244, here p. 223 ff. See for Mauthausen: Andreas Baumgartner, *Die vergessenen Frauen von Mauthausen Die weibliche Häftlinge des Konzentrationslagers Mauthausen und ihre Geschichte*, Vienna 1997, esp. the chapter: "Die ersten Häftlingsfrauen: Zwangsprostituierte", pp. 93–102.

4    Prisoners of the women's camp at Auschwitz-Birkenau worked in the concentration camp of the Auschwitz camp complex. See Hermann Langbein, *Menschen in Auschwitz*, Vienna 1987, p. 455 and Primo Levi, *Ist das ein Mensch? Erinnerungen an Auschwitz*, Frankfurt a. M. 1979, p. 31.

5    In addition to their prisoner number, the concentration camp prisoners were identified with colored cloth triangles signifying categories provided by the SS. Concentration camp prisoners who were persecuted as "asocials" or "gypsies" were marked with the black triangle.

6    Nanda Herbermann, 1903–1979, Catholic, was the secretary of the Jesuit priest Friedrich Muckermann in Münster and arrested in February 1941 by the Gestapo for engaging in "hostile activities against the state". She arrived in the Ravensbrück women's concentration camp in mid July 1941. One of her brothers was able to get her released in March 1943.

7    Nanda Herbermann, Der gesegnete Abgrund. Schutzhäftling Nr. 6582 im Frauenkonzentrationslager Ravensbrück, Nuremberg, undated, (1946), p. 89.

Erika Buchmann,[8] who was the block elder of the punishment block
for two years as of 1942, reports that prisoners from the punishment block[9]
were especially chosen for the brothel commando.[10] "In the FKL [women's
camp] headquarters, they were presented naked and classified by the SS
officers. Naturally this didn't take place without a flood of nasty teasing.
The prisoners had to prove their 'suitability' by retelling their 'experiences'.[11]
The selected women were then prepared for the work in a special room of
the infirmary. They were treated with a sunray lamp there, received better
food, and when they had recuperated enough, a few SS men entered and
tried them out in the operating room. Afterwards they were divided up:
the prettiest ones to the SS brothel, the less pretty to the soldier brothel and
the third-rate women to the prisoners brothel [...]."[12]

Few comments from women who were forced into prostitution have
been recorded.[13] Most the information passed on to us is from the viewpoint

---

8  Erika Buchmann, 1902–1971, member of the KPD of Stuttgart, was first arrested
   by the Gestapo in October 1933. In December 1935 she was again arrested and
   in summer 1937, convicted of "preparing high treason". After two years
   imprisonment in Aichach, she arrived in the Ravensbrück women's concentration
   camp. In November 1940 she was released from the camp on conditions, but in
   January 1942 was arrested again. In July 1942 she was once again in the Ravensbrück concentration camp and, labelled as a "repeat offender", was sent for two
   years to the punishment block. She was liberated in April 1945 during the death
   march of the Ravensbrück prisoners. See Grit Weichelt, *Überleben im KZ Ravensbrück. Zur Geschichte der Erika Buchmann 1942–1945,* published by the
   Mahn- und Gedenkstätte Ravensbrück, Oranienburg 1995.
9  The punishment block was a barrack that was isolated from the rest of the camp
   by a wire fence. Alongside prisoners who were imprisoned for camp misdemean-
   ours of all types, women who had been sent for a second time to a camp, and hence
   regarded as "repeat offenders", were also sent to the punishment block for up to
   two years. The conditions there were dreadful: There was continual overcrowding,
   food rations were cut back and the prisoners sent there were given the hardest
   work. Most of the women imprisoned there were marked as "asocials" or "criminals" in the Ravensbrück women's concentration camp. Mahn- und Gedenkstätte Ravensbrück (MGR), Ravensbrück Archive (henceforth: RA), Erika Buchmann
   collection, vol. 1–47, here: Gefangenen-Stärkemeldungen, vol. 14.
10 Erika Buchmann, *Frauen im Konzentrationslager*, Stuttgart 1959, p. 20. She adds
   that "In no other block and in no other work commando did so many prisoners
   [die] as in the punishment block".
11 Ibid., p. 85.
12 Antonia Bruha, in: Karin Berger/ Elisabeth Holzinger et al., "*Ich gebe Dir einen
   Mantel, daß Du ihn noch in Freiheit tragen kannst*". *Widerstehen im KZ. Öster-
   reichische Frauen erzählen*, Vienna 1987, p. 149.
13 Reports of four female Ravensbrück prisoners who worked in camp brothels are
   known. Frau B. and Frau W., in: Reinhild Kassig/ Christa Paul, Bordelle in deutschen Konzentrationslagern, in: *K(r)ampfader. Kasseler Frauenzeitung*, no. 1, 1991,

of political prisoners in accounts of survivors. Women are occasionally quoted, as in the collection of Austrian Ravensbrück survivors, published in 1945: "A harlot, upon leaving the operating room, once said: 'I have been in this business now for ten years, but this is the first time that I have experienced this kind of smut.'"[14] Erika Buchmann speaks of the "hundreds of women [...] who [were] chosen by the doctors with the eager assistance of the camp commandant, Suhren, and the head of the protective custody camp, Bräuning."[15]

In the prisoners' descriptions, the outrage they felt that a brothel was set up and about the work done there is articulated just as clearly as is their attempt to disassociate themselves from this work. The Luxembourger Lily Unden stresses in the following that no Luxembourgers were among the women working in the brothel: "Except for the block of newborns, the murders, and the contempt for motherhood, the most terrible atrocity in my view was the establishment of SS brothels. Fourteen days after I arrived in Ravensbrück, a female prison guard came elegantly dressed in civilian clothing for the purpose of informing the prisoners in the arrival block of the existence of this enterprise. This enterprise was particularly lucrative for the concentration camp administration, which kept the largest portion of the takings. Recruiting volunteers was carried out regularly and it was mostly the promise of much better living conditions that allured the interests of certain elements. Since there was a number of professional prostitutes among us, there were always a few who took it upon themselves to do this degrading task. But never was there a Luxembourg woman among them."[16]

It is repeatedly made clear that the work done in the brothels was not measured even by the prisoners by the same standard as other forms of slave labor in the concentration camp. Wanda Kiedrzyńska describes the situation of "recruitment" among the Polish women: "When the commandant called all the Polish women together and had the block elder inform them that they could register to work in the brothel, it evoked general outrage and protest. Two Polish women who had answered the appeal had their hair cut off by two others who were then sent to the punishment block."[17] The moral outrage over this "offer" from the SS gave rise to a national collective which,

pp. 26–31, Christa Paul, *Zwangsprostitution*, pp. 45–57. A women who is not named, in: Das große Schweigen, Film, ORB 1995, and Frau F. in the article by Peter Heigl, Zwangsprostitution im KZ Lagerbordel Flossenbürg, in: *Geschichte quer*, no. 6/1998, pp. 44 f.

14   Frauen-Konzentrationslager Ravensbrück, described by Ravensbrück prisoners, Vienna 1945, p. 21.

15   Buchmann, Frauen (1946), p. 18.

16   RA, vol. 28, Report 490 from L. Unden, 1956, p. 29.

17   Wanda *Kiedrzynska, Ravensbrück kobiecy obóz koncentracyjny* (Ravensbrück women's concentration camp), Warsaw 1961 (German translation MGR/ Bibliothek), p. 29.

despite the threat of punishment, saw to it that no Polish women accepted this work.

It is necessary to discuss the "voluntariness" of the work in the brothels that is so often expressed in this context. An unnamed unidentified survivor of Ravensbrück briefly and clearly presents what in her view motivated the women working in the brothel: "Our prostitutes enlisted for this 'work' on their own free will and regarded their being chosen as an honor."[18] In another description, Nanda Herbermann reports with a motherly air on the fate of her "special charge," Frieda, who volunteered to work in the brothel. "You landed in a brothel much too young, the result of tragic life circumstances, and asked me to help you so that you could manage later in life. I did what I could. You knew it. Wasn't it lovely how we said the Lord's Prayer together late at night? [...] But you disappointed me nonetheless and signed up for the brothel [...]. I used all my powers of persuasion on you, reminded you of your sworn good resolutions, of your miserable situation. Yes, I predicted that you would never be able to stand it – and I was right. You never returned from Mauthausen."[19]

With regard to the emphasized voluntariness, it must be added that under the conditions in the camp, every "job offer" from the SS had a compulsory quality. The decision made by the women to register for this commando may have been determined by what they thought would be expected of them. The hope for better living conditions in the camp presented an equally important incentive. But these considerations were significant not only for the brothel commando, but for all the "good" commandos which women tried to get into. Some women were certainly able to enlist themselves for the work in the brothel commando, and many did so because of the promise of release, but many were simply selected by the SS.

The brothels in the concentration camps were established on the basis of an order from Heinrich Himmler, given during an inspection of the Mauthausen concentration camp.[20] The justification given for setting up the camp brothel was that male concentration camp prisoners needed to be given a stimulus for working harder.[21] The brothels were additionally

---

18  RA, vol. 42, report 986, no information on the writer, undated, p. 22.

19  Herbermann, Abgrund, p. 89.

20  Affidavit of Dr. Schiedlausky from August 8, 1945 and March 4, 1947, Nuremberg documents NO-508 and 2332. Schiedlausky was at the time the camp doctor in the Mauthausen concentration camp.

21  Letter from Himmler to Pohl as Head of the SS Economic and Administrative Main Office (WVHA) from March 23, 1942: "I do however consider it necessary that captives who work hard should be provided with women in brothels." German Federal Archives NS 19/2065. See on work stimulus: Hermann Kaienburg, *Vernichtung durch Arbeit. Der Fall Neuengamme*, Bonn 1990 , pp. 330 ff.

used to force male prisoners who, after being convicted of homosexuality in accordance with section 175 StGb (criminal code), were imprisoned in concentration camps and now put to "tests of renunciation." In the battle against homosexuality, methods of forced heterosexual activity were applied to homosexual prisoners within the context of medical experiments.[22]

In the summer of 1942, the first camp brothel was opened in Mauthausen.[23] The construction of additional brothels in other concentration camps followed. The barrack of the camp brothel, referred to as the special building, was situated on the edge of the actual camp grounds. Most of the brothel barracks were enclosed by a fence and the women who worked there were not permitted to leave that area. The barrack also contained a waiting room and a few smaller rooms, a doctor's office and adequate sanitary facilities. The women who worked in the camp brothel were better cared for than most prisoners. It is occasionally reported that the prisoners received food from the SS canteen. Between ten and fifteen women worked in a single brothel commando. After six months they were usually exchanged for new female prisoners from Ravensbrück.

The working and living conditions in a brothel commando are described in a few interviews with women who had to work there and who survived.[24] Frau W. arrived in the Ravensbrück women's concentration camp on a single transport via Rostock on December 15, 1939. She reports that the Gestapo used her acquaintance with a restaurant owner, who was considered a "half-Jew," as a reason for her arrest. In summer 1943 Frau W. was in the punishment block of the concentration camp when, according to her statement, she was selected for the brothel commando by Commandant Koegel; the female head guard, Langefeld; the camp doctor, Schiedlausky and other SS-men who were not familiar to her. Another 15 prisoners were also selected along with her.[25]

---

22  Günter Grau, Die Verfolgung und 'Ausmerzung' Homosexueller zwischen 1933 und 1945. Folgen des rassehygienischen Konzepts der Reproduktionssicherung, in: Achim Thom/ Genadij I. Caregovodcev (eds.), *Medizin unterm Hakenkreuz*, Leipzig 1989, pp. 91–110. Report of a survivor: Heinz Heger, Die Männer mit dem Rosa Winkel. Der Bericht eines Homosexuellen über seine KZ-Haft von 1939–1945, Hamburg 1972. For new research findings see: Verfolgung Homosexueller im Nationalsozialismus, *Beiträge zur Geschichte der nationalsozialistischen Verfolgung in Norddeutschland*, vol. 5, Bremen 1999.

23  On June 11, 1942, the first forced prostitutes from Ravensbrück were transferred to the prisoner brothel in Mauthausen. Baumgartner, *Frauen*, p. 215.

24  In the early nineties, Christa Paul and Reinhild Kassing were able to find three women who were willing to talk about their experiences as forced prostitutes in concentration camps. See Kassing/ Paul, *Bordelle*, and Paul, *Zwangsprostitution*.

25  Paul, *Zwangsprostitution*, pp. 48 f.

In the following excerpt from the interview that Christa Paul tape recorded, Frau W. describes her arrival in Buchenwald and her work situation there: "After travelling a long time, I could see a large gate and a large, long camp road, just like in Ravensbrück. Aha, I thought, so it is a concentration camp. We were driven into the camp along the camp road. There was an extra block there, a barrack, just like the ones everywhere. That is where the truck stopped. Doors open, prisoners out. The block was fenced in by a large wooden wall about 2.2 meters high all the way around. Between the block and the wooden wall there was a distance of about two meters. We went in there. [...] The two female guards then told us the following: We were now in a prisoner brothel, we had it good, we would be given good food and drink, and if we obey then nothing would happen to us. That was what we were told. And there we sat with our wisdom. I was overcome with relief since it wasn't the SS there [...]. At first I had extreme water [retention]. And Captain Gust said, we'll get you back into shape. I then received food from the SS kitchen for an entire week and they really did manage to get me back on my feet. But that is why I didn't have to the first three weeks. The others had to do it right away. When I was well again and had to get to work, I didn't want to do it anymore, and I was constantly thinking about how I could quit. I didn't though and the first time I had to take a prisoner, I defended myself against him. I told him that I had a nail scissors and that I was going to stab him with it. That if he touched me he wouldn't leave in one piece.

"Our clothing consisted of a white pleated skirt, small panties and a bra. We had to let eight men climb on top of us within two hours every evening. How this worked is that they came in, had to go to the doctor's office to get a shot, went to the number, that is, the prisoner, took care of their business there, in, up, down, out, and back again, got another shot and came back again. We had a bathroom with bidet and toilet so there was enough cleanliness there.

What saved me was two political prisoners. I received a lot of privileges from them. They gave other prisoners money and then pushed them in front so that I could get all my numbers, they kept records on it. They told them that the 13, that was me, that she belonged to them. These other prisoners came then in the evening, had to register with the SS man in the guard room in front, were noted in the book and everything. We went into what was called the Kober room, where it all took place, went out again and the prisoner had again to go into the doctor's office. I had to go into the bathroom otherwise they would have noticed. From the very beginning it was agreed: we send the prisoners who won't do anything to you, but when we come we want to get our share. The two, naturally, demanded their right and I agreed to this since that was much preferable to me than the never-ending eight men each evening. They both took turns, one came on one day, the other on the next.

But I still didn't always get away unscathed. There was another one who also had money and who said I want my pleasure too and he couldn't be held off. By some I resisted, I said don't touch me, I have my period, and they believed it, but the next time when they returned ... That is what we were in Buchenwald for, us women."[26]

In the beginning the brothel commandos of the individual concentration camps were supervised by SS female guards from Ravensbrück. They were then replaced by prisoners at the end of 1943 on orders from the SS Economic and Administrative Main Office (WVHA). "In place of guards, older female prisoners were to be brought into the special building. At Ravensbrück FKL [women's camp] there are a number of experienced female prisoners available, who have already managed brothels."[27] When women from the brothel commando became pregnant or caught venereal diseases, they were brought back to Ravensbrück. Abortions were preformed and the women often died during the operation. This is what Antonial Bruha,[28] who worked as a prisoner in the infirmary reports: "They returned to the camp often infected with lues or with gonorrhea. When they suffered from syphilis, for example, they were given injections and were used for various experiments to find cures for lues or they didn't receive any medical treatment and were just left to die."[29] Erika Buchmann also comments from the perspective of the block elder in the punishment block on what was done with the women who returned from the brothel commando: "Most of them went back to detention or the punishment block and if they had a venereal disease or were pregnant, to the extermination transport."[30] The women who worked as forced prostitutes often returned from the brothels to the

---

26  Ibid, pp. 52 ff. Frau W. was refused recognition as a victim of the Nazis according to the federal restitution law with the explanation that she had been arrested as a result of her "asocial behavior". Not until 1988 did she for a short period receive payments from the state hardship fund for Nazi victims of the State of Schleswig Holstein. Frau W. died in October 1990. For more on this, see Paul, *Zwangsprostitution*, p. 57.

27  Secret circular of Nov. 11, 1943 from the SS Economic and Administrative Main Office (WVHA) Amtsgruppe D to the camp commandants, Institute für Zeitgeschichte, Munich, Fa 506/12.

28  Antonia Bruha, born 1915, active since 1934 in the revolutionary socialists' movement in Vienna; since 1938 in a resistance group of Viennese Czechs. Arrested in 1941 and sentenced to death for high treason. Following one year of solitary imprisonment, she was incarcerated in the Ravensbrück women's concentration camp until the liberation in April 1945.

29  Antonia Bruha, in: Berger/ Holzinger, *Mantel*, p. 149 f.

30  Buchmann, *Frauen (1959)*, p. 86.

Ravensbrück concentration camp as "wrecks,"[31] not only humiliated, but also physically broken.

A visit to a brothel by a male concentration camp prisoner was regulated by privileges ordained by official regulations.[32] This "premium ordinance" which handled more than merely the visit to a brothel, was intended to serve the purpose both of increasing work capacity, and also of breaking down solidarity among prisoners and encouraging compliance with the SS. Whether or not these aims were achieved is difficult to judge. An appeal for a boycott against the camp brothel, initiated by the political prisoners, is documented in many of the concentrations camps.[33] The offered explanation for the boycott by the male concentration camp prisoners was "political morals," because they did not want to allow themselves to be corrupted by the SS. Rarely is the situation of the female prisoners who worked as prostitutes given as the reason for the refusal. Instead there are descriptions provided by the male concentration camp prisoners of the women who worked in the camp brothel, depicting the apparent life of luxury in which they worked and — as clients traditionally do — talking shop about the attractiveness of the women and referring to them without exception as whores.[34] The women working in brothels are often not even described as camp prisoners any more.[35] The term "work" is not used in the reports and descriptions of the activity in the camp brothels. The statements are also noticeably similar in their absence of any mention of the violence and terror system in the concentration camps, when they speak of the brothels and the women who work there.

The initial promise of the SS to release the women after six months proved to be a fallacy. The prisoners were usually exchanged for new women after six months. The principle set by Himmler to solely select prostitutes for this commando was not maintained. It can be assumed that following

31  Irma Trksak, in: Berger/ Holzinger, *Mantel*, p. 124.

32  On May 15, 1943, the "official regulation for the granting of privileges to prison-
    ers" also called "premium ordinance" took effect. For special work accomplish-
    ments was to be granted: 1. improved imprisonment conditions, 2. extra rations,
    3. money bonuses 4. purchase of tobacco, 5. visit to a brothel. Nuremberg document
    NO-400.

33  Eugen Kogon, *Der SS-Staat. Das System der deutschen Konzentrationslager*,
    Munich (1974) 1991, p. 214; Christian Meier, *So war es*, Hamburg 1948, pp. 51
    f.; Joseph Joos, *Leben auf Widerruf*, Augsburg 1946, p. 72.

34  Jorge Semprun, *Was für ein schöner Sonntag*, Frankfurt a. M. 1981, p. 361; see
    also Kogon, *SS-Staat*, pp. 214 f.

35  See on the reception of camp brothels: Paul, *Zwangsprostitution*, pp. 89 f. and on
    prostitution as work, Gisela Bock, "'Keine Arbeitskräfte in diesem Sinne!' Prosti-
    tuierte im NS-Staat", in: Pieke Biermann (ed.), *"Wir sind Frauen wie andere auch."
    Prostituierte und ihre Kämpfe*, Reinbek 1980, pp. 70–106.

the first reports from the women returning from the brothels, the number of women to register for this work declined. Rarely is the release of a woman mentioned who had to work as a forced prostitute. The women, as a consequence of their extreme physical and psychological situation, and given the prospect of improved living conditions, were forced as camp prisoners to work in the camp brothel commando. The women who were used as forced prostitutes with the promise of release were, however, by no means released. In fact many of them died from the consequences of the work, for example, from venereal diseases, abortions, and violence.

Because the files are in a fragmentary state, it is only to a limited degree possible to provide data on the number and length of stay of female prisoners from Ravensbrück who worked in the brothels of the other concentration camps.[36] But there is other data available which provides important information. For example, the women's assigned prisoner categories and the breakdown of age groups can be derived from the transfer and arrival lists. Names, birth dates, and prisoner numbers of twelve women are registered on a transfer list from September 17, 1944 drawn up in Ravensbrück under the front page heading "From KL Ravensbrück to KL Flossenbürg special commando Flossenburg."[37] The oldest woman was twenty-nine and the youngest was twenty years old. One of the women had been in Ravensbrück since March 1940, two others were there since April and August 1942 respectively. In the numbers book of the Flossenburg camp, the first six women are each marked as "RD. asocial"[38] and with the entry "S. B." for special building ("Sonderbau"), which is a reference to the brothel commando.[39] Lists that have been retained for the camp brothel in Dachau from November 17, 1944 and December 12, 1944 show thirteen names. Unlike the information for the brothel commando in Flossenbürg of the same year, the Dachau data shows that the women in the commando were

---

36   Ten female Ravensbrück prisoners worked in the prisoner brothel of the Maut-hausen and Gusen concentration camps; in the Buchenwald camp there were 16 women in the brothel commando; in the camp brothel of the Sachsenhausen concentration camp there must have also been ten women; in the Neuengamme camp the initial number of six women doubled to twelve; in Flossenburg, the "special barracks" were divided between prisoner and SS brothel and there is evidence of fifteen women working there in the brothel commando; fourteen female prisoners in Dachau in the "special building", see Paul, *Zwangsprostitution*, pp. 58 ff.

37   United States Holocaust Memorial Museum Archives (USHMM) Washington, DC RG 04.006 M. Reel 20.

38   The initials RD stand for "Reichsdeutsche".

39   An additional six names on the transfer list that were listed separately were marked with the entry "Helmbrechts". They were transferred to the Flossenburg satellite camp near Hof. Archive of the Flossenburg memorial site, MF Numbers Books No. 5.

not drawn solely from the imprisoned group of "asocials." One woman is registered as a Pole; the others twelve as German. Four of them are marked as "asocial," eight as political and one as "criminal." Their ages at the time range between 19 and 38.[40]

The significance of the prisoner categories for the forced prostitution of female concentration camp prisoners becomes clear from the following: In an entry on an arrival list from the Ravensbrück women's concentration camp from February 15, 1944,[41] the remark "returned from Mauthausen" is noted next to the names of two women on the front page. What is interesting about this entry is that in addition to the names, ages and prisoner numbers of the women, their nationality as Polish and their prisoner category as "asocial" is given. One of the women is already on the arrival list from April 10, 1942. There she is listed as a Pole in the prisoner category of political prisoner. This prisoner category on the arrival list is crossed out and replaced with the handwritten remark "asocial." Apparently the work in the prisoner brothel of Mauthausen led to the "correction" of the prisoner category since foreign prisoners were usually marked with the red triangle of the political prisoner. The slave labor in the brothel turned a political prisoner into an "asocial". For the prisoner that meant a considerable loss of status in the hierarchy of prisoner society.

That the availability of the prisoners for work in the brothel commando was established over the claim to their bodies has also to do with their being designated in categories of racial hygienic as "inferior". The following example makes this clear: Of the women who were selected for the brothel commando of the Dachau camp, four were handed over to Dr. Rascher for experiments on hypothermia.[42] These medical experiments, under the direction of Dr. Rascher, were developed in cooperation with the Luftwaffe for the re-warming of pilots suffering from hypothermia.[43] The male prisoners of Dachau, who were artificially inflicted with the anguishing torture of hypothermia, were to be warmed up by having relations with naked women. For this purpose, female prisoners from Ravensbrück were

40 Kerstin Engelhardt, Frauen in Konzentrationslager Dachau, in: *Dachauer Hefte* 14 (1998). Persecution as group experience, p. 218–244, here p. 225
41 USHMM, RG 04.006 M. Reel 22.
42 On orders from Himmler, four women were transferred to Dachau for Rascher's experiments, telex from Oct. 8, 1942, Nuremberg document NO-295.
43 Ino Arndt, Das Frauen-Konzentrationslager Ravensbrück, in: Institut für Zeitgeschichte (ed.), *Studien zur Geschichte der Konzentrationslager*, Stuttgart 1970, new revised edition, in: *Dachauer Hefte* 3 (1987), pp. 125–157, here p. 142; Wolfgang Benz, Dr. med. Sigmund Rascher – Eine Karriere, in: *Dachauer Hefte* 4 (1988), pp. 190–214; Paul, *Zwangsprostitution*, p. 30 f.; Engelhardt, "Frauen", pp. 222 f.

requested. Rascher complained to Heinrich Himmler's adjutant about one of the women that was sent to him. "One of the women designated to me showed perfect northern racial features: blond hair, blue eyes, the corresponding head form and body build, 21 years old. [...] In response to my objection that it was indeed a dreadful disgrace to volunteer oneself as a brothel girl, I was informed: 'a 1/2 year in a brothel is still better than 1/2 year in a camp.' [...] It goes against my racial sensibility that a girl of pure northern appearance, who, perhaps when put to the right work could be set on the right path, should be handed over as a brothel girl to racially inferior camp elements. For this reason I refused to use this girl for my experimental purposes and made the appropriate report to the camp commandant and the adjutant of the Reichsführer-SS."[44]

The fact that this extremely ambitious and utterly ruthless doctor would appear to develop scruples based on racial features suggests more than a curiosity. Himmler, at any rate, uses Rascher's complaint as an opportunity to present the criteria for selection in a letter to Oswald Pohl, the head of the WVHA. "Four girls were assigned, who due to their too loose lifestyles, or because, as harlots, they carried the risk of being infectious, were in the camp. Among these four girls there was a 21 year old, Ursula Krause, who certainly needn't have been assigned. K. was a welfare case and had already been twice infected with venereal disease. Nonetheless she belonged to that type of girl with which at least an attempt should be made to save her for the German people and for her own sake in later life."[45] Pohl was ordered by Himmler to in the future personally inspect the conditions in the camps so that it is not "as is the case in prisons and penitentiaries of the judiciary" that girls who can still be saved are ruined forever as a result of false treatment or repeated poor company.[46]

Ursula Krause, delivered to the Ravensbrück camp in November 1941, was transferred to Dachau on October 13, 1942 and was returned to Ravensbrück on January 19, 1943 with the note "Released for transport."[47]

It remains in conclusion to note that the attributed "racial inferiority" was the criteria for the assigned "asociality" of the women concerned and — this is essential — that this is what legitimized their claim to the women's bodies. The right to physical integrity and freedom from bodily harm was denied these women. In the brothels of the male camps, the bodies of the women were used under force to increase the men's work capacity. Even

44  File comments of Dr. Rascher from Nov. 11, 1942, Nuremberg document NO-323.
45  Nuremberg document NO-1232.
46  Nuremberg document PS-1583.
47  USHMM, RG 04.006 M, Reel 22. Engelhardt, however, notes that Ursula Krause is released on Dec. 8, 1942, see. Engelhardt, *Frauen*, p. 223.

though this complex, presented here on the basis of representative examples, could have affected all the female Ravensbrück prisoners, the women who were incarcerated in the concentration camp as "asocials" were particularly threatened as a result of their designated "inferiority."

It is worth noting that the commando for the "special building" of the various concentration camps is rarely addressed in current research in the context of slave labor.[48] Forced prostitution is also not penalized as such in the prosecution of crimes in the concentration camps. This attitude is not only the result of traditional and still existing moral judgments on prostitution, it is also the consequence of ignorance regarding sexual violence against women.

For years these women fought to be recognized as Nazi victims. The fact that former prisoners often did not tell the authorities about their work in a camp brothel or if they did, only in passing when they spoke of their experiences there, shows what pressure and with what fear of continued discrimination the survivors are confronted still today. That traditional thinking still has a widespread impact is made clear not only in how female sexuality is treated by society today, but also in the fact that the women who were stigmatized as "asocials" continue to be excluded. The assumption that they themselves are to blame for their fate denies them any claim to rehabilitation or recognition.

---

48  Sofsky mentions the camp brothel only in the context of increased work incentives for the male camp prisoners. He notes that it is equally important as the purchase of tobacco in the system of bonuses (p. 197). In the subchapter on the work situation, slave labor in the camp brothels goes completely unmentioned. Wolfgang Sofsky, *Die Ordnung des Terrors. Das Konzentrationslager*, Frankfurt a. M. 1993. In the two volume work on the development and structure of the National Socialist concentration camp system, the subject of forced prostitution in the brothels is also not addressed. Ulrich Herbert/ Karin Orth/ Christoph Diekmann (eds.), *Die nationalsozialistischen Konzentrationslager. Entwicklung und Struktur*, 2 vol., Göttingen 1998.

# Contributors

Ute Benz, psychoanalyst for families, children and young adults, Berlin

Wolfgang Benz, Director of the Center for Research on Antisemitism, Technical University, Berlin

Barbara Distel, Director of the Dachau concentration camp memorial site

Florian Freund, historian, Institute for Contemporary History of the University of Vienna

Detlef Garbe, Director of the Neuengamme concentration camp memorial site, Hamburg

Lee Kersten, Senior Lecturer Dept. of German Studies, University of Adelaide, Australia

Thomas Rahe, Director of the Bergen-Belsen concentration camp memorial site, Bergen-Belsen

Christa Schikorra, historian, lives in Berlin

Robert Sigel, historian, teacher at the Josef-Effner-Gymnasium in Dachau

Johannes Tuchel, Director of the German Resistance Memorial, Berlin

Hermann Weiss, historian, lives in Munich

Jürgen Zarusky, historian at the Institute of Contemporary History in Munich


Mary Ellen Bass translated the article by Hermann Weiss

Paul Bowman translated the articles by Thomas Rahe, Robert Sigel and Johannes Tuchel

Miriamne Fields translated the articles by Wolfgang Benz (Omnipresence of Concentration Camps) and Christa Schikorra

Max R. Garcia (San Francisco, USA), Auschwitz-Buna, prisoners's number 139829 and Mauthausen, prisoners' number 116739 concentration camp survivor, translated the article by Florian Freund

Colleen Hobson translated the article by Detlef Garbe

Herbert Otter and Susan Arase translated the article by Barbara Distel

Olaf Reinhardt (Sydney, Australia) translated the article by Ute Benz and Wolfgang Benz's study on Dachau and the International Public Opinion

Ernest Seinfeld, Auschwitz and Dachau concentration camp survivor, Connecticut, USA translated the article by Jürgen Zarusky

Bruno Schachtner (Dachau) designed the cover

Toby Axelrod and Ingeborg Medaris corrected the proofs